Turbo C++'s Editing Shortcut Keys

Shortcut Key	Description
Ctrl-Delete	Cuts selected text from the editing window. Same as Edit Clear.
Ctrl-L	Repeats the most recent find or replace. Same as Search Search again.
Alt-S R	Opens the Find and Replace dialog box. Same as Search Replace.
Alt-S F	Opens the Find dialog box. Same as Search Find.
F2	Saves the file in the active editing window. Same as File Save.
F3	Brings up the Load a File dialog box. Same as File Open.
Shift-Delete	Copies selected text to the Clipboard. Same as Edit Cut.
Shift-Insert	Pastes clipboard text into the active window. Same as Edit Paste.

Turbo C++'s Menu Shortcut Keys

Shortcut Key	Description
Alt-Spacebar	Displays the System menu.
Alt-C	Displays the Compile menu.
Alt-D	Displays the Debug menu.
Alt-E	Displays the Edit menu.
Alt-F	Displays the File menu.
Alt-H	Displays the Help menu.
Alt-O	Displays the Options menu.
Alt-P	Displays the Project menu.
Alt-R	Displays the Run menu.
Alt-S	Displays the Search menu.
Alt-W	Displays the Window menu.
Alt-X	Exits Turbo C++ and returns to DOS.
F10	Highlights the menu bar.

Turbo C++'s Windowing Shortcut Keys

Shortcut Key	Description
Alt-0	Displays the list of open windows. Same as Window List.
Alt-F3	Closes the active window. Same as Window Close.
Alt-F4	Opens an inspector window. Same as Debug Inspect.
Alt-F5	Jumps to or from the user screen. Same as Window User screen.
F5	Zooms or unzooms the active window. Same as Window Zoom.
F6	Switches to another active window. Same as Window Next.
Ctrl-F5	Changes the size or position of the active window.

Turbo C++'s Help Shortcut Keys

Shortcut Key	Description
F1	Displays an online help screen. Same as Help Contents.
F1 F1	Displays the Help index. Same as Help Index.
Alt-F1	Displays the previous Help screen. Same as Help Previous topic.
Ctrl-F1	Displays language-specific help in the edit window only. Same as Help Topic search.

Turbo C++'s Program Management Shortcut Keys

Shortcut Key	Description
Alt-F7	Displays the previous error. Same as Search Previous error.
Alt-F8	Displays the next error. Same as Search Next error.
Alt-F9	Compiles to an .OBJ file. Same as Compile Compile to OBJ.
Ctrl-F2	Resets the currently running program. Same as Run Program reset.
Ctrl-F3	Brings up the call stack. Same as Debug Call stack.
Ctrl-F4	Evaluates an expression. Same as Debug Evaluate/modify.
Ctrl-F7	Adds a watch expression. Same as Debug Watches Add watch.
Ctrl-F8	Sets or clears a conditional breakpoint. Same as Debug Toggle breakpoint.
Ctrl-F9	Runs the current program. Same as Run Run.
F4	Runs the program to the cursor's current position. Same as Run Go to cursor.
F7	Traces into functions. Same as Run Trace into.
F8	Traces while skipping function calls. Same as Run Step over.
F9	Makes the current program by compiling and linking. Same as Compile Make EXE.

C's Data Types

Data Type	Description
char	Character.
int	Integer.
unsigned int	Unsigned integer.
signed int	Signed integer. Same as int.
short int	Short integer. Same as int.
unsigned short int	Unsigned short integer. Same as unsigned int.
signed short int	Signed short integer. Same as integer.
long	Long integer.
long int	Same as long.
signed long int	Signed long integer. Same as long.
unsigned long int	Unsigned long integer.
float	Floating-point.
double	Double-precision floating-point.
long double	Long double-precision floating-point.

Access Modes for Random Access Files

Access Mode	Description
"r+"	Opens an existing file for reading and writing. The file pointer points to the beginning of the file when you first open the file.
"w+"	Opens a new file for writing and reading. If the file exists, the existing file will be erased and a new version created. Once you write data to the file, you can move the file pointer to a different location and read the data without reopening the file.
"a+"	Opens a new or existing file for appending, reading, and writing. The file pointer points to the end of the file if the file exists. The file is created if it doesn't exist.

printf() Conversion Characters

Conversion Character	Description
%c	For character values.
%d	For integer values.
%i	Same as %d but rarely used.
%f	For floating-point and double values.
%g	For either floating-point or scientific notation (with a lowercase e), depending on the number's value.
%G	For either floating-point or scientific notation (with an uppercase E), depending on the number's value.
%ld	For long integer values.
%lf	For long double floating-point values.
%o	For octal values.
%x	For hexadecimal values.
%e	Scientific notation with a lowercase exponent character.
%E	Scientific notation with an uppercase exponent character.

Data-Type Literal Qualifiers

Literal Qualifier	Description
0	Appears in front of integers to specify octal values.
0x (or 0X)	Appears in front of integers to specify hexadecimal values.
F	Specifies a regular floating-point literal.
L	At the end of an integer, L specifies a long integer literal. At the end of a floating-point literal, L specifies a long double floating-point literal.
U	Specifies an unsigned integer.

Sequential File Access Mode Values

Access Mode	Description
"w"	Opens the file in write mode. If the file exists, the new file you're creating replaces the old one.
"r"	Opens the file in read mode. If the file doesn't exist, fopen() returns an error that you should always check for.
"a"	Opens the file in append mode, letting you add to the end of the file. If the file doesn't exist, a new file is created.

Common C In-Memory Data Type Requirements

Data Type	Byte Requirement
char	1 byte
int	2 bytes
unsigned int	2 bytes
long	4 bytes
unsigned long int	4 bytes
float	4 bytes
double	8 bytes
long double	10 bytes

fseek() origin Values

origin	Description
SEEK_SET	The beginning of the file.
SEEK_CUR	The pointer's current position.
SEEK_END	The end of the file.

textcolor() Arguments

BLACK
BLUE
GREEN
CYAN
RED
MAGENTA
BROWN
LIGHTGRAY
DARKGRAY
LIGHTBLUE
LIGHTGREEN
LIGHTCYAN
LIGHTRED
LIGHTMAGENTA
YELLOW
WHITE

The 12 Easy Elements In 12 Easy Lessons

A *concept* introduces you to a new topic and tells you what you'll learn.

Stop & type lets you know it's time to fire up your compiler and try a program.

Every sample program contains three sections: *input* (the code you enter), *output* (the results you get), and *analysis* (a complete explanation).

Each lesson has three parts—two *units* and a *review project*—designed to make learning C easy.

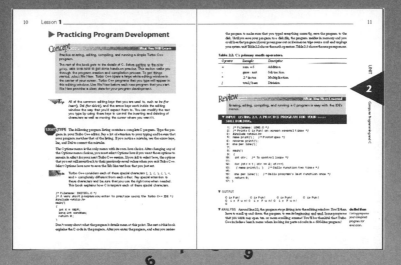

What did you just learn? Each major section wraps up with a *review*, introducing a sample program that applies to the lesson.

Learn from coding *tips*, *notes* about the language, and *warnings* about what to avoid.

Greg Perry makes C fun and easy by providing *real-world analogies* and *examples*.

Each project contains a real-world code example, so you can apply your new C knowledge.

If a line of code in the program confuses you, check the *line-by-line explanation.*

The far-right column looks at *the big picture*, helping you understand coding strategies and techniques.

The enclosed disks contain answers to all the *review questions*, plus the Turbo C++ compiler and all the code in the book.

The *full-color tear-out cheat sheet* at the beginning of the book details syntax and shortcuts.

SAMS
PUBLISHING

C Programming
in **12**
Easy Lessons

Greg Perry

SAMS
PUBLISHING

A division of Macmillan Computer Publishing
201 W. 103rd St., Indianapolis, Indiana 46290

Thanks to Camillo and Loredana Marchi, who make Venice seem like home. Your Costarica coffee is the world's best! This book is for you.

Copyright © 1994 by Sams Publishing

International Standard Book Number: 0-672-30522-4

Library of Congress Catalog Card Number: 94-66282

97 96 95 94   4 3 2 1

Interpretation of the printing code: the rightmost double-digit number is the year of the book's printing; the rightmost single-digit, the number of the book's printing. For example, a printing code of 94-1 shows that the first printing of the book occurred in 1994.

Composed in Stone Serif and MCPdigital by Macmillan Computer Publishing

Printed in the United States of America

Trademarks

Overview

Introduction xx

Lesson 1   Programming with C   **1**

   Unit 1   Computer Programming and C 3

   Unit 2   The Turbo C++ Compiler 15

            Lesson 1 Project 31

Lesson 2   Meeting C Programs   **37**

   Unit 3   Style Issues 39

   Unit 4   Output with `printf()` 59

            Lesson 2 Project 77

Lesson 3   Data Basics   **83**

   Unit 5   Numeric Data 85

   Unit 6   String Data and Input Gathering 107

            Lesson 3 Project 127

Lesson 4   Simple Operators   **133**

   Unit 7   Fundamental Math Operators 135

   Unit 8   Relational and Logical Operators 151

            Lesson 4 Project 171

Lesson 5   Upgraded Operators   **179**

   Unit 9   Special Operations 181

   Unit 10 Advancing with Bitwise Operators 201

            Lesson 5 Project 217

Lesson 6   Looping Back and Forth   **223**

   Unit 11 Spending a While with `while` 225

   Unit 12 Use C `for` Looping 239

            Lesson 6 Project 253

Lesson 7   Taking Charge   **259**

   Unit 13 Controlling Loops and Branching 261

   Unit 14 Power with `switch` 275

            Lesson 7 Project 295

Lesson 8   Breaking It Up with Functions   **301**

   Unit 15   The C Library of Functions 303

   Unit 16   Building Your Own Functions 329

           Lesson 8 Project 355

Lesson 9   Lots of Data   **363**

   Unit 17   Arrays Multiply Storage 365

   Unit 18   Pointers Simplify 383

           Lesson 9 Project 405

Lesson 10   Consolidating Items   **421**

   Unit 19   Structure with `struct` 423

   Unit 20   Allocating Memory..441

           Lesson 10 Project 461

Lesson 11   Long-Term Storage   **475**

   Unit 21   Sequential Files 477

   Unit 22   Random Access Files 495

           Lesson 11 Project 511

Lesson 12   Your C Future   **521**

   Unit 23   Advanced Issues in C..523

   Unit 24   What's This C++ All About? 541

           Lesson 12 Project 555

      A   Installing Your C Compiler 565

      B   ASCII Table 571

      C   C Operator Precedence Table 579

         Index..583

Contents

	Introduction	xx
Lesson 1	Programming with C	**1**
Unit 1	Computer Programming and C	3
	What You'll Learn About	4
	Why Program?	4
	Programming Steps	6
	C: A Brief History of Programming Time	10
	C's Strengths and Weaknesses	10
	Borland and Turbo C++	12
	Homework	13
	General Knowledge	13
	Extra Credit	13
Unit 2	The Turbo C++ Compiler	15
	What You'll Learn About	16
	Starting and Stopping Turbo C++	16
	An Overview of Turbo C++'s IDE	18
	Navigating the Menus	19
	The Control Menu	21
	Dialog Boxes	22
	Practicing Program Development	23
	Getting Help	28
	Homework	29
	General Knowledge	29
	What's the Output?	30
	Find the Bug	30
	Extra Credit	30
	Lesson 1 Project	31
Lesson 2	Meeting C Programs	**37**
Unit 3	Style Issues	39
	What You'll Learn About	40
	An Overview of a C Program	40
	C's Freeform Style	42
	Watch That Caps Lock Key!	42

Comment All Over the Place 43

    How to Comment 44

    C++ Comments 45

    Develop Good Commenting Habits 46

Studying the Big Picture 48

    # Signals a Preprocessor Directive 48

    The `main()` Function 51

    Data and Variables 53

    A Preview of Input and Output 54

    Calling a Function 54

Homework 56

    General Knowledge 56

    What's the Output? 56

    Find the Bug 57

    Write Code That... 57

    Extra Credit 57

Unit 4   Output with `printf()` 59

What You'll Learn About 60

`printf()` Outputs Data 60

    Printing String Literals 61

Other Escape Sequence Characters 64

Printing Single Characters 67

Printing Integer Data 70

Printing Floating-Point Data 73

Homework 75

    General Knowledge 75

    What's the Output? 75

    Find the Bug 75

    Write Code That... 76

    Extra Credit 76

Lesson 2 Project 77

Lesson 3 Data Basics   **83**

Unit 5   Numeric Data 85

What You'll Learn About 86

C's Numeric Data Types 86

    Discussing Data 88

    Numeric Literal Qualifiers 90

Variables 95
   How to Name Variables 96
   Variable Data Types 97
   Defining Variables...98
   Storing Data in Variables 99
Homework 102
   General Knowledge 102
   What's the Output?...103
   Find the Bug 104
   Write Code That… 104
   Extra Credit 105

Unit 6   String Data and Input Gathering 107
What You'll Learn About 108
Characters Versus Strings of Characters.....................................108
   Null Zero 109
   Lengths of Strings 111
Character Arrays 113
Working with Character Arrays 117
Getting Keyboard Input 120
Homework 124
   General Knowledge 124
   What's the Output?...124
   Find the Bug 125
   Write Code That… 125
   Extra Credit 125

Lesson 3 Project..127

Lesson 4   Simple Operators   **133**
Unit 7   Fundamental Math Operators 135
What You'll Learn About 136
Reviewing the Basics 136
   The Unary Operators...137
   Two Divisions and Remainder 138
Order of Operators 141
Advanced Assignments 144
   Multiple Assignments 144
   Compound Operators 145
Homework 148
   General Knowledge 148

What's the Output? 149

Find the Bug 149

Write Code That... 149

Extra Credit 150

Unit 8   Relational and Logical Operators 151

What You'll Learn About 152

Making Decisions with Relational Operators 152

The if Command Tests for Relations 157

Otherwise, There's else 161

Logical Operators 164

Homework 168

General Knowledge 168

What's the Output? 169

Find the Bug 169

Write Code That... 170

Extra Credit 170

Lesson 4 Project 171

Lesson 5   Upgraded Operators   **179**

Unit 9   Special Operations 181

What You'll Learn About 182

Combining Data Types 182

Automatic Promotion 183

The Typecast Operator 184

The sizeof Operator 188

Using the Conditional Operator 190

Adding and Subtracting One 194

Homework 198

General Knowledge 198

What's the Output? 199

Find the Bug 199

Write Code That... 199

Extra Credit 200

Unit 10   Advancing with Bitwise Operators 201

What You'll Learn About 202

An Introduction to the Bitwise Operators 202

Truth Tables 203

The Bitwise Shift Operators 207

Some Uses for Bitwise Operators 209

The Compound Bitwise Operators 213

Homework 214

    General Knowledge 214

    What's the Output? 215

    Find the Bug 215

    Write Code That… 215

    Extra Credit 216

Lesson 5 Project 217

Lesson 6   Looping Back and Forth   **223**

Unit 11   Spending a While with `while` 225

What You'll Learn About 226

The Format of `while` 226

The Other `while`: The `do-while` Loop 230

`break` or an Early `exit()`? 232

Homework 236

    General Knowledge 236

    What's the Output? 237

    Find the Bug 237

    Write Code That… 238

    Extra Credit 238

Unit 12   Use C `for` Looping 239

What You'll Learn About 240

The `for` Loop's Structure 240

Further Control with the `countExpression` 244

Nested Loops 247

Homework 249

    General Knowledge 249

    What's the Output? 250

    Find the Bug 250

    Write Code That… 251

    Extra Credit 251

Lesson 6 Project 253

Lesson 7   Taking Charge   **259**

Unit 13   Controlling Loops and Branching 261

What You'll Learn About 262

Terminating `for` Early 262

`continue` as Opposed to `break` 264

Moving Around with `goto` 267

Homework 272

General Knowledge 272

What's the Output? 272

Find the Bug 273

Write Code That... 273

Extra Credit 274

Unit 14   Power with `switch` 275

What You'll Learn About 276

Multiple Choice with Nested `ifs` 276

Making the `switch` 281

`break` Up That `switch` 284

Using `switch` for Menus 289

Homework 292

General Knowledge 292

What's the Output? 292

Find the Bug 293

Write Code That... 293

Extra Credit 294

Lesson 7 Project 295

Lesson 8   Breaking It Up with Functions   **301**

Unit 15   The C Library of Functions 303

What You'll Learn About 304

Input and Output Functions 304

Printer Output 305

Character I/O Functions 305

String I/O Functions 310

Colorful Text 312

Character-Based Functions 315

Character-Testing Functions 315

Character Conversion Functions 316

String Functions 318

Numeric Functions 322

Integer Functions 322

Other Common Math Functions 323

Trigonometric and Logarithmic Functions 324

Homework 326

General Knowledge 326

What's the Output? 327

Find the Bug 327

Write Code That... 327

Extra Credit 328

Unit 16   Building Your Own Functions 329

What You'll Learn About 330

Separating Code 330

Local and Global Variables 334

Sharing Variables Among Functions 338

Passing by Value 339

Detour for a Moment with Prototypes 341

Passing by Address 343

Returning Values via `return` 347

Homework 351

General Knowledge 351

What's the Output? 352

Find the Bug 353

Write Code That... 353

Extra Credit 353

Lesson 8 Project 355

Lesson 9   Lots of Data   **363**

Unit 17   Arrays Multiply Storage 365

What You'll Learn About 366

Array Basics 366

Searching Through Arrays 373

Homework 379

General Knowledge 379

What's the Output? 380

Find the Bug 380

Write Code That... 381

Extra Credit 381

Unit 18   Pointers Simplify 383

What You'll Learn About 384

Inside Memory 384

Pointer Variables 386

The Marriage of Arrays and Pointers 391

Pointers to Characters 395

Arrays of Pointers 399

Homework 403

    General Knowledge 403

    What's the Output? 404

    Find the Bug 404

    Write Code That… 404

    Extra Credit 404

Lesson 9 Project 405

Lesson 10 Consolidating Items   **421**

  Unit 19   Structure with `struct` 423

What You'll Learn About 424

Grouping in a Structure 424

    The `struct` Statement 425

Initializing Structure Variables 430

Homework 438

    General Knowledge 438

    What's the Output? 439

    Find the Bug 439

    Write Code That… 439

    Extra Credit 440

  Unit 20   Allocating Memory 441

What You'll Learn About 442

The Heap 442

    The Heap Is Critical for Software Developers 444

    Understanding the Terms 444

The Heap Functions 446

Checking `malloc()` for Errors 453

Multiple Allocations 455

Homework 458

    General Knowledge 458

    Find the Bug 459

    Write Code That… 459

    Extra Credit 460

Lesson 10 Project 461

Lesson 11 Long-Term Storage   **475**

  Unit 21   Sequential Files 477

What You'll Learn About 478

About Disk Files 478

The First Step: Opening the File 480

Closing the File with `fclose()` 484

Writing Data 485

Adding to a Sequential File 488

Reading a Sequential File 490

Homework 492

    General Knowledge 492

    Find the Bug 493

    Write Code That... 494

    Extra Credit 494

Unit 22   Random Access Files 495

What You'll Learn About 496

An Introduction to Random Access 496

Opening Random Access Files 497

Seeking the Correct Position 499

Doing the Random I/O 501

Other File-Related Functions...506

Homework 508

    General Knowledge 508

    Find the Bug 509

    Write Code That... 509

    Extra Credit 509

Lesson 11 Project...511

Lesson 12 Your C Future   **521**

Unit 23   Advanced Issues in C 523

What You'll Learn About 524

Sorting for Order 524

Sorting String Data 530

Sorting Structures 533

Finding the Minimum and Maximum 536

Homework 538

    General Knowledge 538

    Write Code That... 539

    Extra Credit 539

Unit 24   What's This C++ All About? 541

What You'll Learn About 542

Building on C 542

Don't Repeat `struct` 543

Define Variables Anywhere 544

Simple I/O 544

Allocate and Deallocate Without Headaches....................546

A Third Way to Pass Data..546

Homework 551

General Knowledge 551

What's the Output?..552

Find the Bug 552

Write Code That… 552

Extra Credit 553

Lesson 12 Project..555

Appendix A Installing Your C Compiler..................................565

What Will Happen 566

Begin at DOS 566

The Installation 567

Modifying Your Path 568

Appendix B ASCII Table 571

Appendix C C Operator Precedence Table............................579

Index 583

Acknowledgments

The editors and production department at Sams Publishing continue to strive for excellence. They want their readers to read only the best computer texts in the world. They work day and night, turning my words into something meaningful.

Rosemarie Graham's hands, eyes, and direction made this book the best introduction to C programming that exists. Dean Miller designed this book. Dean, you're a master at work, and you deserve a salary raise at least monthly, in my opinion! I gave Keith Davenport only moments at the end of this book to get the disk ready, but he came through above par as always. Stacy Hiquet is more in the background now that she's High-Level Super-Executive Management. Everyone gains from her new role except authors who don't get to work as closely with her as before. Poor Gary Farrar must make sense of the writing I do. Gary, you spend more time correcting my writing than I spend writing it! Thanks for your eagle eyes, and I hope that you know I'm grateful. I also wish to thank Gayle Johnson and the production staff, who worked diligently on this book to make it the best possible book on C.

My beautiful bride Jayne and my parents Glen and Bettye Perry continue to support my efforts. My life is great because of them.

About the Author

Greg Perry is quickly becoming one of the most sought-after speakers and writers in the programming field. He is known for being able to take programming topics and bring them down to the beginner's level. Perry has been a programmer and trainer for the past 17 years. He received his first degree in computer science, and then he received a master's degree in corporate finance. Perry is the author of 28 other computer books, including *Teach Yourself Object-Oriented Programming with Turbo C++*, *Teach Yourself Object-Oriented Programming with Visual C++*, *Moving from C to C++*, *QBasic Programming 101* (all Sams Publishing), and *The Complete Idiot's Guide to Visual Basic* (Alpha Books). In addition, he has published articles in several publications, including *Software Development*, *Access Advisor*, *PC World*, and *Data Training*. In his spare time, he wonders around Italy, eating the world's best ice cream and pasta.

Introduction

The book you hold offers something you may not have encountered before. Whereas other books teach you C, this book also includes a C compiler. With this book, there is literally nothing else to buy (except, of course, the computer)! Borland International's Turbo C++ compiler, actually a C and a C++ compiler all in one, turns your computer into a C programming powerhouse. The disk that comes with this book also includes all the code listings in the book, as well as answers to all the exercises at the end of each unit.

Despite the great disk included, this book would be worthless if it didn't teach C. *C Programming in 12 Easy Lessons* begins at the beginning, assuming that you don't know C. By the time you're finished, you will have mastered the C language. You'll be learning how to program, how to perform input and output, how to work with disk files, and how to achieve advanced memory management through C programs.

If you've looked at the computer want ads lately, you've surely noticed the assortment of C programming positions. It seems as if there are always more jobs than C programmers. Why not join the ranks? This book will help get you there.

▶ Who Should Use This Book

C Programming in 12 Easy Lessons is aimed primarily at beginning programmers who either have never programmed or who have never seen a C program. Text, questions, exercises, and numerous program listings are aimed at both beginning programmers and those new to C.

If you already program but have never had the time to tackle C, this book is right for you because it teaches more than just the language. This book attempts to teach you how to program correctly, concentrating on proper coding techniques in addition to the C language.

▶ This Book's Philosophy

C Programming in 12 Easy Lessons extends the traditional programming textbook tutorial by offering all the text and language syntax needed for newcomers to C. It also offers complete program examples, exercises, questions, tips, warnings, notes, and, of course, a full-featured C compiler.

This book focuses on programming correctly in C by teaching structured programming techniques and proper program design. Emphasis is placed on a program's readability rather than on "tricks of the trade" code examples. In this changing world, programs should be clear, properly structured, and well documented. This book doesn't waver from that philosophy.

The format of this book, 12 lessons with two units per lesson, was planned to give you the most out of each sitting. You'll find that you can master each lesson in one evening, taking a short break between the two units. At the end of the lessons are projects. They contain programs that use the lesson's key points, and they also feature a unique line-by-line description of the program.

▶ A Note to the Instructor

If you're an instructor using this book for your class, you'll find that its inclusion of a C compiler lets the entire class participate on the same level, using the same compiler for their programs. When you demonstrate the editing, compiling, linking, and running of C programs, you'll know that your students will be using the same compiler that you use in class.

Each unit offers numerous questions and exercises that provide a foundation for classroom discussions. The answers to all the questions and exercises are on the enclosed disk. In addition, each unit contains one or more "extra credit" programming exercises that you can assign as homework. The answers to these exercises don't appear on the disk.

The typical semester class is divided into 15 or 16 weeks of study. A useful lesson plan that incorporates this book would spend one week on each lesson, with four exams every four weeks. Each lesson contains two units, and one unit can easily be covered in one classroom sitting.

Because *C Programming in 12 Easy Lessons* becomes a part-time teacher, questioning and guiding the student as he or she reads and learns, you can spend more classroom time looking at complete program examples and exploring the theory of C instead of taking time to cover petty details.

▶ Overview

Here is an overview of this book, giving you a bird's-eye view of where you're about to head:

Lesson 1: Programming with C

This lesson explains what C is by giving a brief history of the C programming language and presenting an overview of C's advantages over other languages. You'll learn how to develop C programs and the steps you follow to write and run programs. You'll dive right into working with the C compiler in the second unit.

Lesson 2: Meeting C Programs

This lesson familiarizes you with the format of C programs. Once you master this lesson, you'll be able to recognize C programs and write simple programs that output data.

Lesson 3: Data Basics

C supports all kinds of data. This lesson teaches you about C variables. You must understand the various data types possible in C before you can work with data. You'll see how C supports both numeric and character data.

Lesson 4: Simple Operators

This lesson introduces you to the rich assortment of C operators. These operators make up for the fact that the C programming language is very small. The operators and their order of precedence are more important in C than in most other programming languages. Before you finish this lesson, you'll be using the relational operators to write programs that make decisions based on calculations and data that the user enters.

Lesson 5: Upgraded Operators

This lesson extends your knowledge of the C operators by teaching you some of the more advanced data-manipulation operators and their nuances. C works on a lower level than most programming languages by giving you special operators that control and test internal bit values inside your computer's memory.

Lesson 6: Looping Back and Forth

C data processing is powerful due to the looping and selection constructs it offers. This lesson shows you how to write programs that make decisions that execute certain parts of the program.

Lesson 7: Taking Charge

After learning about the loop control commands in Lesson 6, you'll be ready to control those loops with the commands taught in this lesson. You'll see how to exit a loop early. In addition, you'll learn how a special statement named `switch` improves the readability of your programs when the programs must choose from among many options.

Lesson 8: Breaking It Up with Functions

C contains no commands that perform input or output. To make up for this apparent oversight, C supplies several useful input and output functions. By separating input and output functions from the language, C achieves better portability between computers. This lesson also describes several of the other built-in math, character, and string functions. These functions keep you from having to write your own routines to perform common tasks. Once you learn these built-in functions, the second unit in this lesson teaches you how to write your own functions.

Lesson 9: Lots of Data

C offers arrays that hold multiple occurrences of repeating data but that don't require much effort on your part to process. Unlike many other programming languages, C also uses pointer variables a great deal. Pointer variables and arrays work together to give you flexible data storage that allows for easy sorting and searching of data.

Lesson 10: Consolidating Items

Variables, arrays, and pointers aren't enough to hold the types of data that your programs require. Structures allow for more powerful grouping of many different kinds of data into manageable units. By the time you reach this lesson, you'll begin to see some limitations of regular variables. By mastering an advanced topic called *dynamic memory allocation,* you'll be writing advanced memory-management programs that utilize your system's resources better than most other programming languages.

Lesson 11: Long-Term Storage

Your computer would be too limiting if you couldn't store data to the disk and put that data back into your programs. Disk files are required by most real-world applications. The units in this lesson describe how C processes sequential and random-access files and teaches the fundamental principles needed to effectively save data to disk.

Lesson 12: Your C Future

Where are you headed as a C programmer? Where is C headed? This lesson answers both of these questions. You'll explore a unit that contains advanced programming algorithms that you can use to sort and analyze data effectively. Someday, you'll be ready to move from C to C++. The second unit in this lesson helps smooth that transition. This lesson gives you a taste for the C++ language and shows you how C++ improves on C by offering shortcut commands and procedures.

▶ This Book's Disk

This book contains a full-featured C compiler called *Turbo C++.* Turbo C++ is made by Borland International, a world-famous company known for introducing C and C++ to the most C programmers. The compiler comes with an integrated editor, debugger, and compiler that compile both C and C++ programs professionally.

Note   Appendix A explains how to install the C compiler on your computer.

The disk also contains all the code in all of this book's programs. The first line of every program in this book contains a comment with the program's disk filename.

The disk also contains the answers to all review questions and exercises at the end of each unit, except for the extra credit problems. The answers are organized by lesson and are in a directory named \ANSWERS.

▶ Conventions Used in This Book

This book uses the following typographic conventions:

▶ Code lines, variables, and any text you see on-screen appear in monospace.

▶ Placeholders in statement syntax explanations appear in *italic monospace*.

▶ New terms appear in *italic*.

▶ Filenames in regular text appear in uppercase, such as MYFILE.DAT.

▶ Optional parameters in statement syntax explanations are enclosed in flat brackets ([]). You don't type the brackets when you include these parameters.

▶ Menu commands appear like this: File Open. This command means to select the Open option from the File menu.

definition
Definitions of new terms often appear in margin notes, which are located next to or near the paragraph in which the term first appears.

The following items also appear throughout this book:

Note   When further thought is needed on a particular topic, the note icon brings extra information to your attention.

Tip   A tip shows you an extra shortcut or advantage possible with the command you just learned.

Warning   Sometimes you must take extra care when trying a particular command or function. Warnings point out the dangers before you encounter them yourself.

SIDEBAR

In addition, you'll find several sidebars with useful information that is related to the topic at hand.

Concept   **What You Will Learn**

Concepts, located at the beginning of each major section, provide a succinct overview of the material in that section.

Review   **What You Have Learned**

Reviews, which appear at the end of each major section, recap the material you learned in that section.

 STOP&TYPE This icon provides a description of a subsequent program listing.

▼ INPUT

An input icon marks a program listing that demonstrates the major concepts from the section you just finished.

▼ OUTPUT

This icon accompanies a typical output of the program.

▼ ANALYSIS

A detailed description of the program appears after the output.

Lesson ▶ 1

Programming with C

Unit 1: Computer Programming and C

Unit 2: The Turbo C++ Compiler

Lesson 1 Project

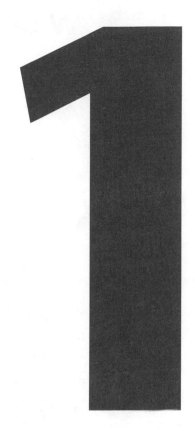

Computer Programming and C

c

compiler

debugging

editor

program

Turbo C++

▶ What You'll Learn About

- ▶ Why program?
- ▶ Programming steps
- ▶ C: A brief history in programming time

Computer people fall into two categories: computer users and computer programmers. Computer users use the computer as a tool for achieving tasks such as word processing and spreadsheet analysis. With the help of this book and Turbo C++, you're going to join the ranks of programmers. Programmers create the programs that users use.

Note Turbo C++ is supplied with this book. C++ is a superset of C. This book teaches C, the programming language that you should learn before C++. Turbo C++ runs C programs. If and when you make the move to C++, you'll already have the C++-compatible language as well.

This unit introduces you to programming by describing the steps programmers go through to create programs for users. You'll also learn why the Turbo C++ programming language was designed and catch a glimpse of your C programming future.

▶ Why Program?

Concept   **What You Will Learn**

It's easy to remove the mystery of programming when you see that writing a program requires familiarization with a simple design process.

definition

A *program* is a list of detailed instructions.

Despite countless science fiction stories and the computer myths floating around, computers have no brains. Perhaps you've heard of a computer's *CPU,* or *central processing unit,* which controls the computer. The CPU does nothing on its own! The CPU is a robot-like computer controller that follows instructions.

The instructions make up a program that you or some other programmer writes. The computer, led by the CPU, which directs all the other components such as the keyboard, screen, and printer, follows the program's instructions meticulously.

Note As you'll soon see, if your program contains an incorrect instruction, the computer will attempt to follow that instruction, producing those computer mistakes you often hear about. Computers really don't make mistakes, but programmers often do.

definition

A program mistake is called a *bug*. When you correct a mistake, you *debug* the program.

A computer program's instructions follow a certain pattern. Your computer can't understand English, Italian, Spanish, or any other spoken language. Maybe someday computers *will* understand such languages, but in the meantime, you must learn to speak in the computer's language. As with spoken languages, there are several computer languages. Each has its own set of grammar and spelling rules, called *syntax* rules.

In the next 12 lessons, you'll learn a foreign language. As you know, that language is C. Luckily, computer languages are easier to learn than spoken languages. Computers are pickier than people, though. Computers require more rigid language rules than people do because the computer can't think; it can only blindly follow your orders.

As Figure 1.1 shows, when the computer follows the program's instructions, the result of those instructions is called the *output*. In other words, the work that a computer does as a result of running the program is the output from the program.

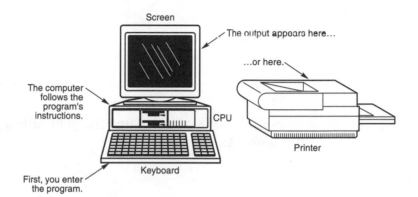

FIGURE 1.1.
The program's instructions produce the output.

Note The output might appear on the screen, printer, modem, or in a disk file.

Listing 1.1 contains a C program. Remember that you can find all of this book's programs, stored under their first-line comment filenames, on the disk that comes with this book. By loading the programs using File Open, you can save a lot of typing time. Listing 1.1 looks cryptic because it is! Don't worry about what the program says or how you make it work. For now, look at its overall format and consider these points:

▶ You must tell the computer to follow a program by *running* that program.

▶ Running a program is also called *executing* a program because the computer executes the program's instructions.

▶ The computer often runs a program sequentially, from the first line to the last, although you can change the order of that execution.

▶ The program often is called *code*.

▶ Each instruction is called a *statement*.

▶ Other than some housekeeping and formatting code, each line in a program typically is a single instruction.

▶ The computer runs only one of your program's instructions at a time.

Review

What You Have Learned

Computers need programs to do work. Without programs, computers would be useless.

▼ **INPUT   LISTING 1.1. GLANCING THROUGH A C PROGRAM.**

```
 1:  /* Filename: INTRO.C */
 2:  #include <stdio.h>
 3:  #include <string.h>
 4:  int main()
 5:  {
 6:    char name[25];
 7:    int n;
 8:    printf("What is your first name? ");
 9:    gets(name);
10:    n = strlen(name);
11:    printf("Your name has %d letters.\n", n);
12:    return 0;
13:  }
```

 Throughout this book, all program listings include a sample output from the program.

▼ **OUTPUT**

```
What is your first name? Clark
Your name has 5 letters.
```

▼ **ANALYSIS**

This program asks the user for a name and prints the number of letters in that name. (The *user* is the person who runs the program. Sometimes the programmer is also the user.) Lines 5 and 13 aren't really instructions, but they help format the program as needed. You'll be able to understand this program completely after just a few lessons.

▶ **Programming Steps**

What You Will Learn

Learn the steps every programmer goes through to design and write programs.

When you want your computer to do something, whether that *something* is manage a checkbook, control inventory, or play a game, you know that you've got to supply a program so that the computer knows what to do. Basically, there are two ways to acquire a program for your computer:

1. Buy a program that someone else wrote.
2. Write the program yourself.

Surely you've bought many programs for your computer already. The operating system itself is a program, Microsoft Windows is a program, your word processor is a program, and programming languages such as Turbo C++ are programs.

Note A programming language is a program that lets you write *other* programs. Hmm, which came first—the programming language or the program?

Store-bought (or mail-ordered) programs don't always do what you want them to. Such programs must be general-purpose to support many different kinds of user needs. Individuals and companies have specific needs that aren't always addressed in store-bought programs. Companies often have large programming staffs. If it were always possible to buy every program that every company needed, there would be no need for such programming staffs. Luckily (for programmers), there will always be a need for programmers who address specific concerns.

THE THIRD OPTION

There is actually a third way for you to obtain a program that addresses your specific needs. Often, firms sell accounting programs that can be modified to work the way the users of those programs want.

Companies might adopt many different accounting procedures. By buying programs that you can modify, you save the trouble of developing those programs from scratch and gain the advantage of being able to change them to work exactly the way you want.

Most programs, however, such as word processors, games, and spreadsheets, can't be modified by the programmers who buy them. Therefore, for most people, the two program-acquiring options just listed are the only choices available.

The rest of this book teaches you how to write programs in the C programming language, using the Turbo C++ language. Before diving directly into the language itself, take a few minutes to learn about the "big picture."

Tip If you are brand-new to the programming process and you want a more in-depth look at how individuals and companies' data-processing departments write programs, check out *Absolute Beginner's Guide to Programming* (Sams Publishing, 1993).

When you want to write a program, where do you begin? Here are the typical steps that most programmers take when developing programs:

1. Decide what you want done.

   This obvious step gets the ball rolling. Formulate a clear and detailed picture of what you want the program to do. Determine what kinds of data the program will need, decide what you want the program's screens to look like, and decide which calculations you want the program to perform.

Warning A builder doesn't construct a building without blueprints because it would be difficult to insert missing rooms once the building were up! Although adding to a program might be *somewhat* simpler than adding a room to a building, the more you plan your program and decide on its contents *before* you write the program, the faster you'll finish the program and be able to move onto other projects.

2. Design the program.

You must take the project you designed in step 1 and translate those abstract needs into a step-by-step list of instructions that your computer can understand. You must use a programming language such as C, because your computer can understand only computer languages.

For beginning programmers, this step is the most difficult. Once you become more familiar with programming specifics, the details of the language itself will get easier. As you practice programming, you'll begin to write longer programs. Then you'll have to spend more time in step 1, laying out the program's overall goals before going to the keyboard to type the program.

definition

To *compile* means to prepare a program for execution. A *compiler* is part of most computer languages.

3. Compile and run the program.

The computer can understand programs written in programming languages, but only after you compile those programs. When you compile the program with your computer language, such as Turbo C++, the compiler helps secure the code from unwanted changes, checks for some errors, and converts the program into an efficient set of instructions that the computer can follow.

definition

A *syntax error* occurs when you misspell a computer-language word or violate the programming language's grammar rules.

Note The program that you write is called the *source code* or *source program*. The computer can run your program only after compiling the source code into *executable* code. Therefore, the source program that you write is not exactly the program your computer runs. The source code makes it easy for you to write a program, and the compiler converts that program into a format that your computer needs to execute the program. Figure 1.2 illustrates the difference between source code and the compiled (executable) program.

FIGURE 1.2.
You must compile your source code before executing the program.

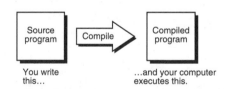

The compiler finds any syntax errors you might have made when writing your program. The compilation won't complete properly until you eliminate all syntax errors in the code.

definition

A *logic error* occurs when you direct a program to do something that it shouldn't, such as computing inventory depreciation incorrectly.

4. Test the program.

Despite your best efforts, there will almost always be logic errors in your program that you must fix. The compiler can't detect your logic errors. Only you can by running the program repeatedly, trying every combination of data.

Logic errors appear when a program produces paychecks with negative amounts, incorrectly zeros bank balances, or erases files that should remain intact. You can write a program free of syntax errors that still contains a number of logic errors.

Warning Test carefully. Some logic errors don't appear for a long time and after lots of testing. Even worse, some logic errors appear long after the user uses the program. Don't be embarrassed by logic errors later; catch as many as you can *before* distributing your program to users.

5. Maintain the program.

As soon as you finish the program, get the bugs out, and distribute the program to whomever will use it (you might be your own user), keep in mind that you'll need to update the program periodically and make changes. Supporting, or maintaining, the programs you write is part of a programmer's life.

Tip Throughout this book, you'll read about ways to improve how you write programs. By writing clear code, you'll decrease maintenance nightmares later.

Figure 1.3 shows the program-creation process. Notice that creating a program often requires an *iterative* approach: You have to repeat certain steps to fix errors that appear during the process.

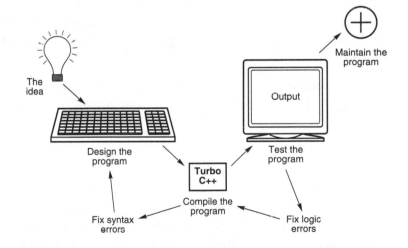

FIGURE 1.3.
Creating a program.

Review **What You Have Learned**

Writing a program requires a five-step design and coding process.

Note There is no input, output, or analysis here due to this section's conceptual nature.

▶ C: A Brief History of Programming Time

Concept   **What You Will Learn**

The C programming language provides many advantages for computer programmers.

C is one of the newest programming languages in existence. C's creators, Dennis Ritchie and Kenneth Thompson, designed C in the early 1970s for the Bell Labs. At the time, there were already many programming languages, but none seemed to provide just what Bell Labs needed for its brand-new operating system, UNIX.

Until C came along, most programmers wrote operating systems in an extremely low-level, difficult, and cryptic programming language called *assembly language*. The worst part of assembly-language programming came during the maintenance of programs. Although assembly-language programs are difficult to write, they're even more difficult to maintain.

C's Strengths and Weaknesses

Ritchie and Thompson wanted to lessen their maintenance chores so badly that they designed a programming language (C) that let them create an efficient operating system that was easier to maintain than operating systems written in other programming languages.

C often is called a *high-low-level language*. Assembly language is considered *low-level* because of its detailed, cryptic commands that are difficult to maintain but extremely efficient. Nonassembly programming languages usually are called *high-level languages* because they more closely match spoken language and are easier to learn and maintain— at the expense of speed and runtime efficiency.

C bridges the gap between low- and high-level languages because of its efficient nature. C compiles to extremely efficient and compact code. A compiled C program runs at execution speeds that almost rival those of an assembly-language program. At the same time, C uses high-level commands and functions that are much easier to master than assembly language—hence C's label as a high-low-level language.

definition

Portability is the capability of a programming language to be compiled on many different kinds of computers.

 Warning   Although a C program is much easier to read and understand than an assembly-language program, C is still one of the most cryptic high-level programming languages. C relies on many *operators* (symbols such as && and +=) and relatively few commands, whereas other programming languages contain many more commands than C. These commands often make the other languages easier to follow than a corresponding C program.

11 UNIT

1

Computer Programming and C

> *Tip* Although C generally isn't as easy to follow as other programming languages, you can learn to write clear and concise C code that's fairly easy to read and maintain. This book always stresses clarity of code over tricky and subtle techniques that detract from a program's readability.

The reason that C uses few commands is to retain its portability across hardware and operating systems. If C relied on lots of specific commands such as screen color commands, another computer might not support that color and the program would have to be rewritten to work on both machines.

The low number of C commands leaves the language lean and less hardware-dependent. When a compiler such as Turbo C++ wants to implement a machine-specific feature, the compiler vendor adds a library function that's not part of the language but a superset of the language, thereby preserving the core C language. The bottom line is that when you learn the fundamental C language, you'll know C on every computer that contains a C compiler.

ANSI C FOR YOU AND ME

The American National Standards Institute (*ANSI*) defines programming-language standards. The ANSI C standard is supported by almost every C compiler on the market, including Turbo C++.

ANSI C defines the fundamental C language and common library routines so that programmers who learn C on one computer using one compiler will be able to move to other computers and compilers with little or no trouble.

There's one problem with strictly adhering to the ANSI C standard. The ANSI committee hasn't defined any screen controls such as color, graphics, or even simple screen-clearing functions or commands. There are too many kinds of hardware for ANSI to write a standard that supports everything.

Therefore, when you learn a compiler's C, such as Turbo C++, you'll almost always learn compiler-specific functions that perform lots of work. Those functions aren't supported by the ANSI committee. Feel free to take advantage of compiler-specific functions so that your programs look good and contain the power they need. If you use these non-ANSI functions, just remember that they might not be available in future compiler releases or on other compilers that you might someday use.

definition
A *library function* is an add-on routine, supplied by the C compiler, that performs a specific task.

definition
I/O, or *input/ output,* is the computer's capability to retrieve and send data using devices such as the keyboard, screen, and printer.

C contains no I/O commands, only I/O functions (routines supplied by Borland). By requiring that all C compiler vendors supply their own I/O library functions, the designers of C helped to ensure C's portability across different hardware. One of the primary ways that computers differ is in their attached I/O devices. Some have mice, some have one-color screens, some have dual printers, some have CD-ROM drives, and so on. If the designers of C added CD-ROM commands, for example, those commands wouldn't work on computers without CD-ROMs. Also, because of the differences between CD-ROM access among different computers, a command that works on one CD-ROM might not work on another.

Good examples of hardware-dependent languages are the versions of BASIC you can find on virtually every computer in existence. Although modern-day versions of BASIC are extremely powerful (such as Visual Basic, QuickBasic, and QBasic), each is directly tied to specific computers and won't work on a different kind of computer. Versions of BASIC for Apple's computers won't work on IBM-compatible computers. If you learn to program in BASIC on an Apple, for example, you have to learn a completely different BASIC language if you switch to an IBM-compatible computer. With C, you don't have an about-face every time you switch computer brands. The fundamental C language is consistent, and each computer version of C comes with its own I/O library functions that work on specific computers.

Borland and Turbo C++

Borland International, the company that developed the Turbo C++ compiler supplied with this book, is a leader in programming languages. The term *leader* isn't just a trite, overused phrase in this case. Open any programming magazine or book and you'll invariably find an article or section on a Borland C or C++ product.

definition

An *editor* is like a simple word processor that you use to type programs.

Borland's first claim to fame was its *Turbo Pascal* language, introduced in the early 1980s. Before Turbo Pascal, programmers had to complete a series of tedious steps to enter, compile, and test programs. Turbo Pascal supplied an integrated editor, compiler, and runtime system that provided one environment with which you could create, compile, and test your programs.

Borland later developed Turbo C (and subsequently Turbo C++), which brought that same ease of programming to the C language for the first time. As you'll soon see, Turbo C provides a simple and integrated tool for programming in C. Figure 1.4 shows the Turbo C++ editor being used to write a C program.

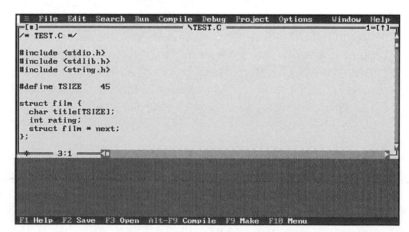

FIGURE 1.4.
With Turbo C, entering, compiling, and running a C program is easy.

 Note   In the next unit, you'll learn how to use Turbo C++'s editor and compiler.

Review

C is a standard and portable language. Once you learn Turbo C++, you'll be able to write C programs on virtually all computers. Borland added the *easy* ingredient to C programming with Turbo C++.

Note There is no input, output, or analysis here due to this section's conceptual nature.

▶ Homework

General Knowledge

1. What is a program?
2. What does a computer do without programs?
3. What is a programming bug?
4. Name the two kinds of computer bugs.
5. What is the difference between the two kinds of computer bugs?
6. Instead of writing your own programs, why don't you purchase every program you need?
7. Why is C called a high-low-level language?
8. How does an editor help you create C programs?
9. What does I/O mean?
10. Why does the C language contain no I/O commands?

Note There are no What's the Output?, Find the Bug, or Write Code That... sections here due to this unit's conceptual nature.

Extra Credit

11. Technically, your computer can't run the source code that you write, even though you supply this source code in the C programming language. Describe what the computer does to your source code before you can run the programs you write.

The Turbo C++
Compiler

dialog box

**Integrated Development
Environment**

linking

menu

on-line help

▶ What You'll Learn About

- ▶ Starting and stopping Turbo C++
- ▶ An overview of Turbo C++'s IDE
- ▶ Practicing program development
- ▶ Getting help

Warm up your keyboard, because this unit jumps into the hands-on waters of the Turbo C++ compiler supplied with this book. This unit shows you how to start the compiler, enter a program, edit a program, and compile a program.

The Turbo C++ compiler's primary strength lies in its *IDE,* or *integrated development environment,* which provides for a full-screen editing system that helps you create your C programs without getting in your way.

Note Although you'll see and type C code in this unit, you won't yet understand the code. Before learning C, you've got to learn how to enter, edit, and run C programs. As soon as you've mastered the IDE, you'll be ready to learn the C language starting in the next lesson.

▶ Starting and Stopping Turbo C++

Concept   **What You Will Learn**

Start the Turbo C++ compiler to begin your exploration of the C language. In addition to starting Turbo C++, you must also learn how to safely terminate Turbo C++ to protect your data and programs.

The Turbo C++ compiler supplied with this book works in your PC's DOS-based environment. If you use Windows, you can use the compiler with no problem as long as you open a DOS window before starting Turbo C++.

Tip To open a DOS window, select the MS-DOS prompt icon from the Main group in Windows Program Manager by double-clicking on the icon or by using the arrow keys to highlight the icon and pressing Enter.

definition
It's at the *DOS prompt* that you issue MS-DOS commands to your PC.

Whether you start the compiler directly from DOS or from a Windows MS-DOS window, you'll see a DOS prompt that looks something like this:

```
C:\>
```

Depending on how your computer is set up, you might see a disk drive letter different from C:, or you might see a pathname after the drive letter. To start Turbo C++, at the DOS prompt type TC and press Enter. (You can use either uppercase or lowercase letters.) After a slight pause, Turbo C++ will load and display the IDE screen shown in Figure 2.1. This screen contains a menu, a large work area in the middle of the screen, and a message area at the bottom of the screen.

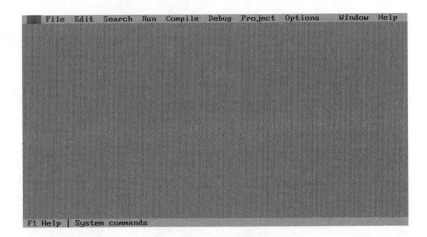

FIGURE 2.1.
The first Turbo C++
screen you see after
starting Turbo C++.

If Turbo C++ doesn't start when you type TC as just described, there are several things you can try to correct the problem. Make sure that Turbo C++ is installed. To do this, type DIR at the DOS prompt and look for a directory file named TCLITE. If TCLITE doesn't appear, turn to Appendix A and install the program using the disk that comes with this book.

IF YOU HAVE PROBLEMS

If Turbo C++ is installed but it doesn't start when you type TC, the pathname might not be set to the correct directory to run the program. Review Appendix A to see how to add Turbo C++'s directory to your computer's pathname. You'll have to reboot your computer to put the pathname change into effect.

If you want to go ahead and start Turbo C++ without rebooting or changing the pathname in your AUTOEXEC.BAT file, you must first change to Turbo C++'s directory by entering the following *change directory* DOS command:

```
CD\TCLITE\BIN
```

and then start the program by typing TC.

When you're through programming with Turbo C++, be sure that you properly exit Turbo C++ before you turn off the computer. To quit Turbo C++, type Alt-X. Alt-X is the shortcut keystroke for selecting File Quit. You'll learn all about Turbo C++'s menu system in the next few sections.

 Warning If you haven't saved to disk the program you were working on, Turbo C++ gives you a chance to do so by displaying a file-saving dialog box before you exit to DOS. From the dialog box, you can either save the file to the disk or ignore the warning and go to DOS without saving the file. Be sure to save your programs to your hard disk, not to a floppy disk. Your hard disk has a lot more free space and is always there when you want to load the program again.

If you don't exit from Turbo C++ before turning off your computer, you could lose part of your program or its data. A good rule of thumb is to exit to the DOS prompt (first exit Windows if it's running), wait a few seconds, and then turn off the machine.

Review   What You Have Learned

You must know how to start Turbo C++ before writing a C program, and you should exit Turbo C++ before turning off your computer.

Note   There is no input, output, or analysis here due to this section's conceptual nature.

► An Overview of Turbo C++'s IDE

Concept   What You Will Learn

Learn what features the Turbo C++ editor includes that help you build C programs.

Before going any further, make sure that you've read Appendix A and followed its instructions on installing Turbo C++ on your computer. The Turbo C++ compiler that you install contains the following components:

▶ An integrated, full-screen, multiwindowed text editor.

▶ A one-step compiler that converts your source code to a compiled executable file with one keystroke.

▶ An integrated debugger that helps you get the bugs out of your programs. (Surely you won't need the debugger. It's only for people who make mistakes!)

▶ An on-line help system.

The following sections look at each of these components. Before going further, you should know that this book's Turbo C++ compiler is limited in some respects compared to other full-functioning C and C++ compilers available from Borland. None of these limitations will hamper your learning C. The enclosed Turbo C++ compiler is extremely powerful and contains a programming system unheard of just a decade ago. Nevertheless, the following items somewhat constrain the enclosed Turbo C++ system:

1. The compiler supports only the small memory model. Other C and C++ compilers that you can purchase contain five additional memory models: tiny, medium, compact, large, and huge. Many powerful programs in use today were

compiled using a small memory model. The small memory model produces faster code than the larger memory models, but your code and data spaces are somewhat limited. The total size of your final executable program can be no larger than 128K.

definition
A *small memory model* limits your code and data size to a total memory size of 64K each.

> *Note* 128K is approximately 128,000 characters. *K* in computer terminology is equal to approximately 1,000 characters of storage.

2. The enclosed compiler supports only DOS-mode programs. You won't find the Windows programming *API (application program interface)* that you get with more extensive (and expensive) C and C++ programming systems. The complexity introduced by Windows programming would hamper a newcomer to C. Learn how to write DOS-based programs while learning C, and you'll be ready to move to Windows programming only after you master the fundamentals of programming.

3. With the enclosed Turbo C++ compiler, you'll find many sample programs supplied by Borland. You can copy and paste code directly from these samples into your own code if you like. A Borland compiler you can purchase also contains the sample code that you'll find here, along with additional samples that explain interfacing routines to combine C and C++ with other programming languages such as Turbo Pascal.

4. Some of the more esoteric debugging options included in the more powerful compilers aren't available.

5. None of the extra utilities, such as the Turbo Assembler, GREP, or Profiler, are included on the enclosed disk.

The rest of this unit takes you through a guided tour of your new Turbo C++ compiler.

> *Note* The Turbo C++ compiler that comes with this book is nicknamed *Turbo C++ Lite* because of its somewhat limited functionality compared to the full-blown version of Turbo C++.

Navigating the Menus

You should first learn the parts of the Turbo C++ screen so that you can use the Turbo C++ IDE effectively. The Turbo C++ *menu bar* appears across the top of the screen, beginning with the File menu and ending with the Help menu. The large blank center area of the IDE is the location of the editing and debugging windows that you'll see as you create and run your programs. The bottom of the screen contains the *message bar* where Turbo C++ often displays helpful hints, explanations, and messages that guide you through your programming experience.

definition
A *menu* is a list of choices offered by a computer program.

> *Tip* Perhaps the most important message on the message bar is the F1 Help reminder, which tells you how to get help. The last section in this unit explains how to use Turbo C++'s help system.

UNIT

2

The Turbo C++ Compiler

Each of the menu bar's options produces a pull-down menu, sometimes called a *submenu*. To use a pull-down menu, you must first display it. There are two ways to do so:

▶ Press and hold the Alt key while pressing the boldfaced letter of the submenu you want to display.

▶ Click on the menu-bar option whose submenu you want to display.

For example, you must display the File pull-down menu before you can choose from it. Click on the menu bar File option, or press Alt-F, and you'll see the File pull-down menu, shown in Figure 2.2.

 Note   Often, this book calls pull-down menus (or submenus) just *menus* to keep things simple.

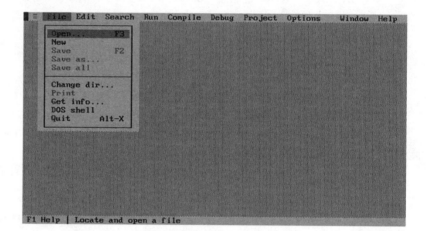

FIGURE 2.2.
Now you can choose from the File menu.

After you display a menu, you can choose from that menu's list of choices. Use the mouse or up and down arrow keys to navigate through the menu choices. For example, if you want to save a program file, the File menu contains a Save option. Once you select the File Save option, you can save to the disk whatever program you're editing at the time.

 Note   Many of the menu options display *dialog boxes,* which are explained a little later in this lesson.

As you display menu options, Turbo C++ updates the message bar, giving you helpful information on the menu choice that's displayed. Table 2.1 explains each of the menu bar's options to give you an overview of the possible menu commands.

Table 2.1. The menu bar's menu options.

Menu	Description
File	Lets you manage your program files by loading, saving, clearing, and printing your programs. The File menu also includes a Get inf. memory availability option, an MS-DOS shell option that lets you temporarily leave the IDE and issue DOS commands, and a Quit option that lets you exit Turbo C++.

Edit	Provides for normal text-editing abilities such as copying, cutting, and pasting commands.
Search	Lets you locate text in your programs.
Run	Contains options to compile and run your program in one step.
Compile	Lets you compile a program without running it.
Debug	Provides single-stepping and variable-watching debugging capabilities to help you eliminate any bugs that might find their way into your programs.
Project	Gives you the ability to manage multifile programs.
Options	Lets you customize Turbo C++'s IDE.
Window	Gives you multiwindowed editing capabilities, letting you edit two separate programs at the same time.
Help	Replaces bulky manuals that come with most compilers. The on-line help system gives you the ability to get information about any Turbo C++ command or library function.

This unit's section titled "Practicing Program Development" walks you through the program-building process, from the initial typing of a program to compiling and running the program, to give you practice in using the menus. This book doesn't discuss every menu command, because some are rarely used.

The Control Menu

There is a special unnamed menu on the menu bar. It's sometimes called the *control menu*. Look to the left of the File menu option and you'll see three horizontal lines. If you click on these lines (or press Alt-F to display the File menu and press the left arrow key), you'll see the control menu, shown in Figure 2.3.

FIGURE 2.3.
The control menu
displays a special set
of choices.

The control menu displays the following three choices:

▶ The About option displays the compiler's version number and copyright date.

▶ The Clear desktop option closes any and all open editing and debugging program windows to prepare the IDE for a new program.

▶ The Repaint desktop option redraws your IDE's screen in case one of your programs overwrites part of the IDE screen with extra output characters (a rare event).

Dialog Boxes

definition

A *dialog box* lets
you supply Turbo
C++ with infor-
mation.

Often, a menu command won't immediately perform an action. Some menu options produce other menus, and others request additional information before a command takes place. Some menu commands produce *dialog boxes* such as the one shown in Figure 2.4. This is the dialog box for the Options Environment Editor menu choice.

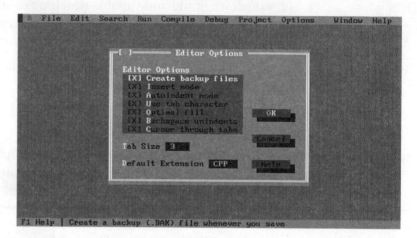

FIGURE 2.4.
A dialog box requests
additional information.

A dialog box is an easy-to-use window where you provide information for Turbo C++. There are several different kinds of data you can enter and options you can select through dialog box *controls*. You can move from control to control by clicking with the mouse or by pressing the Tab key. (Pressing Shift-Tab moves the highlight backward through the dialog-box controls.) Dialog boxes can contain the following types of controls:

▶ Check-box options contain an X at their left when the option is active. You can enable or disable a check-box option by clicking on the option or by pressing the Spacebar when the cursor is over the option.

▶ Text boxes let you type information. The Tab Size text box shown in Figure 2.4 is a text box. When you type a new value, Turbo C++ inserts a different number of spaces (using the Turbo C++ editor) when you press the Tab key.

Tip The default tab size of 8 is too large for most programmers. Change your tab size to 3 so that your Turbo C++ programs won't shift too far to the right when you press Tab before program lines.

▶ Command buttons appear on dialog boxes that contain the captions OK, Cancel, and Help. After making your dialog-box selections, click on the OK command button to activate the new dialog-box choices. Cancel resets your choices to their original values. Help displays information related to the dialog-box controls.

Note   The Options menu has a unique Save choice. After changing any of the Options menu choices, you must select Options Save if you want those options to remain in effect for your next Turbo C++ session. If you fail to select Save, the options that you set will revert to their previously-saved values when you exit Turbo C++. Select Options Save now to save the Tab Size text box that you just set.

Review   **What You Have Learned**

The menus provide you with all the choices possible while working in Turbo C++. By using the different types of controls, you enter new values into dialog boxes that often appear from menu selections.

Note   There is no input, output, or analysis here due to this section's conceptual nature.

▶ Practicing Program Development

Concept   **What You Will Learn**

Practice entering, editing, compiling, and running a simple Turbo C++ program.

The rest of this book covers the details of C. Before you get to the nitty-gritty, however, take time now to get some hands-on practice. This section walks you through the program creation and compilation process. To get things started, select File New. Turbo C++ opens a large white editing window in the center of your screen. Turbo C++ programs that you type will appear in this editing window. Choose File New before each new program that you start. File New provides a clean slate for your program development.

Note   All the common editing keys that you're used to, such as Insert, Delete, and the arrow keys, work inside the editing window the way you expect them to. You can modify the text you type by using these keys to control the insertion and deletion of characters, as well as cursor movement.

The File New command opens one-half of the editing window. Usually, this half window doesn't provide enough screen real estate to present much of a program. Pressing the F5 key (the shortcut key for Window Zoom) enlarges the window to its fullest size. Most Turbo C++ programmers expand the window to full size as soon as they open a new editing window. Press F5 now to see how expanding the editing window gives you more screen real estate.

TYPE The following program listing contains a complete C program. Type the program in your Turbo C++ editor. Use the Tab key to indent more quickly than pressing the Spacebar several times. Pay a lot of attention to your typing and be sure that your program matches that of the listing. If you notice a mistake, use the arrow keys, Insert, and Delete to correct the mistake.

Warning   Turbo C++ considers each of these special characters—[,], {, }, (,), <, and >—completely different from each other. Pay special attention to these characters and be sure that you use the right one. This book later explains how C interprets each of these special characters.

▼ INPUT   LISTING 2.1. USING THE TURBO C++ IDE.

```
/* Filename: INITIAL.C */
/* A program you enter to practice using the Turbo C++ IDE */
#include <stdio.h>
main()
{
  int K = 1024;
  long int convMem;
  convMem = 640L * K;
  printf("Conventional memory holds %ld bytes.\n", convMem);
  return 0;
}
```

Don't worry about what the program's details mean at this point. The rest of this book explains the C code in this program.

After you enter the program and review it to make sure that you typed everything correctly, save the program to the disk. Until you save your program to a disk file, the program resides in memory and you could lose it if your power goes out or if someone trips over a cord and unplugs your system unit!

Okay, perhaps a power loss isn't all that common, but saving your program early and often eliminates lots of potential problems. It's easy to accidentally delete critical text, but once you've safely tucked away the program file, the program will remain intact where you can retrieve it later if you unintentionally mess something up.

To save the file to the disk, select File Save. You'll see the dialog box shown in Figure 2.5. Type the filename. Optionally, you can precede it with the pathname where you want the file stored. Because all C programs end with the .C filename extension, you should get in the habit of saving files with a .C extension from the start.

Note   Turbo C++ uses the default filename NONAME00.CPP until you specify another filename in the File Save dialog box.

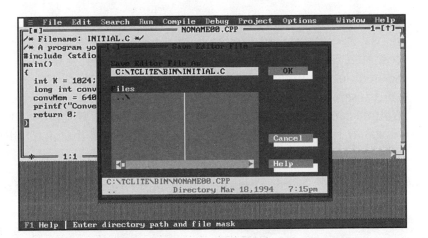

FIGURE 2.5.
Saving a file to the disk.

FILES ON THE ENCLOSED DISK

All the programs in this book are included on the disk supplied with this book. The files are stored by their filename under the directory named \SOURCE. As do all C programs, the files on the disk end with the .C extension.

The programs in this book all contain an initial line with the word Filename followed by a filename ending in .C. The preceding listing contains the file named INITIAL.C. This program is included on this book's disk, but you'll be much better off typing the program yourself instead of loading the program from the disk (using the File Open command). The best way to acquaint yourself with a new editor and programming language is to begin using that editor.

You'll see that Turbo C++ wants to add a .CPP extension. All C++ programs have this extension, but all C programs should have the .C extension.

Now that you've entered and saved the program's source code, it's time to run the program. Before you can run it, Turbo C++ must put the program through the following steps:

1. Compile the source program.
2. Normally, you would link the program at this point. However, the version of Turbo C++ that comes with this book doesn't have a linker. This means that you can't run your programs outside the Turbo C++ environment.
3. Run the program.

definition

Linking prepares your compiled program for execution.

The Compile pull-down menu lets you compile your program. Rarely will you need to access the Compile menu, however, because the Run option on the Run menu performs all these steps automatically. Therefore, to see the program execute, select Run Run. (The shortcut key for Run Run is Ctrl-F9.) When you do, Turbo C++ displays a status dialog box. If Turbo C++ spotted no errors, the compiled program runs.

If you made a typing error, Turbo C++ won't run the program but instead will display a message window at the bottom of the screen that highlights the error or errors that the compiler found. Figure 2.6 shows a message window with error messages displayed. Sometimes, as shown in Figure 2.6, you'll also see warning messages that aren't considered as serious as errors. If you don't make sure that you can safely ignore the warnings, trouble can result. If you get an error, press Enter. Turbo C++ places the cursor on the illegal line in your source code that corresponds to the highlighted error message, and you can fix the problem.

```
≡ File  Edit  Search  Run  Compile  Debug  Project  Options    Window  Help
────────────────────\WINWORD\12EASY\ERRORS2.C ───────────────────2──
/* Filename: ERRORS2.C */
/* Program with two bugs */
#include <stdioo.h>
main()
{
   float regEdCost = .35;
   float spcEdFactor = 1.5;
   int spcNumSold = 100;
   int numSold = 75;
   float spcTotal, regTotal
   /* Compute sales of both papers */
   regTotal = regEdCost * numSold;
   spcTotal = regEdCost * spcEdFactor * spcNumSold;
   /* Display the totals */
   printf("There were %d regular editions sold at $%.2f\n",
─[■]───────────────────── Message ─────────────────────────1─[↑]─■
Compiling C:\WINWORD\12EASY\ERRORS2.C:
•Error C:\WINWORD\12EASY\ERRORS2.C 3: Unable to open include file 'STDIOO.H'
 Error C:\WINWORD\12EASY\ERRORS2.C 12: , expected in function main()
 Error C:\WINWORD\12EASY\ERRORS2.C 15: Function 'printf' should have a prototy
 Warning C:\WINWORD\12EASY\ERRORS2.C 16: Possible use of 'regTotal' before def▼
◄■                                                                    ►
 F1 Help  Space View source  ◄─┘ Edit source  F10 Menu
```

FIGURE 2.6.
This message window contains three errors.

Tip   When Turbo C++ displays errors in the message window, you can press the up and down arrow keys to step through each error message, scrolling if needed to see the entire list.

How do you like the output? Perhaps you don't *see* any output! Turbo C++ doesn't overwrite the editing window with the compiled program's output when you run the program. Turbo C++ displays your program's output in the *user screen*. To see the output, press Alt-F5 (the shortcut key for Window User's screen). Any other keypress returns you to the editing window, where you can edit the file, save or load a program, or exit Turbo C++.

Tip   You can switch back and forth between the editing window and the user screen as many times as you wish.

STOP&TYPE   Listing 2.2 contains a longer program with which you can practice your editing and compiling skills. The program spans more than a single editing window length. Use the arrow keys, Page Up, Page Down, and scroll bars to practice scrolling the text up and down so that you can scan the listing from top to bottom after you enter the program.

Warning   Don't type the program's line numbers.

Review

Entering, editing, compiling, and running a C program is easy with the IDE's menus.

▼ INPUT   LISTING 2.2. A PRACTICE PROGRAM FOR YOUR SKILL-BUILDING.

```
1:  /* Filename: LONG.C */
2:  /* Prints C is Fun! on-screen several times */
3:  #include <stdio.h>
4:  name_print();   /* Prototypes */
5:  reverse_print();
6:  one_per_line();
7:
8:  main()
9:  {
10:   int ctr;   /* To control loops */
11:
12:   for (ctr = 1; ctr <= 2; ctr++)
13:    { name_print(); }   /* Calls function two times */
14:
15:   one_per_line();   /* Calls program's last function once */
16:   return 0;
17:  }
18:
19:  /*********************************************************/
20:  name_print()
21:  {
22:    /* Prints C is Fun! across a line, separated by tabs */
23:    printf("C is Fun!\tC is Fun!\tC is Fun!");
24:    printf("\tC is Fun!\n");
25:    printf("C  i s  F u n! C  i s  F u n! C  i s  F u n!\n");
26:
27:    reverse_print();   /* Calls next function from here */
28:    return 0;   /* Returns to main() */
29:  }
30:
31:  /*********************************************************/
32:  reverse_print()
33:  {
34:    /* Prints several C++ is Fun! messages, */
35:    /* in reverse, separated by tabs */
36:    printf("!nuF si C\t!nuF si C\t!nuF si C\t\n");
37:    return 0;   /* Returns to name_print() */
38:  }
39:
40:  /*********************************************************/
41:  one_per_line()
42:  {
43:    /* Prints C is Fun! down the screen */
44:    printf("C\n \ni\ns\n \nF\nu\nn\n!\n");
45:    return 0;   /* Returns to main() */
46:  }
```

```
C is Fun!        C is Fun!        C is Fun!        C is Fun!
C  i  s  F  u  n!  C  i  s  F  u  n!  C  i  s  F  u  n!
!nuF si C        !nuF si C        !nuF si C
C is Fun!        C is Fun!        C is Fun!        C is Fun!
C  i  s  F  u  n!  C  i  s  F  u  n!  C  i  s  F  u  n!
!nuF si C        !nuF si C        !nuF si C
C

i

s

F
u
n
!
```

▼ ANALYSIS

Around line 22, the program stops fitting into the editing window. You then have to scroll up and down the program to see its beginning and end. Some programs that you write might span 10 or more scrolling screens! You'll be thankful that Turbo C++ includes a Search menu when you're looking for parts of code in a 500-line program!

▶ Getting Help

What You Will Learn

Turbo C++'s on-line help is always just a keystroke away.

Getting help is easy. The Help menu, shown in Figure 2.7, offers several help options. Table 2.2 describes each help option.

FIGURE 2.7.
The Help menu.

Table 2.2. The Help menu options.

Help Option	Description
Contents	Offers an overview of the help, Turbo C++, debugger, editor, and graphics capabilities.
Index	Gives you an alphabetical listing of every topic Turbo C++ provides help on. When you highlight a topic, Turbo C++ displays that topic's help screen.

Help Option	Description
Topic search	Before selecting Topic search, move the cursor to any part of the screen or to a C-language command to get help on that topic. The Topic search option often is called *context-sensitive help* because Turbo C++ looks at the cursor (the context of your requested help) and displays a help window that describes that topic. The Ctrl-F1 keystroke is important to remember for context-sensitive help. When you want help on a command or a library function you just typed the name of, press Ctrl-F1 to see help on that topic.
Previous topic	Displays the previous help screen in case you want to return to the last help message you read.
Help on help	Turbo C++'s help system gives you help on itself! The Help on help option describes how to use the on-line help system.

As mentioned at the beginning of the message bar in the lower-left corner, the F1 key is helpful. While you're editing or displaying a menu, pressing F1 provides context-sensitive help on the editing window or on that menu topic.

Review · What You Have Learned

The designers of Turbo C++ knew that you would want help available at your fingertips, and help is just what you get with the on-line help system.

Note There is no input, output, or analysis here due to this section's conceptual nature.

► Homework

General Knowledge

1. What does IDE stand for?
2. What is the total size of a program and its data that you can create with this book's Turbo C++ compiler?
3. What shortcut key provides help with the editor and menu options?
4. What shortcut key provides context-sensitive help?
5. True or false: You must start Turbo C++ using uppercase letters due to the DOS requirement that commands be uppercase.
6. True or false: When you run a program, the output appears in the user screen, a screen different from the program-editing screen's window.

Note The rest of these questions are more limited than the rest of this book's Homework sections due to the fact that you're not quite ready to analyze C source code.

What's the Output?

7. Terri the Turbo C++ coder left an error in her source code. When she ran the program, errors appeared. Where does Turbo C++ display these errors?

8. After fixing the errors, Terri compiled and ran her program correctly. Where does Turbo C++ display the output of her program?

Find the Bug

9. Richard, owner of Swadley Swindlers, Inc., has decided to take up programming to save payroll costs. After getting the bugs out of his program, Richard followed these steps:

A. He selected File Save.

B. He pressed Enter without typing a filename.

C. He selected File Quit to exit to DOS.

When Richard came in the next day to make changes to his program, he couldn't find the file. Help Richard find his file by telling him the filename under which to look for the program.

Extra Credit

10. Type the following program and attempt to run it. The program has errors. Find the numbers of the offending lines.

```
 1: /* Filename: ERRORS2.C */
 2: /* Program with two bugs */
 3: #include <stdioo.h>
 4: main()
 5: {
 6:    float regEdCost = .35;
 7:    float spcEdFactor = 1.5;
 8:    int spcNumSold = 100;
 9:    int numSold = 75;
10:    float spcTotal, regTotal
11:    /* Compute sales of both papers */
12:    regTotal = regEdCost * numSold;
13:    spcTotal = regEdCost * spcEdFactor * spcNumSold;
14:    /* Display the totals */
15:    printf("There were %d regular editions sold at $%.2f\n",
16:          numSold, regTotal);
17:    printf("There were %d special editions sold at $%.2f\n",
18:          spcNumSold, spcTotal);
19:    return 0;
20: }
```

1

Programming
with C

STOP&TYPE In this lesson, you learned about the fundamentals of the C language, the Turbo C++ compiler, and how to enter and edit programs using Turbo C++'s Integrated Development Editor (IDE). You saw the following:

▶ An introduction to C programming concepts.

▶ How C compares to other languages.

▶ Starting Turbo C++.

▶ Using Turbo C++'s menus.

▶ Entering and editing C programs.

▶ Compiling C programs.

▶ Stopping Turbo C++.

Note   This project reviews entering and editing a C program using the IDE. Future projects concentrate much more on the C language's specifics and use a different format.

Step 1: Start Turbo C++

Before using the C language, you must start the compiler. Follow these steps:

1. Turn on your computer.

2. At the DOS prompt, type tc. You can type the command in uppercase or lowercase letters. The Turbo C++ IDE will appear.

Step 2: Open a Program Window

1. The Turbo C++ IDE is known as a *windowed environment*. You enter and edit programs in one or more windows that appear in the IDE. Before typing a new program, you must open a new file in a new window. Press Alt-F N (File New) to open a new file in a new editing window. Press F5 (Zoom) to enlarge the window.

2. Type the following program. When typing the program, be sure to press Enter at the end of each line. Type as accurately as possible so that no mistakes will appear later. Because the program takes more lines than will fit in the IDE's editing window, you'll see the IDE scroll down when you fill the open window.

Project 1 Listing. The C project program.

```c
/* Filename: PROJECT1.C */

// Prints the first 20 odd, then even, numbers.

// Once done, it prints them in reverse order.

#include <stdio.h>

#include <conio.h>


main()

{

  int num;    // The for-loop control variable

  clrscr();


  printf("The first 20 odd numbers:\n");

  for (num = 1; num < 40; num += 2)

    { printf("%d ", num); }


  printf("\n\nThe first 20 even numbers:\n");

  for (num = 2; num <= 40; num += 2)

    { printf("%d ", num); }
```

continues

Project 1 Listing. continued

```
printf("\n\nThe first 20 odd numbers in reverse:\n");

for (num = 39; num >= 1; num -= 2)

  { printf("%d ", num); }


printf("\n\nThe first 20 even numbers in reverse:\n");

for (num = 40; num >= 2; num -= 2)

  { printf("%d ", num); }


return 0;

}
```

3. When you finish typing the program, you can use Page Up, Page Down, and the arrow keys to scroll the top of the program back into view.

Step 3: Compile and Run the Program

1. Before running the program, you must compile it. Press Alt-R R (Run Run). (Ctrl-F9 is the shortcut key for compiling the program.) A compilation window will display statistics as the program compiles.

2. If errors appear, the compilation window will display Errors: Press any key. Pressing a key and looking at the bottom message window will bring those errors and their offending line numbers into view. You can press Enter and fix any errors that might appear. Recompile the program after you've typed it exactly as the listing shows.

3. If no errors occur, the compilation window disappears. The program's output appears in its own window, called the *user screen*. Press Alt-W U or Alt-F5 (the shortcut key) to view the output. Here's what you'll see:

```
The first 20 odd numbers:
1 3 5 7 9 11 13 15 17 19 21 23 25 27 29 31 33 35 37 39

The first 20 even numbers:
2 4 6 8 10 12 14 16 18 20 22 24 26 28 30 32 34 36 38 40
```

```
The first 20 odd numbers in reverse:
39 37 35 33 31 29 27 25 23 21 19 17 15 13 11 9 7 5 3 1

The first 20 even numbers in reverse:
40 38 36 34 32 30 28 26 24 22 20 18 16 14 12 10 8 6 4 2
```

4. Press any key to switch from the output screen to the IDE's editing window.

Step 4: Save Your Work

1. If you exit Turbo C++ without saving your C program, you'll lose the program and have to reenter it if you want to see the results again. Therefore, you'll want to save your programs to a disk file.

Note   All the programs in this book, including the one shown in Project 1 Listing, are stored on the enclosed disk. Unless you want the practice, you don't have to save this listing, because it's already on the disk.

2. To save a program, press Alt-F S (for File Save). The File Save dialog box appears.

3. Type a program name. Type a pathname as well if you want to store the program in a subdirectory. All Turbo C++ programs should end with the .C filename extension.

Step 5: Exit Turbo C++

1. After saving the program, you can exit Turbo C++ and return to DOS. You should always return to DOS and wait a few seconds (to give any system buffers a chance to clear) before powering off your computer.

2. Select Alt-F X (for File Quit) to return to DOS. If you didn't save your program, Turbo C++ displays a final dialog box that gives you one last chance to save the program.

Lesson ▶ 2

Meeting C Programs

Unit 3:   Style Issues

Unit 4:   Output with *printf()*

Lesson 2 Project

Style Issues

#define

#include

comment

constant

header file

preprocessor directive

▶ What You'll Learn About

- ▶ An overview of a C program
- ▶ Comment all over the place
- ▶ Studying the big picture

This unit describes the "big picture" of C by explaining what C programs look like and by discussing some of the more common elements of C programs. Once you've completed this unit, you'll be able to recognize C programs and understand simple concepts such as comments and preprocessor directives.

As you study this unit, familiarize yourself with the common language pieces and try to get a feel for what comprises a C program. This book leaves many specifics unexplained until you have a more solid C foundation.

▶ An Overview of a C Program

Concept   **What You Will Learn**

Learn about C's freeform style and important elements of all C programs.

STOP&TYPE   For the rest of this unit, you'll be studying the program shown in Listing 3.1. This listing contains a simple C program and provides you with enough starting components of a C program to put you well on your way toward understanding the language.

▼ INPUT   LISTING 3.1. A SIMPLE C PROGRAM.

```
 1:  /* Filename: SIMPLE.C */
 2:  /* The purpose of this program is to give readers an
 3:   introduction to the format of most C programs. */
 4:
 5:  #include <stdio.h>
 6:  #include <conio.h>
 7:  void findRetire(int age);
 8:
 9:  #define RETAGE 65
10:  main()
11:  {
12:    int age;
13:    clrscr();    /* Erase the screen */
14:
15:    printf("How old are you? ");
16:    scanf(" %d", &age);
17:
18:    findRetire(age);    /* Print a retirement message */
19:    return 0;
20:  }
21:  /******************************************************/
22:  void findRetire(int age)
```

```
23:  {
24:    int retire;
25:    /* Find out if eligible for retirement */
26:    if (age < RETAGE)
27:    { retire = RETAGE - age;
28:      printf("In %d years, you'll be able to retire!", retire);
29:    }
30:    else
31:     { retire = age - RETAGE;
32:       printf("You could have retired %d years ago!", retire);
33:     }
34:    return;
35:  }
```

Note Feel free to enter and run this program. The practice will do you good!

Warning Sure, you can cheat (I mean, *save time*) and load the program from the disk. At this stage, getting used to the C language outweighs the advantage of saving a few minutes of typing. Therefore, type the listing instead of loading the program.

Tip Mark the location of Listing 3.1 in your book, because the rest of this unit refers to sections of it.

One of the first things you'll notice about this program is that almost every line ends with a semicolon (;). All executable C statements end with a semicolon. At this point, don't worry about the placement of the semicolons. As you learn the C language, you'll learn what parts of the program need semicolons and what parts don't.

UNIT

3

Style Issues

WATCH YOUR TYPING!

Unit 2 warned you to be careful of C's special characters. C is perhaps more picky about exact typing than any other programming language. Throughout this book, you'll often be required to type a special character. As you can see from Listing 3.1, special characters appear throughout C programs.

Perhaps this would be a good time to learn the names of these special characters so that you'll know what's needed when this book requests one of those characters. The following is a list of characters often confused for one another. After learning their names, you won't have a problem with them again.

(	Left parenthesis	)	Right parenthesis
<	Left angled bracket	>	Right angled bracket
{	Left brace	}	Right brace
[	Left bracket	]	Right bracket
/	Forward slash	\	Backslash
"	Quotation mark	'	Single quote (or apostrophe)
¦	Vertical bar	~	Tilde

Sometimes, programmers substitute the terms *opening* and *closing* for *left* and *right,* respectively.

After you compile a program and start its execution, the program executes line-by-line. Although breakthroughs are being made in parallel processing hardware, most C programs execute one line at a time no matter how fast your computer executes.

C's Freeform Style

definition

Freeform provides for lots of spacing to help a program's readability.

Some programming languages, such as RPG and COBOL, require rigid line-spacing. They require that you start certain program lines in specific columns. C frees its programmers from those alignment shackles by letting you write in a freeform style.

As you can see from Listing 3.1, some lines begin in the first vertical column, and others are indented. Some lines have lots of letters and characters, and other lines are blank. The extra *white space* (the blank lines and indented lines) is there for *you,* not for Turbo C++. Turbo C++ wouldn't care if you squeezed every blank space out of this program and condensed it to just a few lines. If you did squeeze out the extra white space, however, the program would be much more difficult for people to understand, even those well-versed in C.

Throughout this book, lots of attention is paid to maintainable programs. The easier your programs are to read, the easier they will be to maintain in the future. Add ample white space. Insert blank lines to separate sections of code. Indent to show lines of code that work together as a group. Of course, at this point, it's difficult for you to know how to group the lines because you're still learning C. As you learn the language, though, you'll also learn when to add extra spacing to make programs more readable.

Note There is no right or wrong way to code C programs. Programmers use their own freeform style. As you write and maintain more programs, you'll develop a personal style that helps you maintain the programs you write.

Watch That Caps Lock Key!

C makes up for its freeform generosity by being a real stickler for uppercase and lowercase distinctions. On the whole, C prefers lowercase letters to uppercase. Glance back through Listing 3.1 and you'll see many more lowercase letters than uppercase. You *must* type all of C's commands and library functions in lowercase.

Consider line 16 in Listing 3.1, which has no uppercase letters. If you were to change the letters to uppercase, C would refuse to compile the program until you fixed the errors. All of the following are completely different (and wrong) versions of line 16:

```
Scanf(" %d", &age);
SCANF(" %d", &age);
scanf(" %d", &Age);
```

There are some minor exceptions to C's preference for lowercase letters. When you want to display messages to the user or write textual data to a disk file, you can use uppercase or lowercase. Line 15 contains a question that the user will see when he or she runs the program. C lets you begin that question with an uppercase letter. You're free to use any uppercase and lowercase combination you want for text that falls inside quotation marks.

Line 9 illustrates yet another exception to the lowercase rule. You'll use uppercase on virtually all lines that begin with `#define`. A later section explains what `#define` is all about.

Review

Using a freeform style lets you write more readable programs. The more readable a program is, the less time you'll waste changing it later. Don't use the Caps Lock key freely, however, because C considers uppercase and lowercase letters to be entirely different from each other. You also must ensure that you use the correct special characters when C requires them.

Note There is no input, output, or analysis here due to this section's conceptual nature.

► Comment All Over the Place

Concept

Comments supply documentation for your programs.

Perhaps the most important and most common C statement is one that C completely ignores! Program comments are messages that programmers put in their programs to explain what's happening in the program. Remember that Turbo C++ completely ignores comments because comments are for you, the programmer, not for Turbo C++.

Comments are an important part of the C language, but comments aren't C commands. When Turbo C++ reaches a comment, it completely disregards the comment and moves to the next C command or function. Here are several ways that comments can improve your programs:

definition

Comments are messages embedded throughout a program for *programmers,* not for C compilers.

▶ Comments can explain difficult aspects of your code.

▶ Comments at the beginning of a section of code can explain the overall purpose of the section.

▶ Comments can help separate parts of a program from one another.

▶ Comments can contain the programmer's name so that future program questions can be directed to the correct source.

▶ Comments often contain the program's disk filename. If you were to look at a program's printout, you could easily find the file on the disk from the comment.

Warning One thing you *don't* want to do with comments is to put too many of them in your code. Ample comments are important, but don't add a comment just for the sake of adding it.

UNIT

3

Style Issues

Tip   Comments should explain C code in plain language. Don't replicate code in a comment. Instead, use a comment to explain what the code is doing.

How to Comment

The program in Listing 3.1 contains several comments. You can scatter comments throughout code, on lines by themselves or to the right of C statements.

A C comment always begins with a forward slash and an asterisk (/*), and it always ends with an asterisk and a forward slash (*/). Put your explanatory text between the comment's opening and closing symbols. Here is a comment from Listing 3.1:

```
/* Filename: SIMPLE.C */
```

Comments can span more than one line. It doesn't matter how long your comment is, as long as it begins with /* and ends with */. Here is a two-line comment from Listing 3.1:

```
/* The purpose of this program is to give readers an
   introduction to the format of most C programs. */
```

Commenting styles often differ among programmers. The preceding two-line comment also could look like this:

```
/* The purpose of this program is to give readers an */
/* introduction to the format of most C programs. */
```

Do you see the difference? The first is an example of a multiline comment, and the second shows two individual comment lines that make up a description of the program.

Comments can appear to the right of code. Often, tricky code is easily explained by such a comment. Here is a line from Listing 3.1 that contains both a C statement and a comment:

```
clrscr();   /* Erase the screen */
```

Once you master Turbo C++, you'll learn that clrscr() is a built-in library function that clears the screen. Nevertheless, this comment tells you exactly what clrscr() does in plain language. When you look through a multipage program that contains thousands of lines of code, you'll more quickly understand the code inside that program by reading well-placed comments than by interpreting the code each time you glance through the listing.

Here's a useless comment:

```
printf("I like Turbo C++");   /* Print I like Turbo C++ */
```

Even though you don't know about the printf() function yet, does this comment really add anything to your understanding? The printf() shown here prints something (this is obvious even to C newcomers). This comment is a waste of programmer time and detracts more than it adds.

Don't embed one comment in another. For example, the following comment is invalid:

```
/* This is a comment /* (You knew that, didn't you?) */ for you */
```

It appears that this line contains two comments, one embedded in the other. Turbo C++ has a problem with such comments, however. Remember that a comment begins with `/*` and doesn't end until `*/` is reached. Turbo C++ will think that the second `/*` is just another pair of characters inside the comment. When Turbo C++ encounters the first `*/`, it will think that it's reached the end of the comment. The problem arises with the words `for you` that follow the first `*/`. Turbo C++ won't know what to do with the words because they aren't Turbo C++ commands.

> **Note** Many full-featured compilers, such as Borland C++, give you the option of embedding one comment in another. The ability to embed comments, however, is not a standard (ANSI-approved) method of documenting your code, and not all C compilers support embedded comments.

As you learn more about C, you'll see that Listing 3.1 contains two functions, one named `main()` and one named `findRetire()`. (The parentheses are dead giveaways that you're looking at a function's name.) Do you see in Listing 3.1 where `main()` ends and `findRetire()` begins? You might be able to make a good guess thanks to the following weird-looking comment:

```
/*************************************************************/
```

Such separating comments are common in programs. This function separation lets you quickly glance from function to function, finding the function you need more quickly. This book often uses such function-separating comments to help you distinguish between functions in programs.

> **Note** Many of the early programs in this book contain only one function, named `main()`, so you won't see separating comments very much in the early units.

C++ Comments

All of Borland's compilers (and most other vendors' C compilers) let you use a C++ comment in place of the `/*` and `*/` comments, even when you write C code. A C++ comment always begins with two forward slashes (`//`) and ends with the last character on the line. Here are examples of C and C++ comment pairs. Turbo C++ supports both kinds:

```
/* Filename: SIMPLE.C */
```

and

```
// Filename: SIMPLE.C
```

> **Note** Notice that you don't type any special characters to end a C++ comment; the comment ends when the line ends.

```
/* The purpose of this program is to give readers an
   introduction to the format of most C programs. */
```

and

```
// The purpose of this program is to give readers an
// introduction to the format of most C programs.
```

Note Remember that to span comments over more than one line, you must put a new // on each comment line.

Most C programmers feel that the C++ comment is easier to type. This book uses both kinds of comments so that you can get used to each style. This book uses more C++-style comments, however, because of their ease of typing and their full compatibility with the C++ language (for when you move to C++ someday).

Perhaps the only advantage (albeit a questionable advantage) to the C-style comments is that you can embed them in C code:

```
printf(" %d", /* Prints the limit */ n);
```

Without the comment, this line would read

```
printf(" %d", n);
```

Such code-embedded comments often add to readability problems instead of helping to explain the code. Nevertheless, there's no way to embed such a comment with the C++ style because Turbo C++ would consider the entire line to the right of the // a comment that's not part of the code.

 Tip Keep your code clearer by staying away from such tricky comments. Instead of embedding a comment in code, move the comment to the end of the line:

```
printf(" %d", n);    /* Prints the limit */
```

Develop Good Commenting Habits

No book on programming would be worth its price if it didn't stress the importance of commenting *as you write your program.* Too often, programmers are so busy writing their programs that they don't take the time to comment adequately. They think that they'll go back and add the comments later, but when later arrives, there's another program to write, and the comments never get put in.

If you add comments as you write your program, you don't have to add them later. More important, you understand your program *best* when you're writing it, not later. The best time to add explanatory comments is when you understand your program the best, so add comments as you code.

 Note Here's an added bonus for commenting as you code: If you need to look back at code that occurs earlier in the program while you're writing a later section, you can more quickly find the needed code by reading comments instead of reinterpreting your own C code.

 Warning Don't fall into the trap of thinking that you don't need comments if you're the only one who will maintain your programs. A program that you wrote a year ago will be almost as foreign to you as it would be to someone else. Over that year, your coding style will have changed some and you will have written many programs since then. Comments ensure that you'll understand all the code when you need to go back and make changes.

STOP&TYPE Listing 3.2 contains a short program that contains both C and C++ comments.

Review   **What You Have Learned**

Comments help explain a program. When code is tricky, a comment tells a person looking at the code exactly what the program does. The comment also can list a program's filename, programmer, and date of programming.

▼ **INPUT   LISTING 3.2. USING TWO STYLES OF COMMENTS.**

```
 1:  /* Filename: COMMENTS.C */
 2:  // This program contains a short routine and two
 3:  // styles of comments. It asks the user for two
 4:  // letters and displays the letter that appears
 5:  // first in the alphabet.
 6:
 7:  #include <stdio.h>
 8:  #include <conio.h>
 9:
10:  main()
11:  {
12:    char l1, l2;          /* Define variables to hold values */
13:    char low;             // Define a variable to hold low letter
14:    clrscr();             /* Erase the screen */
15:
16:    // Ask the user for each letter
17:    puts("Press a letter... ");
18:    l1 = getche();        // Grab the keystroke
19:    puts("\nPress another letter... ");
20:    l2 = getche();        // Grab the next keystroke
21:    /* The next statement is cryptic but uses a ?: conditional
22:       operator to find the lower of two user values */
23:    low = (l1 < l2) ? l1 : l2;
24:    printf("\n\nThe lower letter in the alphabet is %c\n", low);
25:    return 0;
26:  }
```

▼ **OUTPUT**

```
Press a letter...
t
Press another letter...
w

The lower letter in the alphabet is t
```

▼ **ANALYSIS**

Lines 1, 12, 14, 21, and 22 contain C comments, and lines 2, 3, 4, 5, 13, 16, 18, and 20 contain C++ comments.

UNIT

3

Style Issues

▶ Studying the Big Picture

Concept

All C programs look alike in many ways. These similarities are important elements of the language.

Even though all programs are different, they all contain common characteristics that you'll soon learn to recognize quickly. Here is the general outline of most C programs:

```c
#include <stdio.h>
main()
{
  /* The body of the program goes here */
  return 0;
}
```

Look back at Listing 3.1 and you'll find these same program elements, even though the listing's program is much longer than the short format shown here.

> ***Tip*** In a C program, there is always a right brace for every left brace, a right parenthesis for every left parenthesis, and so on.

Each of the following sections explains different parts of Listing 3.1. Each section duplicates the code being described so that you won't have to flip back and forth between the sections and Listing 3.1.

Signals a Preprocessor Directive

definition

A *preprocessor directive* begins with a # and directs the compiler.

Some lines in a C program begin with a pound sign (#). Those lines aren't C statements, but preprocessor directives. A preprocessor directive runs *before* the rest of your program executes. As a matter of fact, as Figure 3.1 shows, preprocessor directives execute before Turbo C++ even compiles your program.

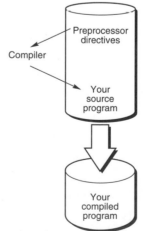

FIGURE 3.1.
Preprocessor directives execute before your program compiles.

You'll use two preprocessor directives the majority of the time. They are

▶ `#include`

▶ `#define`

Although there are additional preprocessor directives, `#include` and `#define` are by far the most common and the only ones that you'll need to understand for a long time. Preprocessor directives never end with semicolons because they're not true C commands.

Listing 3.1 contains the following preprocessor directives:

```
#include <stdio.h>
#include <conio.h>
```

A filename must always follow the `#include` directive. This file is called a header file. The header filename must appear between angled brackets (the most common) or inside quotation marks. The `#include` preprocessor directive instructs the compiler to merge the header file into the source code at the point of the `#include`. In other words, your compiler replaces the `#include` directive with the contents of the header file.

If you put the header file in angled brackets, Turbo C++ looks for the file in a special INCLUDE directory on your disk (set up when you installed Turbo C++). If you use quotation marks, Turbo C++ looks for the header file in the source code's directory before looking in the header file directory.

definition
A *header file* is a file brought into source code by `#include`.

> **Note** Rarely will you use quotation marks around an included header filename. You'll almost always use angled brackets because you'll be including header files supplied by Turbo C++.

You should understand that the inclusion takes place *before* Turbo C++ compiles your program. The `#include` changes your program. For example, the first few lines of your code might look like this:

```
/* My program */
#include <stdio.h>
main()
{
   /* Rest of program follows */
```

Your compiler, however, will *not* see these lines. It will see a greatly expanded source program whose outline will follow this form (the comment starting on the second line explains the inclusion):

```
/* My program */
/*
   All the lines of the file
   named STDIO.H will go here
   instead of these comments,
   no matter how long STDIO.H
   is.
*/
main()
{
   /* Rest of program follows */
```

Turbo C++ actually thinks that *you* typed all those lines (the lines inside the included header file).

Warning The header file *must* be a text file. All header files supplied with Turbo C++ are text files. If you write your own header files, they must contain C program text. If the header file isn't textual, `#include` can't insert the text in the source code before the program is compiled.

You might be wondering why you need header files. For a while, you'll have to trust me when I say that you need a header file to do a certain job. The STDIO.H header file (whose name stands for *standard I/O*) contains lots of needed C descriptions for the input/output routines you'll often use.

Lesson 1 mentioned *library functions,* those Turbo C++-supplied routines that do work for you. You'll learn all about library functions later. Anyway, library functions always need certain header files. Listing 3.1 contains two common library functions, `scanf()` and `printf()`. Both of these functions require that you include the STDIO.H header file.

 Note Throughout the text (as opposed to code listings), this book follows the common convention of stating filenames in uppercase letters. C always requires lowercase filenames inside code statements and directives such as `#include`.

Listing 3.1's `clrscr()` library function (line 13) requires the CONIO.H (which stands for *console I/O*) header file. That's why you see these two `#include` directives near the top of Listing 3.1:

```
#include <stdio.h>
#include <conio.h>
```

As you learn more about C, you'll learn which header file each function requires. In the meantime, this book will describe exactly which header files you need whenever a new library function is first described.

 Tip As illustrated in Listing 3.1, you should put all header files before the `main()` function. (All C programs require a `main()` function, as described in the next section.)

Here's one more use for `#include`: In addition to header file descriptions for library functions, many C programmers put common code in a header file. Instead of typing that code in every program that uses it, the programmer only has to type `#include` to include the code at the exact place in the program that the included file's source code is to appear. If the common code changes, the programmer has to change the code in only one place—the header file—and then recompile the programs that use that file. Without headers, the programmer would have to make the same source code change in every program.

Another very common preprocessor directive is `#define`. `#define` appears in Listing 3.1:

```
#define RETAGE 65
```

definition

A *constant,* sometimes called a *literal,* is a specific, unchanging value in a program.

The `#define` directive is virtually always followed by an uppercase word. This is one of the few times when C programmers use uppercase letters. The `#define` directive defines a *named constant*. In other words, `#define` assigns a name—the word in uppercase letters—to a constant. The constant follows the word. In Listing 3.1's `#define` directive, `RETAGE` is the named constant and `65` is the constant, or literal, being named.

Look through the program listing for the other occurrences of RETAGE. You'll see RETAGE used in three places (lines 26, 27, and 31). Keep in mind that all preprocessor directives execute *before* Turbo C++ compiles your program. The purpose of #define is to tell the C compiler to replace all occurrences of the named constant with the constant value before the program compiles. In other words, everywhere that RETAGE appears, the preprocessor replaces RETAGE with 65. Therefore, here are the three lines that the programmer typed that use RETAGE (after the #define, of course):

```
if (age < RETAGE)

{ retire = RETAGE - age;

{ retire = age - RETAGE;
```

Turbo C++ does *not* see RETAGE, however, because the preprocessor changes those three lines to look like this before the compiler sees your source code:

```
if (age < 65)

{ retire = 65 - age;

{ retire = age - 65;
```

What have you gained by naming the constant? In a small program such as Listing 3.1, perhaps named constants don't add many advantages. However, the longer your programs get, the more helpful that #define becomes.

Use #define when you use a constant value in your program that might, during future maintenance, need changing. For example, the retirement age might change to 68 at a later date. If you had typed 65 throughout the program instead of naming the constant with #define, you'd have to change 65 to 68 in three program lines and recompile the program. In a long program, you could very easily miss one of the 65s. If you use #define to name the constant first, you have to change only *one* source code line from 65 to 68. Therefore, your programs will be easier to modify later, and there's less of a chance that you'll forget something when you have to change a program.

The *main( )* Function

Although this book has reached only its third unit, you've seen the word *function* a lot. C works with several versions of functions. There are the built-in library functions that Turbo C++ comes with. There are also the functions that you write, sometimes called *user-supplied functions*.

C is a language based on the concept of functions. Other programming languages such as FORTRAN and QBasic support functions, but functions are not so integral to those languages as they are to C. As a matter of fact, a C program—even the shortest and simplest C program—is nothing more than a function. Almost all executable C code that you put in a C program must go inside a function that you write.

definition

A *function* is a routine that performs a specific task.

Note A preprocessor directive doesn't always appear in a function because a preprocessor directive isn't a C statement, but an instruction that executes before Turbo C++ compiles your program. Therefore, you'll often see #include and #define directives before the main( ) function.

UNIT

3

Style Issues

Programs require at least one function named `main()`. Every C program contains a `main()` function. You might, as your program grows and becomes more powerful, add additional functions, but you must always keep the `main()` function in the program. When you compile your program and run it, the runtime system always executes `main()` before any other function. It's because `main()` executes first that most C programmers list `main()` before all other functions in their programs. Although `main()` doesn't have to appear first, you should always put it first to follow the standard used by virtually all other C programmers.

The body of all functions that you write always begins and ends with braces. Therefore, you'll always see these lines in every C program:

```
main()
{
   /* The code body goes here */
}
```

If `main()` is the only function in your program, its closing brace will be the last line in your program. If your program contains more than one function, as in Listing 3.1, the second function will always follow `main()`'s closing brace. Listing 3.1 contains two user-supplied functions, `main()` and `findRetire()`. As you can see from a repeat of `findRetire()`, shown next, `findRetire()`'s code body starts and ends with matching braces, just as `main()` does:

```
void findRetire(int age)
{
  int retire;
  /* Find out if eligible for retirement */
  if (age < RETAGE)
    { retire = RETAGE - age;
       printf("In %d years, you'll be able to retire!", retire);
    }
  else
   { retire = age - RETAGE;
     printf("You could have retired %d years ago!", retire);
   }
  return;
}
```

definition

A *block* of code is any code enclosed in braces.

In C, brace pairs don't always signal the beginning and end of a function. As you can see, `findRetire()` contains additional pairs of braces inside the function. These braces signal the location of a code block, not the start or end of a function. Braces always exist in pairs, so when you match up all the left and right braces, you'll be able to determine which ones go together.

*N*ote   Braces always signal a block's beginning or end. Sometimes that block of code is a complete function, and sometimes that block of code contains lines that don't comprise a complete function.

A function's parentheses aren't always empty. The `findRetire()` function contains `int age` in its parentheses. Depending on the function, there might be lots of text inside the parentheses. You'll learn what goes inside parentheses throughout the rest of this book.

Data and Variables

A variable is the opposite of a constant. Variables, just like functions and named constants, have names. Variable data might include your age, weight, and the daily temperature reading. Constant data would be your first name, the mathematical value of pi, and the number of continents in the world. Before you can use a variable, you must *declare* that variable at the top of the body of functions.

The following line appears after `main()`'s opening brace in Listing 3.1:

```
int age;
```

This line tells Turbo C++ that an integer variable is needed in the code that follows. Turbo C++ sets aside memory for that integer variable and names the variable `age`. This book has entire units on variables. This discussion gives you only a preview of variables.

One of the primary purposes of any program is to fill variables with data and display or save those variables after they're filled. Your program might contain math operators that operate on variables. Four of C's math operators work just as their math equivalents do. Table 3.1 describes each of C's four primary math operators.

Table 3.1. C's primary math operators.

Operator	Description	Example
+	Addition	num + 5
-	Subtraction	gross - net
*	Multiplication	.2 * factor
/	Division	total / base

 Note Notice that the math operators often appear with variables, constants, or combinations of both.

One of the most surprising things about C (and about most programming languages) is that it executes some math operations before others when more than one operator appears on the same line. In the following expression:

```
4 + 2 * 3
```

what do you think C computes? If you said 18, you're wrong because C always multiplies before adding. Therefore, C first computes `2 * 3` and gets 6 and then adds 4 to 6 to get 10! You'll see many more examples of this math ordering in Lesson 4.

Lines 27 and 31 in Listing 3.1 (shown next) use the subtraction operator:

```
{ retire = RETAGE - age;
```

```
{ retire = age - RETAGE;
```

There are several more math operators. They will be explained as this book progresses.

definition
A *variable* is a box in memory that contains values that might change as the program runs.

definition
An *integer* is a whole numeric value that doesn't contain a decimal point.

UNIT

3

Style Issues

Warning If you're used to using a lowercase x for multiplication, break that habit fast! C recognizes only ∗ for multiplication.

Variables exist only during program execution, not before. The #define directive does *not* define variables. #define is just a simple search-and-replace directive that replaces named constants with the named constant values before Turbo C++ ever compiles the source code.

A Preview of Input and Output

The two most common I/O functions taught to beginning C programmers are printf() and scanf(). Figure 3.2 shows what both of these functions do. printf() writes data to the screen and scanf() gets data from the user sitting at the keyboard. The data might be textual, numeric, or a combination of both.

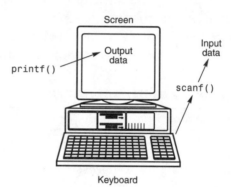

FIGURE 3.2.

printf() outputs data to the screen and scanf() inputs data from the keyboard.

Often, variables hold the data while printf() sends the data to the screen, and variables hold the data that comes from the user via scanf(). Although the details of these functions are covered in the next two units, it's fairly easy to understand what the following pair of lines from Listing 3.1 does:

```
printf("How old are you? ");
scanf(" %d", &age);
```

printf() displays the question and scanf() gets the answer (the age) from the user. You'll almost always see a printf() before a scanf() because your program must tell the user what to type.

 Note Remember that printf() and scanf() are not C commands. They're library functions supplied by the Turbo C++ compiler (and all other C compilers).

Calling a Function

definition

A *function call* occurs when your program executes another function.

Line 18 in Listing 3.1, shown next, calls the findRetire() function. In the preceding section, you saw how printf() and scanf() were called. To call any function, you only need to put the function name on a line by itself.

```
findRetire(age);   /* Print a retirement message */
```

Conceptually, writing your own functions is like adding your own commands to C. A function is *not* a command, but when Listing 3.1's program execution gets to the `findRetire()` function, the code inside `findRetire()` in the program's lower half executes. (A function call is like a program detour.) When the function finishes, its `return` statement (the C command on line 34) causes execution to resume, beginning on line 19, the line following `main()`'s `findRetire()` function call.

The `return` at the end of `main()` doesn't return program control to a function because a function didn't call `main()`. Instead, `main()`'s `return` statement returns control to Turbo C++'s IDE so that you can modify the program if you like.

STOP&TYPE Listing 3.3 contains an additional C program that you can study. Try to locate the different parts of the program before looking at the analysis section that describes the program's components.

Review
What You Have Learned

All C programs contain common coding elements.

▼ INPUT   LISTING 3.3. LOOKING FOR THE COMMON COMPONENTS OF A C PROGRAM.

```
 1:  /* Filename: CSTUDY.C */
 2:  // Program to tell workers how many hours to work
 3:  #include <stdio.h>
 4:  #include <conio.h>
 5:
 6:  #define STORENAME "Disks and Cables"
 7:
 8:  main()
 9:  {
10:    int days, hours;
11:    clrscr();    // Erase the screen
12:    printf(STORENAME);
13:    // Ask the user for the days left
14:    printf("\nHow many days is the sale? ");
15:    scanf(" %d", &days);
16:
17:    hours = days * 24;
18:    printf("That's another %d hours to work!\n", hours);
19:
20:    return 0;
21:  }
```

UNIT 3
Style Issues

▼ OUTPUT

```
Disks and Cables
How many days is the sale? 4
That's another 96 hours to work!
```

▼ **ANALYSIS**

This program contains only a single function, `main()`. In other words, `main()` is the only function written by the programmer. The library functions `printf()` and `scanf()` are called in lines 12, 14, 15, and 18. Another library function named `clrscr()` is called on line 11. This program contains both C and C++ comments. The C comment appears on the first line with the filename, and the remaining comments are C++ comments.

`clrscr()` requires the inclusion of the CONIO.H header file, while `printf()` and `scanf()` require STDIO.H—hence the `#include` directives before `main()`. The `#define` directive associates the store name to a text constant to be printed later on line 12. It's important to realize that the compiler thinks line 12 looks like this:

```
printf("Disks and Cables");
```

due to the preprocessor that defines the text as a named constant.

Two integer variables, `days` and `hours`, are declared and used in the body of `main()`. The only math operator used is the multiplication operator that computes the number of hours left in the sale on line 17.

▶ Homework

General Knowledge

1. What does freeform mean?

2. Is a freeform style more important to the programmer or to the compiler?

3. What are the two most common preprocessor directives?

4. When do preprocessor directives execute?

5. What is meant by a function call?

6. True or false: Lines in a C program must end with semicolons.

7. True or false: A left brace is always followed later in the program by a right brace.

8. True or false: `#define` defines named variables.

What's the Output?

9. Guess the output of this program. Be careful. The results are deceiving if you forget that `#define` occurs before the program is compiled and *not* while the program is being run. Hint: Remember the math ordering that C performs.

```
/* Filename: DEFINE.C */
// Try to determine the printed value
#include <stdio.h>
#include <conio.h>

#define A 3
#define B A + A
```

```
#define C B * B

main()
{
  clrscr();
  printf("%d", C);    // Print value known as C
  return 0;
}
```

Find the Bug

10. Fred just entered his first C program, but the compiler gave him fits. See if you can tell Fred what's wrong with this simple program:

```
/* My first program
   /* At least I'm trying! */
   This program will print a simple message */
#include <Stdio.h>
Main()
{
  Printf("A simple program");
  Return 0;
}
```

Write Code That...

11. Write a comment that includes your name and the date. Use C's style of comments. On the next line, use a C++ comment to do the very same thing.

Extra Credit

12. Jane wants to create a header file that prints her name, address, city, state, and zip code. Write a simple header file that contains three `printf()` function calls that print the following information:

```
Jane Slater
1605 N. 139th Street
Miami, FL  20332
```

The first line in the header file should be a comment that explains the purpose of subsequent statements. Don't put `main()`, preprocessor directives, or anything but the three `printf()` function calls in the code so that Jane can include the file in any program she writes that needs to print her name and address information.

Output with *printf()*

conversion character

escape sequence

format string

literal data

printf()

string data

▶ What You'll Learn About

- ▶ `printf()` outputs data
- ▶ Printing string literals
- ▶ Other escape sequence characters
- ▶ Printing single characters
- ▶ Printing integer data
- ▶ Printing floating-point data

In a nutshell, the `printf()` function prints data to the screen. `printf()` is one of the most common and useful library functions that comes with the C language. This lesson begins to explore `printf()` and shows you how to send different kinds of data to the screen.

`printf()` sends both numeric and text data to the screen. You must tell `printf()` exactly how you want that data to appear. In other words, C doesn't know if you want one decimal place or three decimal places when you print numbers. When printing dollar amounts, you'll want to print two decimal places (for the cents), but how is C to know that the number you're printing is a dollar amount?

definition
Format strings tell `printf()` exactly how to output your data.

Through the use of format strings that you supply in each `printf()`, `printf()` learns how you want your data printed. This unit explains how to print simple data values with `printf()`. This data comes in all shapes and sizes. You'll also learn how to recognize simple data types and see how to print them.

▶ *printf()* Outputs Data

Concept   **What You Will Learn**

Learn the basic format of `printf()`.

All `printf()` function calls take the following format:

`printf("formatString" [, data] [, data...]);`

Notice that the *formatString* appears inside quotation marks. All `printf()` functions require a format string. The brackets in this and all other command and function formats in this book mean that the *data* values are not required. Some `printf()` function calls might have one or more data values to the right of the format string, while other `printf()` calls don't have data values.

definition
String data is text data that might include letters, numbers, and special characters.

The format of your `printf()` format strings and the number of data values you supply varies depending on your program's needs. The kind of data you want to output determines the format of the `printf()` call. The next few sections explain how to print the following types of data:

- ▶ String data. You'll never perform math with string data, even string data that contains digits such as a Social Security number. If you ever need to perform calculations on data, the data must be numeric and not string.

▶ Character data. To C, character data always consists of single, individual characters, never a string of characters. A character may be a letter, a digit that you don't compute with, or a special character.

▶ Integer data. As mentioned in Unit 3, an integer has no decimal place. Integers are useful for whole-number values such as ages and counts.

▶ Floating-point data. Floating-point data is needed when you want high accuracy and fractional numeric results.

definition

Floating-point data contains a decimal place with optional digits to the right of the decimal.

LITERAL DATA

The data printed in the next three sections is all *literal* data. A literal value is sometimes called a *constant* value because it never changes. In Unit 3, you saw how variables can hold values. A variable is like a box whose contents can change. A literal, however, never changes because it's fixed data.

The letters `'A'`, `'B'`, and `'C'` are *character literals*. In C, all character literals must appear within apostrophes (single quotation marks). Regular quotation marks enclose *string literals*. The following sentence is a string literal:

```
"See, I told you so!"
```

This sentence always reads the way you see it here. If you were to change this sentence, you'd have a different literal. These numbers are *numeric literals*: 4, 89.009, and -123.456. If your program makes use of a variable, however, that variable's contents can change. A variable is never a literal.

Printing String Literals

Of all the data you print with `printf()`, string literal data is the easiest. The format string is the data itself. In other words, the following `printf()`

```
printf("The way things ought to be");
```

always displays the string literal The way things ought to be on the screen. The quotation marks don't appear in the output; they only enclose the string literal for the `printf()`. If the string literal is all you want printed, you don't add any data to the right of the format string because the format string contains all the data you want C to print.

Note Remember, all format strings (and all string literals) must appear within quotation marks or C will cough up the error when you attempt to compile the program.

There is one slight "gotcha" with `printf()` that you might as well learn now. At first glance, the following trio of `printf()` function calls appears to send three lines to the screen:

```
printf("A PC with a '386 processor.");
printf("A PC with a '486 processor.");
printf("A PC with a Pentium processor.");
```

If you were to print these three string literals in a program, here is what would appear on the screen:

```
A PC with a '386 processor.A PC with a '486 processor.A PC with a
Pentium processor.
```

That's probably not what you had in mind! C's `sprintf()` function doesn't automatically print on a new line after each subsequent `printf()` function call, even though you'd often like C to do so. `printf()` does nothing more than what you request. If you want the second line printed below the first, you must tell C to print the second literal on a new line. You specify a new line with the *newline escape sequence*.

If you want each line to begin on a new line, you must include an escape sequence that represents a new line, appropriately called the *newline* escape sequence. Here it is: `'\n'`.

There is no error in `'\n'`, although if you've been reading closely, you might think there is. There are two characters, a backslash and an `n`, inside the single quotation marks. Earlier, you learned that only single characters appear inside single quotation marks and that a string of characters must appear inside regular quotation marks. C translates all escape sequences into single characters. Therefore, C considers `\n` a single character, a *control* character, that controls output.

Whenever you specify a newline escape sequence inside a `printf()`, C sends the cursor to the next line. Any subsequent output appears on the next line. The following `printf()` function calls print the three sentences on three separate lines:

```
printf("A PC with a '386 processor.\n");
printf("A PC with a '486 processor.\n");
printf("A PC with a Pentium processor.\n");
```

As you can see, the newline escape sequence doesn't appear inside single quotation marks here because the newline escape sequence is considered just another character inside the string of characters printed with the `printf()`.

definition

An *escape sequence* always consists of a backslash (\) followed by one or more characters that control C.

STOP&TYPE Listing 4.1 contains a program that prints the same three lines different ways. The placement of the newline character differs. Study the program's `sprintf()` function calls and make sure that you see why each newline takes place when it does.

Review

What You Have Learned

C blindly follows your orders. The newline escape sequence makes C move the cursor to the next line whenever the `\n` appears.

▼ INPUT LISTING 4.1. PRINTING SEVERAL MESSAGES WITH `printf()`.

```
1:  // Filename: PRINTRO.C
2:  // Demonstrates the placement options of
3:  // the newline escape sequence
4:  #include <stdio.h>
5:  #include <conio.h>
```

```
 6:  main()
 7:  {
 8:    clrscr();   // Erase the user's output screen
 9:    printf("The first line\n");
10:    printf("The second line\n");
11:    printf("The third line\n");
12:
13:    /* Now, print a blank line by itself */
14:    printf("\n");
15:
16:    // Print the same three lines differently
17:    printf("The first line");
18:    printf("\nThe second line");
19:    printf("\nThe third line\n");
20:
21:    // Print the same three lines differently
22:    printf("\nThe first line\nThe second line\nThe third line");
23:
24:    return 0;   // Return to the IDE
25:  }
```

▼ OUTPUT

```
The first line
The second line
The third line

The first line
The second line
The third line

The first line
The second line
The third line
```

▼ ANALYSIS

The same set of three lines prints three times using three different sets of `printf()` function calls. The `\n` escape character controls every cursor move that the cursor makes in the output.

Notice how the blank line is printed. The `printf()` on line 11 sends the cursor to line 14, where a newline appears by itself, producing a blank line. The same effect could be achieved by eliminating the `printf()` on line 14 and changing line 11's `printf()` to look like this:

```
printf("The third line\n\n");   // Two newlines at the end
```

As you can see from the second trio of `printf()`s (lines 17-19), the newline escape sequence can go at the beginning of the `printf()` string. Finally, line 22 proves that the newline can go *anywhere* inside the `printf()` string. One single `printf()` produced the last set of three output lines.

UNIT

4

Output with *printf()*

▶ **Other Escape Sequence Characters**

Concept   **What You Will Learn**

C's escape characters let you control your program output.

C contains lots of escape-sequence characters in addition to the newline escape sequence that you saw in the preceding section. The newline escape sequence is by far the most used, but Table 4.1 lists the other escape sequences you can use in your printf() function calls.

Table 4.1. The escape sequences.

Escape Sequence	Description
\a	The alarm character (rings the PC's speaker)
\b	Backspace
\f	Form feed (for sending printers to the top of the next page)
\n	Newline (you've seen this!)
\r	Return without line feed
\v	Vertical tab (often called a line feed)
\\	Prints a backslash
\'	Prints a single quote (apostrophe)
\"	Prints a quotation mark
\0	Null zero to terminate strings
\xhh	Hexadecimal value for an ASCII character

Anytime you insert one of these escape sequences within a printf() format string, C performs the action described in place of printing the escape sequence. In other words, when C executes this printf():

```
printf("\a");    // Ring the bell
```

it won't print a backslash followed by the letter a. Instead, C rings the PC's bell. However, what if you *wanted* C to print a backslash followed by an a? As unlikely as that combination of characters might seem, the following message might print in a C-based on-line computer tutorial:

```
The \a rings the bell
```

You can't print the message like this, however:

```
printf("The \a rings the bell");
```

Can you see why? The \a will ring the PC's bell instead of printing directly. That's why the \\ escape sequence character is so important. Whenever C sees \\, it prints a single backslash. Therefore, this printf() prints the previous message:

```
printf("A \\a rings the bell");
```

For the same reason, you must use an escape sequence character when you want to produce a quotation mark or an apostrophe so that C doesn't think that you're ending the format string (with a quotation mark) or trying to embed a character literal inside a string literal (which you can't do if you put apostrophes around the character).

The \b is the backspace escape sequence, as Table 4.1 shows. Anytime C sees a \b inside a printf(), the cursor backs up one space. Backing up the cursor isn't something you'll need to do very often on the screen, but later, in Lesson 8, you'll see how to use the escape characters to affect the printer's output. Sometimes you can even print one character on top of another. Sending / \b= to the printer (despite the odd combination of characters) produces a mathematical *not equal to* sign. The slash prints, the printer backspaces, and the equal sign prints over the slash.

Note You can't print one character on top of another on-screen because only one character can occupy a screen position at one time.

\f, \r, and \v also are useful for printers, so I won't spend a lot of time on them here. (Printing to the printer is discussed in Unit 15.)

\t is useful for aligning columns of data. \t tabs to the next tab space on your PC. Each tab stop is eight spaces wide. Therefore, the following printf() functions

```
printf("Joe\tSusan\tMike\tPauline\n");
printf("Larry\tRed\tFred\tAbe\n");
printf("Kim\tMary\tRusty\tFranklin\n");
```

produce this aligned output:

```
Joe     Susan   Mike    Pauline
Larry   Red     Fred    Abe
Kim     Mary    Rusty   Franklin
```

Notice that each name appears exactly eight columns after the previous name, no matter what the name lengths are. If you want to tab two tab spaces, you can type two consecutive \t escape characters.

As shown here, all escape sequences usually appear inside your format strings. You can now begin to see where format strings got their name: Format strings often contain format codes (escape sequences) that format the output in a specific way.

Note In the next section, you'll see that a format string doesn't always contain data.

\0 is useful for outputting special string data. You'll read why \0 is so important in Unit 6.

Appendix B contains a copy of the ASCII table. Not all of the characters that your PC can produce appear on the keyboard (there are more than 250 characters!). Next to each character in the ASCII table are two columns of numbers, labeled Dec for *decimal* and Hex for *hexadecimal*. The decimal numbers are in the base-10 numbering system you're used to. Computer programmers, however, sometimes use the hexadecimal base-16 numbering system. The hexadecimal numbering system contains the digits 0 through 9, as well as the letters A through F. It's strange that 3C can be considered a number, but that's the nature of the hexadecimal numbering system.

UNIT 4

Output with *printf()*

definition
The *ASCII table* (pronounced *ASK-ee*) contains every character that your PC can produce.

Tip   You can specify the ASCII hexadecimal letters in either uppercase or lowercase. To C, 1A2 and 1a2 are the same hex number.

The primary reason for including the corresponding hexadecimal numbers next to each ASCII character in Appendix B is because of the last escape sequence in Table 4.1. If you put a character's hexadecimal ASCII number after the \x escape sequence, C prints that character even if it doesn't appear on your keyboard. (If the character appeared on your keyboard, you'd just type it, not mess with the escape sequence.)

STOP&**TYPE** Listing 4.2 contains a program that prints several lines of output using many escape sequences. Type this program and study the output.

Review   **What You Have Learned**

The following program produces many characters that are possible only through the use of escape characters.

▼ **INPUT   LISTING 4.2. PRINT SOME OUTPUT USING ESCAPE CHARACTERS.**

```
 1:  // Filename: ESCSEQS.C
 2:  // Prints several lines of output using
 3:  // the escape-sequence characters
 4:  #include <stdio.h>
 5:  #include <conio.h>
 6:
 7:  /* Just to remind you of the purpose of #define */
 8:  #define ALARM "\a"
 9:
10:  main()
11:  {
12:    clrscr();   // Erase the user's output screen
13:
14:    printf(ALARM);
15:    printf("\n\n");   // Two blank lines
16:    printf("Enclose all string literals inside these: \"\n");
17:    printf("Enclose all character literals inside these: \'\n");
18:    printf("In France, they use these all the time: \x80\n");
19:    printf("A newline escape sequence, \\n, prints a newline.\n");
20:
21:    return 0;  // Return to the IDE
22:  }
```

▼ **OUTPUT**

```
Enclose all string literals inside these: "
Enclose all character literals inside these: '
In France, they use these all the time: Ç
A newline escape sequence, \n, prints a newline.
```

▼ ANALYSIS

The first thing you'll notice is that line 8 defines the alarm escape sequence literal with the name `ALARM`. Programmers often assign names to escape sequences and put the `#define` directives in a header file that they then can include (with `#include`) in whatever program needs to use the escape sequences. Some of the escape sequences, especially the ones you define using ASCII values, are difficult to remember if you don't name them with `#define`.

In lines 16 and 17, the backslash is combined with a quotation mark and an apostrophe to print these special characters. Line 18 prints a foreign character that doesn't appear on your keyboard. Finally, a double backslash on line 19 helps produce the `\n` in the printed message.

► Printing Single Characters

Concept

What You Will Learn

You can print individual characters using the `%c` format conversion character.

definition

A *conversion character* tells C what kind of data to print.

If you want to print a single character, such as an initial, you can do so by placing the character inside quotation marks, which turns the character into a string. Consider the following `printf()`:

```
printf("My first initial appears on the next line.\n");
printf("W");   // Print a single character
```

Once you master variables (covered heavily in the next few units), you'll learn how to store character data in its own variable. Instead of printing a character literal, you'll print the variable. Even though we're not discussing variables here, you'll see how to print character data that doesn't appear inside a format string.

To print data that doesn't appear inside a format string, such as some character and all numeric data, you must use special conversion characters inside the format string, one for each piece of data printed. The conversion character for printing character data is `%c`. (All conversion characters begin with a percent sign.)

The following `printf()` prints the letter A:

```
printf("%c", 'A');
```

The `%c` tells `printf()` that a piece of character data appears to the right of the format string. The following `printf()` prints the letters ABC:

```
printf("%c%c%c", 'A', 'B', 'C');
```

The three letters print next to each other because the format string contains three `%c` conversion characters that appear next to each other. If you wanted commas and spaces between the characters, the following would work:

```
printf("%c, %c, %c", 'A', 'B', 'C');
```

UNIT

4

Output with *printf()*

Anything that appears inside a format string that is not a conversion character prints as is. That's why string literals print inside format strings: As long as the string literal doesn't contain a conversion character, the contents of the string print.

Wouldn't it be easier to print the three letters like this:

```
printf("A, B, C");   // Print the same data as before
```

The three letters are much easier to print when you include them in a string and when you don't use conversion characters. Nevertheless, you can't store character variables inside a format string, and you must have some way of printing character variable contents. Have patience: If you can see that a format string with letters is easier, you're ahead of the game, but you still must understand conversion characters and their relationship to printf().

Figure 4.1 illustrates how the three %c conversion characters control the three printed characters. Each character data matches each conversion character. If five characters followed the format string, there would have to be five %c conversion characters to match each character of data.

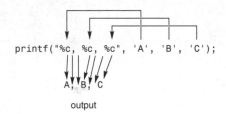

FIGURE 4.1.
Conversion characters control the look of the output.

Figure 4.1 shows that each character inside the format string—whether that character is a conversion character, a comma, or a space—ends up in the output somehow. The character data to the right of the format string replaces each of the conversion characters.

You can include escape sequences inside any format string that contains conversion characters. Also, you can print any ASCII character using the %c conversion character. Consider the following printf():

```
printf("The Spanish N is\t%c.\n", '\xA5');
```

This printf() produces the following output:

```
The Spanish N is        Ñ.
```

Be sure to match your data to your conversion characters. None of the following printf()s is correct:

```
printf("%c %c", 'A', 'B', 'C');   // Too few conversion characters
printf("%c %c %c %c", 'A', 'B', 'C');   // Too many conversion characters
printf('A', 'B', 'C');   // No format string
```

Tip If you want to output a percent sign, you must put *two* percent signs side by side. The following printf()

```
printf("The glass is 50%% full.\n");
```

produces this output:

```
The glass is 50% full.
```

STOP&TYPE Listing 4.3 contains a program that uses the %c conversion character.

Review

To print character data that falls outside a format string, you must use the %c conversion character.

▼ INPUT   LISTING 4.3. PRINTING CHARACTER DATA.

```
 1:  // Filename: CHARCONV.C
 2:  // Prints three initials using
 3:  // character-conversion codes
 4:  #include <stdio.h>
 5:  #include <conio.h>
 6:
 7:  main()
 8:  {
 9:    clrscr();   // Erase the user's output screen
10:
11:    printf("My first initial is on the next line.\n");
12:    printf("%c\n\n", 'G');
13:    printf("My second initial is on the next line.\n");
14:    printf("%c\n\n", 'M');
15:    printf("My last initial is on the next line.\n");
16:    printf("%c\n\n", 'P');
17:
18:    return 0;   // Return to the IDE
19:  }
```

▼ OUTPUT

```
My first initial is on the next line.
G

My second initial is on the next line.
M

My last initial is on the next line.
P
```

▼ ANALYSIS

The printf() functions on lines 12, 14, and 16 contain the %c conversion code and two back-to-back newline escape sequences so that a blank line appears between each pair of output lines.

UNIT 4

Output with *printf()*

▶ **Printing Integer Data**

Concept   **What You Will Learn**

You can print integer values using the %d format conversion character.

Now that you've mastered character data, integer data is easy. To print integer values, you must use %d or %i for the integer's conversion character.

 Warning   Don't use %i to print integer data even though it's allowed and it makes more sense than using %d. (The d in %d stands for *decimal,* and the i in %i stands for *integer.*) C programmers use %d. You'll rarely, if ever, see %i used. If you get into the habit of using %d, you'll never be confused by it when you see everybody else using it. Also, many C programmers probably don't even know that %i is an integer conversion character, because the industry standard is to use %d only.

Here is how you can print the numbers 1 through 5:

```
printf("%d%d%d%d%d", 1, 2, 3, 4, 5);
```

Here is the output:

```
12345
```

With numeric data, you need some spacing so that the user doesn't think you're printing 12,345. Putting commas and spaces in the format string helps separate the output:

```
printf("%d, %d, %d, %d, %d\n", 1, 2, 3, 4, 5);
```

The extra newline puts the cursor on the next line for any subsequent printf(). Here is the output produced by this printf():

```
1, 2, 3, 4, 5
```

Anywhere %d appears, C searches to the right of the format string for data. As with character-conversion codes, you must have a %d conversion code for each integer you want to print. Anything that is not a conversion code prints as is. The following printf()

```
printf("I have %d CD-ROM drives connected to my PC!\n", 4);
```

prints the data, the 4, at the location of the %d:

```
I have 4 CD-ROM drives connected to my PC!
```

Feel free to mix and match conversion characters:

```
printf("I got a letter grade of %c and a score of %d.\n", 'B', 82);
```

Here is the output from this printf():

```
I got a letter grade of B and a score of 82.
```

CHARACTERS AND INTEGERS

Character data and integer data share lots of similarities in the C language. Although you can't (properly) add or subtract with character data, the ASCII table matches characters with a corresponding integer value that lets you substitute conversion codes when you want special output.

For example, if you use the `%d` conversion character to print a character, C prints the decimal ASCII value for that character. If you print an integer (from 0 to 255) and use a `%c` conversion character, C won't print the integer but the letter that corresponds to that integer in the ASCII table.

The following `printf()`

```
printf("%d is the ASCII value for %c.\n", 'H', 72);
```

produces this line of output:

```
72 is the ASCII value for H.
```

You can control the number of spaces that appear between integers. If you put a number between the `%` and the `d`, C treats that number as a width modifier. Instead of printing just the integer, C prints leading spaces and then the integer to fill the total number of places specified by the width modifier. This is one of the many features of C that's easier to understand with an example! The following `printf()`

```
printf("%5d%5d%5d%5d%5d", 1, 2, 3, 4, 5);
```

produces this output:

```
    1    2    3    4    5
```

Notice that each integer falls within a five-column space. C right-justifies each number, meaning that it pushes the number to the far-right of the five-column space. If you want to left-justify the numbers, precede the width modifier with a minus sign:

```
printf("%-5d%-5d%-5d%-5d%-5d", 1, 2, 3, 4, 5);
```

This `printf()` tells C to print the five numbers inside a five-column width as before, but this time C left-justifies each number:

```
1    2    3    4    5
```

If you don't supply enough of a width modifier to hold the entire integer, C ignores the width modifier. The following `printf()` seems to squeeze the integer too much:

```
printf("%3d", 1234);
```

There's no way that C can print `1234` inside a three-column space. C knows this, so it ignores the width modifier of 3 and prints the number as if you didn't use a width modifier.

definition

A *modifier* changes the way a conversion character formats data.

UNIT

4

Output with printf()

Warning   Never put commas in your program's numeric data. C wants you to type the number 3,234 as `3234`.

STOP&TYPE Listing 4.4 contains a C program that prints a few strings, integers, and characters for your review.

Review
What You Have Learned

%d formats integers for printf() format strings.

▼ INPUT   LISTING 4.4. PRINTING STRINGS, CHARACTERS, AND INTEGERS.

```
 1:   // Filename: INTPRINT.C
 2:   // Prints different kinds of data using
 3:   // character-conversion codes and width modifiers
 4:   #include <stdio.h>
 5:   #include <conio.h>
 6:
 7:   main()
 8:   {
 9:     clrscr();   // Erase the user's output screen
10:
11:     printf("Here's a string to get the ball rolling.\n\n");
12:     printf("\aRing the bell to get some attention.\n");
13:     printf("%cOh, ring it again.\n", '\a');
14:
15:     // Print some numbers
16:     printf("Five prime numbers: %d, %d, %d, %d, and %d\n\n",
17:            3, 5, 7, 11, 13);
18:
19:     printf("The same numbers spaced differently: ");
20:     printf(%2d, %3d, %4d, %5d, %6d\n", 3, 5, 7, 11, 13);
21:     return 0;   // Return to the IDE
22:   }
```

▼ OUTPUT

```
Here's a string to get the ball rolling.

Ring the bell to get some attention.
Oh, ring it again.
Five prime numbers: 3, 5, 7, 11, and 13

The same numbers spaced differently:  3,   5,    7,    11,     13
```

▼ ANALYSIS

This program prints a string in line 11. The string in line 12 contains an alarm escape sequence that rings the bell before the string prints. Line 13 also rings the bell, but instead of being embedded in the format string, the escape character appears in the data portion of the printf() as a character literal.

Lines 16 and 20 contain %d integer conversion characters that position the integer data inside the string message. The %ds in line 20 contain width modifiers to control the width that each integer prints within.

Tip You can learn from lines 16, 17, 19, and 20 how to continue long `printf()` functions in C. As long as you break the line after a separating comma (one that doesn't appear inside a format string), you can continue the `printf()` on the next line.

▶ Printing Floating-Point Data

Concept | **What You Will Learn**

You can print floating-point values using the `%f` format conversion character.

Use the `%f` conversion character to print floating-point numeric values. Remember that a floating-point value is a number with a decimal and a fractional portion, such as 72.345 or –0.0003. Here is a `printf()` that prints three stock prices:

```
printf("The prices are %f, %f, and %f\n", 25.75, 8.375, 21.5);
```

`printf()` prints each floating-point value at the location of the `%f`s in the format string. Here is the output:

```
The prices are 25.750000, 8.375000, and 21.500000
```

Already you can see a problem. C insists on printing all floating-point data to six decimal places, whether you want six places or not. However, there's an easy way to modify how `%f` works—use a modifier!

Between the `%` and the `f`, you can type a decimal point and a number that indicates how many decimal places you want in the final floating-point number. For example, the conversion character `%f` prints floating-point values to six decimal places. The conversion character `%.2f` prints floating-point values to two decimal places. Here is the previous `printf()` with some decimal modifiers:

```
printf("The prices are %.2f, %.3f, and %.1f\n", 25.75, 8.375, 21.5);
```

Here is the modified output:

```
The prices are 25.75, 8.375, and 21.5
```

Obviously, limiting the number of decimal places helps the readability of the output a lot. You also can specify a width modifier inside `%f`, just as you can with `%d`, as shown in the preceding section. The width modifier falls after the `%` but before the decimal modifier. The following `printf()`

```
printf("You made $%7.2f last week.\n", 543.12);
```

prints this output:

```
You made $ 543.12 last week.
```

The extra space appears after the dollar sign because 543.12 takes only six columns of output and the `%7.2f` tells C that you want to print the number in seven columns and make two of those columns decimal places.

UNIT

4

Output with printf()

Tip You can round the output of a floating-point number by specifying fewer decimal places than the number contains. The following `printf()`

```
printf("%.3f", 1.2399);
```

prints this rounded-number output:

```
1.240
```

STOP&TYPE Listing 4.5 contains a C program that prints several floating-point values. Each value is labeled with an appropriate string description so that you can tell from the output exactly what the numbers stand for.

Review   **What You Have Learned**

The `%f` conversion character formats floating-point values before you print them.

▼ **INPUT   LISTING 4.5. USING `%f` TO DISPLAY FLOATING-POINT VALUES.**

```
 1:  // Filename: FLTPRINT.C
 2:  // Prints floating-point data
 3:  #include <stdio.h>
 4:  #include <conio.h>
 5:
 6:  main()
 7:  {
 8:    clrscr();   // Erase the user's output screen
 9:
10:    printf("Today's high was %.1f degrees.\n", 31.2);
11:    printf("I have $%6.2f in my pocket.\n", 4.62);
12:    printf("$%.2f USA dollars equals %.0f Italian lire.\n",
13:          10.00, 150000.);
14:
15:    return 0;   // Return to the IDE
16:  }
```

▼ **OUTPUT**

```
Today's high was 31.2 degrees.
I have $  4.62 in my pocket.
$10.00 USA dollars equals 150000 Italian lire.
```

▼ **ANALYSIS**

All three `printf()`s contain decimal-controlling modifiers because you rarely want the six decimal places that C produces without the modifiers. Only one of the `printf()`s, line 11, contains a width modifier on the floating-point value to ensure that the dollar amount prints in six columns even though the number printed, `4.62`, consumes a total of only four columns.

▶ Homework

General Knowledge

1. What do format strings do?
2. What's the difference between string literal data and character literal data?
3. What's the difference between a literal and a variable?
4. Could your age be considered variable or a literal value?
5. What's the difference between an escape sequence and a conversion character?
6. What is the conversion character for each of the following data types?
    A. Integers
    B. Characters
    C. Floating-point values
7. What do the two floating-point modifiers do?
8. What's the purpose of the ASCII table?
9. True or false: You can print the ASCII value of a character using the %d conversion character.
10. True or false: You must have a conversion character for each data value you want to print. (Assume that the data values appear to the right of the format string.)
11. True or false: C automatically left-justifies numeric values inside column widths if you don't override that justification with a minus sign before the conversion-character modifier.
12. True or false: A hexadecimal value can contain letters of the alphabet; therefore, hexadecimal values are not numeric.

What's the Output?

13. Yikes! Programmer Paul tried to be sneaky and put the following printf() in his program. Is there a syntax error here? If not, what gets printed?

    ```
    printf("\\\"\'\\\\\xA5");
    ```
14. Use the ASCII table to determine what prints from the following printf():

    ```
    printf("Now I know my %c, %c, c's", 65, 66, 67);
    ```

Find the Bug

15. What's wrong with the following printf()?

    ```
    printf("I've lived %d days.\n", 11,680);
    ```
16. What's wrong with the following printf()?

    ```
    printf("I am in grade %d and I made an %c on my report card!", 9);
    ```

Write Code That...

17. Write a `printf()` that prints your favorite song titles, one per line, with a blank line between each one.

18. Write a program that prints your initials using only numeric ASCII values.

Extra Credit

19. Write a simple program that prints your IQ (exaggerate), your weight (lie), and your annual salary (brag). Be sure to label the output so that anyone looking at the program's output knows what the data stands for.

**Meeting C
Programs**

STOP&TYPE In this lesson, you learned about the fundamental format of all C programs. You saw the following:

▶ All C programs contain a `main()` function.

▶ Braces determine where the `main()` function begins and ends.

▶ Preprocessor directives direct the way C compiles your program. Preprocessor directives always begin with a pound sign (#).

Project 2 Listing. Introduction to C programs.

```
1:   /* Filename: PROJECT2.C */

2:   // Introduces the format of C programs and demonstrates

3:   // how to use both C and C++ comments, preprocessor

4:   // directives, and the printf() function

5:

6:   #include <stdio.h>

7:   #include <conio.h>

8:

9:   #define CARMODEL "Sleekster"

10:

11:  main()

12:  {

13:     clrscr();   // Erase the user's output screen

14:
```

▶ There are two kinds of comments—C comments, which begin with /* and end with */, and C++ comments, which begin with // and end at the end of the line. Comments are for people, not for C.

▶ The printf() function outputs data to your screen.

▶ Using format strings, conversion characters, and escape characters tells printf() how you want your data to look.

Description

1: A C comment that includes the program's filename.

2: A C++ comment that begins the program's description.

3: The program's description continues.

4: The program's description continues.

5: Extra blank lines make your program more readable.

6: The printf() function needs information in the STDIO.H header file.

7: The screen-clearing function, clrscr(), needs information in the CONIO.H header file.

8: Extra blank lines make your program more readable.

9: The car name string literal is named with #define.

10: Extra blank lines make your program more readable.

11: All functions have names, and the first function in all C programs is main().

12: All functions begin with a left brace.

13: The built-in library function clrscr() erases the output screen so that the screen is clear before the program's output begins.

14: Extra blank lines make your program more readable.

9: Each instance of CARMODEL will be changed to the string literal "Sleekster".

9: Using #defined literals is easier than typing full literals.

continues

Project 2 Listing. continued

```
15:    printf("I have a ");

16:    printf(CARMODEL);                 /* Continue the output line */

17:    printf(" automobile.\n\n");    /* Print a blank line */

18:

19:    printf("I want to sell my car for $%.2f (cheap!).\n", 4800.00);

20:    printf("I have had the car for %d years.\n", 5);

21:    printf("It's really a grade-%c deal!\n\n", 'A');

22:

23:    return 0;    // Return to the IDE

24:  }
```

Description

15: The string literal inside the format string prints. No newline occurs.

16: Model of car prints because `#define` on line 9 makes sure compiler sees this `printf()` as `printf("Sleekster");`.

17: Finishes the output and moves the cursor down two lines.

18: Extra blanks make your program more readable.

19: The `%.2f` ensures that the floating-point value to the right of the format string prints with two decimal places.

20: The `%d` is replaced with the integer data to the right of the format string.

21: The `%c` is replaced with the character literal to the right of the format string.

22: Extra blank lines make your program more readable.

23: The final `return 0;` in `main()` always returns control to Turbo C++'s IDE.

24: A closing brace always terminates the `main()` function.

19: When you format numbers, they appear the way you want your user to see them.

▼ OUTPUT

```
I have a Sleekster automobile.

I want to sell my car for $4800.00 (cheap!).

I have had the car for 5 years.

It's really a grade-A deal!
```

Lesson ▶

Data Basics

Unit 5: Numeric Data

Unit 6: String Data and
        Input Gathering

Lesson 3 Project

Numeric Data

double

int

long

scientific notation

variable

▶ What You'll Learn About

▶ C's numeric data types
▶ Variables

After Unit 4's discussion of integers and floating-point values, what else is there to learn about numeric data? As it turns out, there's *plenty* more to learn. However, most of the additional material presented in this unit is nothing more than a variation on a theme. You'll learn all about the different kinds of integers and floating-point numbers (there are several kinds).

More important, you'll finally get a detailed understanding of C variables. This unit explores numeric variables, and the next unit looks into storing strings in variables.

Computers would be dull (and fairly useless) without variables. Even cheap calculators have memory storage. Variables are nothing more than storage areas for data.

▶ C's Numeric Data Types

Concept   **What You Will Learn**

The numeric data types fall into the two major categories that you already know about: integers and floating-points. This section teaches you about all the different kinds of integers and floating-point data that Turbo C++ supports.

Table 5.1 lists all the numeric data types for the C programming language. Basically, integers and floating-point values each have small versions and large versions.

Table 5.1. C's numeric data types.

Data Type	Description
Integer	Whole numbers that range from –32,768 to 32,767. This is the same data type as signed integer.
Unsigned integer	Whole numbers that range from 0 to 65,535. Notice that unsigned integers hold larger numbers than regular integers, but unsigned integers can't hold negative values.
Signed integer	Whole numbers that range from –32,768 to 32,767. This is the same data type as integer.
Short integer	Same as integer and signed integer. In some languages (not Turbo C++), a short integer holds smaller values than regular integers can hold.
Unsigned short integer	Same as unsigned integer. In some languages (not Turbo C++), an unsigned short integer holds smaller values than regular unsigned integers can hold.

Data Type	Description
Signed short integer	Same as signed integer. In some languages (not Turbo C++), a signed short integer holds smaller values than regular integers can hold.
Long	Whole-number values that range from –2,147,483,648 to 2,147,483,647 (the annual salary of a good C programmer).
Long integer	The same as long.
Signed long integer	The same as long.
Unsigned long integer	Holds values from 0 to 4,294,967,295.
Floating-point	Numbers with decimal portions. The range for floating-points is –3.4E–38 to 3.4E+38. (The following note explains this strange notation.) Floating-point values often are called *floats*. (So are ice-cream-and-soda-pop drinks, but we're not discussing those here.)
Double	Numbers with decimal portions. The range for double is –1.7E–308 to 1.7E+308.
Long double	The largest data type possible in C. The range for long double is –3.4E–4932 to 3.4E+4932.

Note Why are there data types that mean the same thing as other data types (such as signed integer and integer)? Some programmers like to clarify whether or not their data (in variables) can hold signed values. By specifying the full name, the capacity of the number (and ultimately the variables that can hold that number) is made clearer.

WHAT'S THIS FUNNY E+3 BUSINESS?

For the floating-point, double, and long double data types, the range is expressed in scientific notation. Without the shortcut notation provided by scientific notation, the range of long double values would require 34 followed by 4,931 zeros to express one extreme of the range!

To convert from scientific notation to regular numbers, take the number before the E (which stands for *exponent*) and multiply it by 10 raised to the power after the plus or minus sign. For example, to convert 3.4E+38, you would multiply 3.4 times 10 with 38 zeros after the 10. (In math, that's written 10^{38}.) To convert –3.4E–38, you would multiply –3.4 times .000...(38 zeros go here)..., or 10 to the negative 38th power (10^{-38}).

Figure 5.1 shows how 2.45E+13 converts to a regular value. Don't like math? That's fine. The floating-point data types hold virtually any floating-point value that you'll ever need. If you really need accuracy and you're working with extremely large or small numbers (yes, bigger than even the national debt!), you'll need to move to the double or long double data types.

definition

Scientific notation is a shortcut way of expressing extremely large and small values.

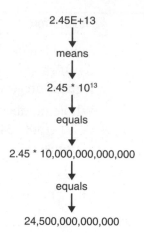

FIGURE 5.1.
The parts of a scientific
notational value.

 Scientific notation provides a shortcut way of representing a wide range of numbers, but you lose some accuracy when you use it, because it doesn't allow for an extended amount of accuracy. Numbers often are severely rounded when they're expressed in scientific notation.

The following sections explain how to represent data types, numeric literals, and numeric variables whose types match those in Table 5.1.

Discussing Data

As Table 5.1 explained, the following are all the same data type in Turbo C++:

> integers
>
> signed integers
>
> short integers
>
> short signed integers

The rest of this book dispenses with all the variations when discussing integers in general by calling them simply *integers*. Therefore, when you see the word *integer*, you'll know that I mean an integer that can have a negative sign. Whenever you see a literal integer that falls within the regular integer range (–32,768 to 32,767), that literal also will be called an integer.

These are both the same data type in Turbo C++:

> unsigned integers
>
> unsigned short integers

The rest of this book calls unsigned integers just that, *unsigned integers*. The *short* qualifier isn't needed, because Turbo C++ treats both unsigned integers and unsigned short integers as the same kind of data.

These are all the same data type in Turbo C++:

> longs
>
> long integers
>
> signed long integers

The rest of this book calls long integers *long integers* because the *signed* notation is always assumed in Turbo C++. If an unsigned long integer is needed, the qualifier *unsigned* is used.

Note Are numbers ever unsigned? There are many examples of values that never become negative. Lengths, ages, and distances are three good examples of data that can't be negative. Using the unsigned data types gives you a greater positive number range than is possible if you use signed data.

Warning There is no such data type as an unsigned floating-point value. In C, only the various integers can be unsigned.

The kind of data type that you use depends on your application's needs. You might write programs that contain examples of every data type that Turbo C++ supports. The data types help keep values stored in their proper formats and locations. When you learn about variables in the last half of this unit, you'll see that you assign a data type to a variable and then only that type of data will fit in that type of variable. Although you must predict the type of data that you'll store in each variable, predicting isn't difficult, because you're familiar with the data your program needs to work with.

The most important thing to remember about data types is that you shouldn't use a larger one than you need. Again, this becomes especially critical when you're working with variables. Table 5.2 lists the amount of memory that each data type consumes. It shows the number of bytes consumed by each data type Turbo C++ supports.

definition

A *byte* is one memory storage location. It takes one byte to hold a character of data.

Table 5.2. Turbo C++'s current data-type requirements.

Data Type	Byte Requirement
Character	1 byte
Integer	2 bytes
Unsigned integer	2 bytes
Long	4 bytes
Unsigned long integer	4 bytes
Floating-point	4 bytes
Double	8 bytes
Long double	10 bytes

You now know that the long double data types hold an extremely large range of numbers. If you tried to store 423E+209 in a floating-point variable (yes, you can use scientific notation in your C programs), you'd get bad results when you ran your program, because a float can't hold that large of a number.

It might seem that you always need to use the long double data type because long double is big enough to hold virtually any number you'll ever use. If you used only the long double data type, however, you would soon discover that even the fastest computer can seem sluggish when each number must be stored or retrieved from 10 bytes of memory.

Using a float when you need only an integer or using a long double when a regular floating-point value will suffice decreases C's efficiency tremendously. Try to use as small of a data type as you think you can get by with and test your programs thoroughly. You'll find that your programs run more smoothly and quickly.

 Warning   The storage taken by each data type differs from compiler to compiler! Even Borland, in a future release, might change the amount each data type takes. Knowing the amount of memory that each data type consumes becomes really important when you learn about pointers in Lesson 9. If you want to write a program today that works on tomorrow's compilers, program as if you don't know the data-type lengths in Table 5.2. The sizeof operator that you learn about in Lesson 5 gives you the ability to find data type storage amounts no matter what C compiler you compile your program with.

Numeric Literal Qualifiers

Turbo C++ supports a special notation that lets you describe how you want Turbo C++ to store your literal data. In other words, when you type the number 7, Turbo C++ uses a two-byte integer storage location to hold the 7. However, what if you wanted C to store the 7 in a long integer four-byte location? (You're probably asking *why* you would want to do that! There are reasons, so have faith.) There's a way to qualify the 7 so that Turbo C++ knows to treat the 7 as a long integer even though it could use a regular integer.

Place the L qualifier at the end of an integer literal if you want to tell C that the literal is a long integer and not a regular integer. The following are all treated like long integers. Each requires four bytes of storage:

```
45L      8L      -603L      0L
```

Place the U qualifier at the end of any integer literal that you want stored as unsigned integer data. All of the following are unsigned integer literals:

```
45U      8U      -603U      0U
```

Of course, you can combine the U and L to specify long unsigned integer literals:

```
45UL      8UL      -603UL      0UL
```

The ordering of the U and the L doesn't matter, and you can use lowercase if you prefer. The following list of numbers matches the preceding one:

```
45ul      8LU      -603Lu      0uL
```

When you print an unsigned long integer, be sure to use the %ld printf() conversion character. The following printf() function calls

```
printf("%ld \n", 45ul);
printf("%ld \n", 8LU);
printf("%ld \n", -603Lu);
printf("%ld \n", 0uL);
```

produce this output:

```
45
8
-603
0
```

C doesn't append the U or L to the end of `printf()`-printed values. The U and L exist solely for the programmer so that she or he can specify explicit data-typed literals.

When you type a floating-point literal, such as 343.456, C stores that literal as a double floating-point, not as a regular floating-point value. Fractional values are difficult to represent accurately in computers, so C automatically uses double floating-point storage to obtain as much literal accuracy as possible. You can use the F qualifier to instruct C to treat a floating-point literal as a simple floating-point instead of as a double floating-point. All of the following values are regular floating-point literals. They would be stored as doubles without the F qualifier:

```
89.0F       12345.567F       34E+5F       34e+5f
```

Note   The last two values, 34E+5F and 34e+5f, are identical in C.

Use the `%f` conversion character to print both floating-point and double floating-point values. The following `printf()` function calls print a floating-point number and a double floating-point number:

```
printf("Float: %f \n", 94.722F);
printf("Double: %f \n", 2934.394409);    // Literals double by default
```

Place the L qualifier at the end of a floating-point literal if you want C to treat the literal as a long double floating-point value stored in 10 bytes of memory. Although none of the following floating-point literals requires long double floating-point storage, the qualifying L ensures that C uses long double floating-point storage for the numbers:

```
89.0L       12345.567L       34E+5L       34e+5l
```

Use the `%lf` conversion character to print long double floating-point values. The following `printf()` prints a long double floating-point literal:

```
printf("%Lf \n", 439.40201984L);
```

As mentioned earlier, C has a rough time handling fractional values. The preceding `printf()` produces this output due to rounding:

```
439.402020
```

By the way, if you ever want to print a value in scientific notation (C never prints in scientific notation if you use any form of the `%f` conversion character), use the `%e` or `%E` conversion characters. The one you use determines whether the value's *e* exponent indicator prints in lowercase or uppercase. Even though the literals listed in the following `printf()` functions aren't written using scientific notation, the conversion characters ensure that C outputs them in scientific notational format:

```
printf("%e \n", 56.7);
printf("%E \n", 56.7);
```

These `printf()` function calls produce this output:

```
5.670000e+01
5.670000E+01
```

You'll want to output in scientific notation when you're working with large data values. If your program will contain a wide range of values, you should consider using the `%g` or `%G` conversion characters. `%g` prints a value in scientific notation if six decimal places aren't enough to print the number with reasonable accuracy. Using `%g` prints a lowercase `e` if the number appears in scientific notation and `%G` prints an uppercase `E` if the number appears in scientific notation. If C prints the value as a floating-point literal (not using scientific notation), there's no difference between `%g` and `%G` because the number appears as if you'd used an `%f` conversion character.

These `printf()` function calls

```
printf("%g \n", 56.7);
printf("%g \n", 123456700.0);
printf("%G \n", 123456700.0);
```

produce this output:

```
56.7
1.23457e+08
1.23457E+08
```

 Note   You're reading about a *lot* of `printf()` conversion characters and literal qualifiers! A little later, some tables summarize what you've learned in order to put things into perspective.

definition

An *octal* value is a base-8 number.

There are two more integer literal qualifiers that some programmers use a lot and others very little. You can specify that an integer literal be either a hexadecimal value or an octal value. (Hexadecimal values are used much more frequently than octal values.)

The `0x` (or `0X`) prefix lets C know that you're specifying a hexadecimal integer literal. All of the following are hexadecimal literals:

```
0x45     0X193     0x6C     0xD2
```

The `0` prefix (a leading zero) always means that the integer literal is an octal constant. Therefore, don't preface your literals with a leading 0 if you don't want C to treat the number as a base-8 number. All of the following are octal literals:

```
010     076     0123
```

Warning   Only integers can be expressed as hex or octal values.

Note   You can begin floating-point numbers with a leading zero, such as `0.283`, without any problem.

Unless you program a lot of system-related programs (such as operating system utilities), you probably won't need hexadecimal or octal values anytime soon. Of course, you might want to use a hexadecimal-based escape sequence to represent an ASCII character, as explained in Unit 4. Rarely will a PC programmer use octal. Octal used to be more popular than it is today. Only a few larger octal-based computers are still in use.

If you want to print values in hexadecimal or octal, use the `%o` and `%x` conversion characters. You don't have to type the data that you print in hex or octal for `%x` and `%o` to output the values in hex and octal. For example, the following `printf()`s print the same number, decimal `192`, in base-10, base-16, and base-8:

```
printf("%d \n", 192);
printf("%x \n", 192);
printf("%o \n", 192);
```

Here is the output from these `printf()` functions:

```
192
c0
300
```

Notice that neither the `%x` nor the `%o` conversion character prints the leading zeros before the hex or octal constants.

Table 5.3 lists all the `printf()` conversion characters that you've seen so far. Table 5.4 lists the literal data-type qualifiers for you to review as well.

Table 5.3. The `printf()` conversion characters.

Conversion Character	Description
`%c`	For character values.
`%d`	For integer values.
`%i`	Same as `%d` but rarely used.
`%f`	Floating-point and double values.
`%g`	Either floating-point or scientific notation (with a lowercase `e`), depending on the number's value.
`%G`	Either floating-point or scientific notation (with an uppercase `E`), depending on the number's value.
`%ld`	For long integer values.
`%lf`	For long double floating-point values.
`%o`	For octal values.
`%x`	For hexadecimal values.
`%e`	Scientific notation with a lowercase exponent character.
`%E`	Scientific notation with an uppercase exponent character.

Table 5.4. Literal data-type qualifiers.

Literal Qualifier	Description
`0`	Appears in front of integers to specify octal values.
`0x` or `0X`	Appears in front of integers to specify hexadecimal values.
`F`	Specifies a regular floating-point literal.

continues

Table 5.4. continued

Literal Qualifier	Description
L	At the end of an integer, L specifies a long integer literal. At the end of a floating-point literal, L specifies a long double floating-point literal.
U	Specifies an unsigned integer.

STOP&TYPE Listing 5.1 contains a program that prints all the literal data types and that uses all the conversion characters.

Review ━━━━━━━━━━━━━━━ **What You Have Learned**

Qualifiers tell C to interpret your literal values differently from the way it would treat those same literals without the qualifiers. Use the conversion characters in `printf()` functions to control how your data appears.

▼ **INPUT   LISTING 5.1. USING QUALIFIERS AND CONVERSION CHARACTERS.**

```
 1:   /* Filename: CONVQUAL.C */
 2:   // Demonstrates the use of both literal qualifiers
 3:   // and printf() conversion characters
 4:
 5:   #include <stdio.h>
 6:   #include <conio.h>
 7:
 8:   main()
 9:   {
10:     clrscr();    // Erase the user's output screen
11:
12:     printf("%c \n", 'X');          // Output a character
13:
14:     printf("%d \n", 42);           // Output an integer
15:     printf("%i \n", 42);           // Output an integer
16:     printf("%x \n", 231);          // Output a decimal integer in hex
17:     printf("%x \n", 0x4f);         // Output a hex integer in hex
18:     printf("%o \n", 94);           // Output a decimal integer in octal
19:     printf("%o \n", 010);          // Output an octal integer in octal
20:     printf("%ld \n", 87532L);      // Output a long integer
21:     printf("%u \n", 453U);         // Output an unsigned integer
22:     printf("%ld \n", 45293UL);     // Output a long unsigned integer
23:
24:     printf("%f \n", 84.57);        // Output a floating-point
25:     printf("%f \n", 5.6e+2);       // Output a scientific-notation
26:                                    // value as a decimal floating-point
27:     printf("%e \n", 5.6e+2);       // Output a scientific-notation
28:                                    // value in scientific notation
29:     printf("%E \n", 5.6e+2);       // Write the E in uppercase
30:     printf("%g \n", 5.6e+2);       // Output as a decimal float or in
31:                                    // scientific notation, whichever
32:                                    // works the best for the data
33:     printf("%lf \n", 54.345e+12);  // Output a long double float
```

```
34:
35:    return 0;    // Return to the IDE
36: }
```

▼ OUTPUT

```
X
42
42
e7
4f
136
10
87532
453
45293
84.570000
560.000000
5.600000e+02
5.600000E+02
560
54345000000000.000000
```

▼ ANALYSIS

The printf()s are separated into three sections. Line 12 prints a character, lines 14 through 22 print integers, and lines 24 through 33 print floating-point values. No width or justification specifiers were used because the previous lesson covered those.

▶ **Variables**

	What You Will Learn

Variables hold data that you can change through assignment or calculation.

Variables are the storehouses for your program's data values. Programs need more than just literals. Your computer would be little more than a calculator without variables. Actually, today's calculators with their multiple memories are more powerful than a computer without variables.

A variable works in the same way that a calculator's memory does. When you store a value in the calculator's memory, that value stays there, ready to be used whenever you want it, until you turn off the calculator or replace the value with a different value. When you store a value in a variable, that value stays there, ready to be used whenever you want it until the program ends, until you turn off the computer, or until the program replaces the variable with another value. As with a calculator's memory, a variable can hold only one value at a time. Like many of today's calculators with multiple memory locations, a program can contain many variables.

A variable is a storage place for a piece of data. That data might be a character, an integer, a floating-point, or any of the other data types that C supports. Although you're limited to a combination of the amount of memory your computer has and the size of your compiled program, in practical terms you can use as many variables in a program as you need.

Think about a program that tracks customer memberships in a fancy health club. (Only C programmers are allowed to join the club because of its prestigious status and location.) Each month, a customer is charged a monthly dues fee. In addition, the customer can charge food or beverage items from the deli. Each customer's monthly balance changes as the customer adds to the bill and pays the bill. The customer's balance would be stored in a variable and would be added to and subtracted from as needed.

Note   Programs use the disk to hold the variable data when the computer is ready to be shut down for the night. You'll learn about the long-term storage of disk data in Lesson 11.

All C variables share these characteristics:

▶ Each variable has a name

▶ Each variable has a data type

▶ Each variable holds a value

The following sections explain these characteristics.

How to Name Variables

Calculators with multiple memories usually label each memory location 1, 2, and so on. Therefore, if you were to store 20 in memory location 1 and store 35 in memory location 2, you could retrieve either value whenever you wanted it by referring to the location number, either 1 or 2. In a way, the memory location number acts like a name for that memory location. The name 1 is the first location, 2 is the second, and so on.

C variables have *much* better names than 1, 2, and 3! Instead of the computer forcing you to use an archaic number-based naming system, *you* get to choose the names for your program's variables. The names you choose must follow some naming guidelines:

▶ All variable names must contain one to 31 characters.

▶ All variable names must begin with a letter of the alphabet. (I lied. Variables also can begin with an underscore character (_), but I don't recommend that.)

▶ After the first letter, a variable name can contain letters, digits, and the underscore character.

▶ You can't give a variable the same name as a function or a command.

▶ A function can't contain two variables with the same name. (There is a minor exception to this rule, but you're safest giving different names to all your variables.) If two variables had the same name, C would have no way of knowing which one you wanted when you used one.

▶ You can use either uppercase or lowercase letters in a variable name (or a mixture of both). Keep in mind, though, that once you give a variable a name, you can't use a different mixture of uppercase and lowercase letters to refer to that variable.

Tip Think of a variable's name as that variable's handle. When you want to use a certain variable, you'll use that variable's name and C will fetch the variable from memory for you.

The following variable names are all valid, legal variable names:

```
myCost      x      Balance94      febSales      total      first_initial
```

Do you see that all of the following are *different names?*

```
aVariable      AVARIABLE      avariable      AvARIABLE
```

Do you see that all of the following are illegal variable names?

```
94total      return      printf      total#amount
```

When you name a variable, you should decide on a name that makes sense. Don't name a variable i when the variable is going to hold a customer balance, because custBalance is a *much* better name! The better your names are, the easier they are to remember, and the fewer bugs that will appear in your program due to variable-name misspellings.

Variable Data Types

Earlier in this unit, Table 5.1 listed every single data type possible in the C language. There are as many numeric variable data types as there are numeric literal data types. Table 5.5 lists all the variable data types that C supports. The first column contains the name that C calls each data type. You'll see how to use the names in the next section. Luckily, the data-type names very closely match the data types themselves, so the data-type names are easier to remember.

Table 5.5. The variable data types.

Data Type	Description
char	Character
int	Integer
unsigned int	Unsigned integer
signed int	Signed integer (same as int)
short int	Short integer (same as int)
unsigned short int	Unsigned short integer (same as unsigned int)
signed short int	Signed short integer (same as integer)
long	Long integer
long int	Same as long
signed long int	Signed long integer (same as long)
unsigned long int	Unsigned long integer
float	Floating-point
double	Double-precision floating-point
long double	Long double-precision floating-point

Warning Don't confuse a variable's data-type name with the variable name. The data type simply describes the type of data the variable can hold. The name sets the variable apart from all other variables. You can have more than one variable with the same data type in a program, but not more than one variable with the same variable name.

In versions of C other than Turbo C++, there is no guarantee that the synonymous data types will match those in Table 5.5. In other words, a `short int` might not be the same data type as an `int` in all versions of C. Choose your variables carefully. You can't tell C that you want an integer variable and then expect to store a floating-point value in that integer variable. C will let you try this, but the value won't look right or compute correctly in a calculation.

Defining Variables

One of the first things proud parents do is name their baby. The first thing proud C programmers should do is name their variables! You must tell C that you want to use a variable before C lets you use that variable. After you tell C that you want to use a variable later in a program, C sets aside memory for the variable, attaches the variable name to that memory, and prepares the proper data type access for the variable.

 Note Some languages, such as QBasic, don't require that you tell the program in advance that you'll need certain variables. QBasic programs often have more data-type logic bugs than C programs because the initial definition of C variables makes you focus on your data better and readies the compiler to look for mistakes for you.

definition

Defining variables means that you place an order with C for a variable with a certain name and data type.

Right after the opening brace of a function, such as `main()`, you must define all variables used within that function. When you define a variable, you do the following:

▶ Tell C to reserve space for the variable

▶ Tell C what you want to call the variable

▶ Optionally, assign an initial value to the variable

C requires that you define all variables right after the opening brace of a function (or a block, but don't worry about that now), before you use the variables. In the middle of a function, you can't store a value in a variable that you didn't define at the top of that function.

Here is the general format of a variable definition:

dataType variableName [= *initialValue*];

As with most code formats, this format looks more difficult than it really is. *dataType* is any data type from the first column of Table 5.5, such as `int` or `float`. *variableName* is the name you make up and assign to the variable. (I'll explain what [= *initialValue*]; means in the next section.) If you don't want to give the variable an initial value, a semicolon appears next. Here is the start of a `main()` function that defines four variables:

```
main()
{
  char initial;
```

```
int makeCode;
int colorCode;
float price;
```

In plain language, here is what this code tells C:

> "C, I want you to define four variables. The first one is a character variable that I'll call `initial`. The second variable is an integer that I'll call `makeCode`. I want another integer that I'll call `colorCode`. Finally, I want you to reserve a floating-point variable that I'll call `price`."

Figure 5.2 shows the memory that Turbo C++ sets up after looking over your variable definitions. Notice that each variable takes the correct amount of storage space needed for its data type. (Refer to Table 5.2 for a list of data-type storage requirements.)

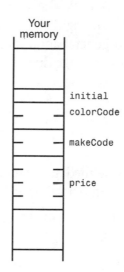

FIGURE 5.2.

The memory after C reserves variables.

Unlike calculator memory, which is zero before you store something in it, there are *not* necessarily zeros in the variables you define! Until you first store a value in a variable, that variable contains whatever value happened to be in that memory location before your program ran. Therefore, you can't assume that a variable holds a certain value until you store a value in it.

It turns out that C is lenient in its variable-defining requirements. If you want to define two variables of the same data type, you can do so on the same line. The following code is identical to the preceding code. Notice how the integers are both defined on the same line and that they are separated by a comma:

```
main()
{
  char initial;
  int makeCode, colorCode;
  float price;
```

Storing Data in Variables

Use the *assignment operator* (=) to put data in variables. Here is the format of the assignment:

```
variableName = expression;
```

variableName is a variable that you've already defined. As you saw in the preceding section, you can store an initial value using = in a variable at the same time that you define the variable. The *expression* can be a literal, another variable that has a value, or a mathematical expression that contains variables, literals, or a combination of both.

 Warning Don't store an expression in the wrong data type or in a variable that's too small to hold the expression. Store only characters in char variables, floating-point values in float variables, and so on.

Figure 5.3 shows exactly how the assignment behaves. The equal sign acts like an arrow that tells C to take whatever is on the right of the = and stick that expression in the variable on the left of the =. A variable and nothing else must *always* appear on the left of an equal sign. In C-speak, the left side of an assignment (the variable) is sometimes called the *lvalue,* and the right is called the *rvalue.* C programmers call variables lvalues when they speak in general about data that can change via an operator. Rvalues are expressions that can't change due to their positioning or type of data.

FIGURE 5.3.
The action of the assignment.

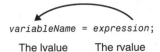

variableName = expression;
The lvalue   The rvalue

Given the variables defined at the end of the preceding section, the following assignment statements put initial values in the variables defined:

```
initial = 'S';    // The apostrophes are required for char literals!
makeCode = 22;
colorCode = 7;
price = 13.75;
```

Of course, you also can use complete expressions to store values in these variables. Later in the program, you might change the numeric values, like this:

```
makeCode = 13 * 4;
colorCode = makeCode / 2;
price = 1.25 * price;    // Update the old price
```

In the last assignment, price is being updated. Notice that the same variable name appears on both sides of the equal sign. The statement tells C to take whatever was in price (13.75 is still in price from the previous assignment) and multiply the price by 1.25. This, in effect, increases the value in price by 25%.

Don't forget that the assignment works at the definition of variables as well. If you need a total of three variables and you want those totals initialized to zero before main() does anything else, you could do this:

```
main()
{
  int total1, total2, total3;
```

but the following code is clearer and slightly more efficient:

```
main()
{
  int total1 = 0, total2 = 0, total3 = 0;
```

If you want to define the three totals but initialize only one of them to zero, C lets you:

```
main()
{
  int total1, total2 = 0, total3;
```

Three totals are now defined, but only `total2` has a known value in it.

Once you define and assign values to variables, printing them is simple. The following `printf()` statement prints whatever appears in the integer variable named `age` and the floating-point variable named `salary`:

```
printf("I am %d years old.\n", age);
printf("I make $%.2f a year.\n", salary);
```

 Warning As with literals, be sure that your `printf()` formatting conversion characters match the data types of the variables you're printing.

STOP&TYPE Listing 5.2 defines and assigns several values to several variables.

Review
What You Have Learned

After you define variables, a program can use those variables to hold calculated results. Once a variable holds a value, you can print the value with `printf()`.

▼ **INPUT   LISTING 5.2. USING VARIABLES FOR STORING AND PRINTING.**

```
 1:  /* Filename: ASSIGNS.C */
 2:  // Defines several variables and assigns
 3:  // values to them before printing the variables
 4:
 5:  #include <stdio.h>
 6:  #include <conio.h>
 7:
 8:  main()
 9:  {
10:    int temp1, temp2, temp3;
11:    float avgTemp;
12:
13:    clrscr();   // Erase the user's output screen
14:
15:    temp1 = 45;
16:    temp2 = 39;
17:    temp3 = 23;
18:
19:    // Print the three temperatures
20:    printf("The first reading is %d\n", temp1);
21:    printf("The second reading is %d\n", temp2);
22:    printf("The third reading is %d\n", temp3);
23:
24:    // Compute the average
25:    avgTemp = (temp1 + temp2 + temp3) / 3.0;
```

continues

LISTING 5.2. CONTINUED

```
26:
27:     printf("\nThe average temperature is %.1f\n", avgTemp);
28:
29:     return 0;   // Return to the IDE
30: }
```

▼ **OUTPUT**

```
The first reading is 45
The second reading is 39
The third reading is 23

The average temperature is 35.7
```

▼ **ANALYSIS**

This program defines all variables in lines 10 and 11, even before clearing the screen. In C, you must define all variables before doing anything else in a function. Lines 15 through 17 then assign initial values to the variables. Perhaps it would have been more efficient to assign the initial temperature values at the time the variables were defined on line 10, like this:

```
int temp1 = 45, temp2 = 39, temp3 = 23;
```

The choice of initializing is up to you. Keep in mind, however, that you can assign only initial literal values to variables when you define the variables. You can't assign expressions or other variables to a variable when you define the variable.

The parentheses around the additions on line 25 ensure that all the addition completes before the division so that the average computes correctly. (Unit 3 briefly described operator precedence. You'll read more about it in Lesson 4.)

Line 27 prints the computed average. Notice that the %f conversion character printed the contents of the float variable named avgTemp.

▶ Homework

General Knowledge

1. What's the difference between a signed integer and an unsigned integer?
2. What's the advantage of scientific notation?
3. What's the disadvantage of scientific notation?
4. Give an example of an unsigned data value.
5. Why not always use the largest data type available?
6. What qualifier specifies a long integer literal?
7. What qualifier specifies a long double floating-point literal?
8. What qualifier specifies an unsigned integer value?

9. What prefix qualifier makes an integer literal hexadecimal?

10. What prefix qualifier makes an integer literal octal?

11. Rank the following numbering systems in order of their use today:

    hexadecimal

    decimal

    octal

12. What does the assignment operator do?

13. True or false: A short integer can't hold as large of a value as a regular integer can.

14. True or false: All C compilers' `int` data types consume the same amount of storage.

15. True or false: A variable can be assigned a literal value.

16. True or false: A variable can be assigned an expression.

17. True or false: You can assign a variable an initial value at the same time that you define the variable.

18. True or false: You can assign a variable an initial expression at the same time that you define the variable.

19. True or false: You must define a variable before you can use it in a program.

What's the Output?

20. Rosemarie G. Cracker, a superb book editor, wants to try her hand at scientific programming. She almost has it right. She needs to print large numbers, but she wants to use scientific notation instead of coding a bunch of zeros. Rosemarie knows that if she uses the `%f` conversion character, C won't use scientific notation in the following `printf()`s. What will C output from the following code?

    ```
    printf("Number 1: %f\n", 4.56e+8);
    printf("Number 2: %f\n", -75.322e-3);
    printf("Number 3: %f\n", 123.4567e+4);
    ```

21. What line of output does the following program print?

    ```
    /* Filename: L3UA21.C */
    #include <stdio.h>
    #include <conio.h>

    main()
    {
        int i, j = 5;
        float x, y = 9.34;

        clrscr();

        i = j * 2;
        x = y + 7.0;
    ```

```
    printf("i is %d and x is %.1f\n", i, x);

    return 0;    // Return to the IDE
}
```

Find the Bug

22. What's wrong with the following assignments?

```
main()
{
  int age;
  char letter = 45.6;
  age = 12.2;
  // Rest of program follows
```

23. What did the programmer fail to do before the following `printf()`?

```
main()
{
  int myAge;
  printf("My age is %d.\n", myAge);
```

24. What's wrong with the following variable definition?

```
unsigned float uf;    // Define an unsigned floating-point value
```

25. What's wrong with the following variable definition and initialization?

```
unsigned int Value 25;
```

Write Code That...

26. Rewrite the following variable definition section of `main()` so that the definitions are grouped in a more orderly fashion:

```
main()
{
  float f;
  char c;
  int i1;
  float x;
  char p;
  double d;
  double e;
```

27. Write a program that defines four variables. The variables will hold your first and last initial, your age, and your tax rate percentage (such as .31 for 31%). Define the age as an unsigned integer. Print your initials and your age. Then, before printing your tax rate, print what your tax rate would be if the government decided to cut your rate in half because you're such a good C programmer.

Extra Credit

28. Change the program that you wrote in question 27 to print the tax rate as a percentage. (For example, print 17% instead of .17.)

29. Write a program that prints the initials, ages, and weights of each person in your family. Initialize the variables at the time that you define the variables. After you print the data, divide all ages by seven and divide all weights by six. You've now adjusted their ages down to doggy years and their weights to lunar weights. Print their initials again, but this time with their new ages and weights. Hint: You must be sure to define all computed dog and weight variables along with the other variables at the top of the program.

String Data and Input Gathering

argument

character array

element

null zero

scanf()

subscript

▶ **What You'll Learn About**

- ▶ Characters versus strings of characters
- ▶ Character arrays
- ▶ Working with character arrays
- ▶ Getting keyboard input

Okay, you know all about numbers. You know how to specify numeric literals and you know how to define and use numeric variables. There's more to data than just numbers, though! This unit explores character-based data.

C's support for character data is somewhat lacking. Actually, C supports character-based data fairly well, but compared to other programming languages, C requires a lot more work from you, the programmer, if you want to manipulate character-string data.

In this unit, you'll learn how C stores character and string data. You might recall from earlier units that string data is nothing more than a bunch of characters strung together, such as a person's name or address or a sentence in this book. To effectively work with strings in C, you have to learn how C stores that string data in memory.

Finally, you'll learn about C's notorious `scanf()` function. `scanf()` takes the user's keyboard input and stores it in variables. Instead of assigning all your data inside the program with assignment statements, your program can get data from the user at the time the program runs. Although `scanf()` isn't everybody's favorite function, it will be fairly easy to learn now that you've mastered the `printf()` function.

▶ **Characters Versus Strings of Characters**

Concept   **What You Will Learn**

Strings and characters share common characteristics, but they also differ in many ways.

C requires that you treat a string of characters differently from a single character. As you know from the preceding two units, you must enclose all character literals in apostrophes, as done with the following character literals:

`'a'        '8'        '\x168'        '\n'        '*'`

`'8'` is a character literal, not a number, because of the apostrophes. The apostrophes are the only way that you and C know that `'8'` is a character. That distinction is important, because you shouldn't store a character literal in a numeric variable. Therefore, single characters are useful when you want to keep track of one-byte data such as symbols, initials, and so on. (Remember from Unit 5 that a byte is a character.)

Note You *can* store a character literal in a numeric variable, but C will actually put that character's ASCII number, not the character, in the variable.

All escape sequences are single characters. Even though there are five characters inside a hexadecimal escape sequence (such as `'\x168'`), C stores the escape sequence as a single byte—hence the need for the apostrophes.

When you want to store character data in a variable, a simple `char` variable is what you need. Here are three character variable definitions:

```
char letterGrade;
char firstInitial;
char lastInitial;
```

Here are three assignments that store characters in those variables:

```
letterGrade = 'A';    // Top student!
firstInitial = 'R';
lastInitial = 'P';
```

String literals require regular quotation marks around them. Here are two string literals:

```
"Excellence in Broadcasting Network"
"Fresh-Squeezed Orange Juice"
```

There is no way that C would let you attempt this:

```
'Bad string!'
```

The apostrophes can contain at most one character (or an escape sequence that translates to a single character).

The strange thing about string literals is that you can specify a one-character *string* in a C program just by enclosing the character in quotation marks. The following are all considered string literals, not character literals:

```
"Q"       "*"       "9"       " "
```

Note As you will see in a moment, C stores one-character string literals differently from character literals. C stores all strings of all lengths in a special way.

The reason that C requires apostrophes around characters and quotation marks around strings is that without these delimiters, C would think that you were typing variable names instead of literals. In C, there might be times when you need zero-length strings. You should delimit empty strings with quotation marks, like this: `""`.

definition

A *delimiter* is a special character that encloses certain programming language elements.

Null Zero

Even though you never see the null zero, all strings end with it. The null zero has the same internal pattern as the integer 0. Here are several special ways to represent the null zero:

```
'\0'      0       '\x0'
```

Here are some names that all mean the same thing as the null zero:

definition

A *null zero* is a zero that appears in memory at the end of all strings.

▶ Binary zero

▶ String terminator

▶ ASCII zero

▶ String-delimiting zero

 Note Note that the null zero is *never* called *zero!* C programmers go to great efforts not to call the string-terminating zero a *zero* because they want to distinguish between the integer zero and the zero that ends all strings in memory.

 Warning Don't confuse the integer zero or the string-terminator with the *character zero!* (Isn't this getting ridiculous?) Look at Appendix B's ASCII table. You'll find that the first entry, the character for ASCII 0, is the null character. ASCII number 48 is the character 0. Here is how you represent ASCII 48: `'0'`. Here is how you represent the null zero: `'\0'`. Here is the number zero: `0`. Because you use them differently, you need to understand how to represent the one you need when you need it.

You can't see the null zero at the end of strings, but it's always there internally. *Whenever* you work with a string, whether it's a string literal or a string stored somehow in a variable (described in the next section), imagine that the null zero is there. (It is; you just won't see it.) C uses the null zero to determine where a given string ends in memory.

Figure 6.1 shows how C stores the string `"ABC"` in memory. Of course, the quotation marks are never stored with a string, because they serve only to delimit the start and end of the string literal in your program. Because of the null zero, `"ABC"` consumes four, not three, bytes of memory.

FIGURE 6.1.

A string always ends with the invisible (to you) null zero.

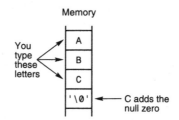

Here's why the null zero character is differentiated from the character zero: There is a null zero at the end of the following string:

```
Made in 1990
```

The null zero isn't the zero inside the number *1990*. It appears right after the character *0* of the year *1990*. Think of the null zero as replacing the terminating quotation mark of any and all string literals, and you'll be ahead of the C programming game.

Figure 6.2 shows how C stores the string that ends with the character zero. The string-terminating null zero never conflicts with actual data inside the string.

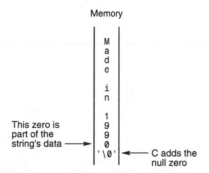

Memory

M
a
d
e

i
n

1
9
9
0
'\0' ← C adds the
         null zero

This zero is
part of the
string's data →

FIGURE 6.2.
The character zero is
never the null zero.

 Tip It's possible to store several individual characters together, such as a list of letter grades, and not treat those characters as if they made up a string. If the characters don't end with a null zero, they don't form a string. All strings end in null zeros. All lists of characters that don't end in a null zero are never considered to be strings. This distinction will become more clear once you learn a few more things.

Lengths of Strings

There will be times during your C programming when you need to know exactly how long a string is. You have yet to see how to store strings in variables. Because storing strings in variables isn't as easy as storing numbers in variables, the next large section of this unit devotes itself to showing you how to store strings. In the meantime, this section uses string constants to show you how to determine the length of a string.

It's true that if you want to know how long a string constant is, you only have to count the characters yourself! Nevertheless, learn how to find the lengths of string literals now. Finding the lengths of string literals uses the very same technique as finding the length of strings stored in variables.

When the term *string length* is used in C programming, it might have a different meaning from what you would expect after reading the preceding section. Although the null zero is *always* present at the end of *all* strings, and although a string isn't a string without the terminating null zero, the null zero is never counted as part of the string length. Only the number of characters before the null zero comprises the string length.

Consider the following string:

`"Four"`

How many characters does it take to store this string? It takes five characters, because the null zero is present. What is the string's length? Four, because the length never includes the null zero. Figure 6.3 shows the difference. No matter how long the string is, the length is always one less than the number of bytes it takes to store the string.

definition
The *string length* is always the number of characters up to but not including the null zero.

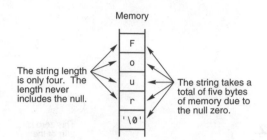

FIGURE 6.3.
The string length never
includes the null zero.

HOW IMPORTANT IS THIS?

In many programming languages, you would never spend this much time learning how strings are represented internally. Most programming languages more fully automate the string-handling process than C does.

In return for a little extra effort, C is highly efficient at manipulating your string data. Therefore, the effort it takes to learn about string storage repays itself in the efficiency of program execution.

Eventually you'll learn to control the placement of the null zero and will also be able to utilize the string space to make the most of your computer's memory while running your programs.

Can you guess how C stores strings containing only a single character? The string "C" is one byte in length but consumes two bytes of storage due to the null zero that must be present. The quotation marks tells C to treat the letter as a string and to add the null zero at the end. If you were to work with the character 'C', C wouldn't add the null zero.

An empty string ("") is zero bytes in length, but it does consume one byte of memory due to the null zero.

Review   What You Have Learned

This section focused on C's storage of string and character literals. The most important thing to remember is that C always puts a null zero at the end of a string. There is no exception to this rule. If the null zero isn't there, the memory holds nothing more than a bunch of one-byte character literals that happen to be located adjacent to one another.

Note   There is no input, output, or analysis here due to this section's conceptual nature.

► Character Arrays

UNIT

6

String Data and Input Gathering

definition
A *character array* is a list of adjacent character variables treated as one entity.

Concept   **What You Will Learn**

If you want to store a string literal in a variable, you must store that string in a character array.

You know about character variables. You know about integer variables. You know about floating-point variables. You know (see a pattern here?) about double floating-point variables. There are, however, *no string variables!* Hey, designers of C, wake up!

Well, in defense of the designers, C really doesn't need string variables. As mentioned in the preceding section, C's lack of support for string variable storage makes it a faster language than other programming languages that support string variables, such as QBasic. Those languages must do a lot of background work (called *garbage collection*) when organizing string variables.

In a way, saying that C doesn't support string variables is technically correct, but in reality, you can store strings in string-like variables called *character arrays*. You can define arrays of any data type, but we'll keep this discussion focused on just character arrays. Later, in Lesson 9, you'll read about the other kinds of arrays (numeric arrays) and the things you can do with them.

A character array is nothing more than a list of character variables. Unlike character variables, however, an array has only one name. The array name is the name for every character stored in the array. You would store characters in an array instead of in separately-named variables if those characters should go together in storage. A string would need such storage. That's what character arrays are mostly used for: holding string data.

Anytime you learn about a new kind of C variable, you must learn how to define that variable. To define a character array, you use the `char` command, just as you do for a character variable. The following definition defines a character variable (tells the compiler that you need one) named `code`:

```
char code;
```

If you want an array (a list of back-to-back character variables), you have to tell C how many characters you want the array to hold, *including the null zero*. You must know in advance the maximum number of characters that a character array will hold, or you'll have problems later.

Tip   One advantage of storing strings in character arrays is that you don't have to type the same string literal all throughout your program. Instead, you only need to use the name of the character array.

The number of elements that you want the array to hold must go inside brackets. Suppose you wanted to hold your pet's name in an array. If your pet's name is `Muffy`, the array would need to be six characters long (the string length plus the null zero). Here's how you would tell C what you needed:

```
char pet[6];   // Define an array
```

 Warning There is *no way* that you can store a string longer than five characters with a null zero at the end in `pet` once you define `pet` as shown here. `pet` can hold a smaller string than that, but never a larger one. Actually, you can *try* to put a larger string in `pet`, and C will act like you're allowed to do so, but then it will damage other data without telling you what's going on! If you want more spaces for string storage, tell C how much you want when you define the array, because later will be too late.

Remember that you can initialize a variable at the time you define the variable. In the previous code's character-variable definition, you can put an initial value in the character variable:

```
char code = 'X';   // Define and store an initial character value
```

If you want to store your pet's name in the array at the time you define the array, you can do so like this:

```
char pet[6] = "Muffy";   // Define and store an initial array value
```

 Warning This bears repeating: Leave room for the string's data *and* the null zero when you define the character array. If you don't leave enough room for the null zero, your program will lose track of data in other variables.

definition

A *subscript* is the number inside an array's brackets.

 Tip If the initial string that you assign is the only string that the character array will hold, or if the initial string is as long as or longer than any other string your program will store in the character array, you don't need to include the subscript when you define the array.

You might as well let C do the counting when you initially define and assign data to a character array. The following character-array definition is identical to the preceding one:

```
char pet[] = "Muffy";   // Define and store an initial array value
```

definition

An *element* is an individual array value.

C counts the length of `Muffy` and gets five. C also knows that the character array must include the null zero or a string can't be stored in the array. Therefore, C knows to define six elements for the array, as shown in Figure 6.4.

Whatever you do, don't define an array with empty brackets and without any initial data assigned to it. C wouldn't know how many elements to reserve in the following array definition, so it wouldn't reserve any. No defined elements in the array makes for difficulties later if you attempt to store data in an array that doesn't have room to hold it:

```
char unknown[];   // C reserves no storage here!
```

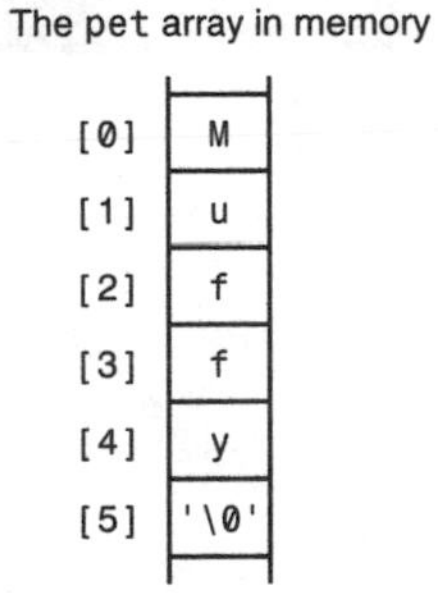

The pet array in memory

[0] M
[1] u
[2] f
[3] f
[4] y
[5] '\0'

FIGURE 6.4.
pet has six elements.

Figure 6.4 shows one more aspect of arrays that you need to know about. Notice the numbers in the brackets next to each array element. These numbers represent the individual subscript numbers for each element. Think about this for a moment: The entire array has a single name, but the array holds multiple characters. The individual characters aren't individually named. To refer to one of the characters, you must use the array name and specify the subscript for the element you want to access.

Even though a string is stored in pet, you might want to access the string's individual characters in the array. There might be times when you want to change a character or print only one or two elements from the array (such as a first initial from a name). Therefore, you need to access individual array elements. The subscript gives you that access.

All arrays begin with a subscript of 0. Therefore, the highest array element always has a subscript one less than the total number of characters in the array. Some programming languages let you change the starting array subscript, but in C, the first array element always has 0 for a subscript, the second always has 1 for a subscript, and so on.

The next section explains how you might use the subscript to change individual array elements.

STOP&TYPE Listing 6.1 contains a program that defines and initializes three arrays using the following three different methods:

▶ An initial string is assigned and a subscript is used.

▶ An initial string is assigned and a subscript is not used.

▶ A character array is defined but no data is stored in the array when it is defined.

The first two character arrays are then printed.

Review **What You Have Learned**

If you want to store string data, you must define a character array to hold that string data.

▼ INPUT   LISTING 6.1. DEFINING AND PRINTING CHARACTER ARRAYS.

```
1: /* Filename: ARRAYBEG.C */
2: // Defines, initializes, and prints three character arrays
3: #include <stdio.h>
4: #include <conio.h>
5: main()
```

continues

LISTING 6.1. CONTINUED

```
 6: {
 7:    char cArray1[6] = "Larry";    // Leave room for null zero
 8:    char cArray2[] = "Moe";       // Let C count
 9:    char cArray3[6];              // No data initialized
10:    clrscr();   // Erase the screen
11:
12:    printf("Here is the first array: ");
13:    printf(cArray1);
14:    printf("\nHere is the second array: ");
15:    printf(cArray2);
16:    printf("\nI cannot print the third array because ");
17:    printf("it has no data!\n");
18:    return 0;
19: }
```

▼ **OUTPUT**

```
Here is the first array: Larry
Here is the second array: Moe
I cannot print the third array because it has no data!
```

▼ **ANALYSIS**

The first array, named cArray1, is both defined and initialized on line 7. Although the length of the string is 5 (the number of characters in Larry), the array requires six elements because of the string data's null zero. cArray1 can never hold a string longer than five characters due to its definition, but it can hold shorter strings if you need it to. On line 8, the programmer didn't have to include the initial subscript. C is smart enough to figure out that Moe requires four array elements to hold the string plus the null zero.

The third array is defined with six elements, but no data is assigned to it. C does initialize the array to *something,* but you have no idea what's in the array and you shouldn't attempt to print an undefined array.

When you compile this program, watch the compilation box carefully. Turbo C++ will compile the program but produce a warning. A warning is not as severe as an error, but usually you should pay attention to warnings to make sure they aren't severe. All warnings appear in the message window, which you can see by selecting Window Message. Figure 6.5 shows the message window that you should see at the bottom of the IDE.

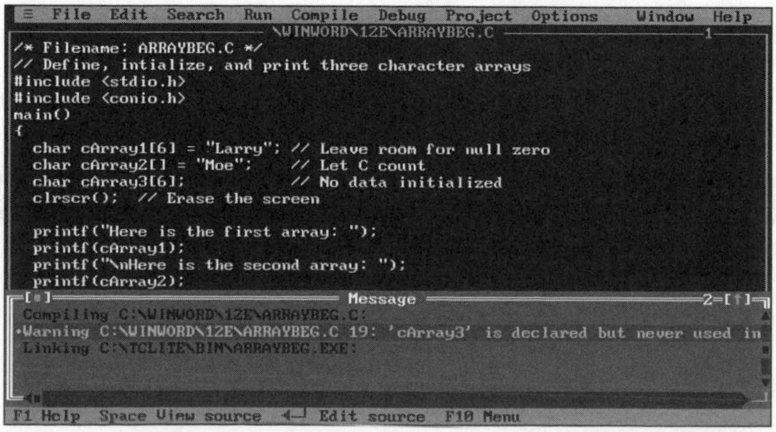

FIGURE 6.5.
Oops! A warning message gives you something to watch for.

The warning is letting you know that you defined an array (cArray3) but you never used it (as if you didn't know). Turbo C++ wants you to know this because your program is less efficient due to the unused variable. This warning is not too severe, but you'll want to remove such an error in your "real-world" programs. As you write longer programs, you'll sometimes think you need a variable at first but it turns out once you finish the program that you didn't need the variable after all. This warning reminds you that you should remove the variable's definition to make your program as efficient as possible.

To the left of the warning message you'll see the number 19. Turbo C++ says that the cause of the warning is line 19. Sometimes warnings are close to the actual offending line numbers, and sometimes they're not. cArray3 is defined on line 9. However, Turbo C++ didn't realize that you hadn't used cArray until the program's final line number—19.

Tip To close a message window, select Window Close or press Alt-F3.

USE %s TO PRINT STRINGS

Listing 6.1 shows that you don't need a format conversion character to print a string stored in a character array. However, you can use the %s conversion character inside printf() functions to print strings.

You could have saved a couple of printf()s in Listing 6.1 by using %s. For example, instead of printing cArray1 on a line by itself (line 13), you could have put cArray1 at the end of line 12's printf(), like this:

```
printf("Here is the first array: %s", cArray1);
```

By using %s, you can embed escape sequences in the string-printing printf(). If you want a newline escape sequence at the end of the printf(), add one after the %s:

```
printf("Here is the first array: %s\n", cArray1);
```

Therefore, if you want to print a character array by itself, you don't need %s. If you want to print the array as well as other kinds of data, use %s.

Working with Character Arrays

Concept   **What You Will Learn**

Store data in character arrays when you define the arrays, through assignment, or with the strcpy() function.

A surprising limitation in C is that you can't assign a string directly to a character array using the assignment operator. For example, once you define an array like this:

```
char cArray3[6];
```

you can't assign a string to the array like this:

```
cArray3 = "Curly";    // Nope, not allowed!
```

This doesn't help any:

```
cArray3[] = "Curly";    // Nope, not allowed either!
```

and neither does this:

```
cArray3[6] = "Curly";    // Nope, not even this!
```

Remember that C doesn't have any string variables. There are character variables and integer variables and floating-point variables, but there are no string variables. A character array is *not* a string variable, although you can store strings inside character arrays.

You can *only* assign a value to a character array using an equal sign at the time that you define the array. There are two ways to change the contents of a character array after you define the array:

▶ Assign one character at a time to each array element.

▶ Assign a new string using the strcpy() built-in library function.

Note You also can store new strings typed by the user at the keyboard. An entire section on keyboard input appears at the end of this unit.

Use an array element's subscript to change an array's contents. If you want to put the name Curly in cArray3, you can do so like this:

```
cArray[0] = 'C';    // Remember that arrays begin at zero subscript
cArray[1] = 'u';
cArray[2] = 'r';
cArray[3] = 'l';
cArray[4] = 'y';
cArray[5] = '\0';    // Without this, there would be no string
```

The null zero must be at the end of the array. Otherwise, you won't have a string; you will simply have assigned five individual characters to the array. Storing characters without the null zero is fine as long as you never attempt to print or treat the array as if it holds a string. Most of the time you'll want to store a string with a terminating null zero.

definition

An *argument* is a value that appears inside a function's parentheses.

Instead of tediously assigning one value at a time to a character array, you can use the library function strcpy(). (Its name stands for *string copy*.) strcpy() requires two arguments: a character array and a string that you want to assign to the character array. Here is the format of strcpy():

```
strcpy(charArray, stringToAssign);
```

charArray must be a character array. (You also can use advanced pointer variables that hold strings, as you'll learn in Lesson 9.) *stringToAssign* can be either a string literal or another character array that holds a string. To assign the string "Curly" to cArray3, you can use strcpy(), which is a lot easier than the previous multiple assignments:

```
strcpy(cArray3, "Curly");    // Assign Curly to cArray3
```

Warning You *must* include the STRING.H header file at the top of any program that uses `strcpy()`!

INITIALIZE ONE CHARACTER AT A TIME

C lets you define and initialize a character array one element at a time using a special *aggregate* initialization notation:

```
char show[7] = {'T', 'V', ' ', 'N', 'e', 'w', 's'};
```

These seven elements *do not* provide for a null zero. A null zero isn't automatically assigned, and show won't hold a string—only seven characters. If you want to define and initialize an array, the initial subscript isn't needed. This is identical to the previous assignment:

```
char show[] = {'T', 'V', ' ', 'N', 'e', 'w', 's'};
```

If you want a string stored in the show array, be sure to include the null zero in the aggregate assignment:

```
char show[8] = {'T', 'V', ' ', 'N', 'e', 'w', 's', '\0'};
```

The 8 initial subscript is optional. Of course, if you were assigning such an initial string, a simple string initialization like this would be easier:

```
char show[] = "TV news";
```

STOP&TYPE Listing 6.2 contains a program that initializes a character array and then assigns two different strings to the array.

Review What You Have Learned

Once you define a character array, you can store strings in that array using `strcpy()` or by assigning one character at a time.

▼ INPUT LISTING 6.2. ASSIGNING TO A CHARACTER ARRAY.

```
1:   /* Filename: CARRINIT.C */
2:   // Defines a character array, then
3:   // initializes the array twice
4:   #include <stdio.h>
5:   #include <conio.h>
6:   #include <string.h>
7:
8:   main()
9:   {
10:    char cArray[30];    // Leave extra room
11:    clrscr();    // Erase the screen
12:
13:    cArray[0] = 'C';
14:    cArray[1] = ' ';
15:    cArray[2] = 'i';
16:    cArray[3] = 's';
```

continues

LISTING 6.2. CONTINUED

```
17:     cArray[4] = ' ';
18:     cArray[5] = 'n';
19:     cArray[6] = 'e';
20:     cArray[7] = 'a';
21:     cArray[8] = 't';
22:     cArray[9] = '\0';
23:     printf("The array holds %s\n", cArray);
24:
25:     strcpy(cArray, "I like programming!");
26:     printf("Now the array holds %s\n", cArray);
27:     return 0;
28:  }
```

▼ **OUTPUT**

```
The array holds C is neat
Now the array holds I like programming!
```

▼ **ANALYSIS**

First of all, notice that more array elements are defined for the array than are ever used (line 10). Defining extra elements is allowed, and doing so will harm nothing—but you do use more memory than you need. Depending on your program, you might not always know in advance exactly how long a string should be; in that case, you must define in advance more array elements than you need. You can use fewer elements than you define, but never more.

As a review, remember that you must define all variables in a program before you can do anything else. Line 10's array definition must appear before line 11's clrscr() function.

Lines 13 through 22 assign a string to the array one element at a time. The array is printed in line 23. Without the null zero assignment in line 22, the printf() in line 23 wouldn't work properly. On line 25, the strcpy() function assigns a different string to the array, which is printed again in line 26.

► Getting Keyboard Input

What You Will Learn

scanf() gets input from the keyboard.

You can't always assign all your program data. Often, you need to get data from the user. The user's input is useful for

- ► answering questions
- ► entering data to be calculated
- ► entering data to be saved to a disk file

Assignment statements are very useful, but they can't handle the day-to-day assigning of data that virtually all programs need. If you were writing a program for a real estate agent that computed commission on homes sold, you would have no idea at the time you wrote the program which homes she will sell, how many she will sell, the price of the homes, or anything else unless you can predict the future. Therefore, you must set up the program to ask the real estate agent for the pertinent data when she runs the program.

There are several ways to get input from the user. The easiest for now is to use the `scanf()` function, which *almost* looks like `printf()`. Here is the format of `scanf()`:

```
scanf("formatString" [, data] [, data...]);
```

As you will soon see, `scanf()` makes a little less sense than `printf()` because it requires a few funny extras.

Tip Always use a `printf()` before a `scanf()` so that your user knows what to type.

After the following `printf()`:

```
printf("How old are you? ");    // No \n so cursor appears after ?
```

you might put this `scanf()`:

```
scanf(" %d", &age);
```

Warning The `&` in front of `age` is *not* part of the variable's name. Remember that all variable names must begin with a letter of the alphabet. The `&` is explained in a moment.

Figure 6.6 shows the action of `scanf()`. The user's input, in this case her age, runs through the format string inside `scanf()` before landing in the variable, called `age`.

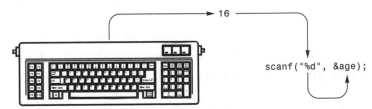

FIGURE 6.6.
How `scanf()` works.

The format string tells `scanf()` exactly what to expect. Here are some problems with `scanf()`:

▶ The user doesn't always type what he or she should. If the user types a floating-point value and `scanf()` expects an integer, `scanf()` won't use the fractional part of the number. If `scanf()` expects two or more values, the user might enter fewer than expected. Worse, the user might enter *more* values than expected, leaving extra input in the keyboard buffer that a subsequent `scanf()` will capture incorrectly. (Those users!) The format string must look exactly like the user's input. If the format string has an integer followed by a comma followed by a floating-point value, like this:

```
" %d,%f "
```

the user needs to enter an integer followed by a comma followed by a floating-point value.

▶ `scanf()` needs the space at the *beginning* of the format string. Well, sometimes the space is needed, so always include it. The user is *not* to enter data with an initial space, despite the format string's initial space. However, all other spaces in the format string, such as one between two conversion characters, must be respected and typed by the user during data input.

▶ `scanf()` requires an ampersand, `&`, before all nonarray variables. For now, accept with blind faith that there is an adequate, albeit advanced, reason that the ampersand is required.

▶ `scanf()` does *not* require an ampersand before array variables! For now, accept this with blind faith also.

▶ `scanf()` can get only a single word at a time, no matter how many array elements are defined in the character array you're entering data into. `scanf()` quits gathering input after the user's first space.

Perhaps you're seeing why `scanf()` doesn't always make a lot of sense. The bottom-line reason for learning `scanf()` now, however, is that it uses the same conversion characters as `printf()`. For now, assume that the user (and let's face it, the user in this book will always be you!) will always enter data in the exact format required by the `scanf()` format string.

Note   As with `printf()`, `scanf()` uses the STDIO.H header file.

Warning   Never use a newline escape sequence (\n) or floating-point precision (a decimal-place position) inside a `scanf()`. The user's newline keypress automatically ends all input, and a \n inside a `scanf()` messes up the input. Also, floating-point decimal precision works only for output, not input.

definition
A *prompt* is a message or question that tells the user exactly what to enter.

STOP&TYPE   Listing 6.3 contains a program that defines an integer, a floating-point, and a character array variable. After appropriate `printf()` input prompts, some `scanf()` functions grab the user's data and print it.

Review
What You Have Learned

`scanf()` is `printf()`'s mirror-like function. Whereas `printf()` sends data, in variables, to the user's screen, `scanf()` gets data from the user's keyboard and stores it in variables.

▼ INPUT   LISTING 6.3. USING `scanf()` **FOR INPUT OF THREE VALUES.**

```
1:  /* Filename: SCANFBEG.C */
2:  // Defines three variables and asks the user
3:  // for values to put in those variables
4:  #include <stdio.h>
5:  #include <conio.h>
```

```
 6:   #include <string.h>
 7:
 8:   main()
 9:   {
10:     char code;
11:     float price;
12:     char city[25];     // Must leave enough room for input and null
13:
14:     clrscr();            // Clear the screen and print a title
15:     printf("Inventory Input\n\n");
16:
17:     // Without the printf()s, the user wouldn't know what to do
18:     printf("What is the one-letter product code? ");
19:     scanf(" %c", &code);
20:     printf("What is the price? ");
21:     scanf(" %f", &price);
22:     printf("In what city was it made? ");
23:     scanf(" %s", city);    // NO ampersand!!!
24:     printf("\nHere is your input:\n");
25:     printf(" Code: %c\n Price: %.2f\n City: %s\n", code, price, city);
26:     return 0;
27:   }
```

▼ OUTPUT

```
Inventory Input

What is the one-letter product code? w
What is the price? 3.45
In what city was it made? Miami

Here is your input:
 Code: w
 Price: 3.45
 City: Miami
```

▼ ANALYSIS

As you can see from this program, scanf() isn't really difficult, despite its nuances. The most important part of the program appears in line 12. You must reserve as much memory as you think you'll need to hold whatever town name the user enters. Also, the town name must be a single word. An input such as St. Louis won't work because scanf() can get only a single word at a time, even though a character array can hold more than one word at a time.

The scanf() variables in lines 19 and 21 both have ampersands as required. The array in line 23 doesn't have an ampersand because arrays don't use an ampersand in scanf() input.

▶ **Homework**

General Knowledge

1. What appears, internally, at the end of every string?

2. What kind of variable holds string data?

3. Is the following a null zero, a binary zero, or an integer zero?

```
0
```

4. Is the following a null zero, an integer zero, or a character zero?

```
'0'
```

5. Is the following a null zero, an integer zero, or a character zero?

```
'\0'
```

6. How many bytes of memory does a character literal take?

7. How many bytes of memory does a numeric integer take?

8. How many bytes of memory does a null string take?

9. How long is the following string?

```
"Rome, Italy"
```

10. How long is the following string?

```
"0"
```

11. How many elements are defined in the following character array definition?

```
char aString[];
```

12. What's the difference between `scanf()` and `printf()`?

13. Which function gets input from the user?

14. True or false: This is a string of zero length: `"0"`

15. True or false: This is a string of zero length: `""`

16. True or false: The following is a string because of the four characters inside the single quotes: `'\xa5'`.

17. True or false: You must initialize a character array when you define the array.

18. True or false: You must define enough characters to hold the array's longest string plus a null zero.

19. True or false: You can store a string in a character array by assigning one character at a time to each array element.

What's the Output?

20. What is printed from the following `printf()`?

```
printf("%s 3 %s\n", "The ", " bears");
```

Find the Bug

21. What's wrong with the following variable definition and assignment?

```
char it;
it = 42;
```

22. Why is the following not a valid string literal?

```
'Something is wrong here...'
```

23. A character array named `person` was defined like this:

```
char person[10];
```

For some reason, programmer Tony's program doesn't work right when he does this:

```
strcpy(person, "Tony Miller");
```

Help Tony find his trouble.

24. In response to the following short program:

```
#include <stdio.h>
main()
{
  char name[25];
  printf("Who are you? ");
  scanf(" %s", name);
  printf("Hi, %s.\n", name);
  return 0;
}
```

Sandra Elliott entered her first and last name. What did she do wrong?

Write Code That...

25. Rewrite the program in question 24 so that it asks for two names, a first and last name.

26. Considering that the character array named `anArray` was defined like this:

```
char anArray[] = "Time for a change";
```

write code that stores the string `"New string"` in `anArray` by assigning one character at a time.

27. Assign `"New string"` to `anArray` using the `strcpy()` function.

Extra Credit

28. Write a program that asks the user for his or her first and last name. Print the last name first and separate the two names with a comma.

29. Write a program that asks the user for his or her first and last name. Print the user's initials. Terminate each initial with a period.

UNIT

6

String Data and Input Gathering

Project

Lesson ▶

Data Basics

STOP&TYPE In this lesson, you learned about the fundamental data variables found in most C programs. You saw the following:

▶ Variables are either numeric or character-based.

▶ There are several types of numeric variables, but all are basically short and long versions of integers and floating-point values.

▶ C includes character variables that hold single characters.

Project 3 Listing. Introduction to data and I/O.

```c
1: /* Filename: PROJECT3.C */

2: // This program defines different kinds of variables and

3: // lets the user's keyboard input fill the variables with

4: // values. Subsequent printf()s print the data in the variables.

5: #include <stdio.h>

6: #include <conio.h>

7:

8: main()

9: {

10:    char prodName[12];

11:    int count;

12:    float price;

13:    float totalInv;

14:

15:    clrscr();

16:    printf("Inventory Calculation\n");
```

▶ If you want to store a string of characters, you must use a character array to hold the string.

▶ `printf()` sends data to the screen.

▶ `scanf()` gets data from the user at the keyboard.

Description

1: A C comment that includes the program's filename.

2: A C++ comment that begins the program's description.

3: The program's description continues.

4: The program's description continues.

5: The `printf()` and `scanf()` functions need information in the STDIO.H header file.

6: The screen-clearing function, `clrscr()`, needs information in the CONIO.H header file.

7: Extra blank lines make your program more readable.

8: All functions have names, and the first function in all C programs is `main()`.

9: All functions begin with a left brace.

10: Defines a character array that can hold a string as long as 11 characters plus a null zero.

11: Defines an integer variable that will hold an inventory count.

12: Defines a floating-point variable that will hold a floating-point price per inventory item.

13: Defines a floating-point variable that will hold a floating-point total price of all the items.

14: Extra blank lines make your program more readable.

15: The built-in library function `clrscr()` erases the output screen so that it's clear before the program's output begins.

16: The first line of a title is printed.

2: Add ample comments at the top of your programs to briefly describe the code.

continues

Project 3 Listing. continued

```
17:    printf("--------------------\n\n");

18:

19:    printf("This program calculates an inventory's product value.\n\n");

20:    printf("What is the product name? ");

21:    scanf(" %s", prodName);

22:    printf("How many %ss are there? ", prodName);

23:    scanf(" %d", &count);

24:    printf("How much does each %s cost? ", prodName);

25:    scanf(" %f", &price);

26:    // Ready to extend the inventory cost

27:    totalInv = count * price;

28:    printf("\nThe total valuation for %s is $%.2f\n",

29:           prodName, totalInv);

30:    return 0;

31: }
```

Description

17: The title appears underlined on the screen due to the well-placed hyphens.

18: Extra blank lines make your program more readable.

19: A printed message to describe the program's goal.

20: A prompt for the item name.

21: Takes the user's input and stores the item name in a character array.

21: There is no ampersand in front of array names in `scanf()` functions.

22: A prompt for the item's inventory count. Notice how the item name, obtained in line 21, is embedded in the prompt.

23: The item's count is entered. As with all nonarray variables, `count` needs an ampersand before its name in `scanf()`.

24: The cost of each item is requested.

25: The user enters the floating-point price per item.

26: A comment describing the upcoming program section.

27: The total inventory price for the item is calculated and stored in `totalInv`.

28: The format string of the two-line `printf()` formats the output with a descriptive message and readies the output for numeric data.

29: The data for the `printf()` is printed.

29: You can continue `printf()`s on more than one line, as done here, as long as you break the line after a comma.

30: The program returns to the IDE.

31: All program functions (`main()` here) end with a closing brace.

▼ OUTPUT

```
Inventory Calculation
- - - - - - - - - - - - - - - - - - - -

This program calculates an inventory's product value.

What is the product name? Widget
How many Widgets are there? 3
How much does each Widget cost? 3.30

The total valuation for Widget is $9.90
```

Lesson ▶

4

Simple Operators

Unit 7: Fundamental Math Operators

Unit 8: Relational and Logical Operators

Lesson 4 Project

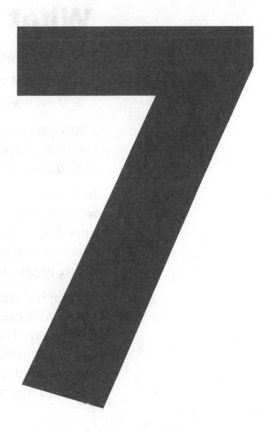

Fundamental Math Operators

binary operator

compound assignment
operator

hierarchy

operator

overloaded operator

unary operator

▶ What You'll Learn About

- ▶ Reviewing the basics
- ▶ Order of operators
- ▶ Advanced assignments

Although you've seen the four primary math operators—+, -, *, and /—there are several more. Appendix C lists all of C's operators. C is a language rich in operators. Not all of them are math-related, but many are.

In this unit, you'll learn about several of the math operators and become more acquainted with the operator precedence that is so important in C. Appendix C's operator table not only describes each of the operators, but it also lists each operator in order of its precedence over other operators. As you might recall from Lesson 2, some operators execute before others, such as division before addition.

Although C computes all your math results for you, you still must understand how to set up your calculations to achieve correct results. If you never thought math was fun, that's okay. There's a lot more to C programming than math. However, programs are extremely useful for computing sales figures, inventory totals, and much more, relieving you from those tedious burdens. Knowing how to use C's operators will let you set up your programs so that you can toss that pocket calculator out the window.

▶ Reviewing the Basics

Concept   **What You Will Learn**

> The primary math operators do what you expect them to. When you need simple arithmetic, the primary math operators will compute many of your needed answers.

Although you understand basic addition, subtraction, multiplication, and division, C presents a few extra considerations that you need to understand. The following sections explore the primary math operators, shown in Table 7.1.

Table 7.1. C's primary math operators.

Math Operator	Description
*	Multiplication
/	Division or integer division
%	Modulus (also called *remainder*)
+	Unary: Specifies a positive amount (optional for positive values)
	Binary: Performs addition
-	Unary: Specifies a negative amount
	Binary: Performs subtraction

Notice that some of the operators are overloaded. For example, the division operator either performs regular division as you know it (sometimes called *floating-point division*) or computes integer division under certain circumstances. The following sections describe the dual operations of +, -, and /.

The Unary Operators

The unary operators, + and -, are almost too obvious to discuss because they're so easy to understand. However, they do appear in different locations in the precedence table than their binary counterparts, so they warrant their own discussions.

 Warning The term *binary operator* has nothing to do with binary numbers. Whereas a unary operator operates on single values, binary operators operate on two values (*bi* is a prefix meaning *two*).

Anytime you put a plus sign in front of a single numeric literal or variable, the plus sign operates as a unary plus sign. The plus sign is optional. Both of the following statements are equivalent:

```
ageLimit = 18;    // Put a positive 18 in a variable
```

and

```
ageLimit = +18;    // Put a positive 18 in a variable
```

You can place the unary plus in front of variables:

```
newLimit = +ageLimit + 3;    // Raise the old age limit
```

Be careful when putting plus signs together. If you rearrange the previous assignment like this:

```
newLimit = 3 + +ageLimit;  // Raise the old age limit
```

C won't care and everything will work fine, but the space between the two plus signs is critical. Without the space, C will complain via a compile error. The ++ (two plus signs without a space between them) is another C operator that you'll learn about in the next lesson.

Again, the unary plus sign is very obvious and is one of the easiest operators to understand. The unary plus sign is also optional because if you omit it, C assumes that the literal or variable is a positive value.

If you want to negate a variable or specify a negative numeric literal, use the unary minus sign. The following statement stores a negative value in a variable:

```
rateOfGrowth = -.23;
```

You can negate (take the negative of) a variable's value like this:

```
factor = amount * -value;
```

value does *not* change in this statement. value is one of the rvalues, and only lvalues (factor in this case) change as a result of assignment statements. This statement tells C the following:

> *"Multiply the value in* amount *by the negative of the number in* value *and store that computed result in* factor. *Don't change either* amount *or* value *from their old values; change only* factor*."*

Feel free to negate any mathematical expression such as the following:

```
a = -(b * c);
```

The quantity b multiplied by c is computed and then the negative of that quantity is stored in a. Again, neither b nor c changes due to the assignment.

As with the unary plus sign, be sure to put a space before the unary minus sign:

```
a = b - -c;    // Without the space, strange things would happen!
```

Note In the preceding statement, the first negative sign is a binary subtraction and the second (the minus before c) is a unary minus. See the difference? As stated before, binary operators operate on two values, while a unary operator operates on only one value.

Two Divisions and Remainder

The division operator, /, actually performs two operations. / performs regular division when you divide two values and at least one of those values is a noninteger. / performs integer division when *both* of its two values are integers. If this sounds like double-speak, you'll see that the difference between regular division and integer division is easy to understand.

The program in Listing 7.1 contains an integer division operator. It's an integer division operator because an integer appears on *both* sides of the /.

▼ **INPUT   LISTING 7.1. PERFORMING INTEGER DIVISION.**

```c
/* Filename: INTDIV.C */
// Computes integer division
#include <stdio.h>
#include <conio.h>
main()
{
  int people, events, avgEv;
  clrscr();

  printf("How many people will attend? ");
  scanf(" %d", &people);
  printf("How many events are scheduled? ");
  scanf(" %d", &events);

  // Compute the average number of people per event
  avgEv = people / events;    // The integer division ensures
                              // that the fractional part of
                              // the answer is discarded
  printf("\nThere will be an average of %d people per event.\n",
            avgEv);
  return 0;
}
```

Here is a sample run of the program:

```
How many people will attend? 14
How many events are scheduled? 3

There will be an average of 4 people per event.
```

Note If an integer variable, literal, or a combination of the two appears on both sides of the /, the / always computes integer division.

If a noninteger appears on one or both sides of the division operator, C computes normal fractional division. For example, the following statement stores 10.5 in the variable named ans:

```
ans = 21.0 / 2;    // Stores 10.5 in ans
```

Each of the following assignment statements also stores 10.5 in ans (notice the different decimal-point placements):

```
ans = 21 / 2.0;    // Stores 10.5 in ans
```

and

```
ans = 21.0 / 2.0;    // Stores 10.5 in ans
```

Tip Do the division operator and the comment slashes confuse you because of their similarity? Of course, you can tell them apart, but perhaps in these statements the regular C-style comments would be a little less confusing:

```
ans = 21.0 / 2.0;    /* Stores 10.5 in ans */
```

Table 7.1 showed the modulus, or remainder, operator, %. The modulus operator performs the opposite of the integer division operator: Instead of returning the integer answer and discarding the remainder, the modulus operator returns the remainder and discards the integer division answer.

Warning Don't use % on floating-point values. % returns the remainder of integer division only.

The following statement stores 1 in ans:

```
ans = 21 / 2;    /* Stores a 1 in ans */
```

If you divide the integer 21 by 2, you will get 10 with a remainder of 1. % discards the integer answer and keeps the remainder (the opposite of what the integer division operator would do).

STOP&TYPE In Listing 7.1, you saw how the integer division operator worked. Listing 7.2 expands on that program by also showing modulus division and regular fractional division.

Review

There are two kinds of division operators, plus a modulus operator. Between these three operators, you can compute both answers and remainders.

▼ INPUT   LISTING 7.2. COMPUTING DIVISIONAL RESULTS.

```
 1:  /* Filename: MOREDIV.C */
 2:  // Computes two kinds of divisions and the modulus
 3:  #include <stdio.h>
 4:  #include <conio.h>
 5:  main()
 6:  {
 7:     int people, events, avgEv;
 8:     int leftOver;    // Will hold modulus
 9:     float floatPeople;   // Needed to force regular division
10:     float exact;    // Will hold exact average
11:     clrscr();
12:
13:     printf("How many people will attend? ");
14:     scanf(" %d", &people);
15:     printf("How many events are scheduled? ");
16:     scanf(" %d", &events);
17:
18:     // Compute the integer average number of people per event
19:     avgEv = people / events;    // The integer division ensures
20:                                 // that the fractional part of
21:                                 // the answer is discarded
22:     printf("\nThere will be an average of %d people per event.\n",
23:           avgEv);
24:     leftOver = people % events;
25:     printf("There will be %d without an event at any one time.\n",
26:           leftOver);
27:     floatPeople = people;  // Converts the integer to a floating-point
28:     exact = floatPeople / events;
29:     printf("The exact average number of people per event is %.1f.\n",
30:           exact);
31:     return 0;
32:  }
```

▼ OUTPUT

```
How many people will attend? 21
How many events are scheduled? 2

There will be an average of 10 people per event.
There will be 1 without an event at any one time.
The exact average number of people per event is 10.5.
```

▼ ANALYSIS

Line 8 defines an integer variable to hold the integer remainder calculated on line 24. Given the user's data-entry values shown in the output, one person will be left without an event.

Line 9 defines a floating-point variable for the sole purpose of assigning the integer number of people entered in line 14 to line 9's floating-point variable, as done on line 27. Once you learn about a C feature named *typecasting* in Lesson 5, you won't need to define such an intermediate variable. When line 27 assigns the integer variable named `people` to the floating-point variable named `floatPeople`, the integer becomes a floating-point value. The conversion of the number of people to floating-point lets line 28 perform exact fractional division instead of integer division only.

► Order of Operators

Concept   **What You Will Learn**

C's operators execute in a certain order.

Just like the math that your high school algebra teacher taught (you *do* remember high school algebra, don't you?), C follows a certain order when evaluating expressions. C doesn't compute all expressions from left to right. Instead, C computes expressions based on the hierarchy in the order of operators table, shown in Appendix C. The higher the operators are in the table, the higher their precedence. Therefore, a unary minus operator is said to have higher precedence than the regular binary subtraction operator.

The following assignment stores 10 in `priority`, not 18 as would be the case if C calculated the expression from left to right:

```
priority = 4 + 2 * 3;
```

Appendix C's precedence table shows that multiplication has a higher precedence than addition; therefore, C computes 2 * 3, getting 6, then adds the 4 to the 6 to get the final answer of 10 to store in `priority`.

You'll notice in the operator precedence table that multiplication and division both appear on the same level, as do addition and subtraction. When two operators of the same level appear in the same expression, as in

```
another = 10 - 8 + 3;
```

C calculates the expression from left to right. 10 - 8 produces 2, and the 2 is added to the 3 to get 5.

Parentheses override most operators because of their high level in the precedence table. If you were to put parentheses in the preceding expression, you could force C to compute the expression differently. The following expression

```
another = 10 - (8 + 3);
```

stores -1 in `another` because the 8 is added to the 3, producing 11, before 11 is subtracted from 10, giving you the -1 answer.

definition

Hierarchy is another name for operator precedence.

Tip Clarify your code as much as possible by using extra parentheses even if they're unnecessary. For example, parentheses aren't really needed in the following expression:

```
another = (10 - 8) + 3;
```

because C calculates the subtraction first due to its position left of the addition in the expression. However, the parentheses show your intent and help you keep straight the order you meant to take place. Also, if you happen to misread the operator precedence table, the extra parentheses force the expression's evaluation to match your desired order just in case C wouldn't have calculated that order automatically.

Perhaps a few more examples of combined operators will help clarify operator precedence even more. Study how Figure 7.1 illustrates the order of expression evaluation.

```
2 * 3 + 3 * 2
  \ /
  6 + 3 * 2
      \ /
      6 + 6
      \ /
       12

20 + 20 / (5 + 5) % 2
            \ /
20 + 20 / 10 % 2
         \ /
20 + 10 % 2
     \ /
   20 + 0
   \ /
    20
```

FIGURE 7.1.
Watch that order
of precedence!

definition

To *nest* operations means to put one calculation inside another.

Sometimes, you might need to nest parentheses inside one another. The innermost parentheses calculate first. Figure 7.2 shows how nested parentheses compute.

```
((2 + 3) + 6 * (3 + (4 - 2))) + 3
   \ /
(5 + 6 * (3 + (4 - 2))) + 3
              \ /
(5 + 6 * (3 +2)) + 3
          \ /
(5 + 6 * 5) + 3
     \ /
(5 + 30) + 3
   \ /
  35 + 3
  \ /
   38
  Whew!
```

FIGURE 7.2.
C calculates the
innermost par-
entheses first.

 Warning Be sure that your expressions have an equal number of opening and closing parentheses.

Tip These examples are great for learning C, but when you write your own C programs, try to keep your expressions simple. Break a long expression into two or more expressions, even if doing so means defining an intermediate variable. The following assignment

```
netPay = grossPay - taxRate * grossPay + bonus;
```

is easier to understand when you break it up like this:

```
taxes = taxRate * grossPay;
netPay = grossPay - taxes + bonus;
```

STOP&TYPE Listing 7.3 contains a program that computes each of the three expressions illustrated in the previous two figures, proving beyond a shadow of a doubt how the order of precedence works (you never doubted the figures, did you?).

Review **What You Have Learned**

C follows the order of operators when computing expressions. You can use parentheses to override many of the expressions' default order.

▼ INPUT LISTING 7.3. CALCULATING LONG EXPRESSIONS IN C.

```
 1:  /* Filename: EXPRESS.C */
 2:  // Computes expressions with C
 3:  #include <stdio.h>
 4:  #include <conio.h>
 5:
 6:  main()
 7:  {
 8:    int ans1, ans2, ans3;
 9:    clrscr();
10:
11:    ans1 = 2 * 3 + 3 * 2;
12:    printf("The first answer is %d\n", ans1);
13:    ans2 = 20 + 20 / (5 + 5) % 2;
14:    printf("The second answer is %d\n", ans2);
15:    ans3 = ((2 + 3) + 6 * (3 + (4 - 2))) + 3;
16:    printf("The third answer is %d\n", ans3);
17:    return 0;
18:  }
```

▼ OUTPUT

```
The first answer is 12
The second answer is 20
The third answer is 38
```

▼ ANALYSIS

As shown here, C computes mathematical results as described in this section and as dictated by the operator precedence table.

In your regular C programming, your programs will be calculating using more variables than numeric literals, but you must understand how the calculating order works by practicing with simple integer literals as shown here.

If you're ever unsure as to how C will order an expression, use parentheses. If you're still unsure, write a simple program to test a sample expression using numeric literals so that you can practice with the expression.

▶ Advanced Assignments

Concept   **What You Will Learn**

Learn other ways to use the equal sign.

The assignment operator has more power in C than in other programming languages. The next two sections explain how the C assignment operator combines with other operators to improve your power and decrease your programming effort.

Multiple Assignments

If you must assign the same value to more than one expression, C lets you string together multiple assignment statements. For example, if you wanted to put zero in several initial `total` variables, you could do this:

```
total1 = 0;
total2 = 0;
total3 = 0;
```

but multiple assignments like these make your work easier:

```
total1 = total2 = total3 = 0;    // Put 0 in three variables
```

Look at Appendix C's operator table and you'll see a column labeled *Associativity*. This column tells you whether an expression works from right to left or left to right. The assignment operator associates from right to left. Figure 7.3 illustrates what a right-to-left associativity means.

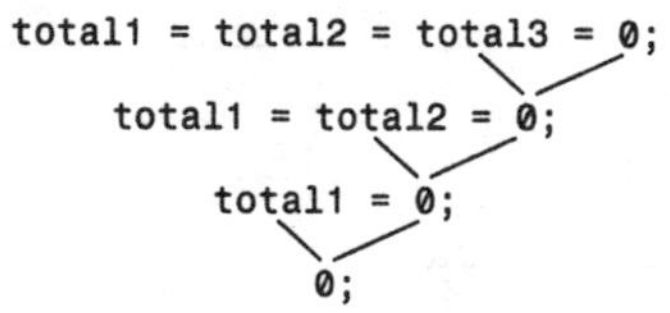

FIGURE 7.3.

The operator associativity describes in which direction to operate.

```
total1 = total2 = total3 = 0;
  total1 = total2 = 0;
     total1 = 0;
        0;
```

As C assigns the zero to each variable on the right, that variable gets the zero and the entire expression becomes zero as well. That expression's zero is then available for the next variable to the left, and so on. Eventually, C assigns the zero to `total1` and the result of that expression is zero. There's nothing to do with that final zero, so C discards it and continues execution at the next statement in the program.

All expressions have values. The assignment statement not only assigns values, but it also creates a value while performing the assignment. Therefore, that value is available for subsequent assignment statements if there are any more assignments to be made to the left of that line. The value produced by the assignment lets you combine two statements such as these:

```
monthAvg = dailyAvg * 30;
yearAvg = 12 * monthAvg;
```

into a single statement such as this:

```
yearAvg = 12 * (monthAvg = dailyAvg * 30);
```

C first computes the monthly average and stores that average in monthAvg. The entire assignment expression in parentheses becomes a value that is then multiplied by 12 and assigned to yearAvg.

Which of the two statement groups do you think is better? The second is more efficient, but too many C programmers go overboard in trying to squeeze efficiency out of their programs. Although the first pair of statements isn't as efficient, it's much easier to read, maintain, and change later if needed.

> *Note* Associativity will come into play more as you learn about more powerful operators.

IS A RULE NOW BROKEN?

Any astute reader (that's *you*, right?) will see right away that right-to-left associativity seems to violate a rule stated earlier in this unit. Earlier, you read that two or more operators in the same expression that appear on the same level in the operator precedence table compute from left to right.

Well, now that you understand associativity, that "rule" can be set in stone with the following definition: "The associativity of operators determines the order in which they compute if two or more operators from the same precedence level appear in the same expression."

All of the fundamental math operators (+, -, *, /, and %) have left-to-right associativity, so they do indeed compute from left to right when they appear on the same level in an expression.

Compound Operators

There are several operations that commonly put the same variable on both sides of the equal sign. Here are some examples:

```
count = count + 1;              // Add 1 to count
salary = salary * bonusFactor;  // Adjust the salary
monthly = monthly + daily;      // Add to daily sales
```

When you see the same variable on both sides of an operator, the variable is being updated in some way. count is being increased by one, salary is being changed to reflect a bonus factor, and `monthly` is being updated with the current day's total sales (thus keeping a running monthly total).

Such updating of variable values is so common that the designers of C added several *compound operators* to C that don't exist in other programming languages. If you want to update the value of a variable, why should you have to go to the trouble of repeating the variable name on both sides of the equal sign? (At least, that was the designers' thinking.)

definition

The compound operators are sometimes called *compound assignment operators.*

Table 7.2 lists each of the compound operators and describes the equivalent assignment statements through examples. As you can see, the compound operators provide you with easier but equivalent updating capabilities.

Table 7.2. The compound operators and their equivalent meanings.

Compound Operator	Example	Equivalent Assignment
+=	a += 100;	a = a + 100;
-=	b -= 0.25;	b = b - 0.25;
*=	c *= 13;	c = c * 13;
/=	d /= 4;	d = d / 4;
%=	e %= 2;	e = e % 2;

Be very careful when using the compound assignment operators! Before going any further, find the compound assignment operator precedence level in Appendix C's precedence table. You'll see that all the compound operators have *lower* precedence than the regular math operators. In other words, `*=` appears several levels down from the multiplication operator, `*`.

Such precedence can cause you agony when you combine the compound assignment operators with other expressions that use the regular operators. For example, given the following variable definitions:

```
int value = 5;
int x = 3;
```

how do you think you would change the following expression to use a compound subtraction operator?

```
value = value - x + 2;    // Be careful!
```

At first, you might be tempted to rewrite such an expression as

```
value -= x + 2;
```

Doing so, however, does *not* yield the same results because the `-=` operator has much lower precedence than the plus sign and the regular minus sign. In the first assignment, the `x` is first subtracted from `value` and then the 2 is added to that result before the final computed 4 is put in `value`.

In the compound version, C computes the `-=` only *after* adding the 2 and the `x`. Therefore, C stores a 0 in `value`! The compound operator, due to its precedence, is actually equivalent to this statement:

```
value = value - (x + 2);   // Equivalent to value -= x + 2
```

As you're beginning to see, precedence can affect everything you compute in C. Earlier, this unit suggested that you enclose as much as you can in parentheses to clarify everything you do, even if normal precedence handles your calculation perfectly. The compound operators and their low precedence really make the use of ample parentheses vital. Instead of writing statements such as this:

```
value -= x + 2;
```

perhaps it would be safer to include parentheses so that both you and C are on the same precedence wavelength:

```
value -= (x + 2);
```

STOP&TYPE Listing 7.4 contains a program that computes interest at the end of five compounding periods.

Review
What You Have Learned

Whenever you need to add to a total or update a variable in some way, the compound assignment operators give you lots of power—as long as you keep the operator precedence in mind.

▼ INPUT   LISTING 7.4. COMPUTING INTEREST FOR FIVE PERIODS.

```
 1:  /* Filename: INTFIVE.C */
 2:  // Computes five periods of interest
 3:  #include <stdio.h>
 4:  #include <conio.h>
 5:  main()
 6:  {
 7:    float intRate;      // Interest rate per period
 8:    float principal;    // Loan amount
 9:    clrscr();           // Erase the screen
10:
11:    printf("Welcome to loan central!\n");   // Title
12:    printf("----------------------\n\n");
13:
14:    printf("How much was the loan for? ");
15:    scanf(" %f", &principal);
16:
17:    printf("What is the period interest rate (i.e., .03 for 3%)? ");
18:    scanf(" %f", &intRate);
19:
20:    printf("Here is the total owed after five periods\n");
21:    printf("(Assuming no payment is made)\n");
22:
23:    principal *= (1 + intRate);   // First period interest
24:    principal *= (1 + intRate);
25:    principal *= (1 + intRate);
26:    principal *= (1 + intRate);
27:    principal *= (1 + intRate);   // Fifth period interest
```

continues

LISTING 7.4. CONTINUED

```
28:
29:     printf("$%.2f total amount owed after five periods.\n",principal);
30:     return 0;
31: }
```

▼ OUTPUT

```
Welcome to loan central!
- - - - - - - - - - - - - - - - - - - - - - -

How much was the loan for? 1000.00
What is the period interest rate (i.e., .03 for 3%)? .10
Here is the total owed after five periods
(Assuming no payment is made)
$1610.51 total amount owed after five periods.
```

▼ ANALYSIS

The heart of this program lies in the computations on lines 23 through 27. Each line increases the loan `principal` by the interest rate for that period. If you were to need the original principal for a printed loan invoice or for an additional kind of calculation later, you would first have to save the original principal in another variable. Each compound assignment operator updates whatever value appears on the left side of the compound assignment, just as the regular assignment changes its lvalue.

 Tip In Lesson 6, you'll learn how to write programs using *loops* that eliminate some of the tedious repetition in Listing 7.4.

▶ **Homework**

General Knowledge

1. What's the difference between a unary operator and a binary operator?
2. Suppose that you stored a **6** in the variable named `amount`. How could you then store the negative of `amount` in a variable called `negAmount`?
3. What is meant by overloaded operator?
4. How many kinds of division can `/` perform? What are they called?
5. Which operator finds the remainder of integer division?
6. What's another name for the remainder operator?
7. Why does an assignment statement produce a value as well as an assignment?
8. What is the associativity of the assignment operator?
9. What is the associativity of the multiplication operator?
10. What value would C compute in the following expression?

    `((7 + 3) + 2)`

11. Why are the parentheses in question 10 not needed?

12. What value would C compute in the following expression?

    ```
    (1 + 2) * 3 / 4
    ```

13. What value would C compute in the following expression?

    ```
    (1 + (10 - (2 + 2)))
    ```

14. What value would C compute in the following expression?

    ```
    22 * 2 - 8 % (3 - 1)
    ```

15. True or false: The unary plus sign is optional.

16. True or false: The unary minus sign is optional.

17. True or false: You can apply the unary minus sign to variables and expressions but not to integer literals.

18. True or false: Binary operators work best for binary values.

What's the Output?

19. Here is a tricky, multiline computational program! See whether you can determine the output.

    ```
    /* Filename: TRCKMATH.C */
    // Computes several layers of expressions
    #include <stdio.h>
    #include <conio.h>
    main()
    {
      int x;
      x = 2 + 5 * 2 - 1 % 2;
      x += 14;
      x -= 5;
      x *= 2 - 7;
      printf("The value of x is %d\n", x);
      return 0;
    }
    ```

Find the Bug

20. What's wrong with the following assignment?

    ```
    netSales = sales--adjustedSales;
    ```

Write Code That...

21. Write the assignment statement that performs the same math as the following formula:

    ```
            (9 - 5)
    a = ----------
            (3 * 12)
    ```

22. Write the assignment statement that performs the same math as the following

formula:

```
        y²
b = --------
      (2 · q)
```

23. Rewrite the following assignment statement so that it takes three separate assignments instead of one:

```
a = (b = x * 12) * (c = 34 + w);
```

24. Oops! You make so much writing C programs that your taxes just went up 8%! Write a statement that takes your current tax rate, stored in a variable named `taxRate`, and increases that rate by 8%. Hint: To increase a variable by 8%, you can multiply the variable by `(1 + .08)`. Write the statement using a regular assignment and multiplication operator, and then write the statement with a compound assignment operator.

25. Rewrite Listing 7.4 to print the principal after *each* period so that the user can see the loan amount building each period.

26. Write a program to calculate the area of a circle whose radius is 2.4. The formula for a circle's area is

area = pi * (radius^2)

Pi is approximately 3.14159. Hint: Pi is an excellent value to define using `#define`.

27. Rewrite question 26 so that the program asks the user for a radius and then computes the area of a circle that has the radius that the user specified.

Extra Credit

28. Write a program that computes the first five powers of 3 (3^1, 3^2, 3^3, 3^4, and 3^5). Print descriptions before each power. The first two lines of output would look like this:

```
3 raised to the power of 1 is 3
3 raised to the power of 2 is 9
```

29. William the worker always works 52 hours a week. He earns $5.65 for the first 40 hours he works. He gets time and a half (1.5 times his regular hourly pay) for the first 10 hours over 40. He gets double time for all hours over 50. He is in the 32% tax bracket. Write a program with appropriate titles that prints William's gross pay, net pay, and taxes.

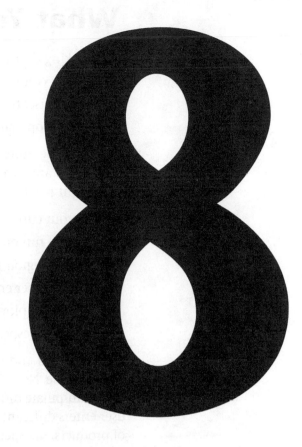

Relational and Logical Operators

else

if

logical operator

pseudocode

relational operator

▶ **What You'll Learn About**

- ▶ Making decisions with relational operators
- ▶ The `if` command tests for relations
- ▶ Otherwise, there's `else`
- ▶ Logical operators

Not all C operators do math. This unit teaches you all about operators that test data. Computers are great not only for making speedy calculations but also for testing data. You might need a program to test data to find the answer to questions such as these:

- ▶ Are our current sales on target with our projected sales?
- ▶ Did we run out of inventory for any items?
- ▶ Which region generated the highest costs last year?
- ▶ Did the user enter a value within an expected range?
- ▶ Which employees will reach retirement age within the next three years?
- ▶ Which salesperson sold the most goods?

The relational and logic operators give your programs the power to answer questions such as these. Now that you understand user input with `scanf()`, you can write programs that manipulate different data values every time someone runs the program in case the user enters different values for each run. Customers don't always buy the same number of products, salespeople don't always sell the same items, and your employees don't always work the same hours.

definition

A *data-driven* program is a program whose data dictates the order of execution.

By being able to test data and act accordingly, your programs can take one of several logic paths. For the first time in this book, you will see data-driven programs that don't necessarily execute sequentially, line-by-line. From now on, many programs that you write will contain code that might or might not execute, depending on the data that gets entered.

▼ *Tip*   Think of data-driven programs as programs that take different paths, just as you do when you drive your car. You rarely drive to the same place each time you get in your car. You might leave your neighborhood using the same path but then turn into the grocer, get gas, take the freeway, or take a detour around construction. Your current needs determine the path you take, just as the data determines the path taken by the statements in your programs.

Making Decisions with Relational Operators

Concept   **What You Will Learn**

Learn how the six relational operators produce true or false results.

Table 8.1 lists the six relational operators that you'll learn about in this section. Unlike the math operators that you learned about in Unit 7, the relational operators don't change data. Instead, relational operators test one data value against another, letting you determine how the values compare.

definition

A *relational operator* tests data values against one another.

 Note The relational operators are binary operators. Therefore, they work between two values, just as the * does.

Table 8.1. The relational operators and their meanings.

Relational Operator	Description
==	Equal to
>	Greater than
>=	Greater than or equal to
<	Less than
<=	Less than or equal to
!=	Not equal to

 Warning Be sure that you compare similar data. For example, you would never compare a character variable to a floating-point variable. Make sure that the value on one side of a relational operator matches the data type on the other side.

As you read through the table's descriptions of the relational operators, perhaps you can begin to get a glimpse of their use. There are many times when you'll want to know if two values are the same, if one is less than another, if one is more than another, or if two values are different.

In everyday life you compare data just as you will do in C programs. For example, here is a list of six statements. Each statement, when spoken, matches the operation of each of the six relational operators shown in Table 8.1.

1. My overcoat sales last month were *equal to* $50,000.
2. Cable television provides fewer channels than satellite television. (The number of cable stations is *less than* the number of satellite stations.)
3. A first-class ticket from New York to Los Angeles is *greater than or equal to* the price of a coach ticket around the world.
4. It rained as much as, or perhaps less than, yesterday. (The amount of rain today was *less than or equal to* the amount of rain yesterday.)
5. Shelly is older than Michael. (Shelly's age is *greater than* Michael's.)
6. The color of your belt is not the same as the color of your shoes. (The belt's color is *not equal to* the shoes' color.)

Note All relational operators return either a *true* value, which is represented as a 1 in C, or a *false* value, which is represented as a 0 in C.

UNIT 8

Relational and Logical Operators

The relational operations are assumed to be true or false. In other words, the overcoat sales in statement 1 were equal to $50,000 or they were not, cable either provides fewer channels or it provides more, and so on. In other words, whenever you compare any two values, either in real life or in a program, there is always a question of whether the comparison is true or not. You'll use the relational operators to test for a true or false result and act accordingly.

definition

Pseudocode is a written description of a program in plain speech, not in C code.

Look at Figure 8.1. It acquaints you with relational logic in a program. The pseudocode in the program checks to see whether the daily sales were more than yesterday's sales. If the sales were more, one section of the program takes over. If the sales were less, a different section of the program takes over. In either case, *only one of the two program sections executes.*

See how the data drives this program outline? One and only one section of the program (in addition to the initial testing of the data) executes, and the data dictates which of those sections executes. Eventually, whatever section took over finishes and the end of the program executes (perhaps to print a sales report) and the program terminates.

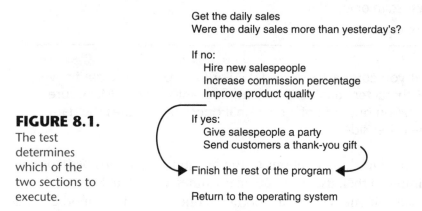

Get the daily sales
Were the daily sales more than yesterday's?

If no:
    Hire new salespeople
    Increase commission percentage
    Improve product quality

FIGURE 8.1.
The test determines which of the two sections to execute.

If yes:
    Give salespeople a party
    Send customers a thank-you gift

Finish the rest of the program

Return to the operating system

Let's move to a more C-like representation of the relational operators. Using the integer variables defined here:

```
int a = 1;
int b = 2;
int c = 3;
int d = 1;
```

can you see that all of the following sentences are true?

1. a == d because they contain the same value.
2. c > b because 3 is greater than 2.
3. c >= b because 3 is greater than or equal to 2. (The *or* implies that c can be greater than b *or* equal to b.)
4. a < c because 1 is less than 3.
5. a <= d because 1 is less than or equal to 1.
6. b != d because 2 is not equal to 1.

All of the preceding sentences about the variables are true. See if you can spot which of the following are *false*:

1. `a >= d`

2. `b != c`

3. `a == c`

4. `c <= a`

The third and fourth statements are false. Working with simple variables like these seems like little more than an easy mental exercise, and testing meaningful values such as sales figures in your C programs isn't much more difficult.

Warning Be sure that you use the double equal sign (==) when testing for equality, and reserve the use of the single equal sign (=) for assignment only. (Some programming languages, such as QBasic, use the single equal sign for both assignment and relational testing.)

STOP&TYPE I want to drive home a final point before you get to *official C code that uses relational operators for actual work*. You saw earlier that C evaluates true relational expressions as 1 and false relational expressions as 0. Listing 8.1 assigns the answers to several relational operators to variables and prints the results. Try to predict the program's output before looking at the answer.

Review
What You Have Learned

The relational operators compare values against other values and determine whether those values compare as true or false based on the specified relational operation. C prints only a 1 or a 0 in Listing 8.1 because 1 and 0 represent true and false relations.

▼ **INPUT   LISTING 8.1. PRINTING THE RESULTS OF RELATIONAL OPERATORS.**

```
1:   /* Filename: RELAT1ST.C */
2:   // Prints the results of several relational operations
3:   #include <stdio.h>
4:   #include <conio.h>
5:   main()
6:   {
7:     int high = 45;
8:     int low = 10;
9:     int middle = 25;
10:    int answer;
11:
12:    clrscr();   // Erase the output screen
13:
14:    answer = high > low;
15:    printf("High > low is %d\n", answer);
16:
17:    answer = low > high;
18:    printf("Low > high is %d\n", answer);
19:
20:    answer = middle == middle;
```

UNIT 8

Relational and Logical Operators

continues

LISTING 8.1. CONTINUED

```
21:     printf("Middle == middle is %d\n", answer);
22:
23:     answer = high >= middle;
24:     printf("High >= middle is %d\n", answer);
25:
26:     answer = middle <= low;
27:     printf("Middle <= low is %d\n", answer);
28:
29:     answer = 0 == 0;
30:     printf("Bonus relation: 0 == 0 is %d\n", answer);
31:
32:     return 0;
33:   }
```

▼ **OUTPUT**

```
High > low is 1
Low > high is 0
Middle == middle is 1
High >= middle is 1
Middle <= low is 0
Bonus relation: 0 == 0 is 1
```

▼ **ANALYSIS**

The 1s and 0s in the output indicate whether or not the relational tests performed were true or false. Most of this program's relational testing should now be obvious to you. The high value is certainly greater than the low value; hence, line 14 stores a 1 (true) in answer. The low value is *not* greater than the high value, so the second assignment, line 17, stores a 0 (false) in answer.

The only possible tricky assignment occurs in line 29. Although 0 is equal to 0, you might be tempted to think that the zero means false. You must remember that the six relational operators return either 1 or 0 based on how two values compare. 0 compares exactly to 0 in line 29. It is because 0 is equal to 0 that == is true. The true result is always 1.

HOW CAN THIS 1 OR 0 BUSINESS HELP ME?

At this point, you might be wondering how a return of 1 or 0 can help you when you write C programs. Have patience, because the next section shows you how to incorporate the six relational operators into useful C code using a new command named if.

To get a taste of 1 and 0's advantages, consider the following section of code:

```
printf("How many tickets were sold? ");
scanf(" %d", &num);
salePay = num * 1.45 + (num > 500) * 25;    // Maybe pay a bonus
```

157

The pay for the salesperson, stored in `salePay`, will always be at least $1.45 a ticket. The trick comes in the statement's second half. If more than 500 tickets were sold, the relation (`num > 500`) is true, or 1, and the `1 * 25` adds an additional $25 to the pay. If, however, the tickets did not total more than 500, (`num > 500`) is false, or 0, and `0 * 25` is $0 so no bonus is paid.

Warning Before you continue, be sure that you understand the code in the preceding sidebar. Some newcomers to C must take a few extra moments to figure out what's going on. Although such relational statements are efficient, some C programmers overuse them. If your code is hard to read and maintain, you don't gain anything with tricks. If you think it's clearer to separate the preceding code's last line into more than one statement, do so for your sake as well as for those who must maintain your program later. The next section's `if` statement gives you a way to break the preceding assignment into two more-readable statements.

Note Obviously, not all relational logic requires that you work with sales figures, but sales totals and bonuses make for great illustrations of relational logic. That's why you're seeing so many such examples here.

definition
A *keyword* is a command's trigger word, such as `if` or `return`.

UNIT 8

Relational and Logical Operators

The *if* Command Tests for Relations

Concept   **What You Will Learn**

The `if` statement uses the relational operators to determine which lines of a program to execute.

Every programming language has some form of `if` statement. The `if` statement tests the relational operators and decides exactly which sections of a program to execute and which to ignore. It is the `if` statement that determines whether a program should detour or go straight.

Although you now have several units of this book under your belt, you don't know a lot of C commands (also called *statements*). You've seen the `return` statement at the end of `main()`. `return` sends control back to the IDE after your program completes its execution. Neither `printf()` nor `scanf()` is a command; they are built-in functions. The assignment statement is a command, but no keyword is associated with the assignment, only an equal sign.

Note The `if` statement lets your programs make decisions at runtime based on data values.

The `if` statement is one of the most important statements in C. Without `if`, C could only sequentially execute statements, limiting the amount of decision-making your programs could do. Now that you understand the relational operators, it's time to see how if can use the true and false relations to take action based on those relations.

The if statement is a multiline programming statement. Unlike return, if almost always takes more than one line of code. Here is the format of the if statement:

```
if (relationalTest)
  { A block of one or more C statements }
```

From the italics, you can tell that if uses a relational test that you must supply inside parentheses. The parentheses are required; without them, C won't compile your program. relationalTest can be the comparison of any two variables, literals, or a combination of both, as shown in the following sample if lines:

```
if (sales < 50000)

if (initial > 'M')

if (amount <= value)
```

 Warning Never put a semicolon after the closing parenthesis! C will think that the if statement is finished and will begin executing the block of statements that follow the if, whether or not the relational test was true or false.

 Tip Semicolons terminate only complete C statements and functions. The if doesn't end after the closing parenthesis; therefore, no semicolon follows the parenthesis. Put semicolons at the end of all statements inside the if's block.

The block of statements that follows the if can contain any valid C statements, including printf()s, scanf()s, assignments, and even additional if statements (meaning that you can nest if statements). If the block of code contains only a single statement, you don't need the enclosing braces. However, good C programmers develop the habit early of including if's braces around even a block of just one statement. If you later add more to the body of the if, you could too easily forget to add the braces, and program logic errors would appear that can be difficult to trace.

C's if reads exactly like you use *if* in real life. Consider the following statement:

"If I learn C, I'll be able to write C programs."

What if you *don't* learn C? You'll never write a C program. The body of that if statement, therefore, will never happen. What if you *do* learn C? You'll be able to write C programs. The truth of the if relational test, *if I learn C* or *if I don't learn C*, determines the next course of action.

Note if needs no header file. Only library functions such as printf() require header files.

Figure 8.2 illustrates how if works. It shows how the body of the if statement might or might not execute, depending on the relation.

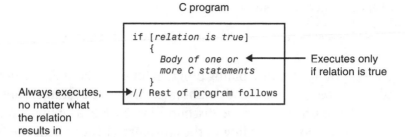

FIGURE 8.2.

The body executes only if the relational test is true.

In the following code, a special message might or might not print:

```
printf("What is your IQ? ");
scanf(" %d", &iq);    // Assume that iq is a defined integer
if (iq >= 140)
  { printf("How brilliant you are!\n"); }
printf("Have a nice day.\n");
```

The program will print either this:

```
How brilliant you are!
Have a nice day.
```

or this:

```
Have a nice day.
```

Do you see how the data drives the program? There is a line in the program, the first `printf()`, that might never execute. The `printf()`'s execution is based solely on the value of the variable `iq` and how that value compares to the number 140. If and only if `iq` holds a value greater than or equal to 140 will the first `printf()` execute.

The preceding code sample's `if` body contained only a single statement to keep things simple initially. The braces aren't required, but they're still recommended. The following `if` statement's body contains four statements:

```
printf("What is your IQ? ");
scanf(" %d", &iq);    // Assume that iq is a defined integer
if (iq >= 140)
  { printf("How brilliant you are!\n");
    printf("Perhaps you should consider learning C\n");
    printf("in order to put your talents and that %d IQ ", iq);
    printf("to good use!\n"); }
printf("Have a nice day.\n");
```

Tip The indentation of the `if`'s code body is not required. As you learned in the first lesson, C is a free-form language, so such spacing is optional. The indentation helps to show you where the `if`'s body begins and ends. Therefore, by indenting the code body, you help improve your program's readability.

Do you remember the following line from an earlier sidebar?

```
salePay = num * 1.45 + (num > 500) * 25;    // Maybe pay a bonus
```

You now know enough to break that tricky line into two more-readable but equivalent statements:

UNIT 8

Relational and Logical Operators

```
salePay = num * 1.45;
if (num > 500)
  { salePay += 25; }    // Pay a bonus if sold enough
```

STOP&TYPE You're writing a billing program for a small hotel. The hotel charges a high rate (called the *rack rate*) and a discount rate. First-time customers are charged the rack rate and repeat customers get the discount. Listing 8.2 contains a program that calculates the cost of a room according to the customer's history with the hotel.

Review   **What You Have Learned**

The if statement chooses whether or not to execute a section of a C program.

▼ INPUT   LISTING 8.2. COMPUTING A HOTEL RATE.

```
 1:   /* Filename: HOTELIF.C */
 2:   // Determines a hotel price
 3:   #include <stdio.h>
 4:   #include <conio.h>
 5:   main()
 6:   {
 7:      char ans;
 8:      int numNights;
 9:      float rackRate = 67.50;
10:      float discRate = 57.65;
11:      float totalCost = 0.0;
12:
13:      clrscr();    // Erase the output screen
14:
15:      printf("How many nights did the customer stay? ");
16:      scanf(" %d", &numNights);
17:
18:      printf("Has the customer stayed here before (Y/N)? ");
19:      scanf(" %c", &ans);
20:
21:      if (ans == 'Y')
22:        { totalCost = discRate * numNights; }
23:
24:      if (ans == 'N')
25:        { totalCost = rackRate * numNights; }
26:
27:      printf("The total cost is $%.2f\n", totalCost);
28:
29:      return 0;
30:   }
```

Note   There are two possible outputs, depending on whether the customer has stayed at the hotel before or not. Therefore, two different runs of the program follow.

▼ OUTPUT

```
How many nights did the customer stay? 2
Has the customer stayed here before (Y/N)? Y
The total cost is $115.30

How many nights did the customer stay? 2
Has the customer stayed here before (Y/N)? N
The total cost is $135.00
```

▼ ANALYSIS

The customer's number of nights is multiplied by either the rack rate, stored in `rackRate`, or the discount rate, stored in `discRate`. These two possibilities require that two statements be made. If the first `if` on line 21 is true, the discount rate is computed. If the second `if` on line 24 tests for a true relation, the rack rate is computed.

This program assumes that the user will enter an uppercase Y or an uppercase N. The initial zero assigned to `totalCost` keeps garbage out of the variable just in case the user doesn't enter an uppercase Y or N. If you ran the program and got a total cost of `$0.00`, you would know that you must enter an uppercase answer to the question. Later in this unit, you will learn how to ensure that the user enters exactly what is expected (such as an uppercase Y or N) through a process known as *input validation*. In Lesson 8, you will learn how to test for either uppercase or lowercase answers. Of course, you could use four sets of `if` statements, testing for Y, y, N, and n, but there are almost always better ways to program instead of duplicating effort.

Notice that the `if` statements test a character variable. Therefore, the `ifs`' relational operators must compare against a character. In this case, the characters tested are the Y and N character literals. The order of the comparison is unimportant; line 21's `if`, for example, could read like this with the same effect:

```
if ('Y' == ans)   // Reverse the comparison order
```

 Never compare floating-point or double floating-point values for equality. It's difficult to represent exact floating-point quantities inside a computer. Therefore, use `>=` and `<=` to compare within a small range of values if you ever want to compare two floating-point values for equality.

There are several ways to improve upon this program. You'll learn how in the sections that follow.

▶ Otherwise, There's *else*

What You Will Learn

`else` determines what happens if the relation is false.

The statement determines whether a block of statements does or doesn't execute. Whatever happens, the statements that follow the `if`'s closing brace execute after the `if` completes its test and possible body of code.

The `if` as you currently know it determines whether or not a block executes, but it's possible to extend the action of `if` so that it executes one block of code or another. To make `if` decide between one of *two* possible blocks of code, add the `else` statement after the `if`'s closing brace. Here is the format of the `if-else` statement:

```
if (relationalTest)
  { A block of one or more C statements }
else
  { A block of one or more C statements }
```

Figure 8.3 shows the action of the `if-else` statement. Notice that either block executes and that the true or false relation determines which block executes. No matter which of the blocks executes, the statements following the `if` execute and the program continues as usual after the `if-else` does its job.

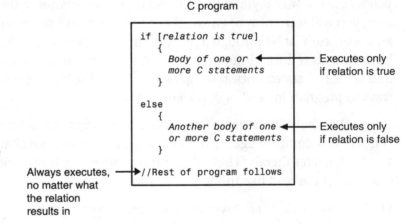

C program

```
if [relation is true]
    {
        Body of one or       ←——  Executes only
        more C statements           if relation is true
    }
else
    {
        Another body of one  ←——  Executes only
        or more C statements        if relation is false
    }
//Rest of program follows
```

Always executes, ——→
no matter what
the relation
results in

FIGURE 8.3.
The body of the `if` or the body of the `else` executes, but never both.

With the simple `if` statement, the block executes if the relation is true. If you add an `else` block, that block of statements executes if the relation is false.

Warning   The `if` can execute only one optional block of code, or one of two blocks if you use `else`. There's no way to make `if` decide between one of *three or more* blocks of code unless you nest one `if` inside another. In Lesson 7, you'll learn about the `switch` statement, which lets your program choose from among more than two possible courses of action.

STOP&TYPE   `else` improves the hotel billing computation program in Listing 8.2. `else` eliminates the need for two `if` statements, as Listing 8.3 shows.

Review   **What You Have Learned**

When your program must select between one of two possible actions, `if-else` handles the job well.

```
 1:  /* Filename: HOTELSE.C */
 2:  // Determines a hotel price by choosing
 3:  // between one of two possible options
 4:  #include <stdio.h>
 5:  #include <conio.h>
 6:  main()
 7:  {
 8:    char ans;
 9:    int numNights;
10:    float rackRate = 67.50;
11:    float discRate = 57.65;
12:    float totalCost;
13:
14:    clrscr();   // Erase the output screen
15:
16:    printf("How many nights did the customer stay? ");
17:    scanf(" %d", &numNights);
18:
19:    printf("Has the customer stayed here before (Y/N)? ");
20:    scanf(" %c", &ans);
21:
22:    if (ans == 'Y')
23:      { totalCost = discRate * numNights; }
24:    else
25:      { totalCost = rackRate * numNights; }   // Only one if needed
26:
27:    printf("The total cost is $%.2f\n", totalCost);
28:
29:    return 0;
30:  }
```

▼ OUTPUT

```
How many nights did the customer stay? 2
Has the customer stayed here before (Y/N)? Y
The total cost is $115.30

How many nights did the customer stay? 2
Has the customer stayed here before (Y/N)? N
The total cost is $135.00
```

▼ ANALYSIS

As you can see, the program got simpler with the else. Two ifs, each testing for an opposite relation, are no longer needed. Basically, lines 22 through 25 say this:

"If the user typed a Y, use the discount rate; otherwise (else), use the rack rate."

UNIT 8

Relational and Logical Operators

Logical Operators

Concept

You can combine relational operators to add power to `if` statements.

definition

A logical operator extends the action of relational if tests.

There is another group of operators called the logical operators. They let you combine two or more relational tests into a single statement or change the value returned from a relation. Table 8.2 lists C's logical operators. The first two logical operators are binary operators, because they work on two values. The last logical operator, `!`, is a unary operator. The values that the logical operators work on are always relational tests.

Table 8.2. The logical operators.

Logical Operator	Meaning	Description
&&	AND	Returns true if and only if both sides of the && are true.
¦¦	OR	Returns true if one or the other side of the ¦¦ is true (or if both sides are true).
!	NOT	Changes a true relation to false or a false relation to true.

> ***Note***   The logical operators are sometimes called the *compound relational operators* because they combine the action of two or more relations.

definition

Input validation ensures that the user entered an appropriate value.

Assume that the user was supposed to enter a value between 1 and 5 that represented his or her department number. How can you ensure that the user enters a value within the range of 1 to 5? You can perform input validation before moving on. Consider the following `if`:

```
printf("What is your department number? ");
scanf(" %d", &dept);    // Get a department number
if (dept < 1 ¦¦ dept > 5)
  { printf("You did not enter a correct department number!\n");
    return 0;   // Return to the IDE early
  }
else
  {   // Put the correct department code here
  }
```

The `¦¦` inside the `if` statement tells C to check that the user's input falls within the range of 1 to 5. If the user enters a value less than 1 or more than 5, the error message prints and the program terminates early. If the user's value falls within the proper range, the user doesn't see the error message and the appropriate department code executes.

The logical operators as well as the relational operators appear in the operator precedence table. C interprets the `if` in the preceding code like this:

```
if ( (dept < 1) || (dept > 5) )
```

because relational operators have higher precedence than logical operators. For clarity, include the extra parentheses as shown here.

Often, there are several ways to write the same program. The preceding code used an || (OR) operator to make sure that the user's entered value fell within the expected range. You can use an && (AND) logical operator to perform a test with the same results. Look at this difference:

```
printf("What is your department number? ");
scanf(" %d", &dept);    // Get a department number
if ((dept >= 1) && (dept <= 5))
  {   // Put the correct department code here
  }
else
  { printf("You did not enter a correct department number!\n");
    return 0;   // Return to the IDE early
  }
```

This `if` tells C the following:

"If the user's value is greater than or equal to 1 and if the user's value is less than or equal to 5, accept the input. Otherwise, print an error message and exit the program."

Without the logical operators, you would have to use a nested `if` to perform the same check, and a nested `if` isn't as easy to read. Here's the same code with a nested `if`:

```
printf("What is your department number? ");
scanf(" %d", &dept);    // Get a department number
if (dept >= 1)
  { if (dept <= 5)
    {   // Put the correct department code here
    }
    else
      { printf("You did not enter a correct department number!\n"); }
        return 0;   // Return to the IDE early
      }
  }
else
  { printf("You did not enter a correct department number!\n"); }
  }
```

The nested `if` requires that both of the first two `if`s be true before the first block of code executes. An `else` is required for both `if`s in this code because if *either* the user's value is less than 1 or the user's value is more than 5, the error should print. As you can see here, a simple logical operator keeps your programming clearer.

The ! (NOT) operator isn't used much because logic is easier to write and maintain if you keep it positive. Virtually any relational test that uses a ! operator is easier to understand if you reverse the logic and remove the . For example, the following if

```
if (!(c >= b))
```

is identical to

```
if (c < b)
```

The second statement is easier to read and write. There is at least one good use for the operator, and you'll read about it in Lesson 11.

C contains a *short-circuiting* feature that sometimes hurts you more than it helps. If the left side of an ¦¦ test is true, C doesn't bother evaluating the right side in order to save run time. In other words, if the following if's amt is more than 70

```
if ((amt > 70) ¦¦ (amt < 100))
```

C doesn't bother checking to see whether amt is less than 100. There's no need to. The ¦¦ requests that C evaluate the if as true if *either side of the* ¦¦ *is true*. If the left side is true, the if is true no matter what the right side evaluates to.

C also short-circuits && operators if the left side is false. Therefore, a statement such as

```
if ((value <= 10) && (value >= 0))
```

takes a shortcut if value is more than 10. There's no need for C to spend the execution time looking at the right side of the && if the left side is false; && requires that both sides be true before the if expression can be true. If the left side is false, the if is false no matter how the right side evaluates.

The short-circuiting feature is fine for efficiency, but make sure that you don't write tricky code that relies on both sides of the logical operator to execute. Consider the following statement:

```
if ((sales > 1000) && (inventoryFlag = 1))
```

If you were to code such an if statement (obviously, the bodies of some of these sample if statements are missing), Turbo C++ would remind you that you're attempting something questionable. Do you see it? An assignment appears to the right of the &&, not an equality relational operator, ==, as was probably intended. Turbo C++ displays only a warning when you do this and goes ahead and compiles your program.

Some C programmers attempt to cram as much as they can into a single statement. Doing so sometimes causes subtle programming errors as well as debugging nightmares. If you leave this statement in your program, and if the sales are more than 1,000, C will go ahead and look at the right side of the &&. C then stores a 1 in the variable named inventoryFlag because of the assignment. The result of the assignment is 1, and 1 is true (any nonzero value in C is considered to be true).

The problem occurs if sales is *not* greater than 1,000. Because of the short-circuiting feature, there's no guarantee that C will assign the 1 to inventoryFlag. Therefore, the programmer must make sure that he or she wants inventoryFlag assigned a 1 only during times when the sales are more than 1,000. The following logic is much clearer:

```
if (sales > 5000)
{ inventoryFlag = 1;
  // Rest of if's body goes here
}
```

STOP&TYPE The program in Listing 8.4 contains a regular `if`, an `if` with an `else`, and an `if` with logical operators.

Review

Use `if` for a simple decision, `if-else` if you need to determine one of two courses of action, and logical operators if you need to combine two or more relational operators.

▼ INPUT   LISTING 8.4. THERE ARE DIFFERENT WAYS TO HANDLE DATA COMBINATIONS.

```
 1:  /* Filename: LOGICALS.C */
 2:  // A program with an if, an if-else,
 3:  // and a logical operator
 4:  #include <stdio.h>
 5:  #include <conio.h>
 6:  main()
 7:  {
 8:      int numCusts;
 9:      float totalSales;
10:      clrscr();    // Erase the screen
11:
12:      printf("How many customers were in yesterday? ");
13:      scanf(" %d", &numCusts);
14:
15:      printf("What were the total sales? ");
16:      scanf(" %f", &totalSales);
17:
18:      // A simple if
19:      if (numCusts > 25)
20:        { printf("Order more snacks for tomorrow.\n"); }
21:
22:      // An if-else
23:      if (totalSales >= 2000.00)
24:        { printf("Reorder stock.\n");
25:          printf("Give sales staff a raise.\n");
26:        }
27:      else
28:        { printf("Replace the sales staff.\n"); }
29:
30:      // An if with a logical test
31:      if ((numCusts >= 50) && (totalSales >= 5000.00))
32:        { printf("Take a day off!\n");
33:          printf("Remodel the store.\n");
34:        }
35:      return 0;
36:  }
```

UNIT

8

Relational and Logical Operators

▼ OUTPUT

```
How many customers were in yesterday? 13
What were the total sales? 675.45
Replace the sales staff.

How many customers were in yesterday? 43
What were the total sales? 1982.34
Order more snacks for tomorrow.
Replace the sales staff.

How many customers were in yesterday? 54
What were the total sales? 9045.67
Order more snacks for tomorrow.
Reorder stock.
Give sales staff a raise.
Take a day off!
Remodel the store.
```

▼ ANALYSIS

As you can see from the three runs shown in the output, very different messages print, depending on the combination of the user's input. The `if` and the logical operators help ensure that every possible option is covered. The `if` on line 19 prints a message only if the number of customers exceeds 25. Whether that message prints or not, line 23 contains the first line of an `if-else` that prints a message based on the quantity of the total sales. Line 31 prints a message only if *both* the number of customers and the total sales exceed certain limits.

▶ Homework

General Knowledge

1. Why don't the relational operators do any math?
2. What values do the relational operators return?
3. Would the following assignment store a 1 (true) or a 0 (false) in `answer`? (This is trickier than it first appears!)

   answer = (4 == 4 == 4);
4. What is input validation?
5. What's the difference between an `if` and an `if-else` statement?
6. Which logical operator works on a single relational value?
7. Why are braces suggested around all `if` bodies, even if the body of the `if` contains only a single statement?

8. How do the logical operators differ from the relational operators?

9. Determine which of the following tests are true and which are false based on the following variable definitions:

```
int a = 0;
int b = 1;
```

  A. `(a < b || b < a)`

  B. `!b`

  C. `!a`

  D. `(!(a == b))`

  E. `(a != b)`

  F. `(a && b)`

  G. `(a || b)`

10. What is the short-circuiting feature of the logical operators?

11. Does the word Hi appear always or sometimes given the following if statement?

```
if (9 > 3);
  { printf("Hi\n"); }
```

12. True or false: You should use the ! operator as often as possible.

13. True or false: if-else lets your program choose from among many possible actions.

14. True or false: A nested if statement lets your program choose from among many possible actions.

15. True or false: The short-circuiting feature helps improve your program's efficiency.

What's the Output?

16. This uses that tricky ! you were told to stay away from. (You'll understand why when you see this problem.) Will the following printf() execute?

```
if (!1)
  { printf("This is tricky!\n"); }
```

Find the Bug

17. What's wrong with the following if statement?

```
if age == 18
  { printf("You can vote\n"); }
```

18. What's wrong with the following if statement?

```
if (amt < 2);
  { flag = 1;
    printf("Everything is not all well...\n");
  }
```

Write Code That...

19. Rewrite the following code to remove the `!` but keep the same `if` logic:

```
if (!(sales != oldSales))
```

20. Write a program that computes pay and overtime pay based on the following conditions:

    A. Pay $5.65 for each hour up to and including 40 hours worked.

    B. Pay time and a half for any hours worked from over 40 to 50.

    C. Pay double time for any hours worked over 50.

Extra Credit

21. Rewrite question 20 so that a special tax of $.02 per hour is deducted from all employees working fewer than 40 hours to help pay for their added training needs.

22. Write a program for a health food store that from this table calculates price based on the number of vitamins sold:

Number Sold	Cost Per Vitamin
Fewer than 25	$.05 per vitamin
26 to 49	$.04 per vitamin over 26
Over 50	$.03 per vitamin over 50

Project

Lesson ▶

**Simple
Operators**

STOP&TYPE In this lesson, you learned about many of C's operators. You saw the following:

► The fundamental math operators perform addition, subtraction, multiplication, and division.

► There are two kinds of division: Integer division and regular fractional division.

► The modulus operator (%) computes a remainder from integer division.

► The precedence of operators affects the order of calculations.

Project 4 Listing. An introduction to operators and `if` testing.

```
 1:  /* Filename: LESSON4.C */

 2:  // Computes a tax amount for the tax preparer's client

 3:  #include <stdio.h>

 4:  #include <conio.h>

 5:  main()

 6:  {

 7:     float earnings;

 8:     float taxOwed = 0.00;    // Stays zero unless changed in computations

 9:

10:     clrscr();    // Erase the screen

11:

12:     printf("Tax Time!\n");    // Title

13:     printf("--------\n\n");

14:

15:     printf("How much did the client earn? ");

16:     scanf(" %f", &earnings);
```

▶ The relational operators let you test data against other data and follow an execution path accordingly.

▶ The logical operators let you combine relational operators to test for a wider range of conditions and perform user input validation.

Description

1: A C comment that includes the program's filename.

2: A C++ comment that describes the program.

3: The `printf()` and `scanf()` functions need information in the STDIO.H header file.

4: The screen-clearing function, `clrscr()`, needs information in the CONIO.H header file.

5: All functions have names, and the first function in all C programs is `main()`.

6: All functions begin with a left brace.

7: Defines a floating-point variable that will hold the client's earnings.

8: Defines a floating-point variable that will hold the client's computed tax.

8: The initial value is zero and remains zero only if the earnings are less than $5,000.

9: Extra blank lines make your program more readable.

10: The built-in library function `clrscr()` erases the output screen so that it's clear before the program's output begins.

11: Extra blank lines make your program more readable.

12: A printed title helps describe the program to the user.

12: Put a title at the top of your screens so that the user knows exactly what the program is about to do.

13: Dashes underline the title.

14: Extra blank lines make your program more readable.

15: A prompt for the client's total earnings amount.

16: Gets the earnings from the user and stores them in `earnings`.

continues

Project 4 Listing. continued

```
17:

18:     if ((earnings < 0.0) || (earnings > 999999.99))

19:       { printf("I believe that you made a mistake. Try again.\n");

20:         return 0;    // Return early to the IDE

21:       }

22:

23:     if (earnings > 20000.00)

24:       { taxOwed = (earnings - 20000.00) * .28;

25:         taxOwed += (9999.99 * .20);    // 20% for $10K to 19.9K

26:         taxOwed += (4999.99 * .10);    // 10% for $5K to 9.9K

27:       }

28:

29:     if ((earnings >= 10000.00) && (earnings < 20000.00))

30:       { taxOwed = (earnings - 10000.00) * .20;

31:         taxOwed += (4999.99 * .10);    // 10% for $5K to 9.9K

32:       }

33:

34:     if ((earnings >= 4999.99) && (earnings < 10000.00))

35:       { taxOwed = (earnings - 4999.99) * .10; }

36:

37:     printf("\nThe client owes a total of $%.2f in taxes.\n", taxOwed);
```

Description

17: Extra blank lines make your program more readable.

18: Checks to see whether the user entered an earnings value between $0.01 and $999,999.99.

    18: If the earnings don't fall within that range, the program assumes that there's a problem with the user's input.

19: Prints an error message.

20: Returns to Turbo C++'s IDE.

21: The closing brace terminates the body of the `if` block.

22: Extra blank lines make your program more readable.

23: Sees whether the earnings are more than $20,000.

24: Computes a 28% rate on all earnings over $20,000.

25: Computes a 20% rate on earnings from $10,000 to $19,999.99.

26: Computes a 10% rate on earnings from $5,000 to $9,999.99.

27: The closing brace terminates the `if`'s body.

28: Extra blank lines make your program more readable.

29: Sees whether the earnings are between $10,000 and $19,999.99.

30: Computes a 20% rate on earnings from $10,000 to $19,999.99.

31: Computes a 10% rate on earnings from $5,000 to $9,999.99.

32: The closing brace terminates the `if`'s body.

33: Extra blank lines make your program more readable.

34: Sees whether the earnings fall between $5,000 and $9,999.00.

    34: Both sides of the && must be true before the body of the `if` executes.

35: Computes a tax rate of 10% on all earnings of $5,000.00 or more.

36: Extra blank lines make your program more readable.

37: Prints the amount of tax computed. A zero remains in `earnings` if all of the `if` tests were false.

38: Extra blank lines make your program more readable.

continues

Project 4 Listing. continued

```
39:    return 0;
40: }
```

Description

39: Returns to the IDE.

40: `main()`'s closing brace terminates the program.

▼ OUTPUT

```
Tax Time!
----------

How much did the client earn? 13443.50

The client owes a total of $1188.70 in taxes.

Tax Time!
----------

How much did the client earn? 28734.99

The client owes a total of $4945.79 in taxes.
```

Lesson ▶ 5

Upgraded Operators

Unit 9: Special Operations

Unit 10: Advancing with Bitwise Operators

Lesson 5 Project

Special Operations

conditional operator

data promotion

decrement

increment

sizeof()

typecast

▶ What You'll Learn About

- ▶ Combining data types
- ▶ The `sizeof` operator
- ▶ Using the conditional operator
- ▶ Adding and subtracting one

Although you now understand a large number of C operators, there are a few left to cover. You won't learn about all the remaining operators in this unit because some of them work only when you write advanced programs (which you will do in this book, but not until Lesson 9).

This unit explores several operators that help you change data from one data type to another. C prefers to work with similar data types, but you can't always ensure that your data will have the same type. Hence, you must use the type-changing operators discussed here to convert between types.

The remaining part of this unit shows you how to use some shortcut operators. In Lesson 4, you saw how the compound assignment operators ease your programming burden. C is the only major programming language with compound assignment operators. C also provides you with additional operators that, although you could write programs without having them, do save you a lot of time. You'll want to use them as much as possible.

▶ Combining Data Types

Concept   **What You Will Learn**

If you must mix data types, you can first convert all the data to the same type so that your expressions operate on similar values.

There's no way to write a program that does much work without mixing data types in some way. Data values come in all shapes, sizes, and forms, and you must be able to work with combinations of data. C converts from one data type to another in the following two ways:

- ▶ Automatic promotion
- ▶ Using the typecast operator

The following sections explain how each method works.

Note   As you eventually move from C to C++, you'll see that C++ is even more stringent about data-type matches than C is. Therefore, learning the data-type conversion methods now helps you today as well as in the future.

Automatic Promotion

Turbo C++ does its best to help you when you mix one data type with another, such as when you add a floating-point to an integer. Much of the time, C assumes that you want the smaller data type converted to the larger one before it evaluates any expression. This automatic promotion of data means that you don't always have to be on guard, watching each and every constant and variable in each and every expression that you write.

C often converts one data type to another. Given the following variable definitions:

```
int i=7;
float f=12.3;
```

you can add, subtract, or combine the data types in virtually any order without worrying about the results. C will automatically promote the integer to a floating-point value before carrying out the evaluation. Therefore, the following expression

```
ans = f + i;    // C converts both to float
```

adds 12.3 to 7.0 (notice the decimal), resulting in 19.3, which is stored in `ans`. For now, assume that `ans` is a floating-point variable that you've defined.

> **Note** `i` is changed to a floating-point only for that single expression. In reality, the compiler doesn't change `i`. Instead, it grabs the integer value out of `i` and then converts that value to a `float` before doing the math. `i` never changes from an integer variable that holds a 7.

definition

The *promotion* of one data type to another occurs automatically when you mix types in an expression.

The promotion of the smaller data type to the larger one provides for as much accuracy as possible. Although you're about to learn a way to promote *down*—for example, from a floating-point to an integer—you almost always want as much precision retained as possible.

Look at Table 9.1 to see how Turbo C++ promotes from each of the smaller data types to the larger ones.

 Warning Other versions of C might promote differently than Turbo C++, but most promotion schemes should be similar to, if not exactly the same as, Turbo C++'s.

Table 9.1. The automatic data-type promotions.

Source Data Type	What It Promotes To
char	`int` or the largest data type if `int` is not the largest data type in the expression
short	`int` or the largest data type if `int` is not the largest data type in the expression
unsigned short	`unsigned int` or the largest data type if `unsigned int` is not the largest data type in the expression
float	The larger of `double` or `long double`, depending on which appears in the expression
double	`long double` if a `long double` appears in the expression

In Lesson 3, you saw how to use the data-type suffix characters such as ʟ and ᴜ to specify numeric literals that you want C to treat as specific data types. C treats all numeric literals such as 2, –0.00002, and 123.45 as floating-point literals, except in these two cases:

▶ When you specify a suffix character to override the default data type.

▶ When the numeric literal is too big to fit within the range of floating-point precision, such as 839495605.5677654323 (floats only handle up to six digits of precision), C treats the literal as if it were a double floating-point value.

The only problem that can arise is when you attempt to store a larger precision value in a smaller precision variable. For example, if you wanted to put a double floating-point value that contained fractional digits in an integer variable, you already know that the integer can't hold the fractional portion. Therefore, C truncates the decimal portion, converting the number to an integer.

In the following code, three variables are defined—two integers and a floating-point value. When C multiplies the integer by the floating-point value, it converts the integer to a floating-point by changing the value of i to 8.000000. C then multiplies the 8.000000 by f to get 55.2. However, the variable that is to hold the resulting 55.2 is an integer variable, and an integer variable can't hold the .2. Therefore, C truncates the fractional portion and stores 55 in result. 55 is approximately equal to the correct answer, but .2 is a large enough truncation to be aware of.

```
int i = 8;
int result;
float f = 6.9;
result = i * f;    // Oops! Puts only 55 in result
```

Warning The order of promotion *does* affect calculated results!

Would result have held a different result if C had first converted f to an integer before multiplying? Think this through. You will see that result would have held an entirely different value. C would have multiplied 8 by 6 and stored only a 48 in result. As you can see, it's vital that you understand C's promotion so that you can mix and match expressions and be able to predict how C will handle the math.

Mixing data types is fairly common. You might need to multiply the number of products sold by a price to get a total price. As a matter of fact, several programs so far in this book have mixed integers and floating-point values, such as multiplying the hours worked times a pay rate. The next section explains an important operator in C that helps with type changes—the typecast operator.

The Typecast Operator

The typecast operator is one of the strangest-looking operators in C. Unlike most of the other operators, the typecast operator doesn't use a traditional symbol such as * or %. Here are some of the typecast operators:

```
(char)
```

```
(int)
```

```
(float)
```

```
(double)
```

As you can see, there is a different typecast operator for every kind of data type in C. The data type must appear in parentheses. By using typecasting, you can specify exactly when and where you want one data type converted to another.

Note In C, you can define your own data types. You'll see how in Lesson 10. You can typecast using your own data types as well as the built-in data types.

To typecast one value's data type to another data type, place the typecast operator right before the value (either a variable, literal, or expression). In the previous expression, you saw how C combined an integer and a floating-point value. If you would like to convert the floating-point value to an integer, you can place an integer typecast operator right before the floating-point variable:

```
int i = 8;
int result;
float f = 6.9;
result = i * (int)f;   // Convert f before multiplying
```

`f` becomes the integer 6. Without the typecast, C multiplies 8.0 by 6.9 to get a result of 55.2 before storing 55 in the integer variable. With the typecast, C multiplies 8 by 6 to get 48 and then stores 48 in the variable named `result`.

Warning Notice that C doesn't round floating-points to the closest integer. It merely truncates the fractional portion when converting from a floating-point value to an integer. If you want to round a floating-point to an integer, you can use a built-in operator, which you'll learn about in Lesson 8.

Can you see that the following typecast is redundant and adds nothing to what C would do without the typecast?

```
result = (float)i * f;   // C first converts i to float anyway
```

Note A typecast doesn't change a value's data type permanently. The value is changed for the location of the typecast only.

If you need to, you also can typecast the result of an entire expression:

```
ans = a + b * (long int)(e / y * 2);
```

In this assignment statement, C computes the result of `e / y * 2` and then converts that result to a long integer. Most of the time, you can let C handle the automatic typecasting for you through its promotion rules, which you read about earlier. However, typecasting gives you exact control over data-type changes when you need those changes. There are specific times in C when you will have to typecast. One of the most important times is when you dynamically allocate data in Lesson 10.

STOP&TYPE The program in Listing 9.1 contains one expression that is typecast several times in different ways. As you will see from the output, the location of the typecast, C's automatic promotion of data types, and the resulting variable's data type all play parts in how C evaluates expressions.

Review
What You Have Learned

Use typecasting operators when you want to control exactly where one type changes to another type.

▼ INPUT   LISTING 9.1. USING TYPECAST OPERATORS.

```
1:  /* Filename: TYPECAST.C */
2:  // Applies the typecast operator to a single expression
3:  // in several different ways to show the different results
4:  #include <stdio.h>
5:  #include <conio.h>
6:  main()
7:  {
8:    double answer;    // Make variable large to hold any precision
9:    int i = 9;
10:   float f = 7.8;
11:   double d = 16.4;
12:
13:   clrscr();
14:   // Apply the typecast in several ways
15:   answer = (i * f * d);
16:   printf("The answer after (i * f * d) is %f\n", answer);
17:
18:   answer = ((float)i * f * d);
19:   printf("The answer after ((float)i * f * d) is %f\n",
20:        answer);
21:
22:   answer = (i * (int)f * (int)d);
23:   printf("The answer after (i * (int)f * (int)d) is %f\n",
24:        answer);
25:
26:   answer = (int)(i * f * d);
27:   printf("The answer after (int)(i * f * d) is %f\n",
28:        answer);
29:
30:   answer = (float)(i * f * d);
31:   printf("The answer after (float)(i * f * d) is %f\n",
32:        answer);
33:
34:   return 0;
35: }
```

▼ OUTPUT

```
The answer after (i * f * d) is 1151.280028
The answer after ((float)i * f * d) is 1151.280028
The answer after (i * (int)f * (int)d) is 1008.000000
The answer after (int)(i * f * d) is 1151.000000
The answer after (float)(i * f * d) is 1151.280028
```

▼ ANALYSIS

The movement of the typecast sometimes changes the answer a little (as shown in the loss of precision in the fourth line of the output, which results from the calculation in line 26) or a lot (as shown in the third line of the output, which results from the calculation in line 22).

When C calculates the expression without any typecasting on your part (line 15), that answer actually is the most accurate. However, the answer C produces might not always be the most accurate, especially if you store the answer in an integer variable. When storing a double floating-point calculation in an integer variable (which you might need to do in some mathematical computations or financial interest rate period calculations), you'll want to control exactly where the precision gets lost.

Be sure that you understand the difference between the third and fourth lines of output. At first, it appears that both calculations are the same because all the multiplied values get converted to integers before being stored in the double floating-point variable. The difference lies in *when* they are converted to integer values. In the third line of the output, the parentheses contain a double floating-point calculation because C promotes the integer and the floating-point value inside the parentheses to double floating-point because double floating-point is the highest precision inside the parentheses. Only after the double floating-point calculation finishes does the typecast change the result to integer, which means truncating only the fractional portion from the result.

In the third line of the output, the floating-point and the double floating-point variables are first typecast to integers. Only after all three values are integers does the multiplication occur. The integer multiplication produces a much smaller result than the same multiplication when three double floating-point values let the fractional portions of f and d stay in the calculation.

Having fun? Typecasting and data-type conversions aren't always the most exciting components of C, but your current understanding is worth the time that you spent. As you progress in C, you'll see why typecasting can become very important as you write longer programs.

THE FRACTIONAL PORTION

By using typecasts, you can store only the fractional portion of a floating-point value if you need to. It's easy to find the whole-number portion of a floating-point number, because you only have to store the value in an integer or long integer variable or typecast the value to an integer.

A simple subtraction does the trick of storing only the fractional portion. Suppose you wanted to store the fractional part of `fract` in a variable named `rightSide`. Here is how to do just that:

```
rightSide = fract - (int)fract;
```

Suppose `fract` held 33.456. Subtracting 33 (the integer portion on the right of the minus sign) from 33.456 (the value on the left of the minus sign) results in the fraction 0.456, which goes into `rightSide`.

Remember that, despite its powerful operator capabilities, C isn't great at storing large precision values with extreme accuracy (very few programming languages are, except for those dedicated to such purposes). Therefore, if you think that 0.456 is going into a variable, don't be surprised if C stores 0.045601 in the variable. You don't have to print the full precision, and besides, 0.000001 is not very big at all. (However, a little 0.000001 here and a little 0.000001 there and you'll wind up with 0.000002 in no time!)

▶ The *sizeof* Operator

What You Will Learn

The `sizeof` operator determines how much memory is needed to hold a value.

C has a second operator that looks a lot like the typecast operator. Instead of using a symbol, as most of the other operators do, the `sizeof` operator uses parentheses. Here is the general format of `sizeof`:

`sizeof(dataValue)`

`sizeof()` looks a lot like a function call because of the parentheses. However, `sizeof` is an operator because it works on built-in data-type names as well as data that you define. Here are some sample `sizeof` expressions:

```
numBytes = sizeof(int);    // Store the number of bytes an integer takes

storage1 = sizeof(myName);    // The amount of memory taken by a string

storage2 = "A string";    // Put 9 in storage2
```

`sizeof()` always returns the total amount of memory it takes to hold whatever value you put in the `sizeof` parentheses.

 Actually, the parentheses are optional if you pass a variable and not a built-in data type to `sizeof`, but `sizeof` is easier to read when you include the parentheses. All examples in this book that use `sizeof()` include the parentheses.

 Don't use `sizeof` to find the length of a string. Use Lesson 8's `strlen()` function if you need to find the length of a string. By definition, `sizeof` returns the number of bytes it takes to hold whatever value you pass it. You'll remember from Lesson 3 that C always needs a null zero byte to hold any string.

Different C compilers store data in different ways. Turbo C++'s sizeof operator might very well return values that differ from those of other C compilers, depending on the data type and the type of machine running the program at the time.

STOP&TYPE Listing 9.2 contains a program that prints the amount of storage it takes to store several built-in data types, variables, and literals in memory using Turbo C++.

Review   **What You Have Learned**

The sizeof operator lets you find the storage requirements of your program's target machine. sizeof returns the number of bytes of storage needed to hold the value that you pass to it.

▼ **INPUT   LISTING 9.2. USE** sizeof **TO RETURN SEVERAL VALUES.**

```
 1:   /* Filename: SIZEOF.C */
 2:   // The sizeof operator always returns the amount of memory
 3:   // (the number of bytes) that it takes to store a value
 4:   #include <stdio.h>
 5:   #include <conio.h>
 6:   main()
 7:   {
 8:     char c = 'x';
 9:     char name[] = "Italy";
10:     int i = 29;
11:     float f = 6.7643;
12:     double d = 9493945.6656543;
13:     clrscr();
14:
15:     // Print the sizes of the data
16:     // Typecast sizeof to an integer because sizeof returns its
17:     // value as a long integer and this program prints with %d only
18:     printf("The sizes of variables:\n");
19:     printf("The size of c is %d\n", (int)sizeof(c) );
20:     printf("The size of name is %d\n", (int)sizeof(name) );
21:     printf("(See, that was not the length of the string!)\n");
22:     printf("The size of i is %d\n", (int)sizeof(i) );
23:     printf("The size of f is %d\n", (int)sizeof(f) );
24:     printf("The size of d is %d\n", (int)sizeof(d) );
25:     printf("\nThe sizes of literals:\n");
26:     printf("The size of 4.3445 is %d\n", (int)sizeof(4.3445) );
27:     printf("The size of Hello is %d\n", (int)sizeof("Hello") );
28:     printf("\nThe sizes of data types:\n");
29:     printf("The size of a long double is %d\n",
30:            (int)sizeof(long double) );
31:     printf("The size of a float is %d\n", (int)sizeof(float) );
32:     return 0;
33:   }
```

▼ OUTPUT

```
The sizes of variables:
The size of c is 1
The size of name is 6
(See, that was not the length of the string!)
The size of i is 2
The size of f is 4
The size of d is 8

The sizes of literals:
The size of 4.3445 is 8
The size of Hello is 6

The sizes of data types:
The size of a long double is 10
The size of a float is 4
```

▼ ANALYSIS

The program is divided into three sections that print these values:

▶ Variable sizes (lines 18 through 24)

▶ Literal sizes (lines 25 through 27)

▶ Data-type sizes (lines 28 through 31)

If `sizeof` were a function instead of a built-in operator, it couldn't return the sizes of data types. Notice that each `printf()` typecasts the `sizeof` operator to an integer because the `printf()`s use `%d` to format the `sizeof` value. `sizeof` normally returns a long integer unless you typecast its return value.

`sizeof` returns the number of bytes that it takes to hold data. `name`'s string has a size of five but `sizeof` returns six in line 20 because `name` requires six bytes with the null zero.

Note   When you learn how to create your own data types in Lesson 10, you'll see that `sizeof` works with those data types as well. (`sizeof` is really smart!)

▶ Using the Conditional Operator

Concept   **What You Will Learn**

You can exchange simple multiline `if-else` code for a single operator—the *conditional operator*.

definition

A *ternary* operator works on three values (called *operands*).

The conditional operator does a lot of work. In fact, it's the only ternary operator in the C language. The other operators are either unary or binary and work on either single values or two values at a time, as you've seen.

When discussing the conditional operator in general, this book writes it like this: `?:`. In programs, however, between the `?` and the `:` are always the operands or values used by the conditional operator. Before looking at an example of the conditional operator, you should see its format:

```
relationalTest ? trueCode : falseCode;
```

> **Tip** Often, C programmers put parentheses around each of the conditional operator's values, as you'll see in a moment.

The relational test is any C expression that uses a relational operator—for example, any relational expression that might appear in an `if` statement. The relational test can include one or more logical operators as well if you want to combine several relational tests into a single test. If and only if the relational test evaluates to a true (nonzero) condition, the `trueCode` executes. If the relational test evaluates to a false (zero) condition, the `FalseCode` executes.

Use the conditional operator in place of simple `if-else` statements such as the following:

```
if (a > b)
  { c = 17; }
else
  { c = 23; }
```

In this `if`, the relational test is `a > b`, the `trueCode` is `c = 17`; and the `falseCode` is `c = 23`;. Here is the very same logic expressed as a conditional statement:

```
(a > b) ? (c = 17) : (c = 23);
```

Notice how the parentheses help distinguish the three parts of the conditional operator. The question mark helps the statement read as follows:

"Is a greater than b? If so, put 17 in c. Otherwise, put 23 in c."

Figure 9.1 shows when the conditional operator's true and false conditions execute. The individual parts (operands) of the conditional don't require semicolons at the end of their statements. Notice, however, that the conditional operator includes a *colon,* not a semicolon, before the third argument.

FIGURE 9.1.
Either the
`trueCode` or the
`falseCode`
executes, but
never both.

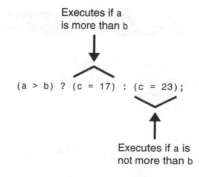

If both the true and false expressions assign values to the same variable, as done here, you can improve the efficiency by assigning the variable one time to the right of the conditional operator. In other words, this:

```
(a > b) ? (c = 17) : (c = 23);
```

becomes this:

```
c = (a > b) ? 17 : 23;
```

You can put parentheses around the 17 and the 23 if doing so improves the code's readability for you. You don't have to put assignment statements in the conditional. Any statement, even a `printf()` or a `scanf()`, will work in the *trueCode* and *falseCode* parts of the conditional operator.

READABILITY AND THE CONDITIONAL

At first, most C programmers feel that multiline `if-else` logic is easier to read than an equivalent conditional operator. Although they're correct, once you accustom yourself to the conditional operator, it becomes just as easy to follow as a multiline `if-else` because you can read the entire statement on one line without having to scan four or more lines. In addition, the conditional is slightly more efficient than `if`.

You can do some very tricky things with the conditional, such as writing a single statement that performs nested `if-else` logic. Such tricks are best left alone, however. A complicated conditional is too difficult to maintain later.

STOP&TYPE Listing 9.3 is a program that prints the minimum and maximum values entered by the user. First the program uses `if-else` logic, and then it uses conditional operators.

Review   **What You Have Learned**

The conditional operator replaces `if-else` logic and is more efficient as well.

▼ INPUT   LISTING 9.3. USING THE CONDITIONAL OPERATOR.

```
1:  /* CONDIT.C */
2:  // Finds the minimum and maximum values
3:  // from the user's entered values
4:  #include <stdio.h>
5:  #include <conio.h>
6:  main()
7:  {
8:     int val1, val2, min, max;
```

```
 9:    clrscr();    // Erase the screen
10:
11:    printf("Enter a value: ");
12:    scanf(" %d", &val1);
13:
14:    printf("Enter another value: ");
15:    scanf(" %d", &val2);
16:
17:    if (val1 < val2)
18:        { min = val1;
19:          max = val2; }
20:    else
21:        { max = val1;
22:          min = val2; }
23:
24:    printf("\nUsing if-else, the minimum is %d and the ", min);
25:    printf("maximum is %d\n", max);
26:
27:    min = (val1 < val2) ? val1 : val2;
28:    max = (val2 > val1) ? val2 : val1;
29:
30:    printf("\nUsing ?:, the minimum is %d and the maximum is %d\n",
31:            min, max);
32:    return 0;
33: }
```

▼ OUTPUT

```
Enter a value: 45
Enter another value: 67

Using if-else, the minimum is 45 and the maximum is 67

Using ?:, the minimum is 45 and the maximum is 67
```

▼ ANALYSIS

Lines 27 and 28 are the focus of this program. The if-else statement group from lines 17 to 22 performs the very same logic as the two lines starting at 27. The user's smaller value is either val1 or val2. The conditional operator in line 27 stores the smaller of the two values in min, and the conditional operator in line 28 stores the larger of the two values in max.

You also can squeeze the same logic into a single line using the *comma operator*, also known as the *sequence point*. It ensures that the statements on either side of the comma execute from left to right. Here is the statement that will assign both values to min and max using a single conditional:

```
(val1 < val2) ? (min = val1, max = val2) : (min = val2, max = val1);
```

Obviously, such code is cumbersome and the individual conditional statements are much easier to write. Semicolons wouldn't work between the inner assignments because the first semicolon would signal the end of the conditional operator, and the remaining part of the statement would be in error as soon as C spotted the colon.

▶ Adding and Subtracting One

Concept
What You Will Learn

The increment and decrement operators add and subtract one from variables.

definition

To *increment* means to add one and to *decrement* means to subtract one.

The increment and decrement operators, ++ and -- respectively, are two of the most distinguishing operators in C. In fact, the ++ in C++ came from C's important increment operator. These operators aren't necessary for C programs; you can use an assignment statement to add one to or subtract one from any value whenever you need to. However, the increment and decrement operators are simple. You can use them in places where an assignment statement could be awkward.

Tip Use the increment and decrement operators for efficiency. Both compile into single low-level *machine instructions* (stuff that's really technical), as opposed to equivalent assignment statements, which sometimes take three low-level machine statements. Efficiency becomes especially important when you need to increment or decrement a variable several hundred or thousand times in a program, as you will do in Lesson 6.

Table 9.2 describes the actions of the ++ and -- operators. It shows equivalent assignment statements. There are actually two sets of increment and decrement operators. One pair is called the *prefix* operators, and the other pair is called the *postfix* operators. The difference lies in where you put the ++ and --, either before or after the variable being incremented or decremented.

Table 9.2. C's increment and decrement operators.

Operator	Example	Order	Equivalent Assignments
++	++i;	Prefix	i = i + 1; or i += 1;
--	--i;	Prefix	i = i - 1; or i -= 1;
++	i++;	Postfix	i = i + 1; or i += 1;
--	i--;	Postfix	i = i - 1; or i -= 1;

There are times when you should use prefix and when you should use postfix. However, as you can see from Table 9.2's Equivalent Assignments column, their actions appear to be exactly the same. The difference between prefix and postfix appears when you combine the ++ and -- with other variables inside larger expressions. When you use the ++ and -- on single variables, as done in Table 9.2's Example column, the postfix and prefix notations are identical.

Warning Use the increment and decrement operators only on integer variables, not on floating-point variables. Also, never use these operators on literal values. The ++ and -- increment only integer variables.

After the following variable definitions:

```
int i = 10;
int j = 20;
```

the following statements add one to and subtract one from i and j respectively:

```
i++;    // i now holds 11
j--;    // j now holds 19
```

If the ++ and -- were expressed as prefix, the results would be the same. Now, after these statements:

```
--i;
++j;
```

i and j hold their original values.

Being able to increment gives you the advantage of changing a variable without dedicating an entire statement to the change. The following statements:

```
printf("The age is now %d.\n", age);
age += 1;
```

can become this statement:

```
printf("The age is now %d.\n", age++);
```

In this printf(), the use of postfix is required. This leads us to why there is a difference between the two categories of increment and decrement operators. In effect, if you specify prefix increment and decrement, C performs the increment and decrement before any other operator in the expression. If, however, you specify postfix, C computes the entire expression, including any assignment, and *then* performs the increment or decrement. In the previous printf(), if you had incremented age using prefix (++age), C would have incremented age before printing the age:

```
age += 1;    // Increment the age before the printf()
printf("The age is now %d.\n", age);
```

The operator precedence table in Appendix C lists the prefix operators early and the postfix operators last to illustrate their precedence relative to the other operators. Technically speaking, the table is incorrect because the prefix operators actually should appear on the topmost level, with the postfix operators immediately following on the next level, to translate such confusing expressions as this:

```
a = +i+++j++;
```

By now, you know that such confusing statements aren't worth the trouble of maintaining later. Practically speaking, the prefix operators execute first in an expression and the postfix operators last.

Prefix and postfix differences become extremely important when you combine the operators with other operators in an expression such as this:

```
int a;
int i = 12;
int j = 6;
a = i++ - j;
```

When the last line finishes executing, you know that i will be 13. There's no doubt about the ++—it adds one to i. However, the timing of that addition is in question. Does the increment occur before or after the assignment to a?

i increments *after* a is assigned its value. Therefore, a gets assigned the value of 6 (12 - 6) and then C increments i to 13. If prefix were used, as in the following:

```
int a;
int i = 12;
int j = 6;
a = ++i - j;
```

i is incremented before a gets its value. Therefore, a is assigned a 7 (13 - 6). Again, i is 13 whether or not prefix or postfix is used, but the surrounding expression differs depending on the prefix or postfix notation.

 Warning   The execution of prefix and postfix is under C's control. Nothing you can do will change the execution of prefix before postfix in your expressions. The following statement wastes a lot of parentheses. They do nothing to force an early execution of the postfix decrement:

```
a = (((i--))) * value;   // Still decrements i LAST
```

Be extremely careful when combining increment and decrement operators inside expressions with logical operators. To be safe, don't use increment and decrement at the same time that you use logical operators. For example, don't do this:

```
if ( (i == 10) || (j <> ++k) )
```

A problem occurs if i is equal to 10. You might recall from Lesson 4 that C short-circuits the || logical operator if the left side evaluates to true. C never looks at the right side if i is indeed 10. Therefore, k isn't incremented if the short circuit happens. Even though k is incremented using prefix, C still doesn't increment k because of the short-circuiting feature. However, k *does* increment if i is *not* equal to 10, because C has to evaluate the right side of the || to see whether the right side is true or false. This "maybe/maybe not" execution provides fertile soil for program bugs. If you want k incremented, pull it out of the if ahead of time like this:

```
++k;   // This can be either prefix or postfix
if ( (i == 10) || (j <> k))
```

STOP&TYPE   Listing 9.4 contains a program that prints the values of integer variables being incremented and decremented. You will see the increment and decrement used much more frequently when you learn in Lesson 6 how C performs loops.

Review

++ adds one to integer variables and -- subtracts one. The prefix and postfix differences determine how the increment and decrement operators affect surrounding operators.

▼ INPUT   LISTING 9.4. USING INCREMENT AND DECREMENT OPERATORS TO CHANGE VARIABLES.

```
 1:  /* Filename: INCDEC.C */
 2:  // Uses increment and decrement
 3:  #include <stdio.h>
 4:  #include <conio.h>
 5:  main()
 6:  {
 7:    int age;
 8:    int lastYear, nextYear;
 9:    clrscr();
10:
11:    printf("How old are you? ");
12:    scanf(" %d", &age);
13:
14:    lastYear = age;
15:    nextYear = age;
16:
17:    printf("Wow, you're a year older than last year (%d)",
18:          --lastYear);
19:    printf("\nand you'll be %d next year.\n", ++nextYear);
20:
21:    return 0;
22:  }
```

▼ OUTPUT

```
How old are you? 32
Wow, you're a year older than last year (31)
and you'll be 33 next year.
```

▼ ANALYSIS

The increment and decrement occur inside each of the printf() calls in lines 17 through 19. The program wouldn't work correctly if postfix were used because C would print the statements before decrementing and incrementing the age as needed. The age is assigned to lastYear and nextYear in lines 14 and 15 without using the increment there. Consider what would happen if you attempted to replace the middle of the program with this:

```
lastYear = --age;
nextYear = ++age;

printf("Wow, you're a year older than last year (%d)",
       lastYear);
printf("\nand you'll be %d next year.\n", nextYear);
```

The printed results wouldn't be correct! The first statement assigns a correct `age - 1` value, but then the `age` variable is off by one. Therefore, `nextYear` would be assigned the current age of the user.

▶ Homework

General Knowledge

1. If you were to multiply an integer by a floating-point and store the result in a floating-point variable, would you get a correct value? If so, why? If not, why not?

2. What is meant by promotion of data types?

3. Given the following variable definitions:

   ```
   int a;
   long b;
   float c;
   double d;
   ```

   What is the resulting data type for the following expressions?

   A. `a + b`

   B. `a + c`

   C. `d + c`

   D. `a * d`

   E. `a + b + c + d`

4. Which of the following is most efficient?

   ```
   i++;
   i+=1;
   i = i + 1;
   ```

5. Which operator replaces simple `if-else` statements?

6. Why is `?:` called a ternary operator?

7. True or false: You don't actually need typecasts because of C's automatic data-type promotion.

8. True or false: C will automatically convert the smallest data type in an expression to the data type of the largest value in the expression unless you override the smallest data type with a typecast.

9. True or false: A typecast changes a variable's data type for the rest of the program.

10. True or false: Postfix and prefix mean the same thing when incrementing or decrementing a single variable and when no other computations are being made in the same expression.

11. True or false: You should nest conditional operators to eliminate nested `if-else` logic.

What's the Output?

12. What value resides in a after the following?

```
int a = 6;
b = ++a - 1;
```

13. What value resides in b after the code in question 12 finishes?

14. What value resides in a after the following?

```
int a = 6;
b = a++ - 1;
```

15. What value resides in b after the code in question 14 finishes?

Find the Bug

16. What's wrong with the following conditional statement?

```
r = (u < 100) ? (r = 12) : (r = 13);
```

17. What's wrong with the following conditional statement?

```
(9 > i || u <= 8) ? (p = 12) ; (p = 13);
```

Write Code That...

18. Given the following variable definitions:

```
char c;
int i;
float f;
double d;
```

rewrite each of the following expressions using typecasts that match the automatic promotion that C would perform without the typecasts. The first one is done for you. Hint: One or more expressions might require two typecasts to match the automatic promotion that C will perform.

```
answer = i * 4.5; becomes answer = float(i) * 4.5;
```

  A. `answer = i * d;`

  B. `answer = c + i + f;`

  C. `answer = d + f;`

  D. `answer = c + i + 2;`

19. Rewrite the following conditional statement using parentheses to help make the three parts of the conditional statement clearer:

```
age <= 18 ? adultCode = 0: adultCode = 1;
```

20. Eliminate the following if-else to use only a conditional operator:

```
if (price > 21.00)
{ salePercent = .12; }
else
{ salePercent = .08; }
```

21. Write a program that asks the user for the number of years, from 1 to 40, that he or she has worked. If the user enters a value that doesn't fall in that range, print an error and terminate the program early. Otherwise, print a message that says the following (assuming that the user enters 13):

```
You have worked 13 years
```

If the user enters 1, print the singular of the message, like this:

```
You have worked 1 year
```

Use a conditional to print the singular or plural of year. Hint: Store an s or a null character in a character variable.

Extra Credit

22. Write a program that prints the final price of purchases at a store where everything costs exactly one dollar. Ask for the number of items purchased. Compute a sales tax of 8% if the user's purchase is less than $100 and 7.5% if the purchase is greater than or equal to $100. Also, if the purchase is over $500, give the customer an additional 10% after-tax discount. Print the purchase price, the amount of the tax, the amount of the discount ($ 0.00 if no discount applies) and the total price. Don't use an if statement in the program. Use only the conditional operator when your program must make a choice. Typecast all operations so that C doesn't have to promote anything to floating-point.

10

Advancing with Bitwise Operators

bit

bitmask

bitwise operator

sign extension

truth table

▶ What You'll Learn About

- ▶ Truth tables
- ▶ The bitwise shift operators
- ▶ Some uses for bitwise operators
- ▶ The compound bitwise operators

definition

A *bit* (short for *binary digit*) is an on or off state of electricity that combines with other bits to form bytes of storage.

This unit teaches you about special operators called the *bitwise operators*. They work on individual bits within a number, not with complete values as the other operators do. It takes a total of eight bits to represent the 256 characters in the ASCII table. If you were to take every combination of eight bits, representing the on states with 1s and the off states with 0s, from 00000000 to 11111111, you would have 256 combinations. Each different combination represents a different character.

The bit patterns also form numbers. By combining two or more bits, your computer stores all representations of numeric values, from integer to double floating-point values. Most often, C programmers use the bitwise operators to manipulate character or integer data.

Warning   Not everybody needs the bitwise operators. As a matter of fact, many C programmers will never need them. The bitwise operators give you access to low-level memory contents. Instead of working with a character value, you can work with individual bits that make up a character inside memory. Although the bitwise operators are extremely efficient, if you don't understand in-memory bit patterns and you don't think you'll ever work with binary values, you can skip this unit without losing any understanding of the primary C language.

▶ An Introduction to the Bitwise Operators

Concept   **What You Will Learn**

Introduce the bitwise operators, their names, and their meanings.

Table 10.1 lists all of C's bitwise operators. The last five operators in the table are nothing more than compound bitwise operators that shorten your expressions when you need to update values.

Table 10.1. The bitwise operators.

Bitwise Operator	Description
&	Bitwise AND
¦	Bitwise OR
^	Bitwise exclusive OR

Bitwise Operator	Description
~	Bitwise 1's complement
<<	Bitwise left shift
>>	Bitwise right shift
&=	Compound bitwise AND assignment
¦=	Compound bitwise OR assignment
~=	Compound bitwise exclusive OR assignment
<<=	Compound bitwise left shift
>>=	Compound bitwise right shift

You probably recognize something about the first two operators. The bitwise AND and bitwise OR operators look like their logical-operator counterparts && (the AND operator) and ¦¦ (the OR operator). The bitwise 1's complement operator is the only unary bitwise operator; the other bitwise operators require two operands.

Be sure that you type the operators exactly right. The bitwise OR is the vertical bar, usually broken. It's often the shifted backslash key on your keyboard. (In other words, type Shift-\ to get the vertical bar.) The bitwise exclusive OR operator, ^, is sometimes called the *housetop* or *carat* operator. It's the shifted number 6 key near the top of your keyboard. The bitwise 1's complement, ~, is called the *tilde* character. It's often found above the Tab key. It's the shifted right-pointing (and hardly ever used) single apostrophe.

Review
What You Have Learned

The bitwise operators work on bit patterns inside values such as characters and integers. The only unary bitwise operator is the 1's complement, ~.

Note There is no input, output, or analysis here due to this section's conceptual nature.

▶ Truth Tables

Concept
What You Will Learn

Truth tables explain how the bitwise operators return true and false results.

The bitwise operators work on individual bit patterns inside values. If you don't know how binary values are formed, you'll have little need for and practically no understanding of the bitwise actions. Nevertheless, the bitwise operators might come in handy some day because you can use them more efficiently than other operators.

Figure 10.1 helps explain the kind of values that the bitwise operators work on. It shows the number 45 represented as a binary number. If you were to apply a bitwise operator to the number 45 (and to a second value if you used any of the operators except for the unary ~), the bitwise operator would work on the 1s and 0s that form the number 45, not the number 45 itself as +, *, and the regular operators would.

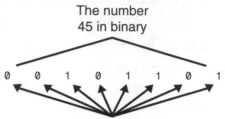

The number
45 in binary

0 0 1 0 1 1 0 1

The bitwise operators
test and change these
individual bits inside
numbers, not the
numbers themselves.

FIGURE 10.1.

The bitwise operators
work on data's internal
bit patterns.

> **Note** The value 45 requires only six bit positions, even though Figure 10.1 includes eight. The first two positions contain zeros. Bit patterns are almost always shown with eight bits even though fewer would hold the value. The eight bits match the width of each byte or memory location in your computer.

definition

A *truth table*
shows how
individual bitwise
truths occur.

Table 10.2 shows the truth table for the bitwise AND operator (&). In truth tables, 1 represents a true value (internally, a 1 represents an on switch that lets electricity flow) and 0 represents a false value (internally, a 0 represents an off switch that stops electricity flow). As with the regular && operator, both sides of a bitwise & operator must be true (there must be a 1 bit) before the result is true.

Table 10.2. The & truth table.

Left Bit	&	Right Bit	Result
1	&	1	= 1
1	&	0	= 0
0	&	1	= 0
0	&	0	= 0

The following assignment places 1 in `ans`:

```
ans = 1 & 1;
```

The following assignment places 0 in `ans`:

```
ans = 1 & 0;   // Both must be true for the result to be true
```

As mentioned earlier, the bitwise operators work on their operands' internal bit patterns, not the operand values themselves. It turns out that a 0 and a 1's internal bit patterns are 0 and 1 as well. When you combine values other than 0 and 1 using the bitwise operators, the results aren't always so straightforward. The following assignment

```
ans = 12 & 5;    // Works on the binary patterns of 12 and 5
```

stores 4 in `ans`. To understand how C stores a 4, look at Figure 10.2. The 12 is represented in binary as 00001100 and 5 is stored as 00000101. When you apply the & bitwise operator to these two operands, it works on each individual bit position, carrying out the & truths shown in Table 10.2.

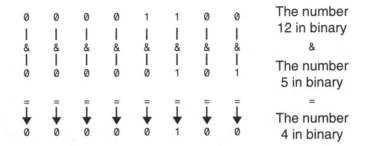

FIGURE 10.2.

Each bit position of 12 and 5 compared using &.

The number 4 is binary 00000100. The single 1 appears in the final eight bits because the third position from the right was the only bit in both 5 and 12 that also had a 1.

Table 10.3 shows the truth table for the bitwise OR operator. Notice that either side (or both sides) of the ¦ can be a 1 and the result will be true. Only if both sides of the ¦ are false will the result be false also.

Table 10.3. The ¦ truth table.

Left Bit	¦	Right Bit	Result
1	¦	1	= 1
1	¦	0	= 1
0	¦	1	= 1
0	¦	0	= 0

Table 10.4 is the bitwise ^ exclusive OR truth table. The ^ returns a true result if one side or the other of ^ is true *but not both sides*. The ^ is mutually exclusive because both sides can't be true and still return a true value.

Table 10.4. The ^ truth table.

Left Bit	^	Right Bit	Result
1	^	1	= 0
1	^	0	= 1
0	^	1	= 1
0	^	0	= 0

The truth table for the bitwise 1's complement, ~, is easy, as Table 10.5 shows. This table has only two lines because the ~ is unary and therefore works on only a single value at a time. The ~ reverses the bits inside its operand: All 1s become 0s and all 0s become 1s.

Table 10.5. The ~ truth table.

~	Operand Bit	=	Result
~	1	=	0
~	0	=	1

There are no more truth tables for the bitwise operators because the remaining bitwise operators are either compound versions of these, or they're bitwise shift operators that don't change individual bits in a way that a truth table can show.

Often, the bitwise operators have very specific purposes, such as system-level programming (operating system utility programs). The rest of this unit shows you a few general uses for the bitwise operators. For additional uses, you'll have to know a lot about the internals of the PC. As mentioned earlier in this unit, many C programmers never have a need for many or any of these operators.

STOP&TYPE The program in Listing 10.1 performs the &, ¦, ^, and ~ on 12 and 5 to show you how the different operators produce different results based on the comparison of the internal bit patterns.

Review
What You Have Learned

The bitwise operators operate only on the internal bit patterns of data, not on the values of the data.

▼ INPUT   LISTING 10.1. PRINTING RESULTS OF BITWISE OPERATORS.

```
1:   /* Filename: BIT1.C */
2:   // Demonstrates &, ¦, ^, and ~ on two values
3:   #include <stdio.h>
4:   #include <conio.h>
5:   main()
6:   {
7:     int i = 5, j = 12;
8:     int answer;
9:     // Although this program applies the bitwise operators to
10:    // variables, bitwise operators also work on literal values
11:    clrscr();
12:
13:    answer = i & j;
14:    printf("The result of i & j is %d\n", answer);
15:
16:    answer = i ¦ j;
17:    printf("The result of i ¦ j is %d\n", answer);
18:
```

```
19:     answer = i ^ j;
20:     printf("The result of i ^ j is %d\n", answer);
21:
22:     // Notice how ~ takes only a single argument
23:     answer = ~i;
24:     printf("The result of ~i is %d\n", answer);
25:     answer = ~j;
26:     printf("The result of ~j is %d\n", answer);
27:
28:     return 0;
29: }
```

▼ OUTPUT

```
The result of i & j is 4
The result of i ¦ j is 13
The result of i ^ j is 9
The result of ~i is -6
The result of ~j is -13
```

▼ ANALYSIS

Most of this program reviews the concepts taught earlier in this section. Notice, however, that the 1's complement operator works on a single value as opposed to two operands (lines 23 and 25). The 1's complement does *not* produce the negative of its operand. (In computer lingo, a *2's complement* would produce the negative of its argument, but there is no 2's complement operator in C. The unary minus sign produces a 2's complement.) The 1's complement simply reverses the bit patterns of the number.

With PCs and most of today's computers, positive values are always expressed with a 0 in the far-left bit position, whereas negative numbers always appear with a 1 in the far-left bit. This 0 and 1 *sign bit* always changes when you apply the 1's complement; therefore, positive values become negative and negative values become positive. Nevertheless, the negation is not a true negative of the operand, but is always a different negative number. In other words, ~5 produces –6, not –5, when the 5 is stored in an integer variable as in Listing 10.1.

 Warning If you store a 6 in an unsigned integer variable, applying ~ produces 851962 because unsigned integers can never be negative. If you store a 5 in a long integer, you'll get –6 again. As you can see, the 1's complement operator doesn't seem to produce consistent results. As you learn more about internal data representation, you'll find uses for the 1's complement even if it seems useless now.

▶ The Bitwise Shift Operators

 *Concept*   **What You Will Learn**

The bitwise shift operators shift internal bits to the left and right.

The bitwise shift operators have special uses in machine-level processing. By shifting bits, you can produce some interesting results (one example is given in a later section). As with the other bitwise operators, important equivalent machine-language statements shift data left and right.

When you use a bitwise shift operator, you must put the value to be shifted on the left side of the bitwise shift operator and the number of bits to shift on the right side of the operator. For example, the following statement:

```
shiftResult = 13 << 2;
```

tells C to shift the internal bits of the value 13 to the left two places. Before the shift, the 8-bit pattern that makes up the number 13 is 00001101. After the shift, shiftResult holds 00110100. Figure 10.3 shows how the left shift produced the result just described.

FIGURE 10.3.
Shifting the bits left twice produces a different value.

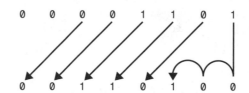

The first two bits in the original value of 13 are sent to nowhere land. They are shifted off the left and discarded. The variable shiftResult gets a 52—the decimal equivalent of the binary number 00110100.

A right shift such as this:

```
shiftResult = 13 >> 2;
```

results in shiftResult holding a value of 00000011, which is equivalent to a decimal 3. The 1 bits shifted off the right are discarded.

When you left- or right-shift negative values, C always extends the sign bit. This behavior is equivalent to the PC's internal machine-level shift operators.

definition

Sign extension is the retaining of a negative or positive sign no matter how many times C shifts a value.

STOP&TYPE Listing 10.2 contains a program that performs the shifting operations just described and also shows the sign bit extension.

Review
What You Have Learned

The left- and right-shift operators move internal bit values to the left or right the number of times indicated by the operator's right value.

▼ INPUT   LISTING 10.2. THE BITWISE SHIFT OPERATORS IN ACTION.

```
1:  /* Filename: BITSHIFT.C */
2:  // Shows the results of several bitwise shift operations
3:  #include <stdio.h>
4:  #include <conio.h>
5:  main()
6:  {
```

```
 7:     int shiftResult;
 8:     clrscr();
 9:
10:     shiftResult = 13 << 2;
11:     printf("13 << 2 is %d\n", shiftResult);
12:
13:     shiftResult = 13 >> 2;
14:     printf("13 >> 2 is %d\n", shiftResult);
15:
16:     shiftResult = -13 << 2;
17:     printf("-13 << 2 is %d\n", shiftResult);
18:
19:     shiftResult = -13 >> 2;
20:     printf("-13 >> 2 is %d\n", shiftResult);
21:
22:     return 0;
23: }
```

▼ OUTPUT

```
13 << 2 is 52
13 >> 2 is 3
-13 << 2 is -52
-13 >> 2 is -4
```

▼ ANALYSIS

The output shows that when you shift a positive value (lines 10 and 13), C keeps the value positive. C accomplishes this by keeping the sign bit a 0 (positive) even if it's time for a 1 bit to shift into the number. C keeps the value negative (as shown in lines 16 and 19) by keeping the sign bit a 1 (for negative numbers) even if a 0 attempts to shift into the sign bit. C discards any 1 bits shifted off the left or right ends of a value.

▶ Some Uses for Bitwise Operators

Concept   **What You Will Learn**

The bitwise operators provide access to highly efficient routines. However, a full understanding of these routines requires an understanding of binary numeric representation.

This book doesn't teach you how to represent numbers in binary. (That's the job of a good book on assembly language such as *Assembly Language: For Real Programmers ONLY!* (Sams Publishing, 1993).) However, you can still follow the next couple of descriptions to find out how to perform common data tests that are more efficient than you would perform without the bitwise operators.

All even numbers end with 0 (a 0 in their rightmost bit position) and all odd values have a 1 in their rightmost bit position. Using a bitmask of 1 or 0, you can test to see whether a number is odd or even.

definition
A *bitmask* is a specific bit pattern you apply that changes another value's bit pattern.

Without the bitwise operators, the following `if` is true if `value` holds an odd value:

```
if ((value % 2) == 1)
```

The remainder of `value` divided by 2 is either 0 or 1 (the remainder of any integer divided by 2 is 0 or 1). If the remainder is 1, the number is odd and the `if` is true. Remember that 1 is always true and 0 is always false. If `value` holds an even number, dividing that number by 2 will produce an even result and the remainder will be 0, producing a false value.

C has to do more work when you compute an integer remainder instead of using a bitwise operator. The following `if` produces identical results but is much more efficient than using `%`:

```
if ((value & 1) == 1)
```

The bit pattern for 1 is 00000001. If that pattern, the bitmask, compares true using a bitwise `&`, the rightmost bit of `value` is a 1, also meaning that `value` is odd. If, however, the rightmost bit of `value` is not 1, the number is even and the `if` will result in a false condition. `if (0)` is always false.

Another useful bitwise operation is to test whether a letter is uppercase or lowercase. Figure 10.4 shows how uppercase ASCII characters differ from their lowercase equivalents by a single bit, the third bit from the left. The bit is a 1 if the letter is lowercase and a 0 if the letter is uppercase.

FIGURE 10.4.
A lowercase letter's third bit from the left is always 1.

Using a bitmask of 32 (in the internal binary equivalent of 32, the only bit turned on is the third bit from the left), you can test to see whether a letter is uppercase or lowercase. Applying 32 against a character value using the `&` operator produces a true result if and only if the character is lowercase.

After defining two character variables like this:

```
int uc = 'C';
int lc = 'c';
```

the following `if` produces a true result:

```
if (uc & 32)    // True if uc is uppercase
```

and the following `if` produces a false result:

```
if (lc & 32)    // True if lc is uppercase
```

Performing a bitwise mask comparison is much more efficient than the equivalent logical operator method, which would work like this:

```
if ((uc >= 'a') && (uc <= 'z'))    // True if uc is lowercase
```

Tip If your program uses a bitmask, you can define the bitmask at the top using #define and then use the defined name instead of the value throughout the program.

During those rare instances when you must multiply an integer by a power of 2 (2, 4, 8, 16, 32, 64, 128, 256, and so on), use the bitwise leftshift operator. The leftshift produces the same result as multiplication, only it does so much faster. The following statements are equivalent:

```
i = answer * 32;    // Multiply by 2 raised to the 5th power

i = answer << 5;    // Multiply by 2 raised to the 5th power
```

The number of places that you shift the value determines the power of 2 that you want to multiply by. Conversely, to divide a number by a power of 2, use the rightshift operator. The following two statements are equivalent, but the bitwise is much more efficient:

```
i = answer / 16;    // Divide by 2 raised to the fourth power

i = answer >> 4;    // Divide by 2 raised to the fourth power
```

Remainders get truncated if you divide an odd number by right-shifting. However, this would also be the case if you divided using integer division, so the shift operators produce the same results as the / and *.

STOP&TYPE Listing 10.3 contains a program that asks the user for three values and then performs the tests described in this section.

Review   **What You Have Learned**

The bitwise operators produce much more efficient operations than equivalent nonbitwise operators.

▼ **INPUT   LISTING 10.3. THE BITWISE OPERATORS WORK ON THE USER'S VALUES.**

```
 1:  /* Filename: BITEQUIV.C */
 2:  // Uses bitwise operators to work with user input
 3:  #include <stdio.h>
 4:  #include <conio.h>
 5:  main()
 6:  {
 7:    int i, result;
 8:    char c;
 9:    clrscr();
10:
```

continues

LISTING 10.3. CONTINUED

```
11:     printf("Enter a number and I'll say if it's odd or even: ");
12:     scanf(" %d", &i);
13:
14:     if ((i & 1) == 1)
15:       { printf("The number is odd\n"); }
16:     else
17:       { printf("The number is even\n"); }
18:
19:     printf("\nEnter a number that you want multiplied by 32: ");
20:     scanf(" %d", &i);
21:     result = i << 5;    // Multiply by 2 raised to the fifth power
22:     printf("%d times 32 is %d\n", i, result);
23:
24:     printf("\nPlease enter your first initial: ");
25:     scanf(" %c", &c);
26:     if (c & 32)
27:       { printf("Always type your initial in uppercase\n"); }
28:     else
29:       { printf("You entered the initial in uppercase, good!\n"); }
30:
31:     return 0;
32:   }
```

▼ OUTPUT

```
Enter a number and I'll say if it's odd or even: 12
The number is even

Enter a number that you want multiplied by 32: 4
4 times 32 is 128

Please enter your first initial: G
You entered the initial in uppercase, good!
```

▼ ANALYSIS

This program simply repeats the logic explained in this section for checking whether a number is odd or even, for multiplying and dividing by powers of two, and for checking for uppercase or lowercase letters. About the only addition that you can make (and you'll be given a chance in the exercises at the end of this unit!) is to use a defined constant for the bitmasks to make the program more maintainable.

Because of their very nature, using bitwise operators is less readable than not using them. A less efficient but equivalent multiplication and division certainly is easier to understand than a bitwise shift operator. Nevertheless, the actions of the bitwise operators are well documented, and their use is well sanctioned by the C community. Once you become familiar with them, feel free to use them for efficiency. Remember too that if you begin writing machine-level systems programs, you'll need the low-level bit manipulation that these operators provide.

▶ The Compound Bitwise Operators

Concept

What You Will Learn

The compound bitwise operators will be easy now that you understand the bitwise operators. When you want to update a variable's value with a bitwise operator, apply a compound operator to speed things along.

The compound bitwise operators work just like their nonbitwise counterparts—+=, /=, and the others—updating values stored in variables. Instead of writing out a complete assignment like this:

```
a = a | bitMask;
```

you can apply the bitmask to a using |=:

```
a |= bitMask;
```

The compound bitwise operators save typing time. They appear low in the precedence table, along with the nonbitwise compound operators, so you'll have to be careful with precedence, just as you are when using *= and the nonbitwise operators. The following statement:

```
a &= 1 - bitMask;
```

is identical to this statement:

```
a = a & (1 - bitMask);
```

because the compound operators have much lower precedence than the subtraction operator.

Warning   There is no compound 1's complement operator.

STOP&TYPE Listing 10.4 asks the user for an even number and then converts that number to the next-highest odd number.

Review

What You Have Learned

The compound bitwise operators let you update values of variables using bitwise operations.

▼ INPUT   LISTING 10.4. USING A COMPOUND BITWISE OPERATOR.

```
1:  /* Filename: EVNTOODD.C */
2:  // Changes the user's value to the next-highest odd number
3:  #include <stdio.h>
```

continues

LISTING 10.4. CONTINUED

```
 4:   #include <conio.h>
 5:   main()
 6:   {
 7:     int num;
 8:     clrscr();
 9:
10:     printf("Enter an even number: ");
11:     scanf(" %d", &num);
12:
13:     num |= 1;    // Turn on the rightmost bit position
14:     printf("The next-highest value is %d\n", num);
15:
16:     return 0;
17:   }
```

▼ **OUTPUT**

```
Enter an even number: 6
The next-highest value is 7
```

▼ **ANALYSIS**

The reason that this program is able to print the next-highest odd value is that whenever you turn on the rightmost bit of an even number, you turn that number into an odd number. All odd numbers have their rightmost bit turned on.

▶ Homework

General Knowledge

1. What is the complete name of each of the following operators?

    A. |

    B. ||

    C. &

    D. &&

    E. ^

    F. ~

    G. |=

    H. &=

    I. ^=

    J. >>

    K. <<

    L. >>=

    M. <<=

2. Why is a binary number often expressed in eight bits even though fewer bits can represent it?

3. Which of the bitwise operators is a unary operator?

4. What is meant by sign extension?

5. Why is there no truth table for the bitwise shift operators?

6. True or false: 7 (which translates to a binary 00000111) can be used to see whether the rightmost three bits of a variable are set to 1.

7. True or false: & and && both do the same thing, but & is more efficient.

8. True or false: The bitwise 1's complement, ~, takes the negative of a number.

What's the Output?

9. Assuming that you know the binary numbering system, what value does C store in result after the following assignment finishes?

```
result = 9 & 14;
```

10. Assuming that you know the binary numbering system, what value does C store in result after the following assignment finishes?

```
result = 9 | 14;
```

11. Assuming that you know the binary numbering system, what value does C store in result after the following assignment finishes?

```
result = 9 ^ 14;
```

12. What's the value of 01010101 after it's shifted left three times?

13. What's the value of 01010101 after it's shifted right four times?

14. What's the value of 11000000 after it's shifted right three times? Hint: Remember the sign extension!

Find the Bug

15. Pauline the programmer wants to apply the bitwise | operator in the following way:

```
answer = 9.3 | 12.3;
```

Something doesn't seem to be working well. Can you tell Pauline what the problem is?

Write Code That...

16. Write a program that asks the user whether he or she likes fresh-squeezed orange juice. If the user answers y or Y, print the message You'll be healthy all your life!. If the user answers n or N, print the message You need vitamin C!.

Test only for an uppercase Y or an uppercase N. In other words, it doesn't matter if the user enters an uppercase or lowercase Y. Your if should check just for uppercase. To let this happen, convert the user's character answer to uppercase using a bitwise & and the bitmask 223. (223 contains all 1 bits except for the third bit from the left.)

17. Add a routine to the BITEQUIV.C program in Listing 10.3 that divides the user's value by 8 (2 raised to the third power). Use a right-shifting bitwise operator for the division.

Extra Credit

18. Rewrite the program you added to in question 17 to use a named constant (via #define) for the bitmasking uppercase/lowercase test.

19. Write a program that prints 5 raised to the first five powers of 2. On the first line print Five raised to the first power of 2 is 25, on the second line print Five raised to the second power of 2 is 125, and so on. Use a bitwise operator for the math.

20. Add error-checking code to the program named EVNTOODD.C (in Listing 10.4) to check the user's input and make sure that the user doesn't enter an odd value when asked for an even value.

Project

Lesson ▶

Upgraded
Operators

STOP&TYPE In this lesson, you learned about many of C's advanced operators. You saw the following:

▶ C performs automatic data-type promotion from smaller to larger data types.

▶ The typecast operator lets you control how data types convert from one to the other.

▶ The `sizeof` operator returns the number of bytes needed to hold data types, variables, and literals.

▶ The conditional operator lets you improve `if-else` efficiency by putting complete relational logic on a single line.

Project 5 Listing. Using the advanced operators.

```
1:   /* Filename: LESSON5.C */

2:   // Shows how the advanced operators give

3:   // you more control and efficiency

4:   #include <stdio.h>

5:   #include <conio.h>

6:   #define MAKEUPPER 223

7:   main()

8:   {

9:      char partCode;

10:     int num, doubleNum;

11:     float price;

12:     double totalInv;

13:     clrscr();

14:
```

▶ The increment and decrement operators provide yet another way that C provides more efficiency than other programming languages.

▶ The bitwise operators aren't for everybody. These operators are important for system-level programmers who need to be able to manipulate individual data bits.

▶ The bitwise operators provide lots of efficiency when you use them to check for odd and even values and uppercase and lowercase letters and to multiply and divide by powers of two.

Description

1: A C comment that includes the program's filename.

2: A C++ comment that begins the program's description.

3: The program's description continues.

4: The `printf()` and `scanf()` functions need information in the STDIO.H header file.

5: The screen-clearing function, `clrscr()`, needs information in the CONIO.H header file.

6: Defines the program's bitmask, which will ensure that the part code is converted to uppercase.

    6: All bits in 223 are on except for the third from the left.

    6: Use a named constant for bitmasks to make your programs more readable.

7: All functions have names, and the first function in all C programs is `main()`.

8: All functions begin with a left brace.

9: Defines a character variable that will hold the part code letter.

10: Defines two integers.

    10: One integer will hold the number in the current inventory and the other will hold what the inventory would be if you doubled the number of goods.

11: Defines a floating-point variable that will hold the item's price.

12: Defines a double floating-point variable that will hold the item's total price.

13: The built-in library function `clrscr()` erases the output screen so that it's clear before the program's output begins.

14: Extra blank lines make your program more readable.

continues

Project 5 Listing. continued

```
15:      printf("** Inventory Valuation **\n\n");

16:      printf("What is the character part code? ");

17:      scanf(" %c", &partCode);

18:      partCode &= MAKEUPPER;     // Ensure that the part

19:                                 // code is uppercase

20:      printf("How many parts are there? ");

21:      scanf(" %d", &num);

22:      printf("What is the price of each part? ");

23:      scanf(" %f", &price);

24:

25:      totalInv = (double)num * (double)price;

26:      printf("\nFor part code %c, ", partCode);

27:      printf("the total valuation is $%.2f\n", totalInv);

28:

29:      doubleNum = num << 1;    // Compute double the current number

30:      printf("\nDoubling our inventory would give us %d new parts\n",

31:             doubleNum);

32:      (num < 20) ? printf("\nWe need to order more inventory!\n") :

33:                   printf("\nWe now have enough inventory\n");

34:      return 0;

35:  }
```

Description

15: A printed title helps to describe the program to the user.

16: Prompts the user for a character part code.

17: Gets the part code.

18: Uses the compound bitwise AND operator to ensure that the part code is uppercase.

19: Extra blank lines make your program more readable.

20: Prompts for the number of total parts.

21: Grabs the total number of parts from the user.

22: Prompts for the price of each product.

23: Grabs the price from the user.

24: Extra blank lines make your program more readable.

25: Uses typecasting to typecast each value on the right of the equal sign to `double`.

26: Prints the item's part `code`. Although the user might have entered the part code in lowercase, it will appear in uppercase.

27: Prints the total price of the items in the inventory.

28: Extra blank lines make your program more readable.

29: Uses the bitwise leftshift operator to compute two times the current number of items.

30: Tells the user what doubling the inventory would mean.

31: Continues printing the doubling of the inventory.

32: Begins a two-line conditional.

33: The conditional's `printf()` continues.

34: Returns to the IDE.

35: `main()`'s closing brace terminates the program.

25: In this case, typecasting isn't needed because C's automatic promotion would handle everything well.

25: Most of the time, you can let C promote such data types for you.

29: In other words, the bitwise leftshift operator multiplies by 2 raised to the first power.

32: As you can see, any C statement can appear inside the conditional, even a `printf()` function call.

32: You can embed `printf()`s in the conditional operator.

33: Whenever a statement gets very long, break it into two lines to make your program more readable.

▼ **OUTPUT**

```
** Inventory Valuation **

What is the character part code? a
How many parts are there? 12
What is the price of each part? 34

For part code A, the total valuation is 408.00

Doubling our inventory would give us 24 new parts

We need to order more inventory!
```

Lesson ▶

6

Looping Back and Forth

Unit 11: Spending a While with *while*

Unit 12: Use C *for* Looping

Lesson 6 Project

11

Spending a While with *while*

break

do-while

exit

infinite loop

iteration

loop

while

▶ What You'll Learn About

- ▶ The format of `while`
- ▶ The other `while`: the `do-while` loop
- ▶ `break` or an early `exit()`

Computers do a lot of things that people find boring. They add and subtract. They print reams of information. They wait patiently while a user sits at the keyboard, trying to find the Enter key. Computers do all these things without complaint as long as their programs contain no syntax errors. (Which, of course, none of your programs will!)

Not only do computers do all these things, they do them very fast. Extremely fast. Their speed gives computers the added advantage of being able to perform multiple repetitions of the same tasks.

definition

A *loop* is a program's repeated execution of the same set of instructions.

When your programs contain loops, they can repeat the same set of code a lot. The computer can repeat the code hundreds, even thousands, of times. Computers repeat so rapidly that the user usually notices no delay at all. Suppose you wrote a program that calculated payroll figures. Instead of running the same program over and over for each employee, the user would have to run the program only once. A loop within the program would keep calculating each employee's data until the entire payroll was finished.

▶ The Format of *while*

Concept   **What You Will Learn**

The `while` loop repeats as long as a relational test is true. As soon as the relational test becomes false, the `while` loop terminates and the rest of the program continues.

The `while` loop requires the `while` statement. `while` is a command, just as `return`, `if`, and `else` are commands.

Note   `while` isn't a library function. Therefore, it doesn't use any header files.

definition

An *infinite loop* never stops executing.

When you want your program to execute the same series of statements over and over, one of the most important points to plan is when the loop should terminate. No matter how fast your computer is, if you write a program that contains a loop that loops without stopping, the endless infinite loop hangs up and the program never lets the user stop the program or return to Turbo C++'s IDE.

To keep loops from executing forever, you write a controlling relational test, just like the relational tests that appear inside `if` statements. The loop repeats as long as the relational test is true. Unlike an `if` statement, a `while` body *keeps repeating* as long as the `while`'s relational test is true. The `if` statement's body executes only once if the `if`'s relational test is true.

Warning You must make sure that something inside the loop eventually changes the while's relational test. If the relation is true when the while first begins, and if nothing inside the body of the while ever changes the relational test, it executes forever. The loop will never stop, and you'll lose your title of "Master C Guru Programmer."

 Tip If you accidentally write a program that contains an infinite loop, you can terminate the program by pressing Ctrl-Break. Turbo C++ then displays the dialog box shown in Figure 11.1. After you press Enter or click on Cancel, Turbo C++ returns you to the IDE.

FIGURE 11.1.

The dialog box you see if you break out of an infinite loop.

Turbo C++ is a fairly smart compiler. Sometimes it can spot an infinite loop ahead of time. If Turbo C++ spots such a problem, it displays a warning during your program's compilation that says Unreachable code. This warning appears on the statement that follows the infinite loop's final line. Don't rely on Turbo C++'s ability to spot your infinite loops, however. Most infinite loops are controlled by runtime data values that the compiler can't be expected to catch. If your program appears to have come to a dead stop when you run it, chances are good that you've entered an infinite loop.

We're a few pages into this unit and you've *yet* to see a while loop. Enough introduction. Here's the format of the while loop:

```
while (relationalExpression)
  { // Block of one or more C statements
  }
```

Just like if, while is a multiline statement. Also like if, parentheses must appear around the relational expression. The relational expression can contain one or more relational operators. If you use more than one relational operator inside the relational expression, use logical operators (&& and ¦¦) to combine the relational tests.

 Tip Indent the body of the while loop so that when you maintain the program, you'll be able to spot where the loop's code begins and ends.

The body of the while loop doesn't require braces if it has only one statement. However, you should get in the habit of using the braces so that you won't forget them later if you add more statements to the while loop.

Warning Don't put a semicolon after the relational test's closing parenthesis. The while loop would then be an infinite loop, because C would think that the body of the loop were a null statement (empty), and null statements can't change the loop's controlling relational test.

The relational test appears at the top of the while loop. The location of the test is important; the while might never execute even once! The body of the while loop executes only if the relational expression is true and keeps executing as long as the relational expression is true. If and when the relational expression becomes false, the program continues at the statement following the while loop's closing brace.

Figure 11.2 illustrates the while loop's action. while is somewhat like a repeating if test. If the relational expression is true, the while body repeats its execution. If the relational expression is false, the while body stops executing and the program continues from there.

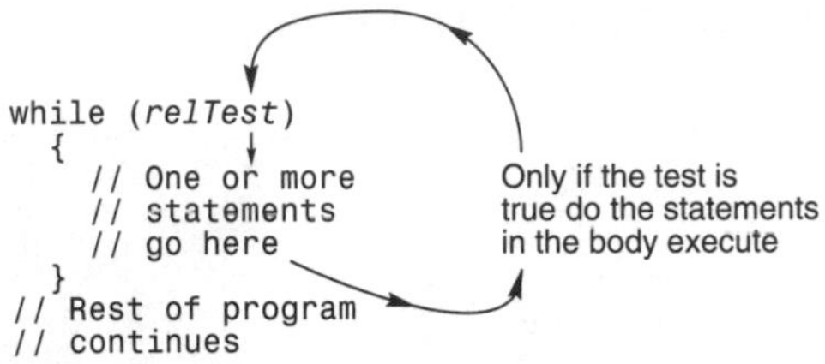

FIGURE 11.2.

The body of the while executes as long as the relational expression is true.

```
while (relTest)
  {
      // One or more
      // statements
      // go here
  }
// Rest of program
// continues
```

Only if the test is
true do the statements
in the body execute

The following while loop prints Happy Birthday! on-screen 10 times. Notice that instead of using 10 separate printf()s, you need to specify only one inside a while loop that loops 10 times:

```
int count = 0;
while (count < 10)
  {
     printf("Happy Birthday!\n");
     count++;   // VERY important!
  }
```

Why is it important to increment the count variable? If you don't increment count, the loop will be infinite! Remember that the body of the loop should always change something in the while's relational test so that the relational test eventually becomes false and the loop can stop.

COUNTERS AND TOTALS

The count variable in the preceding while loop is called a *counter variable*. Each time through the loop, the program increments count. Just as when you count *0, 1, 2, 3,* and so on, count starts out holding a 0, then a 1, 2, 3, and so on, until C increments count to the final value of 10, at which time the relational test becomes false and the loop terminates.

If you add more than one to a variable inside a loop, such as when you add to a daily sales total when customers buy inventory items, that variable is known as a *total variable*. Instead of incrementing by one, keeping a count as counter variables do, total variables increment by whatever value needs to be added to the total variable at the time.

STOP&TYPE Listing 11.1 contains a program that asks the user for an age. If the user enters an age less than 5 or more than 110, the program doesn't believe the user and asks again.

Until now, if the user entered a bad value, the program stopped early. Now, you can keep asking the user until he or she enters a value within an expected range.

Review

The `while` loop lets you repeat sections of your program as long as the relational test is true.

▼ INPUT   LISTING 11.1. USING `while` TO VERIFY USER INPUT.

```
1:  /* Filename: USERAGE.C */
2:  // Uses a while loop to get an age from the user
3:  #include <stdio.h>
4:  #include <conio.h>
5:  main()
6:  {
7:    int age;
8:    clrscr();
9:
10:    printf("How old are you? ");
11:    scanf(" %d", &age);
12:
13:    while ((age < 5) || (age > 110))
14:      { printf("I'm not sure that I believe you are %d\n", age);
15:        printf("Try again...\n\n");
16:        printf("How old are you? ");   // Get the age again
17:        scanf(" %d", &age);
18:      }
19:    // The program continues if the user entered a reasonable age
20:    if (age < 16)
21:      { printf("Your curfew is at 11:30 pm\n");
22:        printf("Have fun!\n");
23:      }
24:    else
25:      {
26:        printf("You're old enough to drive, so be careful ");
27:        printf("out there!\n");
28:      }
29:    return 0;
30:  }
```

UNIT

11

Spending a While with *while*

▼ OUTPUT

```
How old are you? -32
I'm not sure that I believe you are -32
Try again...

How old are you? 192
I'm not sure that I believe you are 192
Try again...

How old are you? 25
You're old enough to drive, so be careful out there!
```

▼ **ANALYSIS**

The user's entered age determines what the program does. First of all, if the user enters an age that isn't within the range of more than 5 and less than 110, the program prints an error message in lines 14 and 15. Actually, the program prints a warning, not an error, because as soon as the user enters a bad age, the program asks the user for another age and tests the age all over again via the loop in lines 13 through 18. The `while` will *continue* looping as long as the user's value isn't within the expected range.

The rest of the program primarily consists of an `if-else` in lines 20-28 that prints one message or another, depending on the user's age. Unlike the `while`, the `if` never repeats its body more than once. When the `if` body finishes, the program always continues.

Note   This program contains two sets of duplicate lines: Lines 10 and 11 are repeated in lines 16 and 17. After mastering the second kind of `while` loop discussed in the next section (there are two), you'll see a way to eliminate the duplication of lines of code.

▶ **The Other *while*: The *do-while* Loop**

Concept   **What You Will Learn**

There is a second `while` loop called the `do-while` loop whose relational test appears at the bottom of the loop's body instead of at the top.

C contains two `while` loops—the `while` loop that you read about in the preceding section and the `do-while` loop. Although these loops are similar, they differ in where they test their relation. Here is the format of `do-while`:

```
do   {   // Block of one or more C statements
} while (relationalExpression);
```

As with the `while` loop, the braces around the body aren't required if it contains a single statement. However, you should use the braces in all cases for clarity and future maintenance. You must put parentheses around the relational expression. The final semicolon after the relational test is required to terminate the `do-while` statement.

definition

An *iteration* is one cycle through the body of a loop.

You should use a `do-while` loop instead of a `while` loop when you want the body of the loop to execute at least once. The location of the `do-while`'s relational test causes execution to fall through and execute the body of the loop at least once. Only after the body executes once can the `do` loop check the relational test to see whether the loop should loop again or terminate. Only after the relational test is false will the rest of the program continue executing.

Note   The `while` loop might never execute because C checks the relational test before the body has a chance to execute. `do-while` doesn't test the relation until the loop executes one full iteration. Figure 11.3 shows how the `do-loop` works as opposed to how `while` works (which you saw in Figure 11.2).

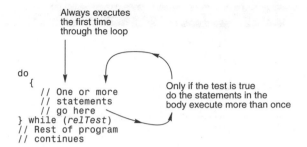

FIGURE 11.3.

The body of a do-while always executes at least once.

```
                              Always executes
                              the first time
                              through the loop
          do
            {
                // One or more
                // statements
                // go here            Only if the test is true
            } while (relTest)         do the statements in the
            // Rest of program        body execute more than once
            // continues
```

Here is a do-while that prints Happy Birthday 10 times:

```
int count = 0;
do
  { printf("Happy Birthday!\n");
    count++;
} while (count < 10);
```

STOP&TYPE Listing 11.1 asked the user for his or her age and printed an appropriate message. Listing 11.2 improves upon that program by using a do-while loop. The use of do-while as opposed to while means that you don't have to repeat the age prompt and the user's scanf(). However, an extra if is needed to capture any mistake the user makes.

Review   **What You Have Learned**

do-while ensures that the body of the loop executes at least once.

▼ **INPUT   LISTING 11.2. KEEP ASKING FOR A CORRECT** age **IF NEEDED WITH** do.

```
 1:  /* Filename: DOUSRAGE.C */
 2:  // Uses a do-while loop to get an age from the user
 3:  #include <stdio.h>
 4:  #include <conio.h>
 5:  main()
 6:  {
 7:    int age;
 8:    clrscr();
 9:
10:    // In the previous listing, two extra lines went here
11:    do
12:      { printf("How old are you? ");   // Get the age
13:        scanf(" %d", &age);
14:        if ((age < 5) || (age > 110))
15:          { printf("I'm not sure that I believe you are %d\n", age);
16:            printf("Try again...\n\n"); }
17:      } while ((age < 5) || (age > 110));   // Quit after good input
18:
19:    // The program continues if the user entered a reasonable age
20:    if (age < 16)
21:      { printf("Your curfew is at 11:30 pm\n");
22:        printf("Have fun!\n");
23:      }
24:    else
25:      {
```

continues

UNIT

11

Spending a While with *while*

LISTING 11.2. CONTINUED

```
26:        printf("You're old enough to drive, so be careful ");
27:        printf("out there!\n");
28:     }
29:   return 0;
30: }
```

▼ **OUTPUT**

```
How old are you? 2
I'm not sure that I believe you are 2
Try again...

How old are you? 3224
I'm not sure that I believe you are 3224
Try again...

How old are you? 12
Your curfew is at 11:30 pm
Have fun!
```

▼ **ANALYSIS**

The use of do-while keeps the program from repeating these lines, as was done in Listing 11.1:

```
printf("How old are you? ");    // Get the age again
scanf(" %d", &age);
```

The use of do-while requires an extra if statement that Listing 11.1 didn't need. The if in line 14 ensures that the age warning message prints only if the user enters an age outside the range. Whether to use while without the extra if or do-while with the extra if is up to you.

▶ ## *break* or an Early *exit()*?

Concept   **What You Will Learn**

The break statement and the exit() function let you terminate programs and loops before their natural conclusion.

So far, when a program has needed to end earlier than its normal termination, this book has ended the program with an extra return statement. return returns control to the IDE whenever the program encounters it. If you were to run a C program directly from DOS and not from the IDE, DOS could capture the integer value to the right of return. The DOS environment variable named errorlevel would get the program's return value. For example, the following return sends the value of 7 to the DOS environment variable named errorlevel:

```
return 7;
```

Often, programmers need to return values to DOS so that a batch file or subsequent program can use the value returned from programs that finish.

Many C programmers prefer to exit from programs early, such as for error processing, using a library function named `exit()`. Once you begin writing multifunction programs in Lesson 8, you'll see that `return` doesn't always return from the entire program. `return` actually tells C to terminate only the current function. When `main()` is the only function in the program, `return` and `exit` do the same thing. Once you begin writing multifunction programs, however, you'll have to begin using `exit()` only for program termination and `return` for function termination.

Note   The `exit()` function requires the header file named STDLIB.H (which stands for *standard library*). Be sure to include that header file in any and all programs that use `exit()`.

Suppose that you were writing a program that computed an average price for products sold in a certain region. You can't divide by zero (mathematically, division by zero is undefined), so the following code makes sure that a zero is never used as the divisor:

```
if (sales == 0)
  { exit(1); }    // Terminate early
```

In this case, the operating system will receive the 1. A `return 0` at the end of the program (triggered at the program's normal conclusion) could indicate that no error exists, while a value of 1 (produced by the `exit()`) would indicate that there was an error. The operating system or subsequent program would have to deal with that return value, stored in the system-level variable named `errorlevel`, as required by the application.

After seeing the `while` loops in the first part of this unit, you know that your program can spot and retry many errors. For example, if the user enters an unexpected value, you can loop back and keep asking him for a better value until he gets it right. Such loops let your programs correct the problem instead of exiting via `return` or `exit()` and making the user rerun the program from the beginning.

The `break` command works like the `exit()` function on a smaller scale. Whereas `exit()` exits a program, `break` exits the current loop in progress. You would use `break` only inside a loop such as a `while` or `do-while` loop. The `break` would exit the execution of only the loop, not the entire program. Therefore, you can now exit a loop in two ways:

▶ Through the normal termination of the loop when the relational test finally becomes false

▶ Through the termination of the loop through the use of the `break` function

No matter how your program's loop finishes, the rest of the program will continue as usual. Figure 11.4 shows the actions of `return`, `exit()`, and `break`.

Warning   `break` terminates only loops, not `if` statements.

```
// An outline of a program
main()
{
   //
   if (i == 10)
      { exit(1); }  ◄──────── Exits the program

   //
   while (a < b)
   { if (i >= 35)
         break;  ◄──────── Exits the current loop
   }

   //
   if (i <= 120)
      { return 0; }  ◄────┐
   //                      ├── Exits the function
   return 0;  ◄───────────┘
}
```

FIGURE 11.4.
The actions of return,
exit(), and break.

You'll almost always enclose exit() and break code in if blocks. You simply don't write code that always executes exit() or break. For example, in both of the following main() code listings, the last printf()s never execute. In the first main(), exit() terminates the program and returns to the IDE (or operating system):

```
main()
{
  int age;
  printf("How old are you? ");
  scanf(" %d", &age);
  exit(1);   // The program terminates here
  printf("I cannot believe that you're already %d!\n", age);
  return 0;
}
```

A break inside a while or do-while loop invalidates the whole use of the loop unless the break appears in an if. The if's relational test lets the loop continue looping until the conditions are right for breaking out of the loop early.

STOP&TYPE Listing 11.3 contains both a break and an exit(). The execution of either depends on the user's response.

Review **What You Have Learned**

break terminates the current loop and exit() terminates the current program.

▼ **INPUT   LISTING 11.3. DEMONSTRATING** break **AND** exit().

```
1:   /* Filename: BREXIT.C */
2:   // Demonstrates both break and exit()
3:   #include <stdio.h>
4:   #include <conio.h>
5:   // Be sure to include STDLIB.H when you use exit()!
6:   #include <stdlib.h>
7:   #define UPPER 223
8:
9:   main()
10:  {
11:     int count = 0;
```

```
12:    char ans;
13:    clrscr();
14:
15:    // The following loop prints "Hi" five times only
16:    // as long as the user keeps requesting the word.
17:    // Whether the user terminates the loop early or
18:    // not, the program continues executing.
19:    while (count < 5)
20:      { printf("Hi\n");
21:        printf("Do you want to see it again (Y/N)? ");
22:        scanf(" %c", &ans);
23:        if ( (ans & UPPER) == 'N')   // Test only uppercase
24:          { break; }
25:        count++;
26:      }
27:
28:    printf("\n");
29:
30:    // The following loop prints "Bye" five times
31:    // as long as the user keeps requesting the word.
32:    // The difference here from the previous section
33:    // is that the entire program, not just the loop,
34:    // terminates if the user requests termination.
35:
36:    count = 0;
37:    while (count < 5)
38:      { printf("Bye\n");
39:        printf("Do you want to see it again (Y/N)? ");
40:        scanf(" %c", &ans);
41:        if ( (ans & UPPER) == 'N')   // Test only uppercase
42:          { exit(1); }
43:      count++;
44:      }
45:
46:    // The following printf() executes ONLY if the user let
47:    // the previous loop execute to its natural termination.
48:    printf("That's all, folks!\n");
49:
50:    return 0;   // Return to the IDE
51:  }
```

UNIT

11

Spending a While with *while*

▼ OUTPUT

```
Hi
Do you want to see it again (Y/N)? y
Hi
Do you want to see it again (Y/N)? Y
Hi
Do you want to see it again (Y/N)? y
Hi
Do you want to see it again (Y/N)? y
Hi
Do you want to see it again (Y/N)? y

Bye
Do you want to see it again (Y/N)? y
Bye
Do you want to see it again (Y/N)? y
Bye
Do you want to see it again (Y/N)? N
```

▼ **ANALYSIS**

The top of the output shows the user letting the while loop continue until its natural conclusion (after five iterations). The bitwise & operators in lines 23 and 41 let the user answer in either uppercase or lowercase (notice the uppercase N in the output's last question). If the user enters n or N in response to the question, the break executes, terminating the while loop on line 24. (The if keeps the break from executing the first time through the loop.)

The second part of the program contains a similar set of lines that print Bye until the user enters n or N (line 40) or until the loop finishes execution after five iterations. If the user terminates the loop early, the exit() in line 42 makes sure that the program terminates completely and the printf() in line 48 never gets a chance to execute. If the user doesn't terminate the loop early in response to line 39's question, line 48's printf() executes because the exit() never executes.

▶ Homework

General Knowledge

1. What is a loop?
2. What's the difference between a loop and an infinite loop?
3. If your program enters an infinite loop, how can you stop the execution?
4. Why should you never put a semicolon at the end of the while loop's closing parenthesis?
5. Why is it recommended that you put braces around the while and do-while loop bodies?
6. What's the difference between exit() and return?
7. What's the difference between exit() and break?
8. Why should an exit() or break fall within an if block instead of residing as regular lines of a C program?
9. Rank the following in the order of seriousness of code termination (list the least serious one first):

    return
    exit()
    break

10. What's the difference between a total variable and a counter variable?
11. Which kind of variable, a counter variable or a total variable, does the ++ increment operator work best with?
12. Which header file does exit() require?
13. What is the name of the operating system variable that captures exit() values?
14. True or false: The body of a while loop might never execute.
15. True or false: The body of a do-while loop might never execute.

16. True or false: Turbo C++ always catches your infinite loops during compilation.

17. True or false: The `break` statement requires a header file.

What's the Output?

18. How many times do the letters `abc` print in the following code?

```
int c = 1;
while (c < 20)
  { printf("abc\n");
    c++;
  }
```

19. How many times do the letters `abc` print in the following code?

```
int c = 0;
while (c < 20)
  { printf("abc\n");
    c++;
  }
```

20. How many times do the letters `abc` print in the following code?

```
int c = 0;
while (c <= 20)
  { printf("abc\n");
    c++;
  }
```

Find the Bug

21. Can you find anything wrong with the following loop?

```
a = 10; b = 4;
while (a >= 10)
  { printf("a is now %d\n", a);
    b += 2;
    printf("b is now %d\n", b);
  }
```

22. Carl the C coder wants to print a special warning message 10 times if his company's costs get too high. Carl coded the following, but the results aren't working exactly as he expected:

```
if (costs >= 25000.00)
  { count = 0;
    while (count < 10)
      printf("** Please lower costs immediately **\n");
      count++;
  }
```

Help Carl fix the problem.

Write Code That...

23. Write a program that defines a character array 80 bytes long. Ask the user for his or her first name (80 bytes is more than enough to hold anyone's response). Using an integer variable and a `while` loop, find the length of the user's name (the string's length). Hint: Add one to the integer variable each time through the loop and stop when you get to the null zero. Note: The string length variable is a counter variable.

24. Write a program that asks the user for test averages. Enter all test values as integers to keep things simple. The program is to continue until the user enters -99 in order to obtain the average or until she enters five values (there were only five tests this term). If the user enters -99, it means that she took fewer than five tests and is ready for the average early. (Hint: `break` might help with the early loop termination.) As the user enters each test average, add the average to a total variable and increment a counter variable (the loop's counter variable will work for the test count). As soon as the user enters five values or -99 (indicating that there are no more test scores), compute a floating-point average and print the result. Be sure that you congratulate the user for an average over 90%!

Extra Credit

25. Write a number-guessing game. Store an integer in a variable. Give the user five tries to guess the variable. If he guesses the variable's value, congratulate him. If he doesn't guess the value in five tries, print the value and stop the program.

26. Modify the program you wrote in question 25 so that the user gets as many tries as it takes to guess the number. Help the user by letting her know if her guess is less than or more than the hidden value. After she finally guesses the number, print the number of tries that it took her to guess the value.

12

Use C *for* Looping

control variable

count expression

for loop

nested loop

▶ **What You'll Learn About**

- ▶ The `for` loop's structure
- ▶ Further control with the `countExpression`
- ▶ Nested loops

C supports the `for` loop, a different kind of loop than the two `while` loops you learned about in Unit 11. The `for` loop requires that you learn the `for` statement. Like the `while` loops, the `for` loop is a multiline loop.

`for` loops give you different mechanisms for loop control. Whereas the `while` loops keep looping as long as a condition is true, you can specify exactly how many times you want a `for` loop to execute. There are many kinds of loops, such as counting loops, in which `for` works better than `while`.

▶ **The *for* Loop's Structure**

Concept   **What You Will Learn**

Learn the format of the `for` statement. A single `for` statement requires three values that control the loop.

The `for` statement makes `for` loops look rather difficult, but as you'll see, `for` loops aren't hard to understand. C's syntax requirements for the `for` statement are a little strange-looking, but C's never been known for being a verbose language. Here is the format of the `for` loop:

```
for (startExpression; conditional; countExpression)
  {
    // Block of one or more C statements
  }
```

When C encounters a `for` statement, it follows these steps to perform a loop:

1. Perform the `startExpression`, which is usually just an assignment statement.
2. Test the `conditional` expression for a true or false result.
3. Perform the body of the loop if the `conditional` is true.
4. Perform the `countExpression`, which usually is an increment or decrement operation.
5. Go back to step 2.

As soon as the `conditional` becomes false, C stops looping and the program continues at the statement following the `for` loop. As with `while`, never put a semicolon right after the `for` statement's parentheses. Semicolons are, however, required *inside* the parentheses. Until now, you've never seen semicolons inside a statement. The `for` loop is the only statement that requires such semicolon placement.

If the body of the `for` statement contains a single statement, the braces aren't required, but as with the `while` loops, braces are recommended even when the body contains only a single statement.

Tip You'll see that the semicolons inside the `for` statement aren't all that strange. Semicolons always terminate executable statements, and the *startExpression* and the *conditional* are individual statements inside `for`. The `for`'s two semicolons help separate the three statements inside the parentheses.

After reading through the action of `for` loops, you might feel as if they're just complicated `while` loops that are controlled by a *conditional* statement just as the `while` loops are. The `for` loop, however, is slightly different from either of the `while` loops, not only in its syntax, but also in the way that it updates its important loop control variable for you.

definition

A *control variable* is a variable controlled and changed automatically by the `for` loop.

Tip Can you see that indenting the body of the `for` loop, as you did with the `while` loops, makes the body of the loop stand out? You can tell at a glance where the loop body begins and ends.

Here is a sample `for` loop:

```
for (i = 1; i <= 10; i++)
  { printf("%d \n", i); }
```

When C gets to this `for` loop, it writes the following output to the screen:

```
1
2
3
4
5
6
7
8
9
10
```

C automatically updates the integer `i` each time the `for` loop executes. The body of this `for` loop executes exactly 10 times, hence the 10 lines in the output. Here are the parts of this `for` loop:

> *startExpression*: `i = 1`
>
> *conditional*: `i <= 10`
>
> *countExpression*: `i++`

Next are the five actions of the `for` loop applied to this specific loop. Follow the actions listed here and you'll see how C produced the numbers from 1 to 10:

1. Assigns 1 to the variable `i`. This two-line `for` loop assumes that you've already defined an integer variable named `i`. C executes this *startExpression* only once before the loop begins.

2. C tests the conditional, `i <= 10`, to see whether it's true or false. The first time C enters the loop, `i` is 1 (due to the assignment just made in step 1) and the *conditional* is true, so C executes the body of the loop.

UNIT

12

Use C *for* Looping

3. The statement inside the loop body executes, the first time printing a 1 for i.

4. The `countExpression` executes, adding 1 to i, storing a 2 in i.

5. C goes back to step 2, testing the `conditional` again and executing the body of the loop nine more times until i contains 11. At that point, C terminates the loop and the program continues.

Here is an equivalent `while` loop:

```
i = 1;
while (i <= 10)
  { printf("%d \n", i);
    i++;
  }
```

The `while` doesn't really require less typing than the equivalent `for`. The increment of i resides in the body of the `while` instead of in the loop's first statement as it does in the `for`. Also, the initial value of i must be set before C ever begins the `while` loop, whereas the first line of the `for` initializes i to its first value.

The biggest difference between `while` and `for` is that you can tell at a glance, in a single statement, how C controls `for`, whereas you must do more searching to find the controlling values of a `while` loop.

> *Note* The `for` loop is not a good loop to use for input validation, but the `while` loops are, as you discovered in Unit 11. `for` is better when you know in advance exactly how many times you want a loop to execute. In the previous `for` loop, the body of the loop executed exactly 10 times, with the expressions inside the `for` statement controlling the 10 executions.

Figure 12.1 helps show the action of the `for` loop. The line traces the loop's execution path. Notice that the `startExpression` executes only once. Also, the loop's test is at the top, similar to a `while` loop's (but not a `do-while` loop, which tests at the bottom of the loop), meaning that there is a chance that the body of the `for` loop might never execute.

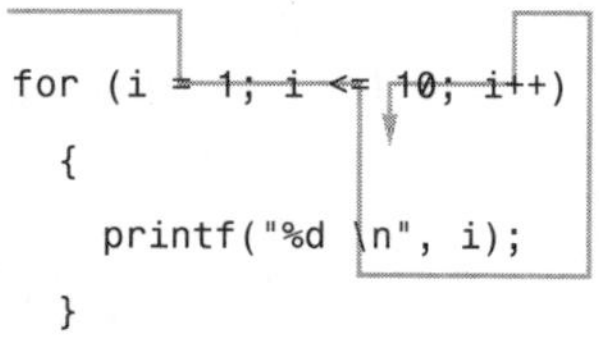

FIGURE 12.1.

The execution path of a for loop.

```
for (i = 1; i <= 10; i++)
  {
      printf("%d \n", i);
  }
```

If the `conditional` is false to begin with, as the following `for` statement's is, the body of the loop never executes:

```
for (i = 15; i <= 10; i++)   // The conditional is false from the start
  {
    printf("This printf never executes!!");
  }
```

When this loop first begins, C stores a 15 in i. The `conditional` test, i <= 10, is false, so C terminates the loop and continues the program right after the loop without ever executing the body of the loop.

STOP&TYPE Listing 12.1 contains a program that asks the user for five values, averages those values, and prints the average. A for loop ensures that the user is asked for the five values.

Review

What You Have Learned

The for loop initializes and increments control variables for you so that you can execute a loop a specific number of times.

▼ INPUT   LISTING 12.1. USING A for LOOP TO COMPUTE THE USER'S AVERAGE.

```
 1:  /* Filename: FORAVG.C */
 2:  // A for loop asks the user for five values.
 3:  // As the user enters each value, a compound
 4:  // assignment statement adds the values.
 5:  // After all five values have been entered and
 6:  // the loop ends, the program prints an average.
 7:  #include <stdio.h>
 8:  #include <conio.h>
 9:  main()
10:  {
11:    int count;    // The for loop's control variable
12:    float value, avg;
13:    float total = 0;
14:
15:    clrscr();
16:    printf("\n** An Average Program **\n\n");
17:
18:    // Loop five times
19:    for (count = 0; count < 5; count++)
20:      { printf("What is the next value? ");
21:        scanf(" %f", &value);
22:        total += value;    // Add to the total variable
23:      }
24:
25:    // Now, compute and print the average
26:    avg = total / 5.0;
27:    printf("\nThe average of your values is %.1f\n", avg);
28:    return 0;
29:  }
```

UNIT

12

Use C *for* Looping

▼ OUTPUT

```
** An Average Program **

What is the next value? 34.5
What is the next value? 65.4
What is the next value? 78.9
What is the next value? 76.5
What is the next value? 43.2

The average of your values is 59.7
```

▼ ANALYSIS

The for loop on line 19 is similar to many that you'll see. This loop iterates exactly five times, as controlled by the loop's control variable, count. count begins at 0, then continues incrementing each time through the loop until its value reaches 5. The *conditional* statement, count < 5, is then false and the loop terminates. Execution of the program then continues at line 26.

What if you wanted to average more than five values? You would have to change only two statements. You would have to change line 19's *conditional* statement to test for a value other than 5 and change the average calculation on line 26 because you could no longer divide by 5.

 Tip To make the program even easier to change and update, change line 26 to this:

```
avg = total / count;
```

To change the number of average values now, you only need to change the loop's *conditional* test. When line 19's for loop finishes, count always holds the number of values that the user entered. To make the program even more maintainable, don't even conditionally test against a numeric literal on line 19. Instead, define a named literal at the top of the program:

```
#define NUMBER 5
```

and make the for loop's *conditional* statement compare against the named literal:

```
for (count = 0; count < NUMBER; count++)
```

After you change the program as suggested here, you'll need to change only one line, the #define preprocessor directive, to make the program work with a different number of values.

▶ Further Control with the *countExpression*

Concept ▮ **What You Will Learn**

for loops don't have to increment. You can decrement the loop control variable as well as update the control variable with a value different from 1.

The third part of the for statement, the *countExpression* in parentheses, doesn't always have to increment the control variable. Inside the *countExpression*, you can decrement or update the control variable by any value your application requires. Consider the following for loop:

```
for (i = 10; i >= 1; i--)
  {
    printf("%d \n", i);
  }
printf("Blast off!\n");
```

Notice that the control variable i begins at 10, not 0 or 1 as has been the case previously. The conditional statement stays true as long as i remains greater than or equal to 1. The *countExpression* decrements i. Here is the output from this loop and the subsequent printf():

```
10
9
8
7
6
5
4
3
2
1
Blast off!
```

STOP&TYPE The program in Listing 12.2 prints the first 20 odd numbers, the first 20 even numbers, and the same values in reverse order. Four for loops are used to produce the four sets of output.

Review
What You Have Learned

By changing the for loop's control variable in various ways, you can produce different kinds of loop constructions.

▼ **INPUT   LISTING 12.2. USE FOUR** for **LOOPS TO PRINT DIFFERENT NUMBER SEQUENCES.**

```
1:  /* Filename: SEQUENCS.C */
2:  // Prints the first 20 odd, then even, numbers.
3:  // Once done, it prints them in reverse order.
4:  #include <stdio.h>
5:  #include <conio.h>
6:  main()
7:  {
8:    int num;   // The for loop control variable
9:    clrscr();
10:
11:    printf("The first 20 odd numbers:\n");
12:    for (num = 1; num < 40; num += 2)
13:      { printf("%d ", num); }
14:
15:    printf("\n\nThe first 20 even numbers:\n");
16:    for (num = 2; num <= 40; num += 2)
17:      { printf("%d ", num); }
```

UNIT

12

Use C for Looping

```
18:
19:     printf("\n\nThe first 20 odd numbers in reverse:\n");
20:     for (num = 39; num >= 1; num -= 2)
21:       { printf("%d ", num); }
22:
23:     printf("\n\nThe first 20 even numbers in reverse:\n");
24:     for (num = 40; num >= 2; num -= 2)
25:       { printf("%d ", num); }
26:
27:     return 0;
28:  }
```

▼ **OUTPUT**

```
The first 20 odd numbers:
1 3 5 7 9 11 13 15 17 19 21 23 25 27 29 31 33 35 37 39

The first 20 even numbers:
2 4 6 8 10 12 14 16 18 20 22 24 26 28 30 32 34 36 38 40

The first 20 odd numbers in reverse:
39 37 35 33 31 29 27 25 23 21 19 17 15 13 11 9 7 5 3 1

The first 20 even numbers in reverse:
40 38 36 34 32 30 28 26 24 22 20 18 16 14 12 10 8 6 4 2
```

▼ **ANALYSIS**

The four `for` loops demonstrate how the expressions inside the `for`'s parentheses can differ, starting at different values, testing different conditional expressions, and changing the control variables in different ways.

Coding such loops using the `while` statement is a lot trickier because you have to be sure to include the control variable's changing code yourself at the right place inside the loop body. Also, you must be sure to initialize the control variables properly. The `for` loop is a compact way to initialize, test, and control a loop in a single statement.

One interesting thing to note is that the `for` loop's parentheses don't have to hold all three expressions. For example, instead of this:

```
for (num = 2; num <= 40; num += 2)
```

you can do this:

```
num = 2;
for ( ; num <= 40; )
   {   // Body of loop goes here
     num += 2;   // Increment the control variable in the loop
   }
```

Taking the expressions out of the `for` statement is sometimes warranted, especially when the user initializes the control variable's starting value with `scanf()` instead of your program initializing the value with an assignment statement. Nevertheless, for most uses of `for` loops, place all three expressions inside the `for` parentheses so that all control information is available at a glance in one statement.

▶ Nested Loops

Concept
What You Will Learn

When you nest `for` loops, one loop can control another, amplifying the power of `for` loops.

Whenever you need to repeat a loop several times, put the loop inside another loop. You learned about nested loops in Unit 11. Many newcomers to programming often find nested `for` loops to be a little tricky, but there is really nothing to them.

Perhaps an analogy to the real world would help introduce the concept of nested `for` loops. Your car's odometer is little more than five or six nested `for` loops, each going from 0 to 9. The far-right number iterates the fastest, visibly moving from 0 to 9 as you drive down the road. A `for` loop that tracked the far-right number would be nothing more than this:

```
for (tenth = 0; tenth <= 9; tenth++)
  { printf("%d \n", tenth); }
```

The far-right number (either a tenth-of-a-mile indicator or a tenth-of-a-kilometer indicator, depending on your country) isn't the only number that moves. All the others do so, but at a slower rate. For every 10 values that move in the tenth-of-a-mile indicator, one of the mile indicators moves. In other words, a nested loop that looks something like this controls the two far-right numbers:

```
for (miles = 0; miles <= 9; miles++)
  {
    for (tenth = 0; tenth <= 9; tenth++)
      { printf("%d%d \n", miles, tenth); }
  }
```

What about the number third from the right? The tens indicator telling you how many tens of miles you've traveled is yet another loop that iterates once for each of the miles iterations, like this:

```
for (tens = 0; tens <= 9; tens++)
  {
    for (miles = 0; miles <= 9; miles++)
      {
        for (tenth = 0; tenth <= 9; tenth++)
          { printf("%d%d%d \n", tens, miles, tenth); }
      }
  }
```

However many digits your odometer contains is the number of nested loops required to imitate the odometer.

Note When you nest `for` loops, the outside loop always loops slower than the inside loops, just as the far-right digits of your odometer change faster than the far-left ones. The outer loop changes only after the inner loop completely finishes.

Figure 12.2 shows how you can picture inside and outside loops. The nested loop at the bottom actually contains two separate `for` loops nested inside an outer loop. Both of the two nested loops completely finish their respective iterations before the outside loop iterates again. When the outside loop changes, the two inner loops start from the beginning to loop again.

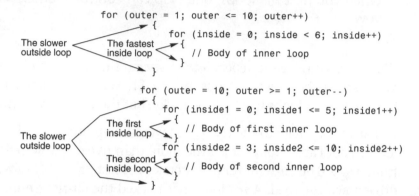

FIGURE 12.2.
Two kinds of nested loops.

STOP&TYPE The program in Listing 12.3 contains two nested loops.

Review
What You Have Learned

Embedding one loop in another produces a nested loop. Nested loops let you execute a loop more than once (a loop of loops).

▼ INPUT   LISTING 12.3. TWO NESTED LOOPS.

```
 1:  /* Filename: NESTFOR.C */
 2:  // Two nested loops
 3:  #include <stdio.h>
 4:  #include <conio.h>
 5:  main()
 6:  {
 7:    int inner, outer;
 8:    clrscr();
 9:
10:    // One loop nested in another
11:    printf("Showing the loop control variables:\n");
12:    printf("Outer    Inner\n");
13:    for (outer = 0; outer < 2; outer++)
14:      { for (inner = 0; inner <= 3; inner++)
15:        { printf("%d\t%d\n", outer, inner); }
16:      }
17:
18:    printf("\n");    // Blank line between loop outputs
19:
20:    printf("Here is a loop from 1 to 10, printed three times:\n");
21:    for (outer = 0; outer < 3; outer++)
22:      { for (inner = 1; inner <= 10; inner++)
23:        { printf("%d ", inner); }
24:        printf("\n");    // Executes once each outer iteration
25:      }
```

```
26:
27:     return 0;
28: }
```

▼ OUTPUT

```
Showing the loop control variables:
Outer   Inner
0       0
0       1
0       2
0       3
1       0
1       1
1       2
1       3

Here is a loop from 1 to 10, printed three times:
1 2 3 4 5 6 7 8 9 10
1 2 3 4 5 6 7 8 9 10
1 2 3 4 5 6 7 8 9 10
```

▼ ANALYSIS

By seeing printed loop control variable values in line 15, you can see how the outer loop variable changes (from 0 to 1) more slowly than the inner loop variable changes (from 0 to 3). The reason that the inner loop changes more rapidly is that the inner loop always completes all its iterations before the outer loop has a chance to iterate again.

The second half of the output shows the values from 1 to 10 being printed. A simple `for` loop in lines 22 through 25 controls the numbers. However, to print that set of 10 numbers three times, an additional outer loop that iterates three times appears, beginning on line 21.

 Tip A clock for football makes a useful analogy for nested loops. The quarter clock moves from 15 minutes down to zero. That countdown happens once each quarter. The quarter count from 1 to 4 increments much more slowly than the minute count within each quarter.

UNIT
12
Use C *for* Looping

► Homework

General Knowledge

1. Which is better for looping a specific number of times: a `while` loop, a `for` loop, or a `do-while` loop?
2. How does a `for` loop differ from a `while` loop?
3. How does the format of a `for` loop help you spot the entire control of the loop in a single statement?
4. When are braces required around a `for` loop's body?
5. What happens when the conditional expression in a `for` loop becomes false?

6. Does the outer loop of two nested loops iterate faster or slower than the inner loop? Why?

7. Which variable controls the inner loop and which controls the outer loop in the following code?

```
for (ctr1 = 10; ctr1 > 5; ctr1--)
  { for (ctr2 = 1; ctr2 < 4; ctr2++)
      { printf("%d  %d", ctr2, ctr2); }
  }
```

8. True or false: A for loop's body might never execute.

9. True or false: The semicolons inside the for loop are optional.

10. True or false: The countExpression portion of the for loop can increment only the loop's control variable.

11. True or false: It's better to use a for loop than a while loop when you know in advance exactly how many iterations a loop requires.

12. True or false: C tests the for's condition before the first iteration of the loop.

What's the Output?

13. What's the output of the following section of code?

```
for (c = 0; c <= 10; c += 3)
  { printf("%d", c); }
```

14. What's the output of the following for loop? Will an error occur?

```
for (i = 5; i; i--)
  { printf("%d \n", i);
  }
```

15. How many times will an x appear in the following nested for loop?

```
for (outer = 0; outer < 5; outer++)
  { for (inner = 0; inner < 3; inner++)
      { printf("X"); }
  }
```

Find the Bug

16. Foster Forsythe is nesting for loops, but they don't seem to be working properly. Will you please help him? Here is the part of the program giving him trouble:

```
for (ctr1 = 1; ctr1 <= 10; ctr1++);
  { for (ctr2 = 1; ctr2 <= 5; ctr2++)
      { value = ctr1 * ctr2;
        printf("%d\n", value);
      }
  }
```

17. Why does Hello not print even once?

```
for (i = 0; i > 10; i++)
  { printf("Hello"); }
```

Write Code That...

18. Change the program FORAVG.C in Listing 12.1 to reflect the suggestions in the tip at the end of the program's analysis.

19. Change the program you completed in question 18. Instead of using a `#define`, ask the user how many values he or she wants to average and make the program work with that value instead of one you define.

20. Use a `for` loop to print the letters of the alphabet in uppercase. To do this, use a character variable, initialize it (within the `for`) with `'A'`, and increment it using `++`. Although applying `++` to a character variable might seem wrong, remember that because C maintains a close relationship between character variables and integer variables, you can interchange simple operations between them.

Extra Credit

21. Write a program with two nested loops that produces the following output:

```
ABCD
ABC
AB
A
```

22. Write a program that asks the user for five values, then prints the average of those five values three times. In other words, write an outer loop that iterates three times and an inner loop that requests and averages the five values.

Looping Back and Forth

STOP&TYPE In this lesson, you learned about C's looping capabilities. You saw the following:

▶ Loops repeat sections of code.

▶ The `while` loop tests a condition at the top of the loop and loops as long as the condition is true.

▶ Loops and the `if` statement differ because the body of an `if` executes one time at most.

Project 6 Listing. Using a `for` loop to compute interest controlled by the user's input.

```
1:   /* Filename: LESSON6.C */

2:   // Computes interest over a number of periods

3:   #include <stdio.h>

4:   #include <conio.h>

5:   main()

6:   {

7:      int periods;      // Number of periods in the loan

8:      int count;        // Loop control variable

9:      float intRate;    // Interest rate per period

10:     float principal;  // Loan amount

11:

12:     clrscr();         // Erase the screen

13:

14:     printf("Welcome to loan central!\n");   // Title

15:     printf("-----------------------\n\n");
```

▶ The do-while loop tests its condition at the bottom of the loop, ensuring that the loop always executes at least once.

▶ The break statement terminates the current loop.

▶ The for loop gives you more control when you know in advance the number of iterations required by the loop.

▶ When you nest loops, the inner loop iterates faster than the outer loop.

Description

1: A C comment that includes the program's filename.

2: A C++ comment that contains the program's description.

3: The printf() and scanf() functions need information in the STDIO.H header file.

4: The screen-clearing function, clrscr(), needs information in the CONIO.H header file.

5: All functions have names, and the first function in all C programs is main().

6: All functions begin with a left brace.

7: Defines an integer variable that will hold the number of periods in the loan.

8: Defines an integer variable that will control the for loop.

9: Defines a floating-point variable that will hold the interest rate.

10: Defines a floating-point variable that will hold the loan principal (the amount borrowed).

11: Extra blank lines make your program more readable.

12: Erases the output screen so that it's blank before the user is prompted with a question.

13: Extra blank lines make your program more readable.

14: Prints a title.

15: Underlines the title on-screen with hyphens.

1: You saw another version of this program in Unit 7, but that program didn't have the looping capability that this program does. As a result, Unit 7's program was longer and less flexible!

8: All for loops require a loop control variable.

continues

Project 6 Listing. continued

```
16:
17:    printf("How much was the loan for? ");
18:    scanf(" %f", &principal);
19:
20:    printf("\nWhat is the interest rate (i.e., .03 ");
21:    printf("for 3%) per period? ");
22:    scanf(" %f", &intRate);
23:
24:    printf("\nHow many periods are in the loan? ");
25:    scanf(" %d", &periods);
26:
27:    for (count = 0; count < periods; count++)
28:      { principal *= (1 + intRate); }   // Compounds the interest
29:
30:    printf("\n$%.2f total amount owed after %d periods.\n",
31:         principal, periods);
32:    return 0;
33:  }
```

Description

16: Extra blank lines make your program more readable.

17: Prompts the user for the amount of the loan (the principal).

18: Gets the principal from the user.

19: Extra blank lines make your program more readable.

20: Prompts for the interest rate. The user is reminded to enter the interest as a decimal.

21: A second `printf()` continues line 20's long `printf()` message.

22: Gets the interest rate.

23: Extra blank lines make your program more readable.

24: Prompts for the number of periods in the loan (called the loan *term*).

25: Gets the term from the user.

26: Extra blank lines make your program more readable.

27: The `for` loop will ensure that the interest calculation computes for the full term entered by the user in line 25.

27: The `for` loop compounds the loan in one step.

28: The body of the `for` loop is only a single statement. The principal increases by the amount of each period's interest rate.

29: Extra blank lines make your program more readable.

30: Prints the computed loan principal, including all accrued interest.

31: Continues the loan balance's printing.

32: Returns to Turbo C++'s IDE.

33: `main()`'s closing brace to terminate the program.

▼ OUTPUT

```
Welcome to loan central!
------------------------

How much was the loan for? 2500.00

What is the interest rate (i.e., .03 for 3%) per period? .11

How many periods are in the loan? 5

$4212.65 total amount owed after 5 periods.
```

Lesson ▶

Taking Charge

Unit 13: Controlling Loops and Branching

Unit 14: Power with *switch*

Lesson 7 Project

Lesson 7

Unit ▶

13

Controlling Loops and Branching

break

continue

goto

spaghetti code

▶ **What You'll Learn About**

- ▶ Terminating `for` early
- ▶ `continue` as opposed to `break`
- ▶ Moving around with `goto`

This unit offers a variation on a theme. You'll see how to use the `break` statement to make an early exit from a `for` loop. With a new command, `continue`, you'll also learn about the opposite of `break`. The `continue` statement tells C to continue with a loop a little earlier than it normally would iterate the loop.

In addition to the looping control that you've mastered, C also includes another command named `goto`. There is much debate about the merits of `goto`, but many veteran C programmers agree that `goto` isn't useful when it's overused. Whether `goto` is good or bad, you need to know how to code `goto` statements in case you run across them someday.

▶ **Terminating *for* Early**

Concept   **What You Will Learn**

The `break` statement forces an early exit from a `for` loop.

In Unit 12, you saw how the `for` statement controls loops a specific number of times via the loop's control variable. The `for` statement does a lot for you. It initializes the control variable, tests the condition, and updates the control variable each time through the loop. You often use the `for` loop when you want a loop to execute a specific number of times. Depending on the data or the user's input, however, your program might have to terminate the `for` loop a little early. Using `break` inside an `if` statement gives you that early termination.

Although the following `for` loop appears to execute 10 times, the first iteration doesn't even complete due to the `break`:

```
for (i = 0; i < 10; i++)
  { break;    // Tell C to ignore the remaining iterations
    printf("%d \n", i);
  }
```

`break` terminates `for` loops in the same manner that it terminates `while` loops (see Lesson 6 for details). When you write nested `for` loops, a `break` statement terminates only the loop it resides in, not any surrounding outer loops. In other words, `break` forces C to break out of the *current* loop, reentering the body of the next-outermost loop:

```
for (out = 0; out < 10; out++)
  { for (in = 0; in < 5; in++)
      { if ((in * out) % 2)
          { break; }    // Terminate inner loop if product is even
        printf("%c", '\x07');    // Ring the PC's bell
      }
  }
```

When the product of the inner loop control variable, in, and the outer loop control variable, out, is an even number, the break statement doesn't force C to terminate *both* loops because break terminates only the current loop. Because the break resides in the innermost loop, the innermost loop is the one that terminates as a result of the break. Figure 13.1 shows how the break works.

FIGURE 13.1.
Breaking out of the current loop.

```
for (out = 0; out < 10; out++)
  { for (in = 0; in < 5; in++)
      { if ((in * out) % 2)
          { break; } ——————————— Terminates the inner
          printf("%c", '\x07');  // Ring the bell    loop and performs
      }                                               another outer loop
  }                                                   iteration
```

STOP&TYPE Listing 13.1 contains a simple program that asks the user for his or her dog's name. The program then prints the name 10 times. The user can terminate the loop early by triggering the break.

Review   **What You Have Learned**

break causes the current loop to quit early.

▼ INPUT   LISTING 13.1. USING break IF THE USER WANTS TO QUIT THE LOOP EARLY.

```
1:  /* Filename: FORBREAK.C */
2:  // Prints a dog's name 10 times
3:  // (or less if the user dictates)
4:  #include <stdio.h>
5:  #include <conio.h>
6:  main()
7:  {
8:    char ans;         // Will hold a Y or N answer
9:    int count;        // The loop control variable
10:   char dName[25];   // Will hold the dog's name
11:
12:   clrscr();
13:
14:   printf("What is your dog's name? ");
15:   scanf(" %s", dName);
16:
17:   printf("I'll now print the name ten times (maybe)...\n");
18:
19:   for (count = 0; count < 10; count++)
20:     { printf("%s\n", dName);
21:       printf("Do you want to see the name again (Y/N)? ");
22:       scanf(" %c", &ans);
23:       if ((ans == 'N') || (ans == 'n'))
24:         { break; }   // Terminate early
25:     }   // Iterate again if not broken out of the loop
26:
27:   printf("That's a nice dog!");
28:   return 0;
29: }
```

▼ OUTPUT

```
What is your dog's name? Luke
I'll now print the name ten times (maybe)...
Luke
Do you want to see the name again (Y/N)? Y
Luke
Do you want to see the name again (Y/N)? Y
Luke
Do you want to see the name again (Y/N)? Y
Luke
Do you want to see the name again (Y/N)? N
That's a nice dog!
```

▼ ANALYSIS

This program is fairly simple. It asks the user for his or her dog's name in lines 14 and 15. Due to scanf()'s limitations, make sure that you enter only a single name and not a name such as Bow Wow.

Tip   Lesson 8 shows you how to get more than one word at a time from the user.

As soon as the user enters the dog's name, the program loops 10 times, with the loop control variable count moving from 0 to 9 before the for loop terminates. Line 19 controls the loop. Inside the loop, however, a question on line 21 asks the user if he or she wants to see the name again. If the user tires of seeing the dog's name before the 10 iterations print, the break on line 24 terminates the loop early and the program ends.

▶ *continue* as Opposed to *break*

Concept   **What You Will Learn**

The continue statement tells C to iterate once again, even if the body of the loop hasn't completed.

C contains a continue statement that performs a job virtually the opposite of the break statement. Whereas break terminates a loop early, continue causes an immediate and new iteration of the current loop.

Here's a simple example. In the following code fragment, the loop iterates only once due to the break statement, and the second printf() never executes:

```
for (i = 0; i < 5; i++)   // Seems to loop five times
  { printf("Adam \n");
    break;
    printf("Eve \n");    // Never executes
  }
```

The next code fragment contains the same code, except a continue statement replaces the break. Of the two printf() function calls, only the first one prints. Unlike the preceding code fragment, however, the continue keeps the loop iterating through all its cycles, unlike break, which tells C to forget the rest of the iterations:

```
for (i = 0; i < 5; i++)    // Does loop five times
  { printf("Adam \n");
    continue;
    printf("Eve \n");     // Never executes
  }
```

This second code fragment prints Adam five times, but Eve never prints. The continue tells C to iterate the loop once again. Of course, on the loop's final iteration (when i is 4), the continue causes the loop to iterate once again, but the loop doesn't iterate because the control variable is *used up,* or past its final value. Figure 13.2 shows the difference between break and continue using these code fragments.

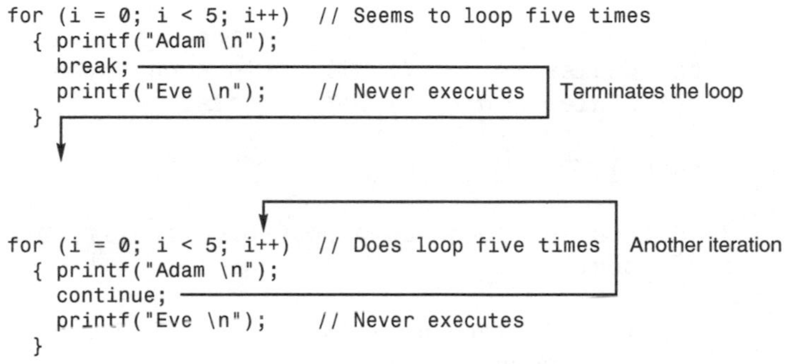

```
for (i = 0; i < 5; i++)  // Seems to loop five times
  { printf("Adam \n");
    break;
    printf("Eve \n");      // Never executes    Terminates the loop
  }
```

FIGURE 13.2.
continue iterates the
loop once again, unlike
break.

```
for (i = 0; i < 5; i++)  // Does loop five times    Another iteration
  { printf("Adam \n");
    continue;
    printf("Eve \n");      // Never executes
  }
```

> *Note* You also can use continue on while loops, just as you can with break, but continue is more often used inside for loops.

There might be times when the body of your loop processes data (through calculations and I/O) and, depending on the values of the data, you don't want to process each data value completely. An early continue statement can make sure that the second part of the loop's body doesn't always execute for every data value.

> *Warning* If you place a break or continue outside an if body, Turbo C++ displays a warning message telling you that there is unused code in your program if any code follows the break or continue. Therefore, programs you compile with loops such as the ones the previous code fragments contain result in compiler warnings because Turbo C++ knows that the second printf() never executes. If, however, you place the break or continue statement inside an if's body, Turbo C++ doesn't display the warnings because the break and continue will change the loop's execution only when the if's conditional is true.

> *Note* As with break, if you place a continue inside a nested loop, the continue executes another iteration of the current innermost loop, not the outer loop.

STOP&TYPE Listing 13.2 contains a program that asks the user for five values that represent each day's sales. A for loop ensures that only five values are asked for. As the user enters the five values, the body of the for loop totals the sales for the week. Not all weeks will have five days' worth of sales, however. If the week had a holiday, the user should enter -99 for that day's sales, which triggers the continue statement.

Review

continue forces an early iteration of the loop.

▼ INPUT   LISTING 13.2. continue LETS THE PROGRAM CONTROL THE EXECUTION OF THE SECOND PART OF A LOOP.

```
 1:  /* Filename: CONTINUE.C */
 2:  // Uses continue when data is missing
 3:  #include <stdio.h>
 4:  #include <conio.h>
 5:  main()
 6:  {
 7:    int count;          // Loop control variable
 8:    float dSales;       // Will hold each day's sales
 9:    float wSales = 0;   // Weekly total
10:
11:    clrscr();
12:
13:    // Set up the loop for a possible five iterations
14:    for (count = 0; count < 5; count++)
15:      {
16:        printf("Enter the sales for day #%d (-99 for none): ",
17:               count + 1);
18:        scanf(" %f", &dSales);
19:        if (dSales < 0.0)
20:          { continue; }
21:
22:        // The following statement executes ONLY if a
23:        // valid daily sales total was just entered
24:        wSales += dSales;
25:      }
26:
27:    // Print the week's total
28:    printf("\nThe weekly total is $%.2f\n", wSales);
29:    return 0;
30:  }
```

▼ OUTPUT

```
Enter the sales for day #1 (-99 to none): 546.77
Enter the sales for day #2 (-99 to none): -99
Enter the sales for day #3 (-99 to none): 434.56
Enter the sales for day #4 (-99 to none): 886.31
Enter the sales for day #5 (-99 to none): 905.42

The weekly total is $2773.06
```

▼ ANALYSIS

This program's continue statement lets the for loop process very intelligently. The for loop in lines 14 through 25 normally will execute five times due to the loop control. Each iteration represents a day of the week. The user is to enter each day's sales value when prompted by the printf() in lines 16 and 17.

Line 17 adds 1 to `count` when printing the prompt for each day's sales because line 14's `for` loop begins at 0, not 1. If, however, there is no sales figure for the user to enter (as would be the case for holidays), the user enters `-99` and the loop iterates again, getting another value.

As soon as the user enters all the values for the week, the program prints the total weekly sales value on line 28.

▶ **Moving Around with** *goto*

Concept   **What You Will Learn**

`goto` lets your program execute in any order you desire.

Many C programmers write all kinds of C programs and never use the `goto` statement. Some programming languages, especially FORTRAN and the pre-QBasic BASIC languages, don't have enough rich control commands such as `while` and `do-while` to eliminate `goto` entirely.

Note   In today's world of modern programming languages, `goto` is rarely used, except when a programmer writes programs in low-level assembly language where `goto`-like statements are mandatory for many operations.

C includes a `goto` just in case you need one. Before studying `goto`, keep in mind that you can write any program without `goto`. Use `goto` only when its meaning is obvious, and don't overdo your use of it. `goto` branches the current program's execution to a different part of the program. In other words, instead of executing a program sequentially, line by line, `goto` tells C what line of your program to execute next.

definition

A branch occurs when one section of a program triggers the execution of a different section.

goto **AND MAINTAINABILITY**

If you put too many `goto` statements in your programs, you will soon find that your programs are virtually impossible to follow. Until you learn about `goto`, all your programs execute in one of two ways:

▶ Sequentially, line-by-line

▶ In a loop, with one or more statements repeating until a condition becomes false

Both of these execution orders are easy to follow, especially if you indent the bodies of your loops. It's very easy to spot where a loop begins and ends. If your program doesn't contain a loop, but instead executes sequentially from top to bottom, it's even easier to follow.

Once you insert `goto` statements in a program, the program's execution is at the mercy of the `goto` statements. The execution might jump from one part of the program to another and do so several times. It's too easy to stick a `goto` in code instead of writing a loop or thinking through the logic to make the program easier to follow. Use `goto` judiciously and sparingly. If you can get by without ever using it, your programs will be better as a result, not worse.

Here is the format of the `goto` statement:

```
goto statementLabel;
```

`statementLabel` follows the same naming rules that variables follow (see Lesson 2 for a review of variable-naming conventions). Here is a sample `goto`:

```
goto getInput;
```

When C encounters this `goto`, it looks, from the top of the current function to the bottom, for a statement label named `getInput`. If C doesn't find a statement label named `getInput`, you get an error message.

A statement label always appears to the left of an executable C statement. For example, all of the following statements have statement labels in front of them:

```
getInput: scanf(" %d", &amount);

here: for (i = 0; i < 10; i++)

Bell: printf("\a");   // Ring the PC's bell
```

Notice that a colon (:) always separates a statement from its label.

 Warning Never put a colon after the label's name in a `goto` statement. Use a colon only after the label name when the label appears before code, as shown in the preceding three statements.

Without the colon, C would be confused by a label right before a legal C statement. The colon tells C, "Here is a label, and it appears before a statement." Never put more than one label with the same name in the same function. Although there can be many `goto` statements that transfer control to the same label, there can never be more than one occurrence of the same label in the same function.

You can name a statement label anything you like, but as with variable names, make up statement labels that give some clue as to the purpose of the statement to the right of the label. In other words, if you must put a label to the left of a payroll computation, because another part of the function will branch to the computation, `payCalc:` is a much better name than `opopop:`. Even though both names work as statement labels, the first is much clearer as to the purpose of the label.

 Tip Start labels in the first column even though other statements within the function are indented. The label will be easier for you to find when you maintain the program.

When C encounters a goto statement, it doesn't continue executing the program on the line following the goto. Instead, C transfers control (*branches*) to the statement label and then continues from there. Unlike loops that always repeat again at the top of the loop, a goto might never come back to its point of origin.

In the following code, a goto skips some code if the user's value is bad:

```
  printf("What is your age? ");
  scanf(" %d", &age);
  if (age < 3)
    { printf("Sure you are %d years old!\n", age);
      goto done;
    }
  dogAge = age / 7;
  printf("In dog years, you are %d\n", dogAge);
done: return 0;
```

If you like, you can place statement labels on lines by themselves. When C encounters a goto to that label, it starts execution on the next executable line following the label. Here is a code fragment identical to the one you just saw, except that the label done: appears on a line by itself to help you find it more easily:

```
printf("What is your age? ");
  scanf(" %d", &age);
  if (age < 3)
    { printf("Sure you are %d years old!\n", age);
      goto done;
    }
  dogAge = age / 7;
  printf("In dog years, you are %d\n", dogAge);
done:
  return 0;
```

Figure 13.3 shows how C interprets the previous code's goto when the if is true.

FIGURE 13.3.
The goto changes the program's order.

Skips the calculation if the user entered a bad value

```
            printf("What is your age? ");
              scanf(" %d", &age);
              if (age < 3)
                { printf("Sure you are %d years old!\n", age);
                  goto done;
                }
              dogAge = age / 7;
              printf("In dog years, you are %d\n", dogAge);
            done:
              return 0;
```

Instead of ignoring the calculation and returning, the programmer of the preceding code fragment should set up a loop and keep asking the user for a value until he or she enters an age value within an expected range (more than three years old). Sometimes, such as when you retrieve data from a disk file, you can't keep asking a user to try again because there is no user. The use of goto would be more justified in such a case.

 Warning A goto can branch only to a label inside the current function. When you begin writing multifunction programs (in Lesson 8), one function can't branch to another using goto.

Watch out for infinite loops! The following statement goes on forever (well, until you press Ctrl-Break):

```
here:  goto here;   // Loop forever
```

Tip break is often considered a much better loop exit than goto. break never sends program execution very far from its location. goto might transfer program execution to 50 lines later in the code and not simply to the bottom of a loop, making the code harder to follow and understand.

STOP&TYPE Listing 13.3 contains an *awful* program. All of its gotos get very confusing. See if you can predict the output before looking at the results that follow the listing.

Review   **What You Have Learned**

The goto statement transfers control to any other part of the current function.

▼ INPUT LISTING 13.3. USING goto TO PRINT MESSAGES.

```
 1:  /* Filename: GOTO.C */
 2:  // Uses goto to print messages in a strange order
 3:  #include <stdio.h>
 4:  #include <conio.h>
 5:  main()
 6:  {
 7:    clrscr();
 8:
 9:    goto Larry;
10:  Final:
11:    printf("What a stooge of a program!\n");
12:    goto EndIt;
13:
14:  Moe:
15:    printf("Moe is here!\n");
16:    goto Curly;
17:
18:  Larry:
19:    printf("Larry is here!\n");
20:    goto Moe;
21:
22:  Curly:
23:    printf("Curly is here!\n");
24:    goto Final;
25:
26:  EndIt:
27:    return 0;
28:  }
```

▼ OUTPUT

```
Larry is here!
Moe is here!
Curly is here!
What a stooge of a program!
```

▼ ANALYSIS

This program is a can of worms! Follow the logic: The program begins, as usual, with `main()`, then clears the screen in line 7. Immediately, line 9's `goto` transfers control to line 18, the location of the `Larry:` label. Once a program transfers control to a label, the execution then begins at that label and continues sequentially. Therefore, line 19's `printf()` executes and another `goto` sends control to line 14, the location of the `Moe:` label. Line 15's `printf()` executes, only to branch once again to line 22's `Curly:` label, where yet another `printf()` prints its message on line 23. Line 24 sends control to line 10's `Final:` label, where a final `printf()` executes before line 26's `EndIt:` label sees the conclusion of the program at line 27's `return` statement.

Note Just because Listing 13.3 used initial uppercase letters for the labels doesn't mean that you have to. As mentioned earlier in this unit, labels follow the same naming rules as variable names.

Figure 13.4 shows you the branching done in this program. Wow! Now you can see why programmers say that too many `goto` statements produce *spaghetti code!* This might seem like an extreme overuse of `goto`s (and it is), but over time, people who use `goto`s too frequently produce code that is even more difficult to decipher than this program.

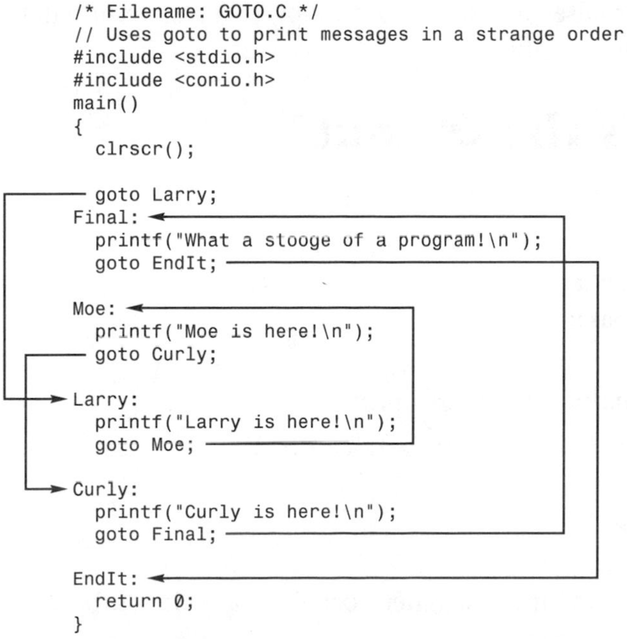

```
/* Filename: GOTO.C */
// Uses goto to print messages in a strange order
#include <stdio.h>
#include <conio.h>
main()
{
  clrscr();

  goto Larry;
Final:
  printf("What a stooge of a program!\n");
  goto EndIt;

Moe:
  printf("Moe is here!\n");
  goto Curly;

Larry:
  printf("Larry is here!\n");
  goto Moe;

Curly:
  printf("Curly is here!\n");
  goto Final;

EndIt:
  return 0;
}
```

FIGURE 13.4.

Making maintenance virtually impossible with a few `goto`s.

▶ Homework

General Knowledge

1. How can you terminate a `for` loop early?

2. How can your program force an early execution of the loop's next cycle?

3. What's the difference between `break` and `continue`?

4. Will `break` and `continue` work for `while`, `do-while`, and `for` loops?

5. Which kind of loop—`while`, `do-while`, or `for`—is usually the one that uses `continue`?

6. Why does `continue` rarely appear without an `if` preceding it?

7. What does `goto` do?

8. What is meant by a program branch?

9. Why is `goto` considered a bad programming statement?

10. What is spaghetti code?

11. True or false: There can be more than one label with the same name, but only one `goto` to that label.

12. True or false: You can't use `continue` in nested loops.

13. True or false: You can't use `break` in nested loops.

14. True or false: Turbo C++ displays a warning message when you compile a program that has a `break` or `continue`.

15. True or false: When you nest loops, `continue` terminates the execution of the inner loop only.

What's the Output?

16. How many times does X print?

```
for (count = 0; count < 5; count++)
  { printf("X");
    break;
  }
```

17. How many times does X print?

```
for (count = 0; count < 5; count++)
  { printf("X");
    continue;
  }
```

18. Here's some more spaghetti code! What's the output?

```
#include <stdio.h>
main()
{
  goto a;
e:
```

```
    goto f;
  c:
    printf("a\n");
    goto d;
  b:
    printf("d\n");
    goto c;
  d:
    printf("c\n");
    goto b;
  a:
    printf("b\n");
    goto e;
  f:
    return 0;
  }
```

Find the Bug

19. Mary Jo Beth can't get her program working. It seems to be hung up on this statement:

```
goto calcPayroll:
```

Help Mary fix the problem.

20. The following three lines appear together in a program. Although there is nothing technically wrong with the statements, something is unnecessary. What is unnecessary and why?

```
  scanf(" %f", &rate);
  goto here;
here: pay = rate * hours;
```

21. When Pete's program gets to the following statement, it seems to hang up. Pete has studied the code for several hours without figuring out the problem. Tell him what he's doing wrong (and why he should consider a different career).

```
makeLoop: goto makeLoop;   // Transfer control
```

Write Code That...

22. Rewrite the following code using a do-while statement:

```
AskAgain:
  printf("What is your first name? ");
  scanf(" %s", fName);
  if ((fName[0] < 'A') || (fName[0] > 'Z'))
    { goto AskAgain; }   // Make sure user enters a word
                         // and not special characters
```

23. Write a program that asks the user for four weekly sales values. Add to a sales total as the user enters a new value and print the total sales after the user enters all four values. Just in case the store closes for repairs one week, see if the user enters a negative value for a sales figure. If so, terminate the sales entry early and average however many weeks the user actually entered.

24. Rewrite Listing 13.2 (CONTINUE.C) so that the loop terminates completely when the user enters -1 for a daily sales figure. The loop will now have both a break and a continue, and the weekly total will update only if neither the break nor the continue executes. Don't check for an exact match for -1 or -99 because the user enters the daily values as floating-point numbers and you can't accurately test for floating-point equality.

Extra Credit

25. Write a program that asks the user for temperature readings for the last 10 days. Compute the average temperature. If the user enters a temperature below freezing, make sure that a continue causes the program to ignore the reading (average in only temperatures above freezing). Keep track of how many above-freezing temperatures the user enters (via a counter variable) and compute the average based on the number of valid values entered.

Unit ▶ 14

Power with *switch*

case

default

menu

switch

▶ # What You'll Learn About

- ▶ Multiple choice with nested `ifs`
- ▶ Making the `switch`
- ▶ `break` up that `switch`
- ▶ Using `switch` for menus

This unit teaches you about the `switch` statement. The `switch` statement is useful for selecting from among many different actions. You've already learned about these two ways that your C program can choose between different courses of action:

- ▶ The `if-else` statement
- ▶ The `?:` conditional operator

The conditional is just an efficient shortcut for implementing simple `if-else` logic. Both the `if-else` statement and the conditional operator are perfect for choosing from between two courses of action, but there are times when your program must select from more than two alternative courses. The `switch` statement provides you with an easy way to set up multiple-choice selection logic from within your program.

▶ # Multiple Choice with Nested *ifs*

Concept   **What You Will Learn**

You can nest `if-else` statements to perform multiple-choice actions.

You'll better understand the advantages of the `switch` statement if you first see how to implement `switch` logic using the `if-else` statement that you already know. Until now, you learned how the `if-else` statement selects from between two courses of actions. Surprisingly, the majority of the time, your programs will choose from between only two actions at a time, so `if-else` (or the simplified conditional operator in many cases) is a statement you'll use a lot. However, when your program must select from among many possible courses of action, you have to stack `if-else` logic, nesting the statements, to achieve a multiple-choice selection.

Suppose that a program you write for a credit-reporting agency needs to charge a different customer-loan percentage based on the current customer's credit rating of A (good) or B (fair). Only two courses of action are necessary, so this simple `if-else` statement works fine:

```
if (rating == 'A')
  { loanRate = .11; }   // Good rating
else
  { loanRate = .13; }   // Fair rating
// Rest of loan program logic would follow
```

Using pseudocode, here is what the preceding `if-else` states:

> *If the customer's rating is A,*
> *the customer's loan rate should be 11%.*
> *Otherwise,*
> *the customer's loan rate should be 13%.*

Tip It's a good idea to use pseudocode to explain program logic. The specific syntax of the programming language doesn't get in the way. Seeing pseudocode with the `if-else` statement that you already know will make it that much easier for you to understand later pseudocode that explains the `switch` statement.

There are two and only two options in this logic. Either the customer's rating is A, or the rating is not A, which means that the rating has to be B. No explicit test for the B has to be made, because there are only two options. If the test for A fails, the rating has to be B.

Let's introduce a third option, a rating of C for a poor credit history. The program must now choose from among three options—A, B, or C. A simple `if-else` won't work. The third option requires a nested `if` like this one:

```
if (rating == 'A')
   { loanRate = .11; }   // Good rating
else if (rating == 'B')        // Must test explicitly
      { loanRate = .13; }    // for the fair rating
    else
      { loanRate = .15; }    // Poor rating
// Rest of loan program logic would follow
```

As soon as you add a nested `if`, the logic gets more convoluted. However, one or even two levels of nesting don't complicate the logic too much for understanding. Here is the pseudocode for this nested `if`:

> *If the customer's rating is A,*
> *the customer's loan rate should be 11%.*
> *Otherwise,*
> *if the customer's rating is B,*
> *the customer's loan rate should be 13%.*
> *Otherwise,*
> *the customer's loan rate should be 15%.*

Do you see why no explicit test was needed to see if the rating was C? It was assumed that there were only three choices—A, B, or C. (Perhaps input validation performed earlier in the program ensured that only these three valid values were entered.) If the rating wasn't A, and if the rating wasn't B, the rating had to be C, and the appropriate loan rate was computed accordingly.

The problem with nested `if-else` logic is that too many levels of nesting introduce difficult-to-follow logic. Although one or even two nested `if` statements aren't impossible to follow, there has to be a better way to represent multiple-choice logic. There is, as you'll see in the next section.

To see how such embedded ifs can really be confusing, what if there are *six* different credit ratings to deal with? Here is a way to represent such a large number of options:

```
if (rating == 'A')
  { loanRate = .11; }
else if (rating == 'B')
       { loanRate = .13; }
     else if (rating == 'C')
       { loanRate = .15; }
          else if (rating == 'D')
            { loanRate = .17; }
               else if (rating == 'E')
                 { loanRate = .19; }
                    else {loanRate = .21; }
// Rest of loan program logic would follow
```

Some credit agencies have many more kinds of credit ratings than the six shown here, so the problem of selecting from multiple-choice logic, with its many possible outcomes, gets to be a real burden for programmers. Some programmers opt to code only if statements without embedded if-else logic, like this:

```
if (rating == 'A')
  { loanRate = .11; }
if (rating == 'B')
  { loanRate = .13; }
if (rating == 'C')
  { loanRate = .15; }
if (rating == 'D')
  { loanRate = .17; }
if (rating == 'E')
  { loanRate = .19; }
if (rating == 'F')
  { loanRate = .21; }
// Rest of loan program logic would follow
```

Such simple sequential if logic might be slightly easier to follow than the previous embedded if-else logic, but the code isn't as efficient. You should agree that readability is more important than efficiency, but this code is *extremely* less efficient than the nested ifs, and it only gets worse as you add more if options. If the credit rating is A, each of the additional ifs is still checked. With nested ifs, however, if the first if is true, none of the other ifs is checked.

Programmers have designed special charts that help demonstrate nested logic, such as the one shown in Figure 14.1. Nothing seems to be as helpful as simply introducing a new statement into the language, however, such as the switch statement, whose very syntax lends itself well to a program's multiple-choice selection.

FIGURE 14.1.

A diagram that helps show embedded if logic.

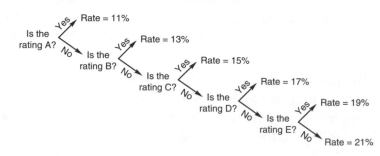

STOP&TYPE Listing 14.1 uses an embedded if-else to perform multiple-choice selection. The user's favorite local TV channel is asked for, and an appropriate message prints accordingly.

Review   **What You Have Learned**

Embedded if-else statements let you select from among several alternatives, but embedded ifs are not very easy to maintain. As soon as you understand how embedded if-else statements work, you'll be ready to learn about the switch statement, which removes much of the multiple-choice selection burden from your programming shoulders.

▼ **INPUT   LISTING 14.1. USING EMBEDDED** if-else **LOGIC TO SELECT AN APPROPRIATE MESSAGE.**

```
 1:  /* Filename: IFELSETV.C */
 2:  // This program uses embedded if-else statements to print
 3:  // a message for the user. The printed message corresponds
 4:  // to the user's favorite television channel.
 5:  #include <stdio.h>
 6:  #include <conio.h>
 7:  main()
 8:  {
 9:    int channel;
10:    clrscr();
11:
12:    printf("In this town, there are five non-cable television ");
13:    printf("channels.\nWhat is your favorite (2, 4, 6, 8, or 11)? ");
14:    scanf(" %d", &channel);
15:    printf("\n\n");    // Output two blank lines
16:
17:    // Use an embedded if to print appropriate messages
18:    if (channel == 2)
19:      { printf("Channel 2 got top ratings last week!"); }
20:    else
21:      if (channel == 4)
22:      { printf("Channel 4 shows the most news!"); }
23:        else
24:          if (channel == 6)
25:             { printf("Channel 6 shows old movies!"); }
26:          else
27:            if (channel == 8)
28:               { printf("Channel 8 covers many local events!"); }
29:            else
30:              if (channel == 11)
31:                 { printf("Channel 11 is public broadcasting!"); }
32:              else   // The logic gets here only if the
33:                     // user entered an incorrect channel
34:                { printf("Channel %d does not exist; it must ");
35:                    printf("be cable."); }
36:
37:    printf("\n\nHappy watching!");
38:    return 0;
39:  }
```

Note   Three different runs of output are shown to demonstrate the program's multiple-choice aspect.

▼ OUTPUT

```
In this town, there are five non-cable television channels.
What is your favorite (2, 4, 6, 8, or 11)? 6

Channel 6 shows old movies!

Happy watching!

In this town, there are five non-cable television channels.
What is your favorite (2, 4, 6, 8, or 11)? 2

Channel 2 got top ratings last week!

Happy watching!

In this town, there are five non-cable television channels.
What is your favorite (2, 4, 6, 8, or 11)? 3

Channel 3 does not exist; it must be cable.

Happy watching!
```

▼ ANALYSIS

If you understand `if`, just multiply that understanding by five and you'll understand this program! Seriously, embedded `if` statements do multiply the difficulty of following a program's logic.

One argument within the C programming community concerns how programmers should indent embedded logic such as that in Listing 14.1. Some prefer to embed as shown here, while others want to put braces around each embedded `if` (which results in a series of several closing braces all grouped toward the end of the program). Still others want to align all the `if` and `else` bodies evenly so that the code doesn't get pushed too far to the right in the last few embedded statements.

If you prefer to embed `if-else` logic, and if you don't have a problem understanding such code (not everyone feels that nested `if`s are difficult), there is certainly nothing wrong with using it as done in Listing 14.1. However, once you learn about the `switch` statement in the next section, you'll probably prefer to use `switch` for much of your multiple-choice processing.

 Note   Despite the advantages of `switch`, nothing beats `if-else` for straight-forward logic when only two choices must be made. Also, if the code is simple, use the conditional operator for efficiency. The `switch` statement can be overkill for simple choices. You shouldn't think that I'm recommending that you cease to use `if-else` logic.

► Making the *switch*

Concept

What You Will Learn

Use the `switch` statement to code multiple-choice logic. You will improve your program's clarity and make future maintenance much easier.

Unlike embedded `if-else` logic, the `switch` statement doesn't need a lot of fancy indentation that causes code to move closer to the right margin as the statement gets longer. Here is the format of `switch`. Even though the format looks a little intimidating, you'll see that `switch` is one of the easiest statements that C offers.

```
switch (expression)
  { case (expression) : {     // Block of one or
                              // more C statements
                        }
    case (expression) : {     // Block of one or
                              // more C statements
                        }
    // If there are more case
    // statements, put them here
    case (expression) : {     // Block of one or
                              // more C statements
                        }
    default :           {     // Block of one or
                              // more C statements
                        }
  }
```

`switch` may span more lines than shown in the format, depending on how many choices must be made. The *expression* following `switch` must evaluate to an integer or character-data type. Here is how `switch` works (using pseudocode again):

> *If the value of the switch expression matches that of the first case expression, execute the first block of code.*
> *If the value of the switch expression matches that of the second case expression, execute the second block of code.*
> *Continue looking for a match throughout the case expressions that compare to the switch's expression and execute the appropriate code.*
> *If none of the case expressions matches the switch expression, execute the default block of code.*

Did the pseudocode help? If not, looking at the following actual `switch` might:

```
printf("What is the customer's credit rating (A, B, C, or D)? ");
scanf(" %c", &rating);
switch (rating)   // The switch value must be an int or char
  { case ('A') : { loanRate = .11;
                   break;
                 }
```

```
        case ('B') : { loanRate = .13;
                        break;
                      }
        case ('C') : { loanRate = .15;
                        break;
                      }
        case ('D') : { loanRate = .17;
                        break;
                      }
        default :     { printf("You didn't enter a valid rating.\n");
                        break;
                      }
  }   // Don't forget this required closing brace!
```

You should be able to read and understand this switch statement with little trouble. Ignoring the breaks for now, the user's credit rating determines exactly which block of code C executes. If the rating is A, the first case block (the one that sets the loan rate to 11%) executes. If the rating is B, the second case block (the one that sets the loan rate to 13%) executes, and so on.

The default portion of switch tells C what to do if *none* of the other case statements matches the switch expression's value. Therefore, if the user didn't enter an A, B, C, or D, the default block of code executes, which is nothing more than an error message for the user.

Warning   switch doesn't perform automatic uppercase and lowercase conversions. Therefore, if the user enters a lowercase a, b, c, or d, switch won't match any of the case expressions due to their uppercase forms.

Tip   Before entering a switch statement, your program should convert the switch expression to uppercase if you're using a character value for the switch expression.

The format and indentation that you see in this switch statement is fairly common. Be sure to remember the closing brace, because it's easy to forget. (Of course, the Turbo C++ compiler won't let you forget it!)

STOP&TYPE   Listing 14.2 contains the television channel program that you saw in Listing 14.1. Instead of embedded if statements, switch makes the logic cleaner and easier to follow.

Note   The next section explains why so many breaks appear in switch statements.

Review

What You Have Learned

The switch statement gives you a maintainable statement that selects from one of many multiple-choice actions. A data value, either an integer or a character, decides which action executes.

▼ **INPUT   LISTING 14.2. THE TELEVISION CHANNEL PROGRAM USING** `switch` **INSTEAD OF** `if`.

```
 1:  /* Filename: SWITCHTV.C */
 2:  // This program uses a switch statement to print a message
 3:  // to the user. The printed message corresponds to the
 4:  // user's favorite television channel.
 5:  #include <stdio.h>
 6:  #include <conio.h>
 7:
 8:  main()
 9:  {
10:    int channel;
11:    clrscr();
12:
13:    printf("In this town, there are five non-cable television ");
14:    printf("channels.\nWhat is your favorite (2, 4, 6, 8, or 11)? ");
15:    scanf(" %d", &channel);
16:    printf("\n\n");    // Output two blank lines
17:
18:    // Use a switch to print appropriate messages
19:    switch (channel)
20:      { case (2) : { printf("Channel 2 got top ratings last week!");
21:                     break; }
22:        case (4) : { printf("Channel 4 shows the most news!");
23:                     break; }
24:        case (6) : { printf("Channel 6 shows old movies!");
25:                     break; }
26:        case (8) : { printf("Channel 8 covers many local events!");
27:                     break; }
28:        case (11): { printf("Channel 11 is public broadcasting!");
29:                     break; }
30:        default  :  // Logic gets here only if
31:                    // user entered an incorrect channel
32:                    { printf("Channel %d does not exist; it must ");
33:                      printf("be cable."); }
34:      }
35:
36:    printf("\n\nHappy watching!");
37:    return 0;
38:  }
```

Note   Notice that the output for this program is identical to that of Listing 14.1, despite the fact that a `switch` statement replaces the embedded `if-else`s.

▼ **OUTPUT**

```
In this town, there are five non-cable television channels.
What is your favorite (2, 4, 6, 8, or 11)? 6

Channel 6 shows old movies!

Happy watching!

In this town, there are five non-cable television channels.
What is your favorite (2, 4, 6, 8, or 11)? 2
```

```
Channel 2 got top ratings last week!

Happy watching!

In this town, there are five non-cable television channels.
What is your favorite (2, 4, 6, 8, or 11)? 3

Channel 3 does not exist; it must be cable.

Happy watching!
```

▼ ANALYSIS

The user's value is either 2, 4, 6, 8, or 11, and only one of the switch statement's blocks executes when one of those values matches a case expression's. If the user doesn't enter a correct value (one that matches the case statement's), the default section takes over and prints an appropriate message. default is a lot like a catch-all if-else statement. It handles any switch value not matched by a case statement.

Both the switch and the case expressions can contain variables and operators if you need to calculate a value, as long as the expression that you use results in an integer or character value.

 Tip   A default section isn't mandatory. If previous input validation ensures that the user's value will match one of the case expressions, no default is needed.

▶ *break* Up That *switch*

Concept   **What You Will Learn**

The switch statement's breaks ensure that each case block doesn't fall through and execute subsequent case blocks.

Although switch statements don't have to contain break statements, they almost always do. break ensures that each case doesn't fall through to the next case blocks. Here is a switch that contains no break statements:

```
switch (value)
  { case (1) : { printf("You entered a 1 \n";); }
    case (2) : { printf("You entered a 2 \n";); }
    case (3) : { printf("You entered a 3 \n";); }
    case (4) : { printf("You entered a 4 \n";); }
    default  : { printf("I don't know what you entered! \n"); }
  }
```

 Tip   Notice the braces around each of the case blocks. Because each block has only a single statement, the braces aren't necessary. However, as with the if, the while loops, and the for loop, braces are always recommended.

Figure 14.2 shows the execution path if the user's value is 1. Notice that *every* printf() executes!

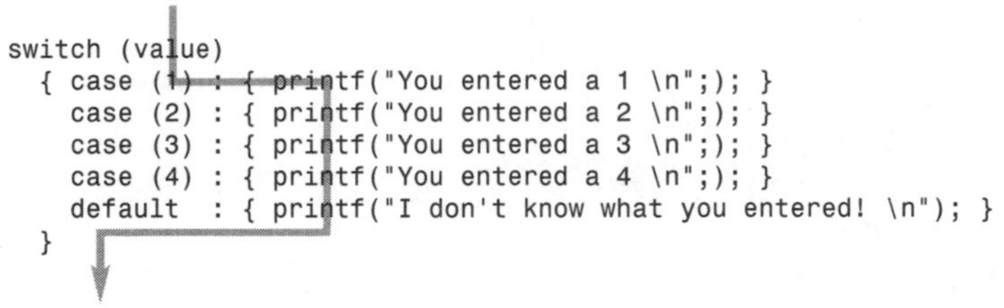

FIGURE 14.2.

Without break, execution falls through all printf()s.

```
switch (value)
  { case (1) : { printf("You entered a 1 \n";); }
    case (2) : { printf("You entered a 2 \n";); }
    case (3) : { printf("You entered a 3 \n";); }
    case (4) : { printf("You entered a 4 \n";); }
    default  : { printf("I don't know what you entered! \n"); }
  }
```

Here is the output when C executes this switch without breaks (assuming that value is equal to 1):

```
You entered a 1
You entered a 2
You entered a 3
You entered a 4
I don't know what you entered!
```

There's a big potential problem here! The switch statement will always fall through each case statement unless a break statement terminates each of the case blocks of code. If value had a 3, this would be the output:

```
You entered a 3
You entered a 4
I don't know what you entered!
```

The first two case statements don't execute, but as soon as C finds a case to match the 3, C executes all remaining case blocks of code.

Note We must now reexamine the break statement's purpose. Earlier you learned that break terminates the current loop. That still holds true. However, break also terminates the current switch statement.

Most of the time, your logic will require that you insert break statements to the end of each case block of code, as done here:

```
switch (value)
  { case (1) : { printf("You entered a 1 \n";);
                 break; }
    case (2) : { printf("You entered a 2 \n";);
                 break; }
    case (3) : { printf("You entered a 3 \n";);
                 break; }
    case (4) : { printf("You entered a 4 \n";);
                 break; }
    default  : { printf("I don't know what you entered! \n");
                 break; }
  }
```

Figure 14.3 shows the action of this switch if value is equal to 1. The case blocks are now truly mutually exclusive; one and only one case block executes for each execution of the switch.

```
switch (value)
  { case (1) : { printf("You entered a 1 \n";);
                 break; }
    case (2) : { printf("You entered a 2 \n";);
                 break; }
    case (3) : { printf("You entered a 3 \n";);
                 break; }
    case (4) : { printf("You entered a 4 \n";);
                 break; }
    default  : { printf("I don't know what you entered! \n");
                 break; }
  }
```

FIGURE 14.3.
With break, execution terminates after one printf().

If the user enters a 1, here is the output:

```
You entered a 1
```

If the user enters a 3, here is the output:

```
You entered a 3
```

Tip Try to put the most-often selected case at the top of the switch statement. The faster case matches the switch expression, the less searching C has to do to find the right match, and the more efficient your code will be.

Note If you happen to put more than one case inside a switch with the *same expression,* C matches only the first one.

The fall-through execution of the case code is actually to your advantage sometimes. For example, there could be a time when your program must calculate five values, or only four, or only three, or only two, or only one (such as when computing a country's, or a region's, or a state's, or a city's, or a person's sales values), depending on the data. You can arrange five case statements without breaks to execute five calculations if the switch expression matches the first case, or four calculations if the switch expression matches the second case, and so on, creating a cascading flow of calculations.

Warning One of the things that a switch can't do is choose from a range of values. For example, if you must execute the same code based on a 1, 2, or 3, and the same code for a 4, 5, or 6, you have to resort to the following coding technique:

```
switch (value)
  { case (1) :
    case (2) :
    case (3) : {    // The case code for 1, 2, or 3
                  break;
                }
    case (4) :
    case (5) :
    case (6) : {    // The case code for 4, 5, or 6
                  break;
                }
```

```
          default :  {    // The code for other values
                        break;
                    }
        }
```

You also can control range-checking by using a menu, as discussed in the Homework section at the end of this unit.

WHY IS THAT FINAL break THERE?

The Pascal programming language contains a CASE statement that works a lot like C's switch. Pascal, however, guarantees that one and only one of the selected values will execute. If one of the options matches the CASE statement, Pascal executes only that code and terminates the statement without the need for break statements.

C requires a little more work on your part if you want only a single case block of code to execute. You must insert break statements at the end of every case code if you don't want the execution to fall through the other case blocks. However, this extra effort gives you the ability to write a switch statement that terminates after a single case or one that cascades through the other case statements, which Pascal doesn't allow.

You might wonder why the default option needs a break. After all, when default finishes, won't C move on to the next statement? There are no more case statements for the execution to fall through to. A break isn't required at the end of the default block of code, but try to get in the habit of including it. If you later rearrange the case blocks for efficiency, and one of the blocks that you rearrange is the default block, the break will already be there.

STOP&TYPE Listing 14.3 contains a program that prints the country's sales value, a region's sales value, a state's sales value, or the local sales value, depending on the user's request.

Review
What You Have Learned

The placement of break statements or the lack of break statements determines whether or not C's case code falls through the other case blocks.

▼ INPUT   LISTING 14.3. PRINTS FIVE, FOUR, THREE, TWO, OR ONE MESSAGE, DEPENDING ON THE USER'S REQUEST.

```
1:  /* Filename: NOBREAKS.C */
2:  // Not using break statements inside a switch lets
3:  // you cascade through the subsequent case blocks
4:  #include <stdio.h>
5:  #include <conio.h>
6:  #define UPPERCASE 223
```

continues

LISTING 14.3. CONTINUED

```
7:  main()
8:  {
9:    int request;
10:
11:   clrscr();
12:   printf("Sales Reporting System\n\n");
13:
14:   printf("Do you want the Country, Region, State, or Local report");
15:   printf(" (C, R, S, or L)? ");
16:   scanf(" %c", &request);
17:   printf("\n");
18:
19:   request &= UPPERCASE;    // A bitmask to convert request
20:                            // to uppercase if needed
21:
22:   switch (request)
23:     { case ('C') : { printf("Country's sales: $343,454.32\n"); }
24:       case ('R') : { printf("Region's sales: $64,682.01\n"); }
25:       case ('S') : { printf("State's sales: $12,309.82\n"); }
26:       case ('L') : { printf("Local sales: $3,654.58\n");
27:                      break; }
28:       default    : { printf("You did not enter C, R, S, or L\n");
29:                      break; }
30:     }
31:   return 0;
32: }
```

> *Note* Three different outputs are shown so that you can see how switch handles the different requests.

▼ OUTPUT

```
Sales Reporting System

Do you want the Country, Region, State, or Local report (C, R, S, or L)?
c

Country's sales: $343,454.32
Region's sales: $64,682.01
State's sales: $12,309.82
Local sales: $3,654.58


Sales Reporting System

Do you want the Country, Region, State, or Local report (C, R, S, or L)?
L

Local sales: $3,654.58


Sales Reporting System

Do you want the Country, Region, State, or Local report (C, R, S, or L)?
x

You did not enter C, R, S, or L
```

▼ ANALYSIS

This program contains four `case` blocks, as well as a `default` block that handles any unmatched expressions. All four sales figures are to be printed if the country's sales are requested, so no `break` appears in the first four `case` blocks to allow the execution to fall through.

There is a `break` on line 27 so that a previous `case` execution doesn't fall through to the `default`'s code. Without that `break`, entering L (for local) would produce this output:

```
Sales Reporting System

Do you want the Country, Region, State, or Local report (C, R, S, or L)?
L

The local sales are $3,654.58
You did not enter C, R, S, or L
```

Obviously, the `break` before the `default` block is needed to keep the error from appearing when the user enters a correct value.

▶ Using *switch* for Menus

Concept

What You Will Learn

Menus are common programming methods that give the user several options from which to choose.

Whenever you sit down in a new restaurant, what must you have before you order food? (From the title of this section, you already know what's coming!) You need a menu. You can't be expected to know in advance what food every restaurant will have.

When your users sit down in front of your program, you can't always expect them to know what's possible either. You need to give them a choice of options that they can order. Such options usually are found on menus.

Obviously, the concept of a menu is nothing new to you, a top-notch Turbo C++ programmer. You've been using the pull-down menus from Turbo C++'s IDE throughout this book. When writing programs, you'll add menus to your programs so that your user can have access to a list of choices, just as you do in the IDE.

I'm not trying to fool you here! The menus that you write using this book won't be the fancy pull-down types that Turbo C++ contains. Such menus are extremely difficult to code, and you have to learn to walk before you can run. The menus you write will do little more than display a list of choices such as these:

```
Here are your choices:
  1. Print an employee report
  2. Enter sales figures
  3. Compute payroll
  4. Exit the program
What do you want to do?
```

> *Tip* Despite the fact that this menu isn't of the fancy pull-down kind, its simplicity is its power. This kind of list menu is easy to code and easy for the user to use.

Once you grab the user's input, your program must figure out what the user entered and execute the appropriate routine. Hey, that's a great job for the switch statement! One of the most common uses for switch is for menu processing. The multiple-choice selection that menus need matches the multiple-choice selection that the switch statement provides.

STOP&TYPE Listing 14.4 contains a menu that calculates different kinds of mathematical results based on the user's menu selection.

Review   What You Have Learned

The switch statement is perfect for writing menu selection code.

▼ INPUT   LISTING 14.4. USING switch TO PERFORM THE USER'S CALCULATION.

```
1:   /* Filename: MATHMENU.C */
2:   // Uses a switch statement to perform
3:   // menu actions for the user
4:   #include <stdio.h>
5:   #include <conio.h>
6:   #include <stdlib.h>
7:   #define PI 3.14159
8:
9:   main()
10:  {
11:     int menu;       // Will hold menu result
12:     int num;        // Will hold user's numeric value
13:     float result;   // Will hold computed answer
14:
15:     clrscr();
16:     printf("Math Calculations\n\n");
17:     do
18:     {
19:       printf("Please enter a number from 1 to 30: ");
20:       scanf(" %d", &num);
21:     } while ( (num < 1) && (num > 30));   // Loop if bad input
22:
23:     printf("Here are your choices:\n\n");
24:     printf("\t1. Calculate the absolute value\n");
25:     printf("\t2. Calculate the square\n");
26:     printf("\t3. Calculate the cube\n");
27:     printf("\t4. Calculate a circle's area\n");
28:     printf("\t   using your radius");
29:     printf("\n\nWhat do you want to do? ");
30:     scanf(" %d", &menu);
31:
32:     switch (menu)
33:       { case (1) : { result = ((num < 0)? -num : num);
34:                         break; }
```

```
35:          case (2) : { result = num * num;
36:                       break; }
37:          case (3) : { result = num * num * num;
38:                       break; }
39:          case (4) : { result = PI * (num * num);
40:                       break; }
41:          default  : { printf("You did not enter 1, 2, 3, or 4\n");
42:                       exit(1);   // Terminate the whole program
43:                       break; }
44:      }
45:
46:    printf("\nHere is your computed value: %.2f \n", result);
47:    return 0;
48: }
```

Note   Two outputs appear.

▼ OUTPUT

```
Math Calculations

Please enter a number from 1 to 30: 10
Here are your choices:

        1. Calculate the absolute value
        2. Calculate the square
        3. Calculate the cube
        4. Calculate a circle's area
           using your radius

What do you want to do? 2

Here is your computed value: 100.00


Math Calculations

Please enter a number from 1 to 30: 6
Here are your choices:

        1. Calculate the absolute value
        2. Calculate the square
        3. Calculate the cube
        4. Calculate a circle's area
           using your radius

What do you want to do? 6
You did not enter 1, 2, 3, or 4
```

▼ ANALYSIS

One of four math calculations is performed, based on the user's request. The menu gives the user a nice display of every option available.

The program first asks for a number in lines 17 through 21. The do-while ensures that the user enters a value from 1 to 30. Once the program captures the user's number, the user sees the menu printed on lines 23 through 29. The user is to enter a value from 1 to 4. No fancy error checking is done. If the user enters a value that isn't in the range of 1 to 4, the program prints an error message (line 41) and exits, via the `exit()` function on line 42. The existence of `exit()` is why the STDLIB.H header file is included on line 6.

> **Note** Without the `exit()` at the end of the `default` option, execution would fall through to print the message in line 46. Line 46's message should be printed only if the user entered a menu option from 1 to 4.

▶ Homework

General Knowledge

1. What is a disadvantage of nested `if-else` statements?
2. How can using a `switch` statement improve the readability of nested `if-else` statements?
3. Are braces required around every `case` block? Why or why not?
4. What kind of data type must the `switch` expression evaluate to?
5. What happens if none of the `case` expressions matches the `switch` expression?
6. Why would a programmer possibly want to reorder the `case` statements in a program?
7. What happens if you don't put `break` statements at the end of `switch` blocks?
8. What happens if more than one `case` block contains the same expression?
9. What do you insert in a `case` statement to capture an expression that doesn't match any of the other `case` expressions?
10. Which `case` block executes if you don't include a `default` block and none of the `case` expressions matches the value of the `switch` expression?
11. Why is it a good idea to put a `break` at the end of a `default` block of code?
12. True or false: The `switch` statement is one of the longest C statements and therefore is the most complicated.
13. True or false: The `default` block is optional.
14. True or false: Forgetting to insert `break` statements at the end of `switch` blocks will introduce bugs into your program.
15. True or false: The `switch` statement requires the STDLIB.H header file.
16. True or false: `switch` statements improve the readability of nested `for` loops.

What's the Output?

17. What's the output of the following `switch` statement?

```
switch ('A') :
  { case ('A') : printf("Apples\n");
    case ('B') : printf("Bananas\n");
```

```
    case ('C') : printf("Carrots\n");
    default    : printf("Onions\n");
}
```

Find the Bug

18. Although the following `switch` doesn't contain a syntax error, each line of code in each `case` is missing a couple of special characters that might come in handy later. What could you add to aid in the future maintenance of this `switch`?

```
switch (ans)
  { case (1) : printf("The answer is 1\n");
    default : printf("The switch statement is not finished.\n");
  }
```

19. Rudy can't seem to get his `switch` statement to work. He's writing a program to control departmental duty reports, but too many departments print at once. Can you help Rudy by rewriting this `switch` so that each `case` block executes independently of the others?

```
switch (ans)
  { case (2) : { printf("Your department isn't on duty today."); }
    case (5) : { printf("Your department begins duty at 4:00."); }
    case (9) : { printf("Your department works overtime Monday."); }
    default :  { printf("Your department is in conference now."); }
  }
printf("\n");
```

20. What's wrong with the following `switch` statement?

```
switch (choice)
  case (1) : { ans = 34 * sales;
               break; }
  case (2) : { ans = 56 * sales;
               break; }
  case (3) : { ans = 78 * sales;
               break; }
  default  : { ans = sales;
               break; }
```

Write Code That...

21. Ask the user for a number from 1 to 5. Using a `switch` statement, print the name of the number (for example, print *two* if the user enters 2). Include an error-checking loop to ensure that the user enters a number in the range of 1 to 5.

22. Wilma coded the following nested `if-else` statement, but she's having a hard time understanding it, even though it seems to be working correctly. Rewrite the statement as a `switch` to help Wilma with future program maintenance.

```
if (num == 1)
  { printf("France\n"); }
```

```
  else if (num == 2)
   { printf("Italy\n"); }
   else if (num == 3)
     { printf("England\n"); }
     else { printf("Greece\n"); }
```

23. Although a switch statement can't deal directly with ranges of values, you can display a menu of ranges, with numbers 1 through the total number of menu options to the left of each range, and base a switch statement on the menu's ranges. Write a program that computes a sales bonus of $0 if the user sold fewer than 100 products, a sales bonus of $50 if the user sold between 101 and 200 products, and a sales bonus of $100 if the user sold more than 200 products.

Extra Credit

24. Write a program that calculates tolls for an interstate toll booth. Ask whether the driver is in a car or a truck. Calculate a charge of $3.00 if the driver got on the toll road within the last 75 miles, $3.50 if the driver got on the toll road within the last 125 miles, and $4.00 if the driver got on the toll road more than 125 miles ago. If the vehicle is a truck, add an extra $1.00 for the added weight. Hint: Use one switch and one if statement.

Taking Charge

STOP&TYPE In this lesson, you learned about C's advanced loop control, branching, and switch capabilities. You saw the following:

▶ Using break to terminate for loops early.

▶ Using continue to force an early end to the current loop, causing the next iteration to occur.

▶ Using goto judiciously to branch from one part of a program to another.

Project 7 Listing. Using a switch statement to control a menu.

```c
1:  /* Filename: LESSON7.C */

2:  // Uses a switch statement to control a user's selection

3:  #include <stdio.h>

4:  #include <conio.h>

5:

6:  main()

7:  {

8:      int menu;

9:      float charge = 0.00;   // Holds total charge

10:

11:     clrscr();

12:     printf("** Computer Repair Center **\n\n");

13:     printf("What work was performed? Here are the choices: \n\n");

14:     printf("\t1. Replaced the CPU and RAM\n");

15:     printf("\t2. Replaced the RAM only\n");

16:     printf("\t3. Repaired the monitor\n");

17:     printf("\t4. Fixed stuck keys\n");
```

▶ The difficulties involved with nested `if-else` statements.

▶ Using `switch` to improve the readability of nested `if-else` statements.

▶ Supplying menus for your users to help them select program options.

Description

1: A C comment that includes the program's filename.

2: A C++ comment that contains the program's description.

3: The `printf()` and `scanf()` functions need information in the STDIO.H header file.

4: The screen-clearing function, `clrscr()`, needs information in the CONIO.H header file.

5: Extra blank lines make your program more readable.

6: All functions have names, and the first function in all C programs is `main()`.

7: All functions begin with a left brace.

8: Defines an integer variable that will hold the user's chosen menu option.

9: Defines a floating-point variable that will hold a charge.

10: Extra blank lines make your program more readable.

11: Erases the output screen so that it's blank before the user is prompted with a question.

12: Prints a title.

13: Prepares to print the menu.

14: The first menu choice.

15: The second menu choice.

16: The third menu choice.

17: The fourth menu choice.

continues

Project 7 Listing. continued

```
18:    do {

19:        printf("\nWhat work was performed? ");

20:        scanf(" %d", &menu);

21:    } while ((menu < 1) || (menu > 4));

22:

23:    // Store the charge based on the repair person's input

24:    switch (menu)

25:    { case (1) : { charge = 200.00; }    // Notice no break here

26:        case (2) : { charge += 150.00;

27:                     break; }

28:        case (3) : { charge = 75.00;

29:                     break; }

30:        case (4) : { charge = 12.00;

31:                     break; }

32:    }

33:

34:    // Print the results

35:    printf("\nThe total charge is $%.2f", charge);

36:    return 0;

37: }
```

Description

18: The do-while loop always executes at least once, ensuring that the body with the user's question will be shown.

18: Always check the user's input for validation.

19: Asks the user for the desired menu option.

20: Get the user's input.

21: Keeps looping if the user doesn't enter a valid menu option.

22: Extra blank lines make your program more readable.

23: Scatter comments throughout your code.

24: Start of the switch statement that will select a case block based on the user's response to the menu.

25: The charge for a CPU repair is stored.

25: Notice that there is no break here. If there is a CPU repair, there will always be a RAM replacement (see the menu), so execution will fall through to the second case as well.

26: The charge for RAM replacement is stored.

25: Removing a break lets you cascade case code blocks.

26: If execution fell through from the previous case, charge will hold $350. Otherwise, if the user selected only RAM replacement, the charge will be only $150.

27: The break ensures that the execution won't fall through to the subsequent case blocks.

28: The charge for monitor repair is stored.

29: The break ensures that the execution won't fall through to the subsequent case blocks.

30: The charge for the keyboard repair is stored.

31: The break ensures that the execution won't fall through to the subsequent case blocks.

32: A final closing switch brace is always required.

33 Extra blank lines make your program more readable.

34: Scatter comments throughout your code.

35: Prints the total charge.

36: Always return from main() to the IDE.

37: A final brace ends all main() functions.

▼ **OUTPUT**

```
** Computer Repair Center **

What work was performed? Here are the choices:

1. Replaced the CPU and RAM
2. Replaced the RAM only
3. Repaired the monitor
4. Fixed stuck keys

What work was performed? 5

What work was performed? 1

The total charge is $350.00
```

Lesson ▶

Breaking It Up with Functions

Unit 15: The C Library of Functions

Unit 16: Building Your Own Functions

Lesson 8 Project

15

The C Library of Functions

character-based I/O
functions

character-conversion
functions

character-testing functions

math functions

numeric functions

string functions

▶ What You'll Learn About

- ▶ Input and output functions
- ▶ Character-based functions
- ▶ String functions
- ▶ Numeric functions

Now it's time to let C do all the work! This unit describes many of the supplied Turbo C++ library functions that you can use to get input, make calculations, and manipulate strings. By using the library functions, you can write less code. For example, if you were writing a mathematical program, you *could* write a calculation that performed a square root, but why not use a built-in function that does that for you? Although no Turbo C++ function does *everything*, Turbo C++ contains functions that perform numerous common (and not-so-common) tasks that eliminate coding on your part.

You already know about many library functions such as `printf()`, `scanf()`, and `clrscr()`. Although Turbo C++ includes far more functions than described here, this unit gives you a sampling of the most important functions and those that you'll most likely need.

Warning   Not all of Turbo C++'s functions are ANSI C-compatible. The ANSI C standard can't support every function because it attempts to stay hardware-independent. For example, Turbo C++ includes functions that write text to the screen in different colors, but ANSI C doesn't support these functions because not all programmers use color monitors.

▶ Input and Output Functions

Concept   **What You Will Learn**

Turbo C++ includes many input and output functions in addition to `printf()` and `scanf()` that you can use to get and display data.

This section explains additional I/O functions that give you added ability to get and display data within a program. Finally, you'll learn how to route output to a printer, display color text, and perform unformatted, character-based input and output that gives you more control over the user's responses to your programs' prompts.

All the I/O functions described here use either the STDIO.H or CONIO.H header files, so you won't have to include more headers in your programs than you already have been including.

Printer Output

Printing to the printer is easy with Turbo C++! As a matter of fact, now that you've mastered the screen's printf() function, you only need to make a minor adjustment to send the same kind of output to the printer. There are actually several ways to send output to a printer, but the easiest is to use the fprintf() function.

The fprintf() function looks just like printf(). It uses the same format string and conversion codes, except you must embed stdprn (which means *standard printer*) before the format string. In other words, if you wanted to print "The 7 hills of Rome" on-screen, you'd do so like this:

```
printf("The %d hills of Rome\n", 7);   // Uses %d just for example
```

If you wanted to print the message on the printer, you'd do so like this:

```
fprintf(stdprn, "The %d hills of Rome\n", 7);   // Uses %d just
                                                // for example
```

The f at the beginning of fprintf() and the stdprn as the first argument to the function are the only changes you have to make in order to print to the printer. The output goes to the printer (assuming that the printer is turned on and has paper).

> **Note**   All of the escape-sequence characters, such as \n, \t, and \f, work for
> the printer just as they work for the screen. Most printers have a bell,
> so \a will even send a ring-the-bell signal to the printer, just as it does
> for the screen.

Character I/O Functions

printf(), scanf(), and fprintf() are all considered *formatted I/O functions*. Through the use of format strings, C modifies the data you input and output with formatted I/O functions to match your format strings.

A few C I/O functions are character-based. Instead of inputting and outputting several digits or letters at once, the character-based I/O functions work with one character at a time. If you use a character-based input routine to get a string, you'll have to get the string one character at a time, adding each character to a character array as the user enters the character.

The advantage of character-based I/O functions is that you get more control over the user's I/O. If you ask for a number and the user enters a letter of the alphabet, you'll know that the user entered a bad number and your program can either ignore the letter or terminate the input routine and tell the user about the problem.

> **Note**   Remember that scanf() requires each user to type data that conforms
> exactly to the scanf() format string.

Table 15.1 describes six common character-based I/O functions.

Table 15.1. Six common character-based I/O functions.

Function Name	Description
getchar()	Buffers the user's input, one character at a time, ending when the user presses Enter.
putchar()	Buffers screen output, one character at a time, ending when \n is output.
putc()	Buffers program output, routing the output to any device one character at a time, ending when \n is output.
getch()	Gets unbuffered user input, without echoing the input, one character at a time.
putch()	Sends (puts) unbuffered output, one character at a time, to the screen.
getche()	Gets unbuffered user input, echoing the input, one character at a time.

getchar() and putchar() are very popular in C programs. They're *buffered,* which gives getchar() a little side effect, but they're easy to understand.

Buffering is the process that getchar() uses to get the user's input. Whenever C encounters a getchar() in your program, it waits for the user to type a character. getchar() inputs only a single character at a time, never more than one. Follow these three lines of code:

```
printf("Please type a character... ");
c = getchar();   // Get the user's character
printf("The character that you just typed is %c", c);
```

At first glance, you would think that as soon as the user presses a key, such as the A key, the printf() would take over, but that's not what happens. Here's a sample of what could happen when the user responds to the prompt:

```
Please type a character... Programming
The character that you just typed is P
```

In other words, C waited for the user's response, and getchar() does get just a single character at a time, but the second printf() didn't print as soon as the user typed a single character. Only after the user presses Enter does getchar() seem to capture the first character of the input.

getchar() works the way it does because it's a buffered input function. When you use a buffered input function, C doesn't respond to any input until the user presses Enter. Until then, C stores the input in a special memory area called a *buffer.* The Enter keypress, or *newline* in C terminology, releases the buffer, letting getchar() finish and continue along its way. Therefore, although it might seem confusing at first, here's what getchar() does:

1. Halts the execution while the user types.

2. When the user presses Enter, getchar() grabs the next character in the buffer.

When `getchar()` appears in a loop, things get a little trickier, as shown in the following `while` loop:

```
printf("What is your first name? ");
while ((c = getchar()) != '\n')   // Loop until the user presses Enter
{   printf("%c", c);
};
```

Here is the pseudocode for this loop. Reading the pseudocode description will give you a better grasp of `getchar()`:

> *Gets a character from the user and stores it in the buffer.*
>
> *While that character is not an Enter keypress, keeps getting characters.*
>
> *Once the user presses Enter, then and only then does `getchar()` release the input and send each character, one character at a time, to the `getchar()` variable.*
>
> *Then `getchar()` prints the results until the character is an Enter keypress.*

What's the advantage of `getchar()` in a loop over `scanf()`? You can control whether or not to take each character the user types. `scanf()` is at the user's mercy, but grabbing characters from a buffer instead of directly from the keyboard lets your program be more selective.

Suppose you wanted the user to enter an address without any special punctuation. The user can use letters, numbers, and spaces, but nothing else. An Enter keypress ends the input. The following code builds an address, skipping anything the user types that isn't a letter, digit, or space:

```
char c;
char addr[25];
int adCtr = 0;
clrscr();

printf("What is your address? ");
while (c = getchar())   // Ignore the warning
{
  if (c == '\n')
    { break; }
  if (((c >= 'a') && (c <= 'z'))   // See if lowercase
   || ((c >= 'A') && (c <= 'Z'))   // See if uppercase
   || ((c >= '0') && (c <= '9'))   // See if a digit
   || (c == ' '))                  // See if a space
    { addr[adCtr] = c;   // Build the address
      adCtr++;
    }
}
addr[adCtr] = '\0';   // Turn the input into a valid string
printf("Your address is %s\n", addr);
```

Given this code fragment, this could be a possible session:

```
What is your address? 6105 E. 46-th Street!
Your address is 6105 E 46th Street
```

> ***Tip*** You also can limit the number of characters the user types by incrementing a counter variable and breaking from the loop after a certain number of characters have been entered.

As you can see, using getchar() lets you filter from the user's input whatever characters you don't want. It's important to note that getchar() *echoes* the user's input: As the user types characters, those characters appear on-screen. Perhaps the program will ignore some of those characters, but the user can see on the screen what's typed.

The putchar() function does the opposite of getchar(). Whereas getchar() inputs one character at a time from a buffer, putchar() outputs one character at a time. Using putchar() results in no noticeable buffering side effects because user input isn't involved.

The following code uses putchar() to print the contents of the name array on-screen, one character at a time:

```
for (i = 0; name[i] != '\0'; i++)
  { putchar(name[i]); }
```

The getchar() and putchar() functions are useful for getting input from the keyboard and sending output to the screen. If you want to send character-based output to the printer, you can do so using stdprn and putc(). putc() works just like putchar(), except that you must supply a destination for the character output. The following loop sends the contents of the name character array to the printer:

```
for (i = 0; name[i] != '\0'; i++)
  { putc(name[i], stdprn); }
```

getch() and putch() are *unbuffered* character-based I/O functions. Instead of sending input to a buffer, getch() sends input directly to variables.

 Tip   The most important thing to remember about getch() is that the program grabs the input *as soon as the user presses a key.*

 Warning   Unlike getchar(), getch() doesn't echo the user's input. When the user types a character in response to a getch() function call, that character doesn't appear on-screen unless you use another function, such as putch(), to print that character.

Think of getch() as getting *faster* input than getchar(). getch() doesn't make use of a buffer. In the following loop, the printf() rings the PC's bell as soon as the user presses * or Enter, but it ignores all other input:

```
while (c = getch() )
  { if (c == '*')
      { printf("\a");
        break; }    // The bell escape sequence
    if (c == 13)    // getch() translates \n to ASCII 13
      { break; }
}
```

This code loops repeatedly, getting input one character at a time. As soon as the user presses *, the loop terminates. Also, as soon as the user presses Enter, the program terminates. Notice that you can't test for a '\n' directly with getch(). Upon getting an Enter keypress, getch() returns a carriage-return character, which is ASCII value 13. When using getch(), you must compare against the value of 13 to check for Enter.

Such loops produce a C compiler warning because of the assignment inside the `while` statement. C is trying to suggest that you might have meant to type `==` inside the `if`. The single `=` is correct, however, because each time through the loop you want to assign the `getch()` input to `c`. Therefore, this is one of the few warnings you can ignore.

Often, C programmers rewrite this code to move the Enter test to the top of the `while` loop:

```
while ((c = getch()) != 13)
   { if (c == '*')
        { printf("\a"); }   // The bell escape sequence
}
```

Putting the check for a carriage return inside the `while` loop eliminates the compiler warning and makes the check more efficient.

If you were to replace this code's `getch()` with `getchar()`, the bell wouldn't ring as soon as you press *. Instead, you'd have to press * and then press Enter to end the input and then the bell would ring as soon as the buffer released the *.

Remember that `getch()` will not echo the input. Here is an address-building routine, similar to one shown earlier, that uses `getch()` instead of `getchar()`:

```
char c;
char addr[25];
int adCtr = 0;
clrscr();
printf("What is your address? ");
while ((c = getch()) != 13)   // Ignore the warning
{
  if (c == '\n')
    { break; }
  if (((c >= 'a') && (c <= 'z'))   // See if lowercase
   || ((c >= 'A') && (c <= 'Z'))   // See if uppercase
   || ((c >= '0') && (c <= '9'))   // See if a digit
   || (c == ' '))                  // See if a space
    { addr[adCtr] = c;   // Build the address
      adCtr++;
    }
}
addr[adCtr] = '\0';   // Turn the input into a valid string
printf("\nYour address is %s\n", addr);
printf("\nUsing putchar():\n");
```

If you were to include this code in a program and run it, you would *not* see the input as you type it. Here is a sample run of this code fragment:

```
What is your address?
Your address is 456 E Elm Street
Using putchar():
```

 One of the biggest advantages of using `getchar()` instead of `getch()` is that the user can correct typing mistakes by pressing the Backspace key. Remember that the `getchar()` input goes to a buffer and not directly to your program. When you're entering a string of input

UNIT

15

The C Library of Functions

characters, if you make a mistake and press Backspace, C removes the previous character from the buffer, and the mistake never gets to the program. If you used `getch()`, you would have to check for the ASCII value of Backspace, eliminate the Backspace character, and eliminate the character to be backspaced over (making input of strings with `getch()` a little tiring). `getch()` is more useful for getting single-keystroke responses than for building strings.

`getche()` is a Turbo C++-supplied function that does exactly the same job as `getch()`, except that `getche()` echoes the input: You see the characters on-screen as you type them.

A `getch()` immediately followed by a `putch()` grabs the user's keystroke and sends it to the screen, simulating `getche()`. The following statement:

```
c = getche();
```

is identical to this:

```
c = getch();
putch(c);    // Echo that character
```

 Tip   Putting a stand-alone `getch()` before the `return 0;` statement keeps Turbo C++ from returning to the IDE editor too quickly. Until now, you've run your programs and then pressed Ctrl-F5 to return to the output screen to see the results. As shown in Listing 15.1, a `getch()` function temporarily halts the output, letting you see the results before returning to the IDE.

CLEARING THE BUFFER

There might be times when you need to clear the input buffer of any text that might still be left. For example, the following statement leaves the Enter keypress, `\n`, still on the buffer after responding to `getchar()` with a single letter followed by an Enter keypress:

```
c = getchar();
```

A subsequent `getch()` won't wait on the user's keypress but instead will grab the `\n` that is still in the input buffer. If you need to get rid of the buffer's contents, use the `fflush(stdin);` statement. `fflush()` flushes the input buffer. Issuing the following `fflush()` right after the preceding `getchar()` clears the input buffer and readies the keyboard for all new input:

```
fflush(stdin);    // Clear the input buffer
```

String I/O Functions

Turbo C++ supplies two string functions to support the input and output of strings into character arrays. They are

▶ `gets()`, for getting strings from the user

▶ `puts()`, for outputting strings to the screen

UNIT

15

The C Library of Functions

Note As with virtually all I/O functions, there is a command, `fputs()`, that sends strings to a device, such as `stdprn` for the printer.

`gets()` doesn't always replace the string-building, character-based I/O functions you read about in the preceding section because you can't filter out certain characters during input using `gets()`. Nevertheless, `gets()` is a lot better for string I/O than `scanf()` because you can get more than one word at a time from the user.

When inputting and outputting string data that is stored in character arrays, use `gets()` and `puts()` instead of `scanf()` and `printf()` because of their simplicity. Only if you need more formatting control should you use a formatted I/O function.

The following code fragment asks the user for her or his first and last names and prints the names. This code wouldn't work if `scanf()` were used because `scanf()` would stop at the end of the first name.

```
char name[45];
puts("Please enter your full name:");
gets(name);
puts(name);   // You also can print string literals with puts()
```

Warning `gets()` will *not* make sure that there are enough character array elements to hold the user's response. In other words, a user could enter a 50-character response to a `gets()` that contains a character array reserved to only 12 elements.

Tip `puts()` automatically puts a `\n` at the end of the string it outputs.

`fgets()` helps eliminate the nasty habit `gets()` has of overwriting memory if a user enters a string that's too long for the character array. Here is the format of `fgets()`:

```
fgets(charArray, length, device);
```

`fgets()` requires a character array that the user's string will go into. `fgets()`'s second argument is the length of the longest string the function should return. The *length* argument must be the number of characters reserved for the array. For example, if you defined a character array like this:

```
char name[25];
```

the maximum *length* argument you could specify for `fgets()` would be 25. `fgets()` always adds a null zero to the end of the string (and ignores the `\n` keypress), so you must leave room for it. The last argument tells C where to go for the input. Most of the time, you'll want input to come from the keyboard, which C calls the *standard input device* or `stdin`.

Here is an `fgets()` function call that gets up to 25 characters of input in the character array named `name`:

```
fgets(name, 25, stdin);
```

The user might enter more than 24 characters. If so, `fgets()` simply discards the extra characters and stores the first 24 in the `name` array. If the user enters exactly 25 characters, C must replace the final one with a null zero to maintain a string in the array.

> **Tip**   In Lesson 11, you'll see how `fgets()` can retrieve data from disk files.

Colorful Text

If you have a color monitor, you can produce text output in color. Adding color to your output gives your programs more appeal and keeps them from becoming too boring.

You don't actually write colored characters. Instead, using the `textcolor()` function, you tell Turbo C++ the color of subsequent text. Once you set a color with `textcolor()`, all future text will appear in that color until you set another color. `textcolor()` doesn't change the color of any text that you've already written to the screen.

Here is the format of the `textcolor()` function:

```
textcolor(int colorCode);
```

colorCode is any value from the following list. You use these defined color names instead of integers for the `textcolor()` argument because in the CONIO.H header file, all the colors are named literal integer constants that produce the colors shown.

```
BLACK

BLUE

GREEN

CYAN

RED

MAGENTA

BROWN

LIGHTGRAY

DARKGRAY

LIGHTBLUE

LIGHTGREEN

LIGHTCYAN

LIGHTRED

LIGHTMAGENTA

YELLOW

WHITE
```

> **Note**   Had you *ever* heard of the color *cyan* before you bought a PC?

`textcolor()` turns only the character a certain color, not the background of the character. To change a character's background, you must call the `textbackground()` function. Here's the format of `textbackground()`:

```
textbackground(int backColorCode);
```

backColorCode can be any of the first eight colors in the previous list. The last eight colors can be used only as foreground colors. `textbackground()` sets the background color of any subsequent text that you print, but it doesn't affect the background of text already on the screen. If you want to turn the entire screen a certain background color before printing text on the screen, call `clrscr()` after `textbackground()`:

```
textbackground(BLUE);
clrscr();
```

Warning There's something you should know before getting too excited about changing the colors of your text. You must use the specialized functions `cprintf()` and `cputs()`, the color-based versions of `printf()` and `puts()`, to maintain the colors you set with `textbackground()` and `textcolor()`. These two color-sensitive functions are a subset of a complete set of text-windowing functions that you will master once you advance a little further in C. (These windowing routines are DOS-based and have nothing to do with Microsoft Windows.)

STOP&TYPE The program in Listing 15.1 uses several of the functions mentioned in this section to get and display data.

Review   What You Have Learned

The character-based and string-based I/O functions often give you added I/O abilities that you don't have with `scanf()` and `printf()`.

Warning Be sure to turn your printer on before running this program. If you don't want to produce printer output, comment out the line that has `fputs()`.

▼ INPUT   LISTING 15.1. USING THE I/O FUNCTIONS TO GET USER RESPONSES.

```
 1:  /* Filename: LOTSIO.C */
 2:  // Performs different kinds of I/O using functions
 3:  #include <stdio.h>
 4:  #include <conio.h>
 5:  main()
 6:  {
 7:    char c;
 8:    char addr[50];
 9:    clrscr();
10:    puts("Getting a single character with getch() \n");
11:    puts("Please type a character... ");
12:    c = getch();
13:    printf("You typed %c\n\n", c);
14:
15:    puts("Getting a single character with getchar() \n");
16:    puts("Please type a character and press Enter... ");
17:    c = getchar();
18:    printf("You typed %c\n\n", c);
19:    fflush(stdin);    // Get rid of the Enter keypress
20:
```

continues

UNIT

15

The C Library of Functions

LISTING 15.1. CONTINUED

```
21:     puts("Please type your address (I'll get it with gets(): ");
22:     gets(addr);    // Get the complete address
23:
24:     printf("\n\nPress any key to send the address to the printer...");
25:     getch();
26:     fputs(addr, stdprn);
27:
28:     textbackground(BLUE);
29:     textcolor(LIGHTRED);
30:     clrscr();
31:     cprintf("\n\n\n T h i s   i s   i n   c o l o r   ! ! !\n");
32:
33:     cputs("\n\n\nPress any key to return to the IDE...");
34:     getch();
35:     return 0;
36:
37:  }
```

▼ **OUTPUT**

```
Getting a single character with getch():

Please type a character...
You typed d

Getting a single character with getchar():

Please type a character and press Enter...s
You typed s

Please type your address (I'll get it with gets():
5675 N. Pine

Press any key to send the address to the printer...

  T h i s   i s   i n   c o l o r   ! ! !



Press any key to return to the IDE...
```

▼ **ANALYSIS**

Listing 15.1 contains examples of many different I/O functions. The getch() on line 12 operates differently from the getchar() on line 17. Whereas line 12's getch() grabs the user's keystroke right away, line 17's getchar() requires that the user press Enter. The Enter keypress is still left on the input buffer. You've read throughout this section about various ways to eliminate the extra newline. This code eliminates the \n with the fflush() on line 19.

Once the buffer is free, line 22 uses gets() to get the user's address and store it in a character array. The full address couldn't be stored with a scanf() if the address contained spaces—and most addresses do contain spaces.

Line 25's getch() simply halts the program until the user presses any key. When the user presses a key, line 26's fputs() sends the address to the printer. Unlike fprintf(), which requires the `stdprn` argument at the beginning of the argument list, `fputs()` requires `stdprn` at the end.

Finally, the foreground text color is set to light red and the background color is set to blue before the screen is cleared and two more messages are printed. Notice that `cprintf()` (line 31) and `cputs()` (line 33) are required to maintain the colors set earlier because neither `printf()` nor `puts()` would respect the colors set in lines 28 and 29 otherwise.

▶ Character-Based Functions

Concept   **What You Will Learn**

C includes several functions that manipulate character data.

In addition to the character-based I/O functions, C includes several character-testing and conversion functions that you'll find useful. Until now, you had to write code that did some of these functions' jobs, but now you can rely on the power that C provides.

Character-Testing Functions

The CTYPE.H header file includes many functions that test character data and return either true or false based on the results of those tests. Table 15.2 describes the more popular functions.

Table 15.2. The character-testing functions.

Function	Description
`isalpha()`	Returns true if its character argument is an alphabetic letter.
`islower()`	Returns true if its character argument is a lowercase letter.
`isupper()`	Returns true if its character argument is an uppercase letter.
`isdigit()`	Returns true if its character argument is a digit from 0 to 9.
`iscntrl()`	Returns true if its character argument's ASCII value is from 0 to 31. The lower 32 ASCII values are called *control characters*.
`isspace()`	Returns true if its character argument is a space, newline (\n), carriage return (\r), tab (\t), or vertical tab (\v).

The following `do` loop ensures that the user types an uppercase letter before it continues:

```
do
  { c = getche();   // Get the character and echo it
  } while (!isupper(c));   // Loop until the user types uppercase
```

This is one of the few times when using the NOT operator, `!`, is more readable than trying to rearrange the logic to eliminate `!`. The `do-while` keeps looping if and only if the user doesn't enter an uppercase character.

These character-testing functions are useful when you need specific input from the user and you're writing input routines that grab specific data in a specific format. Through the use of the character-testing functions, you can ensure that the user types what's expected.

Character Conversion Functions

There are two character conversion functions. Table 15.3 describes them. These functions don't really convert their arguments, but they test them and return either the uppercase or lowercase equivalents.

 Note   If you pass to either function a value that isn't a letter of the alphabet, `tolower()` and `toupper()` simply return their arguments without changing them in any way.

Table 15.3. The character conversion functions.

Function Name	Description
tolower()	Returns the argument converted to lowercase.
toupper()	Returns the argument converted to uppercase.

Both `tolower()` and `toupper()` require that you include the CTYPE.H header file. In Lesson 5, you learned how to test and convert characters to uppercase and lowercase using the bit operators. `tolower()` and `toupper()` are much easier to use. The following loop can check for an uppercase Y or N very easily by using `toupper()`:

```
do
  { printf("Do you want to input the data (Y/N) ?");
    c = getche();
  } while ((toupper(c) != 'Y') && (toupper(c) != 'N'));
```

Tip   Use `toupper()` inside `case` expressions so that you need to check for uppercase letters only when using `switch` statements based on character data.

 STOP&TYPE   The program in Listing 15.2 asks the user for a product code. The company's product codes always appear in the format *CCCNN*, where *C* represents an uppercase letter and *N* represents a numeric digit. Through the use of the character functions taught in this lesson, this program can ensure that the user enters what's expected.

Review   **What You Have Learned**

The character functions give you the ability to test for characters and numbers without resorting to bitmasks and extra `if-else` logic.

▼ **INPUT   LISTING 15.2. GETTING AND CHECKING CHARACTER INPUT.**

```
 1:   /* Filename: PRODCODE.C */
 2:   // Makes sure that the user enters
 3:   // an appropriate product code
 4:   #include <stdio.h>
 5:   #include <conio.h>
 6:   #include <stdlib.h>
 7:   #include <ctype.h>
 8:   main()
 9:   {
10:     char prodCode[6];    // Leaves enough space for null zero
11:     int c;
12:
13:     clrscr();
14:     printf("What is the product code (CCCNN)? ");
15:     fgets(prodCode, 6, stdin);
16:
17:     // Test each character position for validity
18:     for (c = 0; c < 3; c++)
19:       { if (!isalpha(prodCode[c]))
20:           { printf("You entered a bad product code format.\n");
21:             printf("The first 3 characters must be alphabetic.\n");
22:             exit(1);
23:           }
24:       }
25:     for (c = 3; c < 5; c++)
26:       { if (!isdigit(prodCode[c]))
27:           {   printf("You entered a bad product code format.\n");
28:             printf("The last 2 characters must be numeric.\n");
29:             exit(1);
30:           }
31:       }
32:
33:     printf("\nYou entered a correct product.\n");
34:     return 0;
35:   }
```

▼ **OUTPUT**

```
What is the product code (CCCNN)? AB648
You entered a bad product code format.
The first three characters must be alphabetic.

What is the product code (CCCNN)? ABC56

You entered a correct product.
```

▼ **ANALYSIS**

This program uses the fgets() function in line 15 to get a string from the user. fgets() limits the string to a maximum of six characters, and one of those characters is a place for the null zero. If the user enters a string that is more than five characters in length, fgets() ignores the extra characters.

Two for loops control the testing of the user's input. The first for loop in lines 18 through 24 checks the first three characters in the entered string. The isalpha() function in line

19 makes sure that the characters are alphabetic. If any of the three characters aren't alphabetic, the exit() function on line 22 ends the program early.

The for loop in lines 25 through 31 ensures that the final two characters are numeric digits.

Two extra header files that you haven't always needed in previous programs are needed in this program. STDLIB.H is included in line 6 because of the exit(). Line 7's included CTYPE.H header file provides information for the isalpha() and isdigit() functions.

▶ String Functions

Concept   **What You Will Learn**

C has many string functions. The three most helpful are explained in this section.

You'll often use the three useful string functions described in Table 15.4. strlen() is especially simple, but you'll find yourself using this function a lot, especially when you're working with pointers (see Lessons 9 and 10).

Table 15.4. Three useful string functions.

Function Name	Description
strlen()	Returns the length of the string.
strcat()	Concatenates two strings.
strcmp()	Checks to see if two strings are equal.

Note   All these string functions require the STRING.H header file.

The strlen() function (the *string length* function) returns the length of its string argument. As you know, the length of a string is equal to the number of characters up to but not including the null zero. The following statement stores 5 in n:

```
n = strlen("Ditto");
```

strlen() is most useful when you pass strings stored in character arrays. With strlen(), you can check user input and step through every element of a string without hitting the null zero, as done in Listing 15.3.

definition

Concatenation is the merging of one string to the end of another.

strcat() requires two string arguments. The first argument must be a character array or a character pointer like the ones you'll read about in Lesson 9. strcat() changes only its first argument. strcat() takes the second argument and concatenates that string to the end of the first string.

For example, given the following character array definitions:

```
char first[20] = "Chris";
char last[20] = "Smith";
```

you can concatenate the second string to the end of the first like this:

```
strcat(first, last);
```

After C completes the concatenation, the `first` array contains `ChrisSmith`. From this result, you can deduce the following characteristics of `strcat()`:

▶ `strcat()` doesn't insert a space for you. If you want a space between the concatenated strings, you have to add one to the end of the first string or to the beginning of the second string before you concatenate.

▶ `strcat()` concatenates the second string to the end of the first string. The number of bytes reserved for either string, in this case 20, has no bearing on the concatenation.

 Warning `strcat()` doesn't make sure that the first argument can hold the fully concatenated string! If you want to ensure that the first string contains enough room for both strings, perform a `sizeof` and a `strlen()` to compare the strings before you concatenate:

```
if (sizeof(first) >= (strlen(first) + strlen(last) + 1))
  { strcat(first, last); }
```

The size of the first string (the total number of bytes reserved) must be at least large enough to hold both of the strings, and this `if` ensures that is the case.

The `strcmp()` function compares one string to another. You use it to see whether two strings hold the same value. Here is the format of `strcmp()`:

```
strcmp(string1, string2);
```

Be careful, because `strcmp()` doesn't return a simple true or false result. `strcmp()` returns one of these three results, depending on the result of the comparison:

▶ `strcmp()` returns a 0 if both its arguments are equal.

▶ `strcmp()` returns a negative value if the first string is alphabetically higher than the second string, according to the ASCII character set.

▶ `strcmp()` returns a positive value if the first string is alphabetically lower than the second string, according to the ASCII character set.

The following `strcmp()` stores a zero in `result`:

```
result = strcmp("Lake", "Lake");
```

Remember that 0 is false, so if you want to use an `if` to compare strings, as you often do, you have to use the NOT operator to achieve a true comparison:

```
if (!strcmp(s1, s2))
  {   // Body of the if goes here
  }
```

This `if` will be true (not zero) if and only if the two strings are identical.

Note   Be sure to include the STRING.H header file when using these three string functions.

STOP&TYPE Listing 15.3 contains a program that asks the user for his or her first and last names. strlen(), strcat(), and strcmp() are then used to work with the names.

Review   **What You Have Learned**

The string functions help you manage and change strings.

▼ **INPUT   LISTING 15.3. USING THE STRING FUNCTIONS TO WORK WITH TWO NAMES.**

```
 1:   /* Filename: NAMESTR.C */
 2:   // Uses the user's first and last names to
 3:   // demonstrate the common string functions
 4:   #include <stdio.h>
 5:   #include <conio.h>
 6:   #include <string.h>
 7:   #include <ctype.h>
 8:   main()
 9:   {
10:     int c;    // Loop control variable
11:     char first[25];
12:     char last[25];
13:
14:     clrscr();
15:     puts("What is your first name? ");
16:     gets(first);
17:     puts("What is your last name? ");
18:     gets(last);
19:
20:     if (!strcmp(first, last))
21:       { puts("You have the same first and last name???\n"); }
22:
23:     if (strcmp(first, last) < 0)
24:       {
25:         puts("Your first name is before your last alphabetically\n");
26:       }
27:
28:     if (strcmp(first, last) > 0)
29:       {
30:         puts("Your last name is before your first alphabetically\n");
31:       }
32:
33:     // Concatenate only if there's room
34:     if (sizeof(first) >= (strlen(first) + strlen(last) + 1))
35:       { strcat(first, " ");    // Insert the space
36:         strcat(first, last);    // Merge the names
37:         puts("Your full name is ");
38:         puts(first);
39:       }
40:
41:     puts("\nHere is your last name in all uppercase:\n");
42:     for (c = 0; c < strlen(last); c++)
```

```
43:     {
44:         putchar(toupper(last[c]));
45:     }
46:     putchar('\n');
47:
48:     puts("\n\n\nPress a key to return to the IDE...");
49:     getch();   // Press a key to return to the IDE
50:
51:     return 0;
52: }
```

▼ OUTPUT

```
What is your first name?
Sam
What is your last name?
Jones
Your last name is before your first alphabetically

Your full name is
Sam Jones

Here is your last name in all uppercase:

JONES

Press a key to return to the IDE...
```

▼ ANALYSIS

Notice that Listing 15.3 contains several included header files in lines 4 through 7. This program relies on several functions, and several of those functions require the headers shown here. Turbo C++ is nice about letting you know when a header file is missing. If you were to omit the header file inclusion for the toupper() function, for example, Turbo C++ would display the following compiler warning:

```
Function 'toupper' should have a prototype in function main()
```

You'll learn what a prototype is in the next unit. For now, just remember that you can fix such a problem by including the appropriate header file for whatever function Turbo C++ lists in the error message.

After lines 15 through 18 get the user's first and last names, the rest of the program works with the two character arrays that hold each name. A series of ifs in lines 20 through 31 tests to see how the first and last names compare alphabetically. Without strcmp(), you would have to write a tedious character-by-character comparison routine.

As soon as line 34 determines that the first-name array can hold both names plus an additional byte for the space between the names, the strcat() function in line 35 adds a space to the end of the first name, and the strcat() function in line 36 puts the last name after the first name.

A for loop in lines 42 through 45 then converts each letter in the last name to uppercase. The strlen() function is used in the for to ensure that the for loop doesn't look at characters that fall after the last name's final character. The return value of toupper(), after being applied to each character in the last-name array, converts the last name to all uppercase before line 46 prints the newly converted name on-screen.

► **Numeric Functions**

Concept   **What You Will Learn**

C's numeric functions help general-purpose, business, and scientific programming by offering a wide assortment of numeric capabilities.

You might never use all the mathematical functions described here, but you'll surely use some of them. The math routines are broken into the following three sections:

► Integer functions

► Common computational functions

► Trigonometric and logarithmic functions

Note   All the math functions described here require the inclusion of the MATH.H header file.

Integer Functions

The integer functions let you change the way C stores integer values. Most programmers use these functions to round numbers in a specific way. Table 15.5 describes the integer functions.

Note   These functions take floating-point arguments.

Table 15.5. The integer functions.

Function Name	Description
ceil()	Rounds numbers up to the nearest integer. This function is often called the *ceiling* function.
fabs()	Returns the absolute value of its argument. If the argument is either positive or negative, fabs() returns the positive value.
floor()	Rounds numbers down to the nearest integer.

Given that f contains 4.4, ceil(f) returns 5 and floor(f) returns 4. When rounding values with ceil() and floor(), you must keep in mind that negative values consistently round with positive values, even though they don't appear to at first glance. Given the following definition:

```
float f = -4.4;
```

`ceil(f)` returns –4, not –5, because –4 is the next highest integer above –4.4. `floor(f)` returns –5 because –5 is the next lowest integer below –4.4.

The absolute value function is useful for calculating differences. The difference between two people's ages is always a positive value, no matter which number you subtract from the other, as the following code fragment shows:

```
puts("How old are you? ");
scanf(" %d", &ageYou);
puts("How old is your sister? ");
scanf(" %d", &ageSis);
diff = fabs((float)ageYou - (float)ageSis);
printf("There are %.0f years between you.", diff);
```

Don't let the `(float)` typecasts in the last assignment throw you. They're there just to ensure that `fabs()` gets the floating-point argument it expects. No matter which variable is higher, `ageYou` or `ageSis`, the absolute value will be the positive representation of the difference.

Other Common Math Functions

C includes three more useful functions that you will use at some point. Table 15.6 describes these functions. Each requires floating-point arguments and returns floating-point values.

Table 15.6. Three common mathematical functions.

Function Name	Description
`fmod()`	Requires two arguments. Returns the remainder of the first argument divided by the second argument. In a way, `fmod()` works like a floating-point modulus remainder operator (`%` works only for integer data). The second argument can't be zero because division by zero is undefined.
`pow()`	Requires two arguments. Returns the first argument raised to the power of the second.
`sqrt()`	Returns the square root of the argument.

`fmod()` doesn't produce a fractional remainder, even though you might expect it to. For example, the following assignment stores 1.0, not .5, in `result`:

`result = fmod(11.0, 2.0);`

11.0 divided by 2.0 is 5.0 with 1.0 left over as a remainder—hence the result of 1.0.

Often in financial calculations you need to raise a number to another power. To compute 4 raised to the fifth power, or 4^5, you could do this:

`ans = pow(4.0, 5.0);`

`ans` holds 1024.0 after the assignment.

The sqrt() function computes the square root of its argument. The following assignment stores 12.0 in result:

```
result = sqrt(144.0);    // Find the square root of 144.0
```

 Tip If you want to take a root other than the square root of a number, raise that number to a fractional power. For example, to find the cube root of 125, raise 125 to the (1/3) power using pow():

```
result = pow(125.0, (1.0/5.0));
```

Trigonometric and Logarithmic Functions

No calculator would be complete without trigonometric and logarithmic functions, and neither would C. Although they're not useful for everybody, C has them just in case you need them. Table 15.7 describes the most common trig and logarithmic functions.

Table 15.7. Common trigonometric and logarithmic functions.

Function Name	Description
cos()	Returns the cosine of the argument whose angle must be given in radians.
sin()	Returns the sine of the argument whose angle must be given in radians.
tan()	Returns the tangent of the argument whose angle must be given in radians.
exp()	Returns e, the base of the natural logarithm, raised to a power specified by $x(e^x)$. e is the mathematical expression for the approximate value of 2.718282.
log()	Returns the natural logarithm of the argument, mathematically written as $\ln(x)$ where x is a positive argument.
log10()	Returns the base-10 logarithm of the argument, mathematically written as $\log10(x)$ where x is a positive argument.

 Tip If you must find the trigonometric value of an angle expressed in degrees, convert the degrees to radians by multiplying the degrees by (pi / 180.0) where pi equals approximately 3.14159.

 Listing 15.4 contains a list of math function results for various arguments.

Review ████████████████████████ **What You Have Learned**

The math functions are great because you don't have to write complicated mathematical algorithms yourself.

```
1:   /* Filename: MATHALL.C */
2:   // Demonstrates the math functions
3:   #include <stdio.h>
4:   #include <conio.h>
5:   #include <math.h>
6:   main()
7:   {
8:     float result;
9:     clrscr();
10:
11:    // integer functions that still take float
12:    // arguments and return float results
13:    result = ceil(-8.9);
14:    printf("ceil(-8.9) produces: %.1f\n", result);
15:    result = floor(-8.9);
16:    printf("floor(-8.9) produces: %.1f\n", result);
17:    result = fabs(-34.6);
18:    printf("fabs(-34.6) produces: %.1f\n", result);
19:    result = fabs(34.6);
20:    printf("fabs(34.6) produces: %.1f\n", result);
21:
22:    // Common mathematical functions
23:    result = fmod(25.0, 3.2);
24:    printf("fmod(25.0, 3.2) produces: %.1f\n", result);
25:    result = pow(4.0, 7.0);
26:    printf("pow(4.0, 7.0) produces: %.1f\n", result);
27:    result = pow(4096.0, (1.0/3.0));   // Same as cube root of 4096
28:    printf("pow(4096.0, (1.0/3.0)) produces %.1f\n", result);
29:    result = sqrt(1000.0);
30:    printf("sqrt(1000.0) produces: %.1f\n", result);
31:
32:    // Trig functions
33:    result = cos(-1.0);
34:    printf("cos(-1.0) produces: %.1f\n", result);
35:    result = sin(-1.0);
36:    printf("sin(-1.0) produces: %.1f\n", result);
37:    result = tan(-1.0);
38:    printf("tan(-1.0) produces: %.1f\n", result);
39:
40:    // Log functions
41:    result = exp(12.0);
42:    printf("exp(12.0) produces: %.1f\n", result);
43:    result = log(12.0);
44:    printf("log(12.0) produces: %.1f\n", result);
45:    result = log10(12.0);
46:    printf("log10(12.0) produces: %.1f\n", result);
47:    getch();
48:
49:    return 0;
50:  }
```

▼ **OUTPUT**

```
ceil(-8.9) produces: -8.0
floor(-8.9) produces: -9.0
fabs(-34.6) produces: 34.6
fabs(34.6) produces: 34.6
fmod(25.0, 3.2) produces: 2.6
pow(4.0, 7.0) produces: 16384.0
pow(4096.0, (1.0/3.0)) produces 16.0
sqrt(1000.0) produces: 31.6
cos(-1.0) produces: 0.5
sin(-1.0) produces: -0.8
tan(-1.0) produces: -1.6
exp(12.0) produces: 162754.8
log(12.0) produces: 2.5
log10(12.0) produces: 1.1
```

▼ **ANALYSIS**

There is little going on with this program except function calls and printed results. Note that on line 27, the cube root of 4096.0 is computed by raising 4096.0 to the third power (the only way to find a cube root in C).

► **Homework**

General Knowledge

1. Which function sends formatted output to the printer?
2. What is the name of the printer device you use to specify the printer in C functions?
3. What does input buffering mean?
4. What's the difference between `getchar()` and `getch()`?
5. What's the difference between `getch()` and `getche()`?
6. What value must you use to test whether the user pressed Enter during a `getch()`?
7. What keystroke releases the `getchar()` buffered input?
8. What statement removes all data from the input buffer?
9. What are the two string input functions?
10. What is the string output function called?
11. What function sets the text color?
12. What function sets the background text color?
13. Describe how you can find the *nth* root of a number.
14. What does concatenation mean?
15. `strcat()` isn't considered a safe function by itself. Why?
16. Which function finds the length of a string?
17. True or false: When you select a text color, any text on-screen at that moment will become the new color.

18. True or false: All the functions mentioned in this unit are approved by the ANSI C committee.

19. True or false: A program receives input as the user types it when `getchar()` is used.

20. True or false: A program receives input as the user types it when `getch()` is used.

21. True or false: Both `floor()` and `ceil()` round values the same way.

22. True or false: The trigonometric functions require that their values be expressed in radians.

23. True or false: `strcmp()` returns a false result (0) if its two string arguments don't match.

What's the Output?

24. What is the value of each of the following function calls?

    A. `floor(2.3)`

    B. `floor(2.999)`

    C. `floor(-2.3)`

    D. `floor(-2.999)`

    E. `ceil(-2.3)`

    F. `ceil(2.3)`

Find the Bug

25. Paula just defined an array to hold an inventory product code. The array is defined as 10 elements long and is called `prodCode`. She coded the following `gets()` to get the product code from the user:

`gets(prodCode);`

The user sometimes enters too many letters and overwrites the array. Rewrite the `gets()` as `fgets()` so that you can limit the number of characters input at any one time.

26. Jim Perkins can't seem to set his color screen's background color to yellow. Tell him what the problem is.

27. Marty the mathematician wants to use the trig functions, but he can't because his angle, stored in the variable `angle`, is expressed in degrees and C's trig functions require radians. Show Marty the calculation he must perform on `angle` before any of C's trig functions will work with that variable.

Write Code That...

28. Write a program that asks the user for his or her full name using `gets()`. Print the name to the screen using `putchar()` and print the name to the printer using `fprintf()`.

29. Repeat the program in question 28, but write a character array-building routine similar to the one in this unit that gets the user's address a single character at a time.

30. Write a program that prints C is fun on-screen 16 times in 16 different colors. Only 15 occurrences will show because the background color will match the foreground text color in one instance.

Extra Credit

31. Write a program that asks the user for a password. As the user types each character, display an asterisk, *, not the actual character, but keep track of the character typed. If the user's password matches that stored in the program's character array, make the computer beep twice and tell the user congratulations.

32. Write a program that prints the cube root, square root, square, and cube of every number from 1 to 10.

16

Building Your Own Functions

function

global variable

local variable

prototype

return

structured program

▶ **What You'll Learn About**

- ▶ Separating code
- ▶ Local and global variables
- ▶ Sharing variables among functions
- ▶ Returning values via `return`

In Unit 15, you learned a lot about C's built-in library functions. This unit teaches you how to write your own functions. Once you write a function, you can call that function from a program just as you call a library function.

So far, every program you've written has contained one and only one function that you wrote—`main()`. C programs can contain many more functions that you write. The longer your program is, the better it is to break it into several small functions. By following a *building-block approach,* you separate routines into their own areas and make debugging easier because you can focus on specific problems without letting the rest of the code get in your way.

Writing a function in addition to `main()` does require a little fancy programming footwork, but writing multiple functions isn't difficult at all.

▶ **Separating Code**

Concept   **What You Will Learn**

> A program with many small functions is a lot easier to maintain than one long program. When writing separate functions, you have to manage the communication between those functions so that they can "talk" to each other.

Why does a book contain separate chapters? For one thing, one long, continuous book would seem to drag on and on. Chapters give the reader breaks, even if the reader starts another chapter right after finishing one. Chapters give the reader a sense of accomplishment.

More important, separate chapters, especially in a technical book such as this one, allow the reader to zero in on specific topics. Suppose that you picked up this book already knowing how to program in C but you'd never taken the time to master bitwise operators. You wouldn't need to read the entire book. Instead, you could turn directly to Unit 10 and get exactly the information you needed without the rest of the text getting in the way.

Structured programming becomes a habit once you begin to use it. People are used to breaking large tasks into smaller, more manageable ones. Programs often need to be broken down.

definition

A *structured program* is a modular program that contains one function for each task the program does.

Suppose that you were to write a program that computed and printed payroll figures for employees. As the payroll clerk entered each person's payroll figures, the program would perform input validation, compute payroll results, compute tax amounts, and print the results.

Here is a skeleton version of what such a program might look like:

```
main()
{
  // This is only an outline of a program
  //
  // C code to validate employee data
  //
  // C code to calculate payroll amounts
  //
  // C code to compute taxes
  //
  // C code to print the results
}
```

Note This program would more likely contain a large loop that continued running until all employee data were entered, validated, and printed, but we're keeping things simple for now.

There's nothing wrong with building a program such as this. For a real-world payroll system, however, this program would be extremely long. If the employee payroll figures were computed incorrectly, you would have to find exactly where in main() the problem occurred. Tracking such a bug would require you to make sure that the input validation code, the calculation code, and the printing code all worked properly.

If, however, you structured the program into separate functions, putting only one task in each function, you could more easily test each routine separately. Changing one routine wouldn't be likely to introduce as many bugs in other areas, as would be the case with one long program.

Tip Each separate function might be several lines long. The important thing to keep in mind when writing separate functions is that each function should do, at most, one task. As a rule of thumb, each function shouldn't be longer than a single screen length. Any longer and the function probably does too much work and you should break it into more functions.

When you write a function, you must start it with a name, parentheses, and surrounding braces, just like with main(). For example, here is the familiar outline of main():

```
main()
{
  // First, define any variables
  // The body of main() goes here
}
```

When writing additional functions, keep this format in mind. Here is the outline of a function called calcWages():

```
calcWages()
{
  // First, define any variables
  // The body of calcWages() goes here
}
```

You never explicitly call the `main()` function. The runtime system always begins at the `main()` function. However, if you want to execute (or *call*, in C terminology) another function in your program, you call that function by name, just as you call the library functions (such as `printf()`) by name. For example, if you wanted `main()` to call the `calcWages()` function, `main()` could do so with this statement:

```
calcWages();   // Call the calcWages() function
```

Once `calcWages()` finished, `main()` would regain control and continue on its way. Of course, any function can call any other function. Once `main()` calls a function, that called function might, in turn, call yet another function.

Tip   In really good programs (the ones that you write), `main()` should be little more than a controlling function for the other functions. In other words, `main()` should contain very few C statements other than function calls to other functions. In a way, `main()` acts like a table of contents for your program, controlling the execution of the rest of the code. If you need to change the program later, `main()` gives you the "big picture" that shows you how the rest of the program operates.

One additional advantage of separate functions is that you can call a routine more than once from different places in the program. For example, if you wanted to print your company's name and address at the top of every screen and report produced by a program, you could write a single function named `prCompInfo()` and call it from anywhere in the program that the company information needed to appear.

STOP&TYPE Listing 16.1 contains a version of the payroll program described earlier. Instead of having one long `main()` function, this program is broken into several separate functions, each of which accomplishes a single task.

Review   **What You Have Learned**

Break your programs into several small functions to aid in debugging and to decrease the number of bugs.

Warning   Listing 16.1 isn't a working program, only an outline of one.

▼ INPUT   LISTING 16.1. AN OUTLINE OF A STRUCTURED PAYROLL PROGRAM.

```
1:  main()
2:  {
3:     // This is only an outline of a program
4:     //
```

```
 5:    getInput();    // Get and validate the input data
 6:    calcWages();    // Calculate the payroll results
 7:    calcTaxes();    // Calculate the payroll taxes
 8:    prResults();    // Print the results
 9:    return 0;       // Return to the IDE
10:  }
11:
12:  //*********************************************
13:  getInput()
14:  {
15:    // C code to validate employee data
16:    return;   // Return to main()
17:  }
18:
19:  //*********************************************
20:  calcWages()
21:  {
22:    // C code to calculate payroll amounts
23:    return;   // Return to main()
24:  }
25:
26:  //*********************************************
27:  calcTaxes()
28:  {
29:    // C code to compute taxes
30:    return;   // Return to main()
31:  }
32:
33:  //*********************************************
34:  prResults()
35:  {
36:    // C code to print the results
37:    return;   // Return to main()
38:  }
```

> **Note** There is no output for Listing 16.1 because the program is incomplete as shown.

▼ ANALYSIS

Look at main() (lines 1 through 10). It controls the flow of the rest of the program. You can glance at main() and tell what the rest of the code does without wading through the rest of the code! Of course, using meaningful function names and ample comments helps make main() a true "control panel" that describes the rest of the code.

After the program is broken into separate functions, the code is certainly longer than the all-in-one function version you saw earlier. However, brevity isn't the key to structured programs—readability is.

In this listing, main() is the only function shown that calls another function. However, that doesn't have to be the case. Any of the subsequent functions could call any other function. The separating asterisk comments aren't required, but they do help you find where each function begins and ends.

UNIT

16

Building Your Own Functions

definition
Recursion occurs when one function calls itself or when two functions call each other.

 Warning As with infinite loops, you can get into trouble if a function calls itself or if function A calls function B and function B then calls function A. Recursive techniques can be helpful in advanced programming, but for now you'll want to stay away from them. (You'll be *cursing* your *recursive* programs!) If you write recursive functions without knowing exactly how to eliminate infinite recursion calls, you'll get a runtime error called *stack overflow*. Believe me, you don't want to overflow your stack!

▶ Local and Global Variables

Concept   **What You Will Learn**

Variables have either local or global scope. Their scope determines whether or not another function can use them.

definition
A *local* variable can be used only within the block you define it in.

All variables that you've defined in this book have been local variables. In other words, if you were to define a variable after main()'s opening brace, another function couldn't use that variable for anything. Only main() could use it. Perhaps you can see a problem: If separate functions are better than one long function, how can those functions work with the same data? If the user enters payroll values in one function, how can another function calculate with those values?

definition
A *block* is code between braces.

The concept of a block becomes important when discussing local variables. Variables aren't local to functions, but variables *are* local to blocks. For example, all the variables you've defined so far have been local to main() simply because you defined them at the top of main()'s primary block. A function always contains at least one pair of braces; therefore, a function always contains at least one block.

You can define variables at the top of any block, not just at the top of a function. Once the block ends, all variables defined at the top of that block *go away forever!* Once a block ends, all variables defined at the top of that block disappear and can *never* be used again unless you define them again elsewhere and reinitialize the variable with a new value.

Consider the following main() function:

```
main()
{
  int i = 9;        // Local to main()'s large block
  printf("i is %d\n", i);
  {                 // Begin a new block
    int j = 17;     // Local to this block only
    printf("j is %d\n", j);
  }                 // j goes away!
  printf("i and j are %d and %d\n", i, j);   // Error!!!
  return 0;
}                   // i goes away here!
```

`i` is local to the entire `main()` function because it's defined right after `main()`'s opening brace. `i` doesn't go away until its block ends at the end of `main()`. Therefore, from `main()`'s opening brace to its matching closing brace, `i` is active and is said to be *visible*.

`j` is a different story. Notice that the code doesn't define `j` until a new block begins. `j` is defined at the top of `main()`'s inner block; therefore, `j` is available (visible) *only within that block*. At the location of the inner block's closing brace, `j` disappears, causing an error on the subsequent `printf()` that occurs right before `return`.

Now, you might not be opening new blocks in the middle of a function and defining new variables inside them as done here, but it's vital that you understand the following:

▶ All local variables are available from their point of definition down in whatever block they appear in.

▶ When a local variable's block ends, that variable goes away completely. If two or more variables are defined inside a block, they all go away when the block ends.

The opposite of a local variable is a global variable. At first, it seems as if global variables are the answer for multifunction programs, because they let more than one function see the same variable. However, global variables lend themselves to sloppy programming practices, so you should avoid defining too many of them.

You must define a global variable before a function begins. That is, you must define the variable before a function name or between two functions (after one function's closing brace and before another's beginning line). If you define global variables, define all of them before `main()` even though C lets you define them later between other functions. Putting all your global variable definitions in one location helps you find them later.

All global variables are visible from their point of definition down in the source code. That is, once you define a global variable, any statement in any function that follows that global variable will be able to use it. The global variable won't go away until the program ends.

> **Warning** You can't use a global variable *before* its definition.

The problem with global variables is that they're *too visible*. All functions that follow their definition can access the global variables whether they need to or not. Local variables keep data on a need-to-know basis. Only functions that define local variables can use them, but any function can use visible global variables. One problem with global variables is that you can too easily change a global variable in one function and then inadvertently reinitialize that variable in another function. Also, global variables are sometimes difficult to find. If you define global variables at the top of a 20-page program, and you're working in the middle of that program, you'll have to flip back and forth from the beginning to the middle to see how those variables were defined. When you use local variables, their definitions always appear close to their usage.

The only time you should use global variables is when *all* functions (or a large majority of them) need access to the same variable. (You'll read in Lesson 11 that global variables find a good but limited use in file processing.)

definition
A *global* variable is visible throughout the rest of the program.

UNIT

16

Building Your Own Functions

All this discussion of local and global variables presents the following problem: With rare exceptions, you should use only local variables, but doing so keeps other functions that need access to those variables from using them. Luckily, you can teach C to share data between *only* those functions that need access to certain variables. You'll learn how C shares data between specific functions in the next section.

STOP&TYPE Listing 16.2 contains a program with both local and global variables.

Review

What You Have Learned

Local variables are safe, but they're visible only within the block you define them in. Global variables often are messy and lead to program bugs, but they allow for mass sharing of data.

▼ INPUT   LISTING 16.2. A SIMPLE PROGRAM WITH TWO GLOBAL AND THREE LOCAL VARIABLES.

```
1:  /* Filename: LOCGLO.C */
2:  // Defines four variables, two local and two global
3:  #include <stdio.h>
4:  #include <conio.h>
5:
6:  // Define two global variables
7:  int g1 = 10;    // Global variables can be any data
8:  int g2 = 20;    // type, just as local variables can be
9:
10: main()
11: {
12:   int l1 = 14;
13:   clrscr();
14:
15:   // The next line shows that globals are available
16:   printf("At the top of main(), \n");
17:   printf("The globals are %d and %d\n", g1, g2);
18:   printf("The local variable l1 is %d\n", l1);
19:
20:   // Create a new block
21:   {
22:     int l2 = 21;    // Local to this block only
23:     printf("\nIn main()'s inner block, the globals are");
24:     printf(" %d and %d\n", g1, g2);    // Still available
25:     printf("The local variable l1 is %d\n", l1);
26:     printf("The local variable l2 is %d\n", l2);
27:     printf("(l2 is about to disappear...)\n\n");
28:   }    // This terminates all valid use of l2
29:
30:   printf("Toward the end of main(), the globals are");
31:   printf(" %d and %d\n", g1, g2);    // Still available
32:   printf("The local variable l1 is %d\n", l1);
33:   printf("The local l2 is no longer valid.");
34:
35:   return 0;
36: }    // All variables go away now
```

▼ OUTPUT

```
At the top of main(),
The globals are 10 and 20
The local variable l1 is 14

In main()'s inner block, the globals are 10 and 20
The local variable l1 is 14
The local variable l2 is 21
(l2 is about to disappear...)

Toward the end of main(), the globals are 10 and 20
The local variable l1 is 14
The local l2 is no longer valid.
```

▼ ANALYSIS

Figure 16.1 helps show where each of the variables in Listing 16.1 are defined and where they lose their visibility. It's important to note that if the program contained additional functions below main(), the global variables g1 and g2 would be fully visible to those functions.

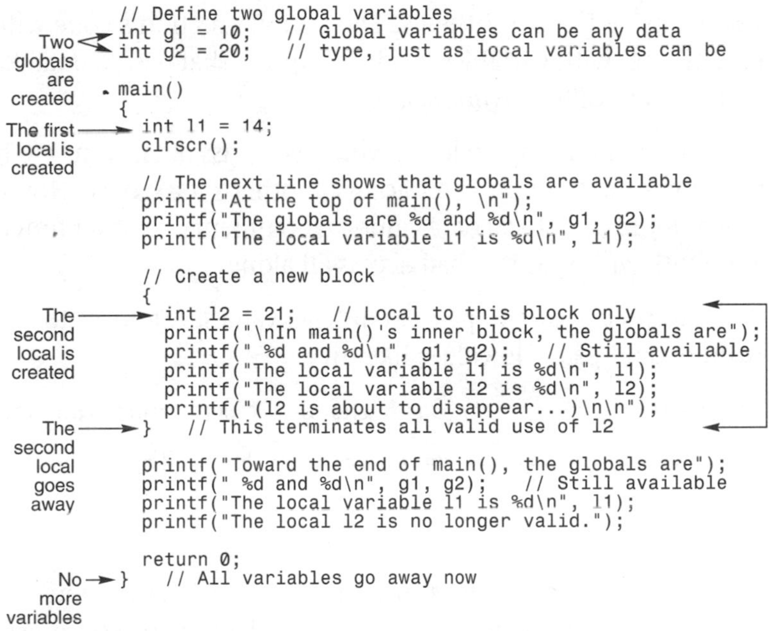

```
                              // Define two global variables
              Two  ◄── int g1 = 10;   // Global variables can be any data
            globals ◄── int g2 = 20;   // type, just as local variables can be
              are
            created    • main()
                       {
         The first ──────► int l1 = 14;
          local is        clrscr();
          created
                          // The next line shows that globals are available
                          printf("At the top of main(), \n");
                          printf("The globals are %d and %d\n", g1, g2);
                          printf("The local variable l1 is %d\n", l1);

                          // Create a new block
                          {
            The ──────►   int l2 = 21;    // Local to this block only
          second          printf("\nIn main()'s inner block, the globals are");
          local is        printf(" %d and %d\n", g1, g2);    // Still available   The
          created         printf("The local variable l1 is %d\n", l1);           inner
                          printf("The local variable l2 is %d\n", l2);           block
                          printf("(l2 is about to disappear...)\n\n");
            The ──────►   }      // This terminates all valid use of l2
          second
           local          printf("Toward the end of main(), the globals are");
           goes           printf(" %d and %d\n", g1, g2);    // Still available
           away           printf("The local variable l1 is %d\n", l1);
                          printf("The local l2 is no longer valid.");

                          return 0;
            No ──►  }    // All variables go away now
          more
          variables
```

FIGURE 16.1.
Pointing out the local and global variables.

Once main()'s inner block finishes in line 28, l2 goes away completely. The program defines l2 at the top of the inner block, right after the opening brace in line 21, and l2 goes away when the block ends (where the matching closing brace appears in line 28). If you were to open a second additional block inside main() after the first one finished, you could define another variable named l2 and no conflict with the first l2 would occur because the first l2 goes away in line 28.

▶ Sharing Variables Among Functions

Concept

To share local variables between two functions, you must pass the variables, not unlike a quarterback does with a football, from the calling function (the quarterback) to the receiving function (the receiver).

This section shows you how to pass data from one function to another. The passing described here is one-way. In the next section, you'll learn how to return a value from one function to another function. This section also finally tells you why you have to put parentheses after function names!

Actually, the parentheses aren't difficult to figure out now that you've used library functions. When a library function needs to work with values, your program passes the values inside the parentheses. The library function's code will have a similar group of parentheses with variables inside to capture that passed data. Remember that the values you pass are called *arguments*.

Arguments are the vehicles in which you pass data from one function to the next. Ordinarily, one function can't access another's local data. However, if a function passes one or more of its local data values as arguments, another function can receive that data and work with it as if it had access all along.

If you wanted `main()` to pass two integer values, `v1` and `v2`, to a function called `getThem()`, `main()` could pass the values like this:

```
getThem(v1, v2);    // Call the getThem() function and pass two values
```

The first two lines of `getThem()` would look something like this:

```
getThem(int v1, int v2)
{
```

definition
A function *definition* is the function's first line, which names the function and describes the arguments.

When a function receives one or more arguments, you can't leave the function's definition line with empty parentheses. The parentheses must describe to the function exactly what data is coming, as well as the data types. Figure 16.2 helps describe the process and terminology of passing data from `main()` to `getThem()`.

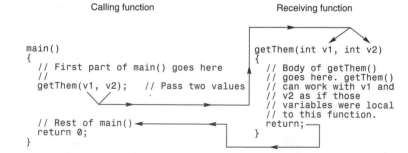

FIGURE 16.2.
Passing data requires a little setup in the function's definition line.

There are two ways to pass data from one function to another:

▶ By value

▶ By address

The method you use depends on your data and application. The majority of the time, you'll pass nonarray variables by value and array variables by address. The following sections explore each of these methods.

Passing by Value

Passing by value is sometimes called *passing by copy*. When you pass an argument from one function to another, the argument's value is passed to the receiving function, but the variable itself isn't passed.

It's vital that you understand that passing by value means that the receiving function can't change the passing function's variable in any way. Only the value of the passing function's variable, not the variable itself, is passed. Once the value gets to the receiving function, the receiving function accepts that value into its own local variable argument and works with its own variable that contains the passed value. However, nothing the receiving function does will change anything in the passing function.

STOP&TYPE Study the program in Listing 16.3. main() is the passing function and getIt() is the receiving function. The argument i is passed from main() to getIt(). No special syntax is needed. When you pass a nonarray as shown in Listing 16.3, C passes the data by value.

Note Passing by value is safer than passing by address. When you pass by value, the "owner" of the original variable, the passing function, passes the variable's value but retains all rights to that variable. The receiving function simply uses the value in its own variable without changing the passing function's version of the variable.

▼ **INPUT   LISTING 16.3. PASSING FROM** main() **TO** getIt() **BY VALUE.**

```
 1:  /* Filename: VALUPASS.C */
 2:  // Passes an argument from main()
 3:  // to another function by value
 4:  #include <stdio.h>
 5:  #include <conio.h>
 6:  getIt(int i);   // The function's prototype
 7:
 8:  main()
 9:  {
10:    int i;
11:    clrscr();
12:
13:    printf("I'm now in main()... \n");
14:    printf("Please enter a value for i: ");
15:    scanf(" %d", &i);
16:
```

continues

LISTING 16.3. CONTINUED

```
17:     getIt(i);   // No data types, just the variable
18:
19:     printf("\n\nBack in main(), the value is still %d\n", i);
20:     printf("Press a key to return to the IDE...");
21:     getch();
22:     return 0;    // Return to the IDE
23: }
24: //***********************************************************
25: getIt(int i)
26: {
27:     // getIt() now has a local variable called i also
28:     printf("\n\nJust got to getIt() and i is %d\n", i);
29:
30:     i *= 5;
31:
32:     printf("After multiplying by 5, i is now %d\n\n", i);
33:     return 0;    // Return to main()
34: }
```

▼ **OUTPUT**

```
I'm now in main()...
Please enter a value for i: 3

Just got to getIt() and i is 3
After multiplying by 5, i is now 15

Back in main(), the value is still 3
Press a key to return to the IDE...
```

▼ **ANALYSIS**

By studying the output, you can see that getIt() can change i only inside getIt(). Once getIt() returns control to main(), you see that main()'s i was left intact with its original value. main()'s i and getIt()'s i are two completely different variables. One is main()'s local variable and the other is getIt()'s local variable.

One interesting thing to note is that getIt() didn't even have to call the variable i. If getIt()'s definition line read like this:

```
getIt(int myVal)
```

getit() would print and multiply myVal by 5, and the results would be identical to the preceding output. Only the *value* of main()'s i was passed, not the variable itself.

main() didn't have to list i's data type in the parentheses in line 17 because main() already knows i's data type. Only the receiving function, which knows nothing about the argument before the pass, must be told the data type of the value being sent.

 Warning   Never put a semicolon at the end of a function's definition line. For example, line 25 would never have a semicolon at the end of it. At the point where you call a function, however, you must put a semicolon, as done in line 17.

Figure 16.3 helps show how `main()` sends the value of the variable to `getIt()` and not the variable itself. This figure assumes that the user entered a 3, as shown in the previous output.

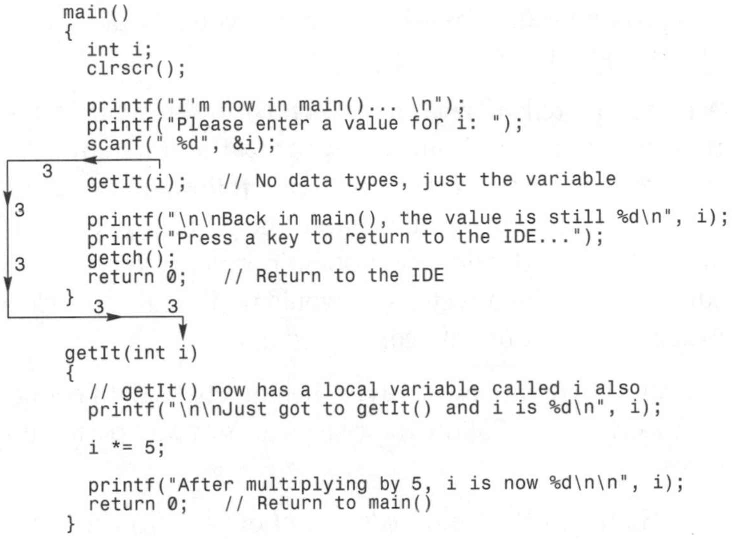

```
main()
{
  int i;
  clrscr();

  printf("I'm now in main()... \n");
  printf("Please enter a value for i: ");
  scanf(" %d", &i);

  getIt(i);    // No data types, just the variable

  printf("\n\nBack in main(), the value is still %d\n", i);
  printf("Press a key to return to the IDE...");
  getch();
  return 0;    // Return to the IDE
}

getIt(int i)
{
  // getIt() now has a local variable called i also
  printf("\n\nJust got to getIt() and i is %d\n", i);

  i *= 5;

  printf("After multiplying by 5, i is now %d\n\n", i);
  return 0;    // Return to main()
}
```

FIGURE 16.3.
`main()` passes the value of 3, not `i`.

If more than one value were passed from `main()` to `getIt()`, all the values would be sent, but the receiving function couldn't change `main()`'s copy of the variables. When you pass more than one variable, separate the variables with commas. When a function receives more than one argument, separate the receiving data types and arguments with commas. For example, if `main()` passed an integer named `i`, a character named `c`, and a floating-point value named `x` to `getIt()`, the line in `main()` might look like this:

```
getIt(i, c, x);    // Pass three values
```

The definition of `getIt()` would look like this:

```
getIt(int i, char c, float x)    // Definition line
```

As mentioned earlier, `getIt()` could have renamed the argument values and used the new names as its variables, but `getIt()` could never change `main()`'s copy of any of the variables.

Detour for a Moment with Prototypes

We're not done with Listing 16.3. Aren't you curious about the duplication of `getIt()`'s definition line in line 6? Line 6 is called a prototype. All functions that you write using Turbo C++ must include a prototype. Some C compilers don't always require prototypes, but you'll develop much better habits and many fewer bugs if you start prototyping all functions that you write now.

As you know, you must define all variables before you can use them. Also, you must define all functions before you call them! `main()` is the exception because it's already known by the runtime system that runs your program. (`main()` is known as a *self-prototyping function*.)

UNIT

16

Building Your Own Functions

definition
A *prototype* models a function's definition.

Defining (prototyping) a function almost seems like overkill because it's so easy. To prototype a function, you must copy the function's definition line (the function's first line with arguments and everything else) to the top of your program. The best place to prototype your program's functions is right after your #include directives. As long as you prototype anywhere before main(), you'll be okay, but most people prototype right after the #includes.

A prototype tells C what to expect. For instance, if you tell it, via a prototype, that a particular function should receive a float followed by a double, but in the program you inadvertently pass the function a char followed by a double, C will be able to catch the error during compilation. Without the prototype, C would have to promote the value any way it could, and a char doesn't promote very well to a double! Your program results would be incorrect, and it would be difficult to track down the error and figure out exactly where your data got messed up.

Many C programmers prototype their functions right before compiling. With Turbo C++, that's easy to do. Follow these steps to copy and paste function definitions into prototypes:

1. Highlight the function's definition (the first line in the function) by clicking on it or by holding down the Shift key and pressing the arrow keys until the line you want is highlighted.

2. Select Edit Copy (Ctrl-Ins) to copy the highlighted line to Turbo C++'s IDE clipboard.

3. Move the cursor to the top of the program and insert a new line where you want the prototype to go.

4. Select Edit Paste (Shift-Ins) to copy the clipboard's line to the prototype area.

5. Add a semicolon to the end of the prototype. All prototypes require semicolons so that C can distinguish a prototype from a function's definition line.

AH, IT MAKES SENSE NOW!

You've been dutifully including the appropriate header files such as STDIO.H and CONIO.H as needed. Until now, you've never fully understood why they're needed. Each time you learned a function that required a different header file, you began using that header. Now you know enough to understand *why* those header files are so important.

As mentioned a moment ago, you must prototype *all* functions before you can use them. The only exception is main(). That means that you must prototype functions that you didn't even write, such as printf() and clrscr()!

What does the prototype for printf() look like? You don't know, yet you've already been prototyping printf() and all the other library functions. When Turbo C++ supplies a library function, it prototypes that function for you in one of the header files. Therefore, when you include a header file, you're including a ton of prototypes for all functions you might use that are related to that header file. By including STDIO.H, for instance, you started prototyping printf() from the very beginning.

If, in the beginning, I had gone into a lot of detail about the need to define all functions with a prototype before you call them, you might have given up too early. Now that you understand prototypes, the header files should make a lot more sense.

A prototype doesn't have to have the actual argument names listed inside its parentheses, only the data types. The following are considered to be identical prototypes for a function named `calcIt()`:

```
calcIt(float i, double d, char c);
```

```
calcIt(float, double, char);
```

A prototype helps C with data types, not variable names, so names aren't needed in the prototype itself. Argument names are needed, however, in the function's definition line. Most programmers use the cut-and-paste method described earlier to create their prototypes; therefore, most programmers' prototypes do contain argument names.

Passing by Address

C passes all arrays by address. In other words, when you pass an array, such as a character array, to a function, the function receives the array by address automatically. As you read earlier, all nonarray variables are passed by value.

The *address* in *passing by address* is the starting location, in memory, of a variable. All variables begin at a specific address. The exact address isn't important. What *is* important, however, is that you know the following: When C passes a variable by address, it passes the variable itself (in effect), meaning that the receiving function can change the calling function's variable. When the calling function regains control, any variable just passed by address might be changed if the called function changed the argument.

STOP&TYPE Passing by value is safer than passing by address because the called function can't change the calling function's variables. However, there are times when you want the called function to change the calling function's variables. For example, Listing 16.4 contains a program that asks the user for his or her name in `main()`. The user's name is then passed to `changeIt()`, where the first and last characters in the name are changed to #. When `main()` regains control, it prints the name array, showing that the called function did indeed change `main()`'s version of the array.

definition

Passing by address means that the variable itself (its location in memory) is passed and received.

UNIT

16

Building Your Own Functions

▼ INPUT   LISTING 16.4. PASSING AN ARRAY BY ADDRESS.

```
1:  /* Filename: PASSADDR.C */
2:  // Passing an array means that the called function
3:  // can change the same variable as in the calling function
4:  #include <stdio.h>
5:  #include <conio.h>
6:  #include <string.h>
7:  changeIt(char userName[30]);    // Prototype
8:
```

continues

LISTING 16.4. CONTINUED

```
 9:  main()
10:  {
11:    char userName[30];
12:
13:    clrscr();
14:    printf("What is your name? ");
15:    gets(userName);
16:
17:    // Send the name to changeIt() by address
18:    changeIt(userName);
19:
20:    puts("After a return to main(), here is your name:");
21:    puts(userName);
22:    return 0;
23:  }
24:  //*********************************************************
25:  changeIt(char userName[30])
26:  {
27:    int endPlace;
28:    userName[0] = '#';    // Change first letter in name
29:    endPlace = strlen(userName) - 1;   // Find location of
30:                                       // final letter in name
31:    userName[endPlace] = '#';
32:
33:    return 0;    // Return to main()
34:  }
```

▼ **OUTPUT**

```
What is your name? Ronald Bush
After a return to main(), here is your name:
#onald Bus#
```

▼ **ANALYSIS**

The user fills the array named userName with a value in line 15. In line 18, main() passes the array named userName to the function named changeIt(). changeIt() changes the first and last letter of the name to a pound sign.

changeIt() changes main()'s array because all arrays are passed by address. Therefore, when changeIt() overwrites two letters with pound signs, main() knows about the change. When changeIt() returns to main(), the array is still changed. main() displays the array in line 21. As you can see from the output, the array that main() displays is indeed the array that changeIt() changed.

 Tip   It turns out that, when you pass an array to a function, you don't have to put the subscript in the receiving function's argument brackets. The 30 in line 25 is optional.

You can't pass an array by value. Therefore, you must be on guard when passing arrays. Always be aware that the called function could change the array. If the called function does change the array, the calling function's array will reflect those changes.

There's a way to override the passing of nonarrays by value. If you need to, you can pass a regular integer variable (or any nonarray variable) to a function by address. You would do so if you wanted the function to change the variable in both places.

Passing a nonarray variable by address requires some really strange syntax. Perhaps it's best that the designers of C included the extra syntax, because maybe that will make you pass by address only when you need to. It's important when writing long, structured programs (especially if you're on a team of programmers writing a large system) to make sure that only functions that need to change variables get a chance to do so.

To pass a nonarray variable by address, precede the argument in the calling function with an ampersand (&). (You'll learn in the next lesson that the ampersand is called the *address of operator*.) The ampersand tells C that you want that specific nonarray variable passed by address. C therefore passes the variable by address and lets the called function change the variable in both places.

STOP&TYPE In addition to including an ampersand in the calling function, you must also (get this!) precede the variable with an asterisk (*) in the receiving function wherever the variable appears! In this context, the * is called the *dereferencing operator* (as you'll see in the next lesson). It looks really crazy, as you can see in Listing 16.5.

▼ INPUT   LISTING 16.5. PASSING AN INTEGER BY ADDRESS AND A CHARACTER BY VALUE.

```
 1:  /* Filename: OVERRIDE.C */
 2:  // Overrides the default method of passing
 3:  // a nonarray variable. This program passes
 4:  // a nonarray variable by address and,
 5:  // therefore, requires some extra notation.
 6:  #include <stdio.h>
 7:  #include <conio.h>
 8:  changeIt(int *i, char c);
 9:  main()
10:  {
11:    int i;
12:    char c;
13:
14:    clrscr();
15:    // Assign two values in main()
16:    i = 10;
17:    c = 'X';
18:
19:    printf("Before leaving main(), i and c are %d and %c\n",
20:          i, c);
21:
22:    changeIt( &i, c);    // Pass the integer by address
23:
24:    printf("Back in main(), i and c are %d and %c\n", i, c);
25:    return 0;
26:  }
27:  //**********************************************************
28:  changeIt(int *i, char c)
29:  {
```

UNIT

16

Building Your Own Functions

continues

LISTING 16.5. CONTINUED

```
30:     *i = 26;
31:     c = 'p';   // main()'s version of c won't change
32:
33:     return 0;   // Return to main()
34:  }
```

▼ **OUTPUT**

```
Before leaving main(), i and c are 10 and X
Back in main(), i and c are 26 and X
```

▼ **ANALYSIS**

If `changeIt()` were longer and had referred to `i` several times throughout the function, `i` would have needed an asterisk (`*i`) every place it appeared. Again, overriding the passing of nonarray data requires some strange syntax, but when a function has to change another function's data, passing by address is a good way to accomplish that change.

YET ANOTHER MYSTERY SOLVED!

You've seen the preceding ampersand (&) before, haven't you? `scanf()` requires it. Well, `scanf()` requires the ampersand before all nonarray variables. What's going on? You know now that `scanf()` must have a requirement that you pass all variables to it by address!

Think for a moment why. Doesn't `scanf()` need to be able to change the variables you send it? For instance, when `main()` calls `scanf()`, `scanf()` must fill `main()`'s variables with the user's values. `scanf()` takes care of the keyboard input and stores the data in `main()`'s variables. The only way that `scanf()` could store data in the calling function's variables is via passing by address.

Hmm, perhaps `scanf()` isn't so cryptic after all. (Just between friends, though, `scanf()` still stinks!)

Note Not every function requires arguments. Sometimes you might write a function that prints a report from a data file without needing to rely on variables from elsewhere in the program. If you write a function that accepts no arguments, put `void` in its argument list both in the function definition and in the prototype. For example, the following function receives no arguments:

```
aFunction( void )
{
   // Body of function goes here
}
```

Of course, if you don't pass values to a function, you can leave the function's parentheses empty, as you've seen throughout this book with `main()`.

Review **What You Have Learned**

In this section, you learned that there are two ways to pass variables from one function to another. When you pass by value, the called function can't change the calling function's variables. When you pass by address, the called function can change the calling function's variables.

Note There is no Stop and Type section here. Before you pass variables in a larger example, you need to read the next section.

► Returning Values via *return*

Concept **What You Will Learn**

The `return` statement gives your functions the ability to return a single value from a called function.

Until now, you've seen the passing of data *to* a function. Using the `return` statement, you can see how to return a value to the calling function. Every program in this book has returned a 0 to the IDE by placing this `return` statement at the end of `main()`:

```
return 0;
```

Sometimes, C programmers put the `return` value in parentheses:

```
return (0);
```

You can return, at most, one and only one value from a function! As Figure 16.4 shows, you can pass several arguments to a function, but you can return only one.

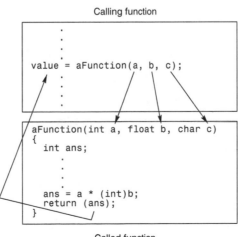

FIGURE 16.4.
At most, you can return only a single value.

Although Figure 16.4 contains an outline of two functions, you can see that the calling function's function call looks unlike any you've seen so far. Instead of calling `aFunction()` on a line by itself like this:

```
aFunction(a, b, c);
```

`main()` assigns `aFunction` to a variable like this:

```
value = aFunction(a, b, c);
```

The assignment is needed to hold `aFunction()`'s return value. In other words, when a function returns a value, you should have some way to capture that return value.

> **Note** If a function returns a value, the calling function doesn't *have* to capture the value. However, if the calling function ignores the return value, there is little reason to return anything. Nevertheless, every function in this unit other than `main()` has returned a 0 to `main()`, and `main()` has done nothing with the 0. You'll see why 0 was returned, even though `main()` ignored it, in a moment.

When you learned about the mathematical library functions in Unit 15, you saw many functions that returned values. You learned about `pow()`, useful for raising a number to a power, whose usage looks something like this:

```
ans = pow(4.0, 3.0);    // Raise 4.0 to the third power
```

In this assignment, `pow()` is passed two values, and `pow()`'s single return value is captured and stored in `ans`.

Before you look at a program that uses a return value, there's one more thing you must know. If a function returns a value, you must tell C what kind of value that function is returning. Put the return value data type before the function name. If a function isn't going to return a value, you must put `void` before the function name.

Therefore, you know from the following function definition, without looking at its `return` statement, exactly what kind of data the function returns:

```
double functionA(int i, float j)
```

This function returns a `double` value. The return data type appears on the same line as the function definition so that you can specify the return data type in the prototype as well. Here is the prototype for the preceding function:

```
double functionA(int i, float j);
```

If you don't specify a return value, C assumes that you're returning an integer. Therefore, the following function prototypes are identical:

```
int compute(int age, float factor);
```

```
compute(int age, float factor);    // Assumed to return an int
```

Given the default return data type of `int`, what kind of value do you think `main()` is assumed to return? In all of this book's programs, the first line of `main()` looks like this:

```
main()
```

Therefore, C assumes that `main()` will return an integer value. That's the purpose of the `return 0;` at the end of every `main()` in this book. The operating system discards the 0, but if you ran your program from a batch file, you could capture the 0 or any other return value and process it accordingly.

Throughout this book, `main()` could have started like this:

```
void main(void)
```

Such a definition of `main()` would be extremely pure, because no `main()` function in this book has received arguments or needed to return a value. With the `void` return data type, `main()`'s `return` could look like this:

```
return;    // Nothing returned
```

The ANSI C committee requires that a program's `main()` function return a value, even if that value is ignored. Therefore, you'll find that most C and even C++ programmers let `main()` return 0 instead of putting `void` before `main()`'s definition.

STOP&TYPE Listing 16.6 contains a program that uses three functions (including `main()`). The first function that `main()` calls asks for the user's name, and the second calculates the number of years left until the user's retirement.

Review   **What You Have Learned**

The passing and returning of data provide C's vehicle for sharing data. You can pass data by value or by address. The method you use depends on whether you want the receiving function to be able to change the calling function's variables.

▼ INPUT   LISTING 16.6. PASSING AND RETURNING VALUES.

```
 1:  /* Filename: PASSRET.C */
 2:  // Program that passes by value and by address.
 3:  // This program also demonstrates prototypes and
 4:  // how to return a value from one function to
 5:  // the calling function.
 6:  #include <stdio.h>
 7:  #include <conio.h>
 8:  void getUserName(char uName[50]);
 9:  int computeRetire(int age);
10:
11:  main()
12:  {
13:    char uName[50];
14:    int age;
15:    int yrsToRetire;
16:
17:    clrscr();
18:    getUserName(uName);    // Fill the array in the function
19:
20:    printf("How old are you, %s? ", uName);
21:    scanf(" %d", &age);
```

UNIT

16

Building Your Own Functions

continues

LISTING 16.6. CONTINUED

```
22:    yrsToRetire = computeRetire(age);   // Pass and return values
23:
24:    printf("You have %d years until retirement at 65\n",
25:         yrsToRetire);
26:
27:    return 0;
28: }
29: //********************************************************
30: void getUserName(char uName[50])    // 50 is optional here
31: {
32:    printf("What is your name? ");
33:    gets(uName);
34:    return;   // No need to return anything
35: }
36: //********************************************************
37: int computeRetire(int age)
38: {
39:    return (65 - age);   // Return the number of years until 65
40: }
```

▼ **OUTPUT**

```
What is your name? Ted
How old are you, Ted? 41
You have 24 years until retirement at 65
```

▼ **ANALYSIS**

Lines 8 and 9 contain the prototypes for the two functions that follow main(). Always put main() first in your programs. Not only is main() executed first, but other C programmers who might maintain your programs expect main() to appear first.

In line 18, main() calls the next function in the program, getUsername(). main() passes the character array to this function so that the function can fill the array. C receives all arrays by address, so when the user enters a value into the array within the getUserName() function, main()'s array also gets filled at the same time. When you pass an array, a copy of the array values doesn't get sent. Instead, C passes the actual array.

The printf() in line 20 shows that the user's name resides in main()'s array when getUserName() returns control to main(). Once the user enters her or his age, main() passes the age in line 21 to the computeRetire() function. The body of computeRetire() consists of a single statement, the return statement on line 39, that computes the number of years until the user reaches 65. As you can see from line 39, you can return an expression from a function instead of a single variable if you wish.

There is no reason for main() to pass age by address to computeRetire(), because computeRetire() doesn't need to change main()'s age value. It only uses age to compute the retirement years. You won't find any global variables in Listing 16.6 because they're not needed. There usually is never a need for them.

Note This unit began by separating a payroll program into different functions. This lesson's project contains the full code for and a description of the program.

▶ Homework

General Knowledge

1. Which is better, a program with one long `main()` function or a program with lots of smaller functions?

2. What's one advantage of structured programs?

3. Why are modular programs with lots of functions easier to maintain than programs with only one or a few long functions?

4. What is recursion?

5. Variables can be defined two places in a program. List the two places.

6. What's the difference between local and global variables?

7. What's a block?

8. Which variable is safer, a local or a global variable?

9. When does a local variable go away?

10. When does a global variable go away?

11. What are the two ways you can pass variables?

12. Which is safer, passing by address or by value?

13. What's another name for passing by value?

14. How can you pass a nonarray variable by value?

15. How can you pass a nonarray variable by address?

16. What's a prototype?

17. How can prototypes help eliminate bugs?

18. How can you prototype library functions such as `printf()`?

19. How many values can a function return at any one time?

20. Why don't you need to prototype `main()`?

21. Why don't you need to return global variables?

22. Suppose `main()` passes a variable by value. If the called function changes the argument, will `main()`'s value also change?

23. Suppose `main()` passes a variable by address. If the called function changes the argument, will `main()`'s value also change?

24. True or false: A function that returns a value can be passed only a single argument.

25. True or false: Once you define a local variable, all functions in the program can use the variable.

26. True or false: You can't use a global variable before its definition.

27. True or false: The following is a prototype.

```
void aFunction(void)
```

28. True or false: The following is a prototype.

```
void aFunction(void);
```

29. True or false: You can pass an array by value.

What's the Output?

30. What's the output of the following program?

```
/* Filename: L8BOUT1.C */
#include <stdio.h>
void doubleIt(int i);

main()
{
  int i = 19;

  doubleIt(i);
  printf("i is now %d\n", i);
  return 0;
}
//*************************************************
void doubleIt(int i)
{
  i *= 2;
  return;
}
```

31. What's the output of the following program?

```
/* Filename: L8BOUT2.C */
#include <stdio.h>
void doubleIt(int *i);

main()
{
  int i = 19;

  doubleIt(&i);
  printf("i is now %d\n", i);
  return 0;
}
//*************************************************
void doubleIt(int *i)
{
  *i *= 2;
  return;
}
```

Find the Bug

32. What's wrong with the following function?

```
sqThem(i, j)
{
  i = i * i;
  j = j * j;
  printf("i squared is %d\n", i);
  printf("j squared is %d\n", j);
  return 0;
}
```

Write Code That...

33. Write a prototype equivalent to the following that explicitly includes the return data type:

```
event(int a);
```

34. Write a program that prints, in `main()`, the double-precision area of a circle given that a user's double-precision radius is passed to the function. The formula for calculating a circle's area is

```
area = 3.14159 * (radius * radius)
```

35. Rewrite the following function to receive and process its arguments by address instead of by value:

```
void doubleThem(float x, float y)
{
  x *= 2.0;
  y *= 2.0;
  printf("The first argument is now %f\n", x);
  printf("The second argument is now %f\n", y);
  return;
}
```

36. Write a program whose `main()` function calls a function that asks the user for a number from 1 to 80. (Keep looping if the user enters a value outside that range.) Return to `main()` and pass that number to a function named `asterisk()`, which will print that number of asterisks in a line across the screen.

Extra Credit

37. Write a program that in `main()` asks the user for the number of vacation days he or she has left at work this year. As soon as the user enters the number of days, pass that value to a second function. In the called function, print the number of hours of vacation that the user still has (24 times the number of days). Print the message `Enjoy!` if the user has more than five days' worth of vacation time. Return to `main()` and terminate the program as usual.

UNIT

16

Building Your Own Functions

38. Write a function that receives two integers by address. Switch the values of the two integers in the function. Due to the passing by address, when the called function returns control to the calling function, the values will still be swapped in the calling function.

Breaking It Up with Functions

STOP&TYPE In this lesson, you learned about several more library functions, as well as how to write your own functions. You saw the following:

▶ Input and output functions that help you control the user's data.

▶ Character-based functions that manipulate character data.

▶ String functions that compare and test null-terminated string data.

▶ Numeric functions that include rounding, mathematical, trigonometric, and logarithmic calculations.

Project 8 Listing. A multifunction program that passes data between functions.

```
1:  /* Filename: LESSON8.C */

2:  // A multifunction program that computes payroll amounts

3:  #include <stdio.h>

4:  #include <conio.h>

5:  void getInput(float *rate, int *hours);

6:  float calcWages(float rate, int hours);

7:  float calcTaxes(float pay);

8:  void prResults(float pay, float taxes);

9:  main()

10: {

11:    int hours;

12:    float rate, pay, taxes;

13:    getInput(&rate, &hours);    // Get and validate the input data
```

▶ How to write your own functions.

▶ How to determine the difference between local and global variables.

▶ How to pass data to a function.

▶ How to return data from a function.

Description

1: A C comment that includes the program's filename.

2: A C++ comment that contains the program's description.

3: The printf() and scanf() functions need information in the STDIO.H header file.

4: The screen-clearing function, clrscr(), needs information in the CONIO.H header file.

5: Prototype of a function.   5: Prototype all functions.

6: Prototype of another function.

7: Prototype of another function.

8: Prototype of another function.

9: main() begins.

10: All functions begin with an opening brace.

11: An integer variable that will hold the number of hours worked.

12: Variables to hold various payroll values.

13: Passes rate and hours by address so that getInput() can change them and keep those changed values in main().

continues

Project 8 Listing. continued

```c
14:     pay = calcWages(rate, hours);    // Calculate the payroll results

15:     taxes = calcTaxes(pay);          // Calculate the payroll taxes

16:     prResults(pay, taxes);           // Print the results

17:    return 0;    // Return to the IDE

18:  }

19:  //*************************************************************

20:  void getInput(float *rate, int *hours)

21:  {

22:     int scanfHours;

23:     float scanfRate;    // Needed to grab scanf()

24:     // Code to validate employee data

25:     clrscr();

26:     printf("How many hours did this employee work? ");

27:     scanf(" %d", &scanfHours);

28:     printf("What is the pay rate per hour? ");

29:     scanf(" %f", &scanfRate);

30:     *rate = scanfRate;

31:     *hours = scanfHours;

32:     return;    // Return to main()

33:  }

34:  //*************************************************************
```

Description

14: `calcWages()` uses the `rate` and `hours` figures to calculate and return the gross pay. `main()` captures the return value in `pay`.

15: `calcTaxes()` uses the gross pay to calculate and return the taxes. `main()` captures the return value in `taxes`.

16: The gross pay and taxes are sent to `prResults()` to be displayed on-screen.

17: Always return from `main()` to the IDE.

17: Keep `main()` as simple as possible.

18: A final brace ends all `main()` functions.

19: A line of asterisks helps to separate functions.

20: The definition (first line) of `getInput()`. Receives two arguments by address.

21: All functions begin with an opening brace.

22: Creates a local variable to use for `scanf()`.

23: Creates another local variable to use for the `scanf()`.

24: Scatter comments throughout your code.

25: Clears the user's screen.

26: Prompts the user for the hours.

27: Gets the hours.

27: Without the extra local variable named `scanfHours` (and `scanfRate` in line 29), you'd have to eliminate the ampersand in the `scanf()` variables, and that would confuse you more than help you at this point.

28: Prompts the user for the pay rate.

29: Gets the rate.

30: Assigns to `main()`'s variable the value entered by the user.

30: When passing by address, always use the *.

31: Assigns to `main()`'s variable the value entered by the user.

32: Returns to `main()`.

33: A final brace ends all functions.

34: A line of asterisks helps to separate functions.

continues

Project 8 Listing. continued

```c
35:   float calcWages(float rate, int hours)

36:   {    // Code to calculate payroll amounts

37:     return (rate * (float)hours);    // Return to main()

38:   }

39:   //**********************************************************

40:   float calcTaxes(float pay)

41:   {    // Code to compute taxes

42:     float taxRate = .34;

43:     return (pay * taxRate);    // Return to main()

44:   }

45:   //**********************************************************

46:   void prResults(float pay, float taxes)

47:   {    // Code to print the results

48:     printf("\nThe employee earned a total of $%.2f\n", pay);

49:     printf("Before $%.2f in taxes.\n", taxes);

50:     return;    // Return to main()

51:   }
```

Description

35: Defines the function that calculates gross pay.

35: This function receives a floating-point and an integer argument passed by value.

36: Scatter comments throughout your code.

37: Returns the wages (the number of hours multiplied by the rate per hour).

38: A final brace ends all functions.

39: A line of asterisks helps to separate functions.

40: Defines the function that calculates taxes. This function requires one argument passed by value.

41: Scatter comments throughout your code.

42: Stores the current tax rate percentage.

43: Returns the taxes to main(), which are simply the gross pay multiplied by the tax rate.

44: A final brace ends all functions.

45: A line of asterisks helps to separate functions.

46: Defines the function that prints the results. This function requires two arguments passed by value.

47: Scatter comments throughout your code.

48: Prints the employee's gross pay.

49: Prints the employee's tax requirement.

50: Returns to main().

51: A final brace ends all functions.

▼ OUTPUT

```
How many hours did this employee work? 40
What is the pay rate per hour? 12.34

The employee earned a total of $493.60
Before $167.82 in taxes.
```

Lesson ▶

Lots of Data

Unit 17: Arrays Multiply Storage

Unit 18: Pointers Simplify

Lesson 9 Project

Lesson 9

Unit ▶

17

Arrays Multiply Storage

array

element

key

parallel array

single-dimensional array

▶ What You'll Learn About

▶ Array basics

▶ Searching through arrays

There is little need to explain arrays in great detail here because you already know all about them! You've been working with character arrays since Lesson 3. This unit simply explains more about how C stores arrays and introduces arrays of data types that are different from the `char` data types you've been working with.

In addition to character arrays, you can create arrays of any data type. You can define an integer array, a floating-point array, and a double floating-point array. Anytime you need lists of values, it's a lot easier to define the list as an array instead of as differently named variables. You can step through all the elements of an array with a `for` loop, and you'll often need to process and print elements throughout an array.

▶ Array Basics

Concept   **What You Will Learn**

Review the terminology of arrays and explain how arrays reside in the computer's memory.

Figure 17.1 shows a character array named `cArray` with five values. Each individual value in the array is an *element*. The subscripts range from 0 to 4 for a five-character array. No matter what kind of array you define, each value in the array is called an element, and the number that references each element is also a subscript.

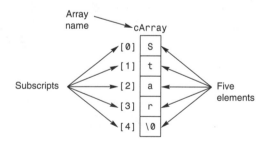

FIGURE 17.1.
A five-element character
array holding a string.

As you know, character arrays hold strings. In C, arrays can be taught much earlier than in other programming languages (or at least character arrays can be). When a character array holds a string value, treating the array as a single but aggregate string value, with the individual elements holding individual characters, makes a lot of sense. (Other programming languages store strings in string variables.)

You might not see the need for numeric arrays at this time. After all, if you defined an array of 25 integers, you would never refer to the entire integer array as a single entity.

The concept of doing something with a single group of 25 numbers doesn't make as much sense as treating a character array holding a string as a single group.

In reality, you work with lists of numbers all the time. When your program must process several numeric values, array storage is perfect for holding and stepping through those values. Although you don't refer to the array aggregately in the same way that you do a character array holding a string, numeric arrays are extremely important in computing.

To help with your understanding of numeric arrays, let's review the basics of character arrays. The array in Figure 17.1 might be initialized like this:

```
char cArray[5] = "Star";
```

C's syntax for initializing strings in character arrays, as shown here, doesn't apply to numeric arrays. There's no need to worry about a null zero at the end of numeric arrays because only strings need null zero values at their termination. If you define and initialize a numeric array at the same time, you must initialize the array's individual elements one at a time. Use braces to initialize individual elements in the array.

Here's how you would initialize cArray one element at a time:

```
char cArray[5] = {'S', 't', 'a', 'r', '\0'};
```

This definition is identical to the previous one, except that it's a little more tedious for you to type. Nevertheless, this character-by-character initialization will prepare you for the syntax required for all numeric array initialization. C automatically adds the null zero to the end of the string when you assign an initial string value.

When you define and initialize an array at the same time, you don't need the initial subscript. The following definition is identical to the preceding one:

```
char cArray[] = {'S', 't', 'a', 'r', '\0'};   // C counts the elements
                                               // for you
```

When you (or C) reserve five array elements, don't try to store six or more elements in the array! If you do, you will overwrite memory that might be holding other kinds of variables. If you need to define a large array, you can always define the array with extra elements. The following array definition holds the four-character string Star, with a trailing null zero, but it also has extra reserved room in case you need to store a longer string in the array later:

```
char cArray[35] = {'S', 't', 'a', 'r', '\0'};
```

Character arrays might hold individual characters and not strings. If that's the case, don't worry about the null zero. It exists only to terminate strings.

Note   String functions such as strlen() and strcpy() rely on the null zero. If you define an array to hold a list of individual characters, such as a class's letter grades, you'll never treat the array as if it holds a string; therefore, you don't have to make sure the null zero is at the end of the array.

Warning   Unlike most programming languages, C doesn't complain if you store a value in an undefined array element. For example, the following statement:

```
cArray[3200] = 'X';    // Oops!
```

puts an X approximately 3,200 memory locations after the start of the 35-character array named cArray. Who knows *what* the X will overwrite? Whatever happens, you'll realize something has gone awry when your computer freezes or reboots because the X overwrote an important area of memory or changed a critical internal program value!

Moving to numeric arrays is now easy. If you want to define a five-element integer array named nums, you can do so like this:

```
int nums[5];    // Define an integer array
```

You also can initialize the array at the same time you define it:

```
int nums[5] = {2, 4, 6, 8, 10};    // Define and initialize the array
```

Figure 17.2 shows how the integer array looks in memory. Notice that an integer array and a character array are the same except for these two things:

▶ Numeric arrays contain numeric values and not character values.

▶ Numeric arrays don't use a terminating null zero.

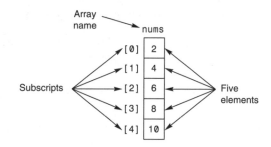

FIGURE 17.2.
A five-element integer array holding five integers.

As with character arrays, you don't need to specify the initial subscript if you define the array with its maximum number of values up front. This array definition matches the preceding one:

```
int nums[] = {2, 4, 6, 8, 10};    // Define and initialize the array
```

 Warning   If you define an array without assigning initial values at the time of definition, be sure to use an initial subscript. The following array definition is incorrect. C reserves *no* storage for the array!

```
int array[];    // There must be a subscript
                // or initial values
```

Here is another integer array definition:

```
int values[] = {10, 9, 8, 7, 6, 5, 4, 3, 2, 1, 0};
```

Despite the fact that a 0 is in values's last element, that zero is considered an integer zero, not a null zero, because there is no string in the array.

If you don't initialize an array when you define it, you must fill the array one value at a time. For example, this is not possible in the body of the program:

```
values[] = {10, 9, 8, 7, 6, 5, 4, 3, 2, 1, 0};
```

and neither is this:

```
values = {10, 9, 8, 7, 6, 5, 4, 3, 2, 1, 0};
```

In the body of the program, you must assign each value to each array element one at a time. Later in this unit, you will learn some techniques that most programs use to initialize arrays.

The following two array definitions reserve two numeric arrays. The first array is a `double` array and the second is a `long int` array:

```
double factors[25];      // Define an array of 25 doubles

long int weights[100];   // Define an array of 100 long integers
```

At the time you define these arrays, you could initialize them with a few values, like this:

```
double factors[25] = {4244.56, 78409.21, 2930.55433, 569401.34};

long int weights[100] = {43567, 70935, 32945, 102, 49059};
```

If you define an array of a specific size but initialize fewer elements as shown here, C zeros out every remaining element in the array. In other words, the first five elements of `weights` contain the values inside the braces (from 43567 to 49059), and the remaining elements will hold zero.

If you don't initialize any elements, don't rely on C to initialize them for you! C doesn't automatically initialize `vals` to zeros given this definition:

```
int vals[100];   // Defines but doesn't initialize vals
```

Tip If you want to initialize an array to all zeros, initialize it with a single zero:

```
int vals[100] = {0};   // The entire array now holds 0
```

ARRAY SPACE

Each element in an array requires a different subscript. All arrays, no matter what data type they are, start at subscript 0. The next array element is subscript 1, and so on.

Each element in an array of double values will consume more memory than each element in an array of character values. A five-element character array will consume much less space than a five-element double floating-point array. You reference both, however, with the subscripts 0 through 4.

If you want to know how much memory an array consumes, use the `sizeof` operator on the array name. The following statement stores in `mem` the total amount of memory taken by the array named `factor`:

```
mem = sizeof(factor);
```

If `factor` were a character array, `mem` would hold a much smaller number than if `factor` were a floating-point array because each element in the character array would take much less memory. `sizeof` returns the total amount of memory an array is defined as. `sizeof` has nothing to do with how many values you've actually initialized with data.

Many times, you can't initialize an array when you first define it. The user's input or data from a disk file or calculations might fill the array with values in the body of the program. The assignment operator stores values in arrays. Given the following array definition:

```
float ara[10];    // Define an array of 10 floating-point values
```

you can later store a number in the first element with an assignment like this:

```
ara[0] = 293.05;
```

You also can pass an element to `scanf()` and let the user assign to the element:

```
printf("What is the next value? ");
scanf(" %f", &ara[4]);
```

The following `for` loop stores the values 0 through 450 in an integer array that's assumed to be defined to hold at least 451 elements (one for element 0):

```
for (s = 0; s <= 450; s++)
  { iArray[s] = s; }
```

 **STOP&TYPE** Listing 17.1 contains a simple program that defines an array of seven floating-point values. The user initializes each value with a daily temperature in Fahrenheit. The program then applies a calculation to each element to convert those Fahrenheit values to Celsius. When all values have been converted, the program prints the Celsius readings.

Review   **What You Have Learned**

You can define an array of any data type and step through each element.

▼ **INPUT   LISTING 17.1. CONVERTING A WEEK'S WORTH OF TEMPERATURE READINGS.**

```
 1:  /* Filename: ARRTEMP.C */
 2:  // Fills an array with seven temperature readings, converts
 3:  // those readings to Celsius, and prints the results
 4:  #include <stdio.h>
 5:  #include <conio.h>
 6:  void fillTemps(float temps[7]);
 7:  void calcCelsius(float temps[7]);
 8:  void prCelsius(float temps[7]);
 9:
10:  main()
11:  {
```

```
12:
13:     float temps[7];    // The user will initialize the array
14:     clrscr();
15:
16:     fillTemps(temps);     // Get the seven values from the user
17:     calcCelsius(temps);   // Convert the values to Celsius
18:     prCelsius(temps);     // Print the Celsius readings
19:
20:     return 0;
21: }
22: //**********************************************************
23: void fillTemps(float temps[7])
24: {
25:   int ctr;
26:   printf("** Temperature Conversion **\n");
27:   printf("-----------------------------\n\n");
28:   for (ctr = 0; ctr < 7; ctr++)
29:     { printf("What is the Fahrenheit reading for day #%d? ",
30:               ctr + 1);
31:       scanf(" %f", &temps[ctr]);
32:     }
33:   return;
34: }
35: //**********************************************************
36: void calcCelsius(float temps[7])
37: {
38:   // Change each temperature to Celsius
39:   int ctr;
40:   for (ctr = 0; ctr < 7; ctr++)
41:     { temps[ctr] = (temps[ctr] - 32.0) * (5.0 / 9.0); }
42:   return;
43: }
44: //**********************************************************
45: void prCelsius(float temps[7])
46: {
47:   // Print the Celsius readings
48:   int ctr;
49:   printf("\nHere are the equivalent Celsius readings:\n\n");
50:   for (ctr = 0; ctr < 7; ctr++)
51:     { printf("Day #%d: %.1f\n", ctr + 1, temps[ctr]); }
52:   printf("\nStay warm!\n");
53:   puts("Press any key to return to the IDE...");
54:   getch();
55:   return;
56: }
```

▼ OUTPUT

```
** Temperature Conversion **
-----------------------------

What is the Fahrenheit reading for day #1? 65.7
What is the Fahrenheit reading for day #2? 45.4
What is the Fahrenheit reading for day #3? 32.1
What is the Fahrenheit reading for day #4? 28.3
What is the Fahrenheit reading for day #5? 24.5
What is the Fahrenheit reading for day #6? 67.8
What is the Fahrenheit reading for day #7? 76.2
```

```
Here are the equivalent Celsius readings:

Day #1: 18.7
Day #2: 7.4
Day #3: 0.1
Day #4: -2.1
Day #5: -4.2
Day #6: 19.9
Day #7: 24.6


Stay warm!
Press any key to return to the IDE...
```

 Warning   A Turbo C++ bug might show up when you compile this program! If you run the program and get this output:

```
** Temperature Conversion **

---------------------------


What is the Fahrenheit reading for day #1? 32
 scanf : floating point formats not linked
Abnormal program termination
```

you'll have to add the following lines right before `main()`:

```
#pragma warn -aus
void LinkFloat(void)
 { float f = 0, *ff = &f; }
#pragma warn .aus
```

Sometimes Turbo C++ doesn't link proper floating-point code into your program, even when that code is required to print floating-point numbers. This strange `#pragma` line begins a four-line workaround to this Turbo C++ bug. `#pragma` is an advanced preprocessor directive that's used here to force Turbo C++ to link the floating-point library.

▼ ANALYSIS

One of the first things to note about this program is that all the temperature readings are asked for in advance, all at once, before any calculation is performed. You could never program this way without arrays. Arrays give you the ability to capture all your data in a loop and then process that data all at once. Without arrays, you would have to use separate variable names for each temperature and ask for the seven readings using seven different sets of the same I/O code.

`main()` is a controlling function that dictates what the rest of the program is to do. If you hadn't read the description of the program beforehand, you could still figure out the entire program's job by studying `main()`. One of the many advantages of structuring your program into smaller modules is the readability of the `main()` function.

The `fillTemps()` function in lines 23 through 34 gathers all the temperature readings in one `for` loop. As you begin to write longer and more powerful programs (this is one of the longest programs in this book so far), you'll see that gathering data up front, before processing, often helps eliminate messy get-a-value, calculate-a-value code. By storing data in an array first, you can better structure your programs. When you begin to write *really* big programs (several pages long), everything you can do to help streamline the code will save you time during both program development and debugging.

> ***Tip*** Do you think this long program is difficult to understand? On the contrary—you probably think it's rather simple. However, this program is one of the most complex in this book so far! You're now at the point where more-advanced C code seems easy. The structuring of programs into smaller functions helps you see "the big picture" better than before.

This program always passes the array by address. Therefore, the functions can all change the array. When they do, `main()`'s version also is changed because the functions operate on the same array as `main()`, not on a copy as would be the case with data passed by value.

> ***Note*** You might think that a global array of temperatures would be better than passing the same local array through all the functions. It's true that a global variable makes sense if every function in the program, or at least most of the functions, needs access to the variable. However, my desire to shy away from global variables as much as possible dictated the use of one local array instead. The extra practice at passing data between functions is good for you.

▶ Searching Through Arrays

Concept   **What You Will Learn**

One of the most important features of array processing is searching through an array for specific values. You can tell your computer to find a customer balance, receivable amount, or payroll figure, and it responds in a snap, even if the program has to search through hundreds of values.

Searching an array for a particular value is simple. Array searching requires no new commands, just an application of the commands you already know. Once an array is filled, finding a value requires starting at the beginning of the array and comparing the next array element with a key value.

definition
A *key* is a value you're looking for in an array or a file.

> ***Note*** All kinds of searching techniques for computers have been developed. The technique discussed in this unit, the *sequential search* technique, is the most popular and one of the easiest, but it's also one of the slowest. Unless your programs often search through huge arrays of data, however, the sequential search gives you more than enough power to find a match in a short time.

For example, suppose you need to see whether a customer properly filled out his or her customer number on a mailing that you recently sent. You can scan the customer ID list, an array of values, looking for the customer's ID (the key).

When you search an array for a key value, one of three things will happen:

▶ You'll find a match.

▶ You won't find a match.

▶ You'll find more than one match.

Your data will dictate whether you'll allow duplicate keys. In other words, you don't want two customers with the same customer ID number. Therefore, every time you add a customer to your files, through array processing you'll want to make sure that the customer isn't already on the list. Other times, you'll want to allow two or more equal values in an array. A list of student test scores might produce two or more students who happened to make the same grade on a test.

Searching an array makes the assumption that the array already has data. There are three primary ways that you fill arrays with values:

▶ Assignment statements

▶ Data entry from the user

▶ Disk file input

This book has spent a lot of time assigning values with the assignment operator, but most real-world data comes from the user or the disk. You can't know when you write a program exactly what values that program will eventually process, so you can rarely assign data in assignment statements. You can't predict how much a customer will buy, so you have to wait for the clerk at the computer to enter the amount.

The rest of the programs in this unit assign array values directly or through user input because you have yet to learn about file I/O. Lesson 11 explains how to use disk files for storage. When you start a program that manages disk file data, probably one of the first things the program will do is read the disk values into an array. Therefore, a prerequisite for learning about disk files is learning how to work with arrays.

 Tip In Lesson 11, you'll learn about *random file access,* which is a fancy term that basically means treating a disk file as if it were one large array. Instead of taking up valuable memory, you can keep the data on the disk and apply this lesson's array techniques to the file itself. As you can see, array processing is vital for your future programming.

Here is a simple loop that searches an array with MAX values, looking for the user's match:

```
printf("What is your customer code? ");
scanf(" %d", &userKey);
match = 0;    // No match is made yet
for (c = 0; c < MAX; c++)
  { if (customers[c] == userKey)
      { match = 1;
        break; }   // 1 is true
  }
if (match)
```

```
    { printf("You are already in the list\n"); }
else
    { printf("You are not in the list\n"); }
```

In this code fragment, userKey is the key value that you're looking for. Searching almost always involves a variable that holds a true or false result. Either the search key was found in the array (true) or it was not found (false). In this code, the match variable begins as false before the search begins. If there is a match of the customer's number to an array element, match is set to 1 (true) and the break terminates the for loop because there is no reason to look through the remaining elements.

Note If you were applying this sequential search against an array that holds duplicate keys, you wouldn't break out of the loop but would continue searching. Such searches often add all of the matches found (using a counter variable). A weather center might look through an array of last year's temperature readings for all values below freezing, counting the number of values that meet that criteria. Because two or more days could be below freezing, you wouldn't stop the search after finding just one.

ARE YOU "JUST A NUMBER"?

Do you get tired of feeling as if utilities and credit card companies think of you as just a number instead of a real person? Blame the computer!

Many names, such as McNeal and St. John, have far too many variations to be used as a key when searching with a program. McNeal might be entered as McNeal, Mc Neal, Mcneal, or Mc.Neal, depending on the person doing the data entry. An integer or character string is a much more accurate way of assigning specific values to people. The customer code of 734AB has little ambiguity other than the possibility of the user entering lowercase letters, which your program can test for with isupper() and fix with toupper().

When businesses computerize their records, they must assign their customers, vendors, and products unique IDs (key-searching values) to speed up the searching. Ideally, these computerized filing systems ultimately save you lots of money over file-cabinet organization. Can you imagine how long it would take a credit card company to go through miles of filing cabinets, looking for your balance when you wanted to charge something? Computers speed up important business processing, and that saves you, the customer and consumer, lots of dough.

Before looking at code that searches an array, you've got one more concept to understand. Look at Figure 17.3, a spreadsheet-like representation of a customer file. The first column is a list of customer IDs, the second column contains customer balance amounts, and the third column is the customers' last purchase amount.

Rarely will you have to search a single array to look for a value. More likely, you'll have to search several parallel arrays. Figure 17.3 contains three parallel arrays. The first array is the customer ID, the second array is the balances, and the third array is the last purchase amount. Each array would be parallel, meaning that the first element ID in the

definition

Parallel arrays are several arrays with the same number of elements that work in tandem to produce data.

first array would have the balance shown in the first element of the second array. That same customer's last purchase amount is listed in the first element of the third array. For example, customer number 4967 has a balance of $3,249.55 and last made a purchase of $573.68.

Customer ID	Balance	Last purchase amount
4543	5,567.65	656.78
2934	345.43	19.83
1902	1,001.34	1,001.34
4967	3,249.55	573.68
8092	657.84	657.84
4234	2,384.56	1,290.45

FIGURE 17.3.
A three-array representation of customer data.

Here's how parallel arrays work: The data from the arrays would probably come from a disk file, as discussed earlier. Once the arrays are filled with their values, a customer comes into your store to buy something. The first thing you'll do is have a program look through the customer ID array. When the customer's ID is found, use that element number to look in the balance array to see if the customer's balance is too high to buy something. If so, the customer must pay some of the balance. You could use this same procedure to see if the customer's last purchase was large, in which case you might want to give a special discount today.

The arrays that you've learned about in this book are called *single-dimensional* arrays. C supports multidimensional arrays, which hold data in a tabular format, but multidimensional arrays aren't as commonly used in C as they are in other programming languages. You can rarely replace parallel arrays with multidimensional arrays, even though multidimensional arrays have a tabular format similar to that of Figure 17.3. Multidimensional array elements must all be the same data type, which limits their use as a replacement for parallel arrays.

Also, C doesn't really have built-in support for multidimensional arrays as other languages do. To create a multidimensional array, you must create an array of arrays, which can greatly increase program complexity without adding a lot of benefit.

If you're lost, that's fine because this book doesn't discuss multidimensional arrays any further. Again, their use is limited, and taking the time to discuss them in detail here would take away space from more important material. If you'd like to know more about C's advanced internal data representations, such as multidimensional arrays, check out *Advanced C* (Sams Publishing, 1992).

STOP&TYPE Listing 17.2 contains an inventory program. Initialization statements fill the parallel arrays with product ID numbers, product amounts, product prices, and product reorder levels. The user enters a product ID, and the program then displays the product's inventory figures.

Review

Searching parallel arrays requires that you look for a match on a key value. If a match is found, the matching elements in the other arrays provide additional data.

▼ INPUT   LISTING 17.2. DISPLAYING INVENTORY INFORMATION.

```c
 1:  /* Filename: INVSRCH.C */
 2:  // Demonstrates the sequential parallel array searching
 3:  // technique. An inventory ID number is asked for. If
 4:  // the ID is found in the arrays, that product's
 5:  // inventory data is displayed for the user.
 6:  #include <stdio.h>
 7:  #include <conio.h>
 8:  #include <stdlib.h>
 9:  int getKey(void);
10:  int searchInv(int keyVal, int prodID[]);
11:  void prData(int foundSub, int prodID[], int numItems[],
12:          float price[], int reorder[]);
13:  #define INV 10    // Number of products in this sample array
14:  main()
15:  {
16:    // First, initialize a few sample elements
17:    // Product IDs
18:    int prodID[INV] = {32, 45, 76, 10, 94,
19:                       52, 27, 29, 87, 60};
20:    // Number of each product currently in the inventory
21:    int numItems[INV] = {6, 2, 1, 0, 8,
22:                         2, 4, 7, 9, 3};
23:    // Price of each product
24:    float price[INV] = {5.43, 6.78, 8.64, 3.32, 1.92,
25:                        7.03, 9.87, 7.65, 4.63, 2.38};
26:    // Reorder levels
27:    int reorder[INV] = {5, 4, 1, 3, 5,
28:                        6, 2, 1, 1, 4};
29:    int keyVal, foundSub;
30:
31:    // The program's primary logic begins here
32:    keyVal = getKey();    // Ask the user for an ID
33:    foundSub = searchInv(keyVal, prodID);   // Search the inventory
34:    if (foundSub == -99)
35:      { printf("That product is not in the inventory.");
36:        exit(1);
37:      }
38:    // Here only if the item was found
39:    prData(foundSub, prodID, numItems, price, reorder);
40:    return 0;
41:  }
42:  //*********************************************************
43:  int getKey(void)
44:  {
45:    // Ask the user for an ID
46:    int keyVal;
47:    clrscr();
```

continues

LISTING 17.2. CONTINUED

```
48:     printf("** Inventory Search Program **\n");
49:     printf("\n\nEnter a product ID: ");
50:     scanf(" %d", &keyVal);
51:     return (keyVal);
52: }
53: //**********************************************************
54: int searchInv(int keyVal, int prodID[])
55: {
56:     // Search the ID array and return the subscript of
57:     // the found product, or return -99 if not found
58:     int foundSub = -99;
59:     int c;
60:     for (c = 0; c < INV; c++)
61:       { if (keyVal == prodID[c])
62:         { foundSub = c;
63:            break;
64:         }
65:       }
66:     // The -99 will still be in foundSub
67:     // if the search failed
68:     return (foundSub);
69: }
70: //**********************************************************
71: void prData(int foundSub, int prodID[], int numItems[],
72:         float price[], int reorder[])
73: {
74:     // Print the data from the matching parallel arrays
75:     printf("\nProduct ID: %d\tNumber in stock: %d\n",
76:         prodID[foundSub], numItems[foundSub]);
77:     printf("Price: $%.2f\tReorder: %d\n",
78:         price[foundSub], reorder[foundSub]);
79:     return;
80: }
```

▼ **OUTPUT**

```
** Inventory Search Program **

Enter a product ID: 13
That product is not in the inventory.

** Inventory Search Program **

Enter a product ID: 94

Product ID: 94    Number in stock: 8
Price: $1.92      Reorder: 5
```

▼ **ANALYSIS**

main(), from lines 18 through 29, consists primarily of array initialization. As mentioned earlier in this unit, your real-world programs will probably initialize arrays from disk files or user input. Inventory programs are almost always designed to initialize from a disk file because the user shouldn't be expected to enter the inventory data each time he or she runs the program.

Once the arrays are initialized, main() controls the rest of the program. The user enters a customer ID in the getKey() function. getKey() searches the customer ID array, looking for a match. If the customer ID isn't found, getKey() stores –99 for the subscript, which indicates that the ID isn't in the list and which causes an error to appear in main(). If a match is found, the subscript for that customer's parallel arrays is returned to main(), where it's passed on to the prData() function, along with the four parallel arrays.

prData() then uses the subscript of the found customer to print the inventory information from the arrays. When main() regains control, the program quits and returns to the Turbo C++ IDE.

The logic in this program is fairly complicated, yet you should have little trouble understanding what's going on. No new commands or library functions were needed. Arrays make stepping through and searching a list of values simple. Once you add file I/O to a program such as this, reading that file's data directly into the arrays, you have a full-featured inventory searching program.

When you complete the questions at the end of this unit, try your hand at the last two Extra Credit exercises. They require that you write a program similar to this inventory program and add some updating and reporting functions. You'll develop a full-featured customer-balance control system based on what you already know.

Note Fewer than eight lessons ago, you were figuring out the difference between an integer and a floating-point value. Now you're writing high-level business programs!

► Homework

General Knowledge

1. Besides char, what other data types can you store in arrays?
2. Do numeric arrays end with null zeros? Why or why not?
3. What is the starting subscript value for integer arrays?
4. How many array elements does the following array definition reserve?

   `double values[16];`
5. How many array elements does the following array definition reserve?

   `int ages[] = {23, 54, 32, 39, 40, 69, 74, 57, 12};`
6. Why will the following array definition fail to reserve storage?

   `float weights[];`
7. How can you find out how much memory the following array consumes?

   `long double scientific[25];`
8. What's the easiest way to initialize a 100-element integer array with zeros?
9. Why do arrays usually make programs more readable instead of less so?
10. What is a key?

11. If you allow for no duplicate values in an array, what are the two possible results of an array search?

12. If you allow for duplicate values in an array, what are the three possible results of an array search?

13. What are the three ways that programs initialize arrays?

14. Why do computerized systems often rely on integer- or character-based keys instead of people's names?

15. Why would you use parallel arrays?

16. If you pass a floating-point array to a function and the function changes it, does the array change in the calling function also?

17. True or false: The following array named `values` terminates with a null zero:

    ```c
    int values[] = {5, 2, 1, 9, 8, 0};
    ```

18. True or false: An error message displays when you attempt to store a value in an array subscript higher than the number of elements you've defined.

19. True or false: Both of the following arrays consume the same amount of memory:

    ```c
    int vals[8];
    double vals[8];
    ```

20. True or false: Both of the following arrays contain nine elements:

    ```c
    int vals[8];
    double vals[8];
    ```

21. True or false: All elements in an array must be the same data type.

22. True or false: C initializes all arrays with zeros if you don't store values in arrays when you define them.

What's the Output?

23. Given the following array definition and initialization:

    ```c
    int ara[] = {1, 2, 3, 4, 5, 6, 7, 8, 9};
    ```

    what does the following code produce?

    ```c
    for (c = 8; c >= 0; c--)
      { printf("%d \n", ara[c]); }
    ```

Find the Bug

24. Mike has written an array-searching routine that doesn't work consistently. Perhaps you can help him spot the problem:

    ```c
    scanf(" %d", &keyVal);
    for (i = 0; i < NUM; i++)
      { if (ara[i] == keyVal)
          { found = 1; }    // Found a match
        else
          { found = 0; }    // Not at this element
      }
    ```

Write Code That...

25. This one's easy! Rewrite the temperature conversion program in Listing 17.1, changing all the hardcoded literal 7s to one defined constant named DAYS. After you replace 7 with the named constant, change the constant to 21 and rerun the program. The program now asks for three week's worth of data. It's important to realize what you just accomplished; with arrays, the total number of items you have to process is a trivial concern. Once you write a program that contains array processing, all you have to do is modify the array size and for loop limits with the defined constant, and none of the rest of the program has to change. Without arrays, you would have to add more variables and more sections of repeated code.

26. Rewrite the INVSRCH.C inventory-searching program in Listing 17.2 to allow for more than one search with each run. Put a do-while loop in the main() function so that the user can look up more than one product. If the user enters an incorrect product ID, print an error message but don't terminate the program. Only when the user enters –99 for the product ID (and let the user know that a –99 will terminate the program) should the loop, and therefore the program, terminate.

Extra Credit

27. Write a customer balance program using the parallel array data shown in Figure 17.3. You can use a lot of the code from the inventory program in Listing 17.2 as a basis for this program. Ask the user (in a loop) for a customer number. Print the customer's balance and previous purchase amount, and ring the bell if the user's balance is over $3,000 (which indicates that the balance is too high for another purchase).

28. Add the following menu to the program you wrote in question 27:

```
Here are your choices:
    1. Display a customer's balance information
    2. Update a customer's balance with a payment
    3. Print a list of all customer IDs with a balance over
       $3,000
    4. Exit the program
What do you want to do?
```

If the user selects the second option, ask him or her for the ID of the customer who wants to make a payment. If the ID exists, ask for the payment amount and apply that payment to the customer balance (which requires a simple subtraction from that array element). If the user requests the third option, step through the array, testing only the balance array for any values greater than $3,000, and print the matching customer ID and the high balance in a list on-screen.

18

Pointers
Simplify

address

dereference

pointer array

pointer

RAM

▶ What You'll Learn About

- ▶ Inside memory
- ▶ Pointer variables
- ▶ The marriage of arrays and pointers
- ▶ Pointers to characters
- ▶ Arrays of pointers

definition

Pointer variables point to other variables.

This unit takes you into the world of advanced C programming by teaching you about pointer variables. Be warned: At first, pointer variables seem to add more work without offering any advantages. Be patient! Before this unit ends, you'll see how pointers let you write programs that manipulate string data in arrays. Until you learn about pointers, you can't keep track of string data using an array.

> *Note*   Pointer variables are often just called *pointers*.

Although pointers are considered advanced, the true power of C doesn't appear until you master pointers. Many programming languages, such as COBOL, FORTRAN, and QBasic, don't support pointers. Those languages can't provide for the advanced data management that you'll read about in Lesson 10.

Enough convincing! Let's get to the point.

▶ Inside Memory

Concept   **What You Will Learn**

To understand pointers, you must understand your PC's memory.

definition

RAM stands for *random access memory*.

The memory inside your PC, often called RAM, holds your program, data, and operating system. There are really two types of memory if you count the disk drive. The disk, however, is long-term memory. Your PC can't process any program or data on the disk until you or another program reads the disk contents into RAM.

> *Note*   To keep things simple, RAM will be called *memory* throughout the rest of this book. ROM, a special kind of read-only memory, isn't discussed here.

Your computer can process only data stored in memory. Therefore, your computer's memory is vital and closely tied to your computer's processor. Until now, you didn't need to know much about memory to run C programs. However, a thorough understanding of pointers isn't possible until you really understand the makeup of your computer's memory storage.

If your computer contains 640K of memory (640K is approximately 640,000 bytes of storage), it's capable of storing up to 640K characters, or bytes. The operating system always resides in the lower part of memory. The operating system is like a control system that makes sure your computer talks to the other devices properly. What's left is free memory that you can use to load a program and its data.

Perhaps you've heard of *extended memory* or *expanded memory*. These days, probably all computers being sold offer at least a few megabytes of extended memory, but expanded memory is now considered fairly outdated. Although extended memory is different from your regular, *conventional* 640K of memory, the details of that difference aren't extremely important now. Future operating systems promise to meld extended and conventional memory into a single continuum. Because that hasn't happened yet, the programs in this book stick to the conventional 640K memory because that's the default behavior of the Turbo C++ compiler that you get with this book.

Figure 18.1 shows an overview of memory as viewed by C. If you run Windows or OS/2, you'll have to give up even more memory for your operating environment, but usually there's enough memory still left to write virtually any program you need.

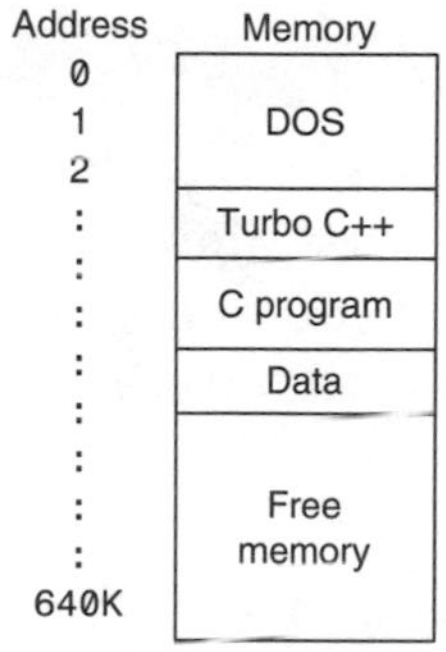

FIGURE 18.1.
Your PC's
memory layout.

```
Address     Memory
    0
    1        DOS
    2
    :      Turbo C++
    :
    :      C program
    :
    :        Data
    :
    :        Free
    :       memory
 640K
```

The *Address* column in Figure 18.1 is very important for this unit. Each memory location in your PC has a different address, just as your house has an address different from the rest of the world's. The PC's addresses are sequential numbers that begin at 0 and increment at each memory location through the highest memory location.

When you define a variable, C finds the next empty address in the data area and sticks the variable at that location. C keeps track, through an internal table, of where each variable resides. As you already know, C's data types consume different amounts of memory, so variables are rarely stored in back-to-back addresses. Integers take two bytes, long integers take four, and so on.

After these variable definitions:

```
main()
{
  int i = 19;
  char c = 'X';
  float f = 3.453;
```

C would store the data in memory to look something like the memory in Figure 18.2. Of course, the variables probably wouldn't be placed exactly at the addresses in the figure, but the important thing to note is that each variable starts at a given address and that different data types take different amounts of memory.

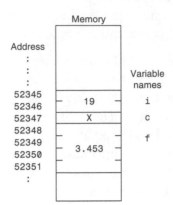

FIGURE 18.2.
Three defined
variables in
memory.

Aren't variable names great? Without variable names, you would have to remember the address of every data value your program worked with.

Review **What You Have Learned**

Each memory location in your computer contains a specific address. When you define variables, C finds unused memory locations and stores the variables there. When you refer to a variable by name, C finds that variable's address and works with the value stored there.

Note   There is no stop and type section here due to this section's conceptual nature.

▶ Pointer Variables

Concept **What You Will Learn**

As with all other kinds of variables, you must define and initialize pointer variables before you can use them.

A pointer variable is just that—a *variable*. You already know that you must define all variables before you can use them, and pointers are no exception. When you define variables, the following things happen:

▶ You tell C to find an empty place in memory.
▶ You tell C what to call the variable.
▶ You might put something in the variable.

You don't always put a value in every variable at the time you define the variable, but you can, as you already know.

Nothing's new here so far. It's important to realize that when you request a pointer variable, you do exactly the same thing as when you request a nonpointer variable. If you were defining an integer variable, you'd do this:

```
int i;    // No initial value
```

When you define pointer variables, you must tell C that the variable is a pointer. C knows that this variable named i is a simple integer variable.

To define a pointer variable, you must include one extra symbol. Here's how you would define a pointer variable named ip:

```
int * ip;    // No initial value
```

The * is *not* the multiplication operator! It's called a *dereferencing operator* when used in this context. The * is an *overloaded* C operator because of its double duty for both multiplication and pointers. Without the *, C wouldn't know that ip is supposed to be a pointer variable. Without the *, C would think that ip was another integer variable; therefore, you couldn't perform pointer access with ip.

 Tip The spacing around the * isn't important. All of the following variable definitions are equivalent:

```
int * ip;

int *ip;

int* ip;
```

The * must be there when you define pointers just so that C will know that the variable is a pointer and not a regular variable. The * is *not* part of the pointer variable's name.

The purpose of pointer variables is to point to other variables. When you define a pointer variable, you must tell C what type of data the pointer will point to. In the previous definition, ip is a pointer to integer data. ip can't point to anything other than integers. If you wanted to define a pointer to a floating-point variable, you could do so like this:

```
float * fp;    // A pointer to a floating-point variable
```

You can define pointer variables for all of C's data types. In the next lesson, you'll learn how to define your own data types. C even lets you define pointers to data types that you define.

You can give pointer variables any name you want. Often, programmers develop special naming conventions for their pointer variables so that they can more easily distinguish between pointers and regular variables without having to refer often to the program's definition section.

As with all variables, defining pointer variables is only half your job. You also must initialize pointer variables before you can do anything with them. When you define a pointer variable, initializing it with a value, the value you store in the pointer variable is always the address of another variable. Pointers don't hold data in the normal sense of the word. The data that a pointer variable holds is always an address.

To store the address of another variable, you must learn about one additional operator. The *address of* operator, &, returns the address of (good name, huh?) other variables. Once you define a pointer variable named fp, as done earlier, you can store the address of a floating-point variable named aFloat like this:

```
fp = &aFloat;   // Link the pointer to the floating-point variable
```

The following code defines an integer variable named count. The value 135 is stored in count as count is defined. Immediately after that integer is defined, a pointer to an integer variable named iPnt is defined. The third line then stores the address of count in iPnt:

```
int count = 135;
int * iPnt;
iPnt = &count;   // Make iPnt point to count
```

Figure 18.3 shows what the memory would look like after these three lines execute. This figure assumes that count appears at the address of 456212, but the address probably would be something else, of course, depending on the makeup of the PC's memory. The important thing to know is that *whatever* address count is stored at is assigned to iPnt.

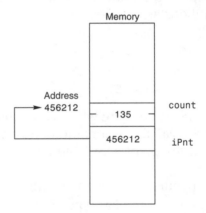

FIGURE 18.3.
iPnt points to
count.

Notice that you don't use the * again when assigning the address of count to iPnt. The second line contains the * just to tell C that iPnt is a pointer variable. If you want to, you can initialize the pointer variable at the time you define it. The following variable definitions are equivalent to the previous code:

```
int count = 135;
int * iPnt = &count;   // Initialize iPnt and make iPnt point to count
```

Once you've defined a pointer, what can you do with it? Well, through the pointer, you can manipulate the variable being pointed to. Given the count and iPnt definitions just shown, the following statement stores a 7 in count:

```
count = 7;
```

That's no big deal. However, now that the iPnt pointer points to count, the following statement *also* puts a 7 in count:

```
*iPnt = 7;   // Stores a 7 in the variable pointed to
```

Perhaps you can now see why the * operator, when used with pointers, is called the *dereference operator*. The pointer variable iPnt is dereferenced so that the address pointed to by `iPnt` gets the 7. Without the `*`, what would have happened? C would think that you wanted to store the address 7 in `iPnt`! Always keep in mind that pointers hold only addresses. When you assign to a pointer, you will assign only addresses. However, when you assign to a dereferenced pointer, you assign data that you want to go in the pointer's pointed-to location.

You've now seen three uses of the `*` operator:

▶ A multiplication operator, such as `ans = p * u;`

▶ A pointer definition operator, such as `char * cPtr;`

▶ A dereference operator, such as `*cPtr = 'X';`

> **Note** The `*` is called the *dereference operator* both when you use it to define pointer variables and when you use it to store data in memory pointed to by the pointer.

If you want to use the value pointed to by a pointer variable, you can. Given the previous variable definition, both of the following `printf()` statements are equivalent:

```
printf("%d", count);   // Print the value of count

printf("%d", *iPnt);   // Print the value of count
```

The first `printf()` prints the contents of the variable `count`. The second `printf()` prints the same value by dereferencing the `iPnt` variable.

You can now define pointer variables and work with variables pointed to by pointer variables. Right now, you might wonder why there's any need to use pointer variables. After all, it's a lot easier to work directly with a specific variable by name than to dereference a pointer to that variable. You're right that variable names are easier to use than dereferenced variables. In the next lesson, however, you'll learn how to store data in *unnamed* memory locations! The only way to get to those locations is through pointer variables. Therefore, you should learn all about pointers now. In the next lesson you'll be glad you did.

STOP&TYPE Listing 18.1 contains a program that defines several variables and pointers to those variables. Different values are then printed using dereferenced pointer variables.

Review

What You Have Learned

Pointers point to other data values. Pointers always hold addresses of other variables, and you store only addresses in pointers. When you define a pointer, using `*`, you must also tell C what data type that pointer variable will point to. You also use the `*` to store and retrieve data values in the memory pointed to by pointer variables.

▼ INPUT   LISTING 18.1. WORKING WITH POINTERS.

```
1:   /* Filename: DEFPNTS.C */
2:   // Defines several variables and pointers to those variables
3:   #include <stdio.h>
4:   #include <conio.h>
5:
6:
7:
8:   main()
9:   {
10:    int i1 = 14;        // Define and initialize an integer
11:    int *ip1;           // Define a pointer to an integer
12:    int i2 = 20;
13:    int * ip2 = &i2;    // Define and initialize the pointer
14:    float f = 92.345;
15:    float * fp = &f;
16:    double d;
17:    double *dp;
18:
19:    clrscr();
20:    ip1 = &i1;
21:    printf("i1 is %d and *ip1 is also %d \n", i1, *ip1);
22:    printf("i2 is %d and *ip2 is also %d \n", i2, *ip2);
23:    printf("f is %.3f and *fp is also %.3f \n", f, *fp);
24:    *fp = 1010.10;
25:    printf("After changing f through fp, \n");
26:    printf("f is now %.3f and *fp is also %.3f \n", f, *fp);
27:    dp = &d;
28:    *dp = 83949443.54333;   // Change dp
29:    printf("d is now %.5f and *dp is also %.5f \n", d, *dp);
30:    return 0;
31:  }
```

▼ OUTPUT

```
i1 is 14 and *ip1 is also 14
i2 is 20 and *ip2 is also 20
f is 92.345 and *fp is also 92.345
After changing f through fp,
f is now 1010.100 and *fp is also 1010.100
d is now 83949443.54333 and *dp is also 83949443.54333
```

▼ ANALYSIS

This program simply defines and assigns variables and pointers to those variables. In lines 10 and 11, integer i1 is defined and assigned 14 and the pointer to an integer named ip1 is defined. ip1 isn't assigned anything until later in the program. Line 12 defines another integer named i2 and stores 20 in the variable. Line 13 defines and links the ip2 pointer to i2.

Lines 14 and 15 define and initialize a floating-point variable f and a pointer to that floating-point variable named fp. Line 16 defines a double variable without initializing it. Line 17 defines a pointer that can point to a double, but no address is placed there yet.

Line 20 links ip1 to the address of i1. Although this could be done in line 11, the initialization occurs here for your review. The printf()s that follow in lines 21 through 23 print both the regular variable and the regular variable's value using the pointer.

Line 27 finally connects dp to d, and line 28 stores a value in d, indirectly, through a dereferenced dp. A subsequent printf() prints the result.

It wouldn't make a lot of sense to print the contents of a pointer variable. The actual address stored in a pointer isn't a meaningful number. If you do try to print a pointer directly instead of by dereferencing the pointer for the data value, use the %p conversion character in the printf(). Due to a sectioned addressing scheme that the PC uses, the address appears in hexadecimal and therefore isn't a true representation of what the pointer holds.

▶ The Marriage of Arrays and Pointers

Concept

What You Will Learn

Arrays share common storage methods with pointers. As this section explains, an array is nothing more than a special kind of pointer.

Often, C programmers use array subscript notation and pointer notation interchangeably. This is possible because C stores both arrays and pointers in the same way. Once you master the similarities between arrays and pointers, you'll be able to understand how to represent an array of string values, something not possible in C without pointers.

Until now, an array was considered a list of values. That's still what an array is conceptually, but internally an array name is a *pointer* to the first element in the array. Such a pointer is a fixed pointer (called a *constant pointer*). Unlike with a pointer variable, you can't change the contents of an array name pointer.

When you define an array such as this:

```
int ages[] = {32, 45, 42, 19, 67};
```

C really stores *six* values in memory. C stores the five data values in the array, as you already know. It's important to realize that C stores every array element in back-to-back memory. In other words, ages[0] always comes right before ages[1], ages[1] always comes right before ages[2], and so on.

The sixth value that C stores, a value that you didn't need to know about until now, is the array name itself. The array name is a separate variable that is always a pointer to the array's first element. A picture is worth a thousand words (although I'll throw both at you!). Figure 18.4 shows how C stores the ages array in memory.

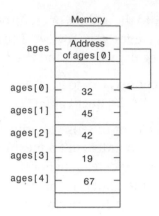

FIGURE 18.4.
When C stores an array, it stores the data and a pointer to the array.

Suppose that you want to print the array's first element. The following `printf()` does the trick:

```
printf("The first element is %d \n", ages[0]);
```

The following `printf()` *also* prints the array's first element!

```
printf("The first element is %d \n", *ages);
```

If you want to change the contents of the array's first value, you can do so using either notation:

```
ages[0] = 24;    // Store a new value in the first element
```

and this also is possible:

```
*ages = 24;    // Store a new value in the first element
```

The array name is nothing more than a pointer! The only limitation is that you can't change where an array name points because its value is always a fixed constant. (Perhaps now you can see why you can't put an array name on the left side of an equal sign!) Given the following pointer definition:

```
int i = 9;
int j = 10;
int *pt = &i;
```

you can change where `pt` points:

```
pt = & j;    // pt now points to j
```

You could never switch an array name to another value, however. Given the previous `ages` array definition, the following is not allowed:

```
ages = &j;    // Invalid! Arrays must keep pointing to their first value
```

You can use the pointer notation to step into the array elements, accessing the remaining elements, without using the actual array notation. For example, you can print the contents of the `ages` array using the familiar subscript notation:

```
printf("ages[0] is %d \n", ages[0]);
printf("ages[1] is %d \n", ages[1]);
printf("ages[2] is %d \n", ages[2]);
printf("ages[3] is %d \n", ages[3]);
printf("ages[4] is %d \n", ages[4]);
```

You also can print them by adding to and dereferencing a pointer:

```
printf("*(ages + 0) is %d \n", *(ages + 0));
printf("*(ages + 1) is %d \n", *(ages + 1));
printf("*(ages + 2) is %d \n", *(ages + 2));
printf("*(ages + 3) is %d \n", *(ages + 3));
printf("*(ages + 4) is %d \n", *(ages + 4));
```

The parentheses are important because the dereferencing operator, *, has higher precedence than the addition operator, +, as shown in Appendix C. To print the second array element, you want C to first add one integer memory location to the address stored in ages before dereferencing that location to print its value.

Of course, astute C programmers would never print the five elements one at a time when a for loop does more work in less code:

```
for (c = 0; c < 5; c++)
{  printf("ages[c] is %d \n", ages[c]); }
```

The same for loop will print the array using pointer notation also:

```
for (c = 0; c < 5; c++)
{  printf("*(ages + c) is %d \n", *(ages + c)); }
```

The whole key to being able to point into an array is that all array elements are stored back-to-back with no padding between them. Even though most data types require more than one byte of memory, when you add one to a subscript or a pointer's value, C adds one data type location and not just 1. ages[2] is two bytes away from ages[3]; therefore, *(ages + 2) is also two bytes away from *(ages + 3) even though they lie back-to-back in sequential array element locations.

STOP&TYPE Listing 18.2 contains a program that defines a floating-point array and then uses lots of pointer notation to print various values from the array. You'll see that you can use some strange notation to get to individual array elements using pointers. If you keep in mind that a pointer contains an address, you'll be able to figure out how the program works.

Tip Keep in mind that the following equivalent notations:

```
ara[3]
*(ara + 3)
*(ara + 1)[2]
```

all reference the same value! Just do the math and then subscript accordingly from the answer, and you'll see for yourself.

Review

What You Have Learned

You can reference arrays as if they were pointers. However, you can't change where an array name points. An array name always points to the array's first element.

▼ INPUT   LISTING 18.2. REFERENCING AN ARRAY THROUGH POINTER NOTATION.

```
1:   /* Filename: FLOTARPT.C */
2:   // Defines a floating-point array and then
3:   // accesses elements from the array using
4:   // pointer notation
5:   #include <stdio.h>
6:   #include <conio.h>
7:
8:   main()
9:   {
10:     float ara[6] = {11.1, 22.2, 33.3, 44.4, 55.5, 66.6};
11:     int ctr;    // for-loop counter
12:     clrscr();
13:
14:     // First, print the array using subscripts
15:     printf("Here is the array using subscripts:\n");
16:     for (ctr = 0; ctr < 6; ctr++)
17:       { printf("%4.1f  ", ara[ctr]); }
18:
19:     // Print the array using simple pointer notation
20:     printf("\n\nHere is the array using pointers:\n");
21:     for (ctr = 0; ctr < 6; ctr++)
22:       { printf("%4.1f  ", *(ara + ctr)); }
23:
24:     // You can even combine pointer and array notation!
25:     printf("\n\nHere is the array using a combination:\n");
26:     printf("%4.1f  ", (ara + 0)[0] );  // ara[0]
27:     printf("%4.1f  ", (ara + 1)[0] );  // ara[1]
28:     printf("%4.1f  ", (ara + 0)[2] );  // ara[2]
29:     printf("%4.1f  ", (ara + 0)[3] );  // ara[3]
30:     printf("%4.1f  ", (ara + 3)[1] );  // ara[4]
31:     printf("%4.1f  ", (ara + 2)[3] );  // ara[5]
32:
33:     printf("\n\n\n\nPress any key to continue...");
34:     getch();
35:     return 0;
36:   }
```

▼ OUTPUT

```
Here is the array using subscripts:
11.1  22.2  33.3  44.4  55.5  66.6

Here is the array using pointers:
11.1  22.2  33.3  44.4  55.5  66.6

Here is the array using a combination:
11.1  22.2  33.3  44.4  55.5  66.6

Press any key to continue...
```

▼ ANALYSIS

Familiar subscript notation in line 16's `for` loop prints the contents of the floating-point array as you're used to. Then the fun begins.

Lines 21 and 22 print the same array using pointer notation. Being able to reference the array as `*(ara + 1)` instead of `ara[1]` proves beyond a shadow of a doubt that an array is nothing more in C than a pointer to the first element in the array. The expression `*(ara + 1)` tells C to add one floating-point memory location (which takes four bytes) to the address stored in `ara`. That references the array's second element, which the `*` then dereferences to print the value stored there.

This program uses some strange notation to print the array in lines 25 through 31, but as you can see from the output, the array elements appear as if you used subscripts to print them. An array name is nothing more than an address, so you can add to that name, as in `ara + 2`, and subscript from there instead of from the start of the array (`ara`) like this: `(ara + 2)[1]`. To bring the expression back down to simple subscript notation, just do the math. In other words, the expression `(ara + 2)[1]` references the same element as `ara[3]` (2 plus 1 is 3). Likewise, an expression such as `(ara - 25)[27]` references nothing more than `ara[2]` (–25 + 27 is 2).

Although this program doesn't change any of the array elements using pointer notation, it could do so. All of the following assignments store 8.9 in `ara[4]`:

```
ara[4] = 8.9;

*(ara + 4) = 8.9;

(ara + 4)[0] = 8.9;

(ara + 2)[2] = 8.9;

(ara + 3)[1] = 8.9;
```

 *Tip* You'll never use the dereference operator and a subscript at the same time. `*(ara + 4)` and `ara[4]` and `(ara + 4)[0]` and `(ara + 1)[3]` all refer to `ara[4]`, but notice that the `*` is never used when a subscript in brackets is used also.

Master pointer notation now, because in the next lesson, you'll be defining data that has no variable or array name. Sometimes, the only way to access data is to use pointer notation.

▶ Pointers to Characters

Concept   **What You Will Learn**

Using pointers to characters, you can assign string literals directly to variables.

Never before could you assign a string literal to a variable in C. Before this unit, the only variables you knew of that held strings were character arrays, and an array name can never appear on the left side of an equal sign. In C terminology, an array name isn't an *lvalue* (*left value*) and therefore can't be changed. You learned in this unit that an array name is a constant. Thus, you see why an array name can't appear on the left side of an equal sign.

A pointer variable, however, doesn't have that limitation! Pointers are variables, and variables can appear on the left side of equal signs. Consider the following character array definition:

```
char name[] = "I like C!";
```

Nothing is new here. A pointer constant, name, points to the array's first value, I. Now consider how the following variable definition differs from the preceding one:

```
char * nameP = "I like C!";
```

In this case, nameP is *also* a pointer that points to the first letter, I. The difference is that nameP is a variable! Therefore, if you want to change the string pointed to by nameP, you can do so like this:

```
nameP = "I love C!";
```

To change the name array, you have two choices:

▶ Use strcpy():

```
strcpy(name, "I love C!";
```

▶ Change the array one character at a time:

```
name[3] = 'o';   // Change "like" to "love"
name[4] = 'v';
name[5] = 'e';
```

Note   We got lucky here, because only three letters needed changing. Usually, it's not so easy because you have to change many more over several assignment statements just to put a new string value in an array.

Changing arrays is tedious. Changing strings pointed to by pointer variables is extremely easy with a simple assignment statement.

Note   As long as the character pointer's string ends with a null zero, all the string functions work for both arrays and character data pointed to with pointers. You can use strcpy() to make pointer variables point to new strings with some limitations, as described in a moment.

To print a string pointed to by a character pointer, use the regular %s format code. After all, an array is nothing more than a pointer, and you print strings in character arrays with %s. The following printf() prints the contents of nameP:

```
printf("%s", nameP);
```

C always replaces string literals in memory with the address where they're stored. In other words, this assignment:

```
nameP = "I love C!";
```

stores a null-terminated I love C! in memory and then assigns that string literal's address to nameP. The %s format code works the same way, but you weren't prepared to understand that earlier. %s tells C to find the address in the data—either a string literal, a character array, or a character pointer—and print that string until the null zero is reached.

Some warnings are in order before we go any further. Only string literals work in assignments such as the ones just shown. If you use any of the array-changing functions, such as gets(), fgets(), or strcpy(), you must treat the character pointer as if it were an array because those functions all assume that they're working with an array.

Consider what happens if you define a character pointer like this:

```
char *myName;
```

and then assign it a string literal like this:

```
myName = "Sam";
```

C finds the address of Sam and stores that address in myName. Everything is fine. However, what if, instead of using that assignment, you initialized myName like this:

```
gets(myName);    // Oops!
```

The user might enter a long name or a short name, but whatever she enters, something bad will probably happen! gets() knows that you *might* pass it a character array. Therefore, gets() knows that it should never change the address of myName. Even though in this case myName happens to be a character pointer, C doesn't detect that myName is a pointer. Therefore, C stores the user's name wherever myName points. myName could have anything in it, even an address that's pointing to part of the operating system. Remember that C doesn't initialize variables for you, so the definition char myName; simply reserves a character pointer that points to an unknown location!

If you want to use a character pointer inside character array functions, the easiest way is to reserve a character array and assign a character pointer to the first element of that array:

```
char largeArray[101];      // Can hold a string as long as 100 bytes
char *cPtr = largeArray;   // cPtr now points to the
                           // array's first element
```

You can now store strings up to 100 bytes long in cPtr using gets(), strcpy(), and fgets(), because the data will go to the memory already reserved for the array.

STOP&TYPE Listing 18.3 contains a program that demonstrates what you can and can't do with pointers to characters. Remember that none of the string functions change their argument's address because the functions might be working with arrays.

Review

What You Have Learned

You can directly assign string literals to character pointers. You also can use character pointers in all string functions as long as the character pointer is already pointing to a string long enough to hold the result.

```
 1:  /* Filename: CHARFUNS.C */
 2:  // Uses character arrays and character pointers
 3:  #include <stdio.h>
 4:  #include <conio.h>
 5:  #include <string.h>
 6:  main()
 7:  {
 8:    char c;
 9:
10:    char * cpt0;    // A stand-alone character pointer
11:    char * cpt5 = "abcd";          // Points to 5 bytes
12:    char * cpt12 = "Programming";  // Points to 12 bytes
13:    char ara27[27];                // Points to 27 bytes
14:    char * cpt27 = ara27;          // Points to 27 bytes
15:
16:    clrscr();
17:
18:    cpt0 = "cpt0 is pointing to this string\n";
19:    puts(cpt0);    // No problem
20:    cpt0 = "A new string for cpt0";   // Still no problem
21:    puts(cpt0);
22:    // You couldn't
23:    // strcpy(cpt0, "This is a string for cpt0 that is too long")
24:    // though!
25:
26:    printf("\nPlease type your name (up to 12 characters): ");
27:    fgets(cpt12, 12, stdin);    // Okay because of fgets() limit
28:    // gets(cpt12) would be dangerous!!!
29:    printf("You typed %s\n\n", cpt12);
30:
31:    // fgets(cpt5, 12, stdin) wouldn't work either because
32:    // all characters after the fifth one would overwrite
33:    // memory not pointed to by cpt5
34:
35:    // Fill the 27-character array
36:    for (c = 'A'; c <= 'Z'; c++)
37:      { ara27[c - 65] = c;  }    // ASCII A is equivalent to decimal 65
38:    ara27[26] = '\0';;
39:    strcpy(cpt27, ara27);    // Okay because they point to
40:                             // the same number of bytes
41:    // strcpy(cpt12, ara27) would NOT be okay
42:    puts("cpt27 contains:");
43:    puts(cpt27);
44:
45:    printf("\n\n\nPress any key to continue...");
46:    getch();
47:    return 0;
48:  }
```

▼ OUTPUT

```
cpt0 is pointing to this string

A new string for cpt0

Please type your name (up to 12 characters): George Lake
```

```
You typed George Lake

cpt27 contains:
ABCDEFGHIJKLMNOPQRSTUVWXYZ

Press any key to continue...
```

▼ ANALYSIS

The numbers at the end of this program's character pointers indicate the maximum number of bytes each character pointer can point to. Remember that once you assign a string literal to a character pointer, or once you make a character pointer point to the starting location of a character array, you can never make the pointer point to more bytes than it already points to except by assigning a string literal to the pointer.

Lines 18 through 21 show an uninitialized character pointer being assigned two different string literals. Everything works fine. Note the comment in lines 22 through 24. Although you can assign a string literal of any length to cpt0, you can't use strcpy() to assign a string longer than what cpt0 already holds at the time. If you do, C would store the longer string directly over the existing one, overwriting other data or code that might appear behind the existing string.

It's okay to use fgets() to enter strings into character pointers as done on line 27 because fgets(), unlike gets(), ignores any characters longer than fgets()'s second argument. cpt12 already points to a string 12 bytes long, so there's no problem using fgets() to get a string up to 12 bytes long.

The for loop in lines 36 and 37 stores the letters A through Z in ara27, adding the null zero at the end of the letters to turn the data into a 26-byte string. Notice how the character variable c is used as the character data (holding A, B, and so on), as the loop counter, and as part of line 37's subscript expression. C lets you interchange char data and int expressions to create such a loop.

Line 39's strcpy() has no problem copying the array to the character pointer because both happen to be pointing to data that's the same length. You also could use strcpy() to assign an array to a pointer that's pointing to a longer string, but not to a shorter string.

▶ Arrays of Pointers

Concept   **What You Will Learn**

When you need lots of pointers, define an array of pointers.

You can define an array that holds any data type, including pointers. When you want a list of pointers, you'll want to use an array to hold that list of pointers. Figure 18.5 gives you a general idea of what such an array looks like. A pointer contains addresses to other memory locations. When you have an array of pointers, you have an array that acts like the one in the figure.

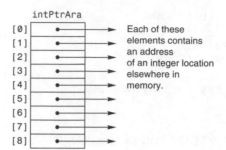

FIGURE 18.5.

You can define an
array of pointers!

Figure 18.5 shows an array of nine integer pointers. The array is named `intPtrAra`, and each element in the array is a pointer to an integer somewhere else in memory. The arrows indicate that each element holds an address of another value somewhere.

Defining such an array is easy. As long as you keep in mind the difference between a nonpointer definition and a pointer definition, you can remember how to define an array of pointers. You define a nonarray integer like this:

```
int i;
```

You define a pointer to an integer like this:

```
int * ip;
```

You define an array of nine integers like this:

```
int iAra[9];
```

Finally, you define an array of nine pointers to integers like this:

```
int * intPtrAra[9];    // Defines an array of 9 pointers to integers
```

 Tip   Reading all variable definitions from right to left makes understanding them easier. The preceding definition defines an array of nine elements. That array is named `intPtrAra`. The array contains pointers (indicated by the *). The pointers can point to only integers.

To write advanced programs, you'll need to be able to define several pointer variables at once. Although you could define several nonarray pointers with different names like this:

```
int *ip1, *ip2, *ip3, *ip4, *ip5, *ip6, *ip7, *ip8, *ip9;
```

you already know that an array gives you much more power than separately-named variables because you can use a `for` loop to step through an array.

We'll return to numeric pointers in the next lesson. For now, it's important to learn how to store an array of pointers to characters. There's really nothing different about pointers to characters, except that you can now hold an array of strings! (Well, you can *simulate* holding an array of strings.)

Study the following definition. See if you can figure out what's being defined (remember to read from right to left):

```
char * cities[5];
```

This definition builds a memory layout similar to that in Figure 18.5, with these two exceptions:

▶ Only five elements are defined

▶ Each element points to character data

Here is how you could initialize such an array at the same time that you define it:

```
char * cities[5] = {"San Diego", "Miami", "New York",
                    "Oklahoma City", "St. Louis"};
```

Remember that C treats all string literals as an address. In other words, C stores the five city names somewhere in free memory. C then assigns the address of each of those string literals to each element of the cities array. The end result is that each element in cities points to one of the cities.

Note   The array named cities doesn't end in a null zero because the array holds pointers, not strings. However, the strings *pointed to* by each element in cities do end in null zeros, as all strings do.

Figure 18.6 shows what the cities array looks like in memory. Each element, cities[0] through cities[4], holds an address to a city name. You can print each of the names using the %s format code.

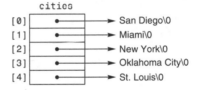

FIGURE 18.6.
What the cities array looks like in memory.

STOP&TYPE Listing 18.4 defines the array of pointers to five cities and prints the cities on-screen.

Review   **What You Have Learned**

An array of character pointers lets you work with lists of strings as if those strings were stored inside the array.

▼ **INPUT   LISTING 18.4. STORING AND PRINTING DATA IN AN ARRAY OF CHARACTER POINTERS.**

```
1:  /* Filename: CITYNAME.C */
2:  // Stores and prints a list of city names
3:  #include <stdio.h>
4:  #include <conio.h>
5:  main()
6:  {
7:    int ctr;
8:
9:    char * cities[5] = {"San Diego", "Miami", "New York",
```

continues

LISTING 18.4. CONTINUED

```
10:                                 "Oklahoma City", "St. Louis"};
11:    clrscr();
12:
13:    // Print the cities
14:    // Anywhere a character array can appear, so can the
15:    // elements from the cities array of pointers
16:    puts("Here are the stored cities:");
17:    for (ctr = 0; ctr < 5; ctr++)
18:      { puts(cities[ctr]); }
19:
20:    // Change the cities with literals
21:    // These assignments store the address of
22:    // the string literals in the elements
23:    cities[0] = "Tulsa";
24:    cities[1] = "Boston";
25:    cities[2] = "Indianapolis";
26:    cities[3] = "Las Vegas";
27:    cities[4] = "Dallas";
28:
29:    // Print the cities again using pointer notation
30:    puts("\nAfter changing the pointers:");
31:    for (ctr = 0; ctr < 5; ctr++)
32:      { puts( *(cities + ctr) ); }
33:
34:    printf("\n\n\nPress any key to continue...");
35:    getch();
36:    return 0;
37:  }
```

▼ OUTPUT

```
Here are the stored cities:
San Diego
Miami
New York
Oklahoma City
St. Louis

After changing the pointers:
Tulsa
Boston
Indianapolis
Las Vegas
Dallas

Press any key to continue...
```

▼ ANALYSIS

After assigning pointers to the city names in lines 9 and 10, the for loop in line 17 prints the five cities using a subscript notation. Each element holds the address of a city, so the %s format conversion code works great.

Lines 23 through 27 then assign new strings to the array. In reality, the *addresses* of the new strings are assigned to each array element. A strcpy() function wouldn't work reliably in place of the assignment if the new string literal were longer than the string being pointed to at the time by each element.

Notice that the `for` loop body in line 32 prints the names of the five new cities using pointer dereferencing instead of subscript notation.

▶ Homework

General Knowledge

1. What is an address?
2. What is a pointer?
3. What is the `&` operator called?
4. What does a pointer variable hold?
5. What are the three uses of `*`?
6. What is `*` called when it's used with pointer variables?
7. What do arrays have in common with pointers?
8. Assume that `iptr` is a pointer to an integer and that integers take two bytes in Turbo C++. How many bytes does C really add to `iptr` in the following assignment? Hint: Remember that pointer arithmetic adds enough for each data type when you increment a pointer.

   ```
   iptr += 2;
   ```

9. Which of the following are equivalent, assuming that `iary` is an integer array and that `iptr` is an integer pointer pointing to the start of the array?

   A. `iary` and `iptr`

   B. `iary[3]` and `iptr + 3`

   C. `iary[2]` and `*iptr + 2`

   D. `*iary` and `*iary[0]`

   E. `iary[5]` and `(iary + 4)[1]`

10. How does C simulate holding arrays of string data?
11. Explain what kind of data the following definition defines:

    ```
    float * measures[250];
    ```

12. Given the following floating-point array and pointer to a `float` definition:

    ```
    float fAra[] = {1.1, 2.2, 3.3, 4.4, 5.5, 6.6, 7.7, 8.8};
    float * fPtr1, *fptr2;
    ```

    which of the following assignments are allowed?

    A. `iPtr1 = fAra;`

    B. `iPtr2 = iPtr1 = &fAra[2];`

    C. `fAra = 19.45;`

    D. `*(iPtr2 + 2) = 19.45;`

13. True or false: Two or more memory locations can have the same address.

14. True or false: A pointer variable can point to floating-point values only.

15. True or false: An array name is nothing more than a pointer variable.

What's the Output?

16. What is in i after the following executes?

```
int i = 18;
int *ip = &i;
*ip = 99;
```

17. Describe what is in ip after the preceding code executes.

Find the Bug

18. Given these variable definitions:

```
int i;
long int j;
int * ip1;
int * ip2;
```

why will the following not work?

```
ip1 = &i;
ip2 = &j;
```

19. Given the following array definition:

```
int num[5] = {1, 2, 3, 4, 5};
```

why doesn't the following printf() produce a 3?

```
printf("%d", *num + 2);   // Tries to print num[2]
```

Write Code That...

20. Write two printf()s that print the first value in a double array named values. Use subscript notation for the first printf() and use pointer notation for the second.

21. Write a program that stores the names of your all-time favorite movies in an array of character pointers. Print the names of the movies.

22. Write a program that stores your favorite temperature for each of the four seasons in an array of floating-point pointers. Print the array forward, then backward, using only pointer notation.

Extra Credit

23. Pretend that you're a teacher who just gave 15 students a hard pop quiz. Write a program that defines an array of 15 pointers to float values that you initialize when you define the array. Print the values for your grade sheet. Search the array for the highest score and the lowest score and print both. Step through the array again and compute the average test score. Use only pointer notation.

Lots of Data

STOP&TYPE In this lesson, you learned about advanced variable access techniques. You saw the following:

▶ How to define and access numeric arrays.

▶ How to search arrays to find key values.

▶ Storing data in a series of parallel arrays advances the kinds of programs you write so that you can search tables of information.

▶ Each memory location in your PC resides at a unique address.

Project 9 Listing. Searching through arrays for property data.

```
1:  /* Filename: LESSON9.C */

2:  // A simple in-memory property database program. Through a menu,

3:  // the user decides if he or she wants to see a property

4:  // database on the screen or search for a specific property.

5:  #include <stdio.h>

6:  #include <conio.h>

7:  #include <stdlib.h>   // For exit()

8:  #include <string.h>   // For strcmp()

9:  void dispMenu(void);

10: int getAns(void);

11: void diProps(char * code[], float price[],

12:             char * addr[], float commPer[]);

13: void seProps(char * code[], float price[],

14:             char * addr[], float commPer[]);

15:

16: // Eight properties maximum due to next #define
```

▶ Using pointer variables, you can access data by its address instead of through the variable's name.

▶ Arrays are nothing more than pointer constants. You can access arrays with pointer notation and you can access pointers with array notation.

▶ Once you learn to define arrays of pointers, you can keep track of lists of string data.

Description

1:	A C comment that includes the program's filename.
2:	A C++ comment that contains the program's description.
3:	The program's description continues.
4:	The program's description continues.
5:	The printf() and scanf() functions need information in the STDIO.H header file.
6:	The screen-clearing function, clrscr(), needs information in the CONIO.H header file.
7:	The exit() function requires STDLIB.H.
8:	The strcmp() function requires STRING.H.
9:	The functions written by the programmer are prototyped.
10:	The second prototyped function.
11:	The third prototyped function.
12:	The third prototype continues here to provide lots of white space.
13:	The fourth prototyped function.
14:	The fourth prototype continues here to provide lots of white space.
15:	A blank line helps separate the prototypes from the rest of the program.
16:	Comments the defined constant that follows.

continues

Project 9 Listing. continued

```
17:   #define NUM 8

18:

19:   main()

20:   {

21:      int ans;

22:      // Define the program's data in parallel arrays

23:      // A code that uniquely identifies each property

24:      char * code[NUM] = { "231DV", "821WQ", "1990I", "294JU",

25:                           "901RE", "829BN", "483LQ", "778AS" };

26:      // The price of each property

27:      float price[NUM] = { 89432.34, 123029.34, 321293.95,

28:                           214293.20, 68402.92, 421034.53,

29:                           232456.54, 432123.40};

30:      // The address of each property

31:      char * addr[NUM] = { "919 N. Elm", "2202 West Sycamore",

32:                           "7560 E. 26th Pl.", "213 W. 104th Ave",

33:                           "123 Willow Rd.", "5629 S. 188th",

34:                           "45 North Harvard", "17093 Lansford" };

35:      // The broker's commission on each property

36:      float commPer[NUM] = {.072, .07, .065, .091,

37:                            .078, .0564, .102, .0834 };
```

Description

17: Defines a named integer constant that holds the number of properties in the database.

18: A blank line helps separate the opening code from `main()`.

19: `main()` begins.

20: All functions begin with an opening brace.

21: An integer variable that will hold the user's menu response.

22: Comments that describe the data.

23: Comments that describe the data.

24: The first of four parallel arrays that hold property data. `code` contains a unique code number for each property.

25: The `code` array's values are still being initialized.

26: Scatter comments throughout your code.

27: The parallel array that holds the price of each property.

28: The `price` array's values are still being initialized.

29: The `price` array's values are still being initialized.

30: Scatter comments throughout your code.

31: The parallel array that holds the address of each property.

32: The `addr` array's values are still being initialized.

33: The `addr` array's values are still being initialized.

34: The `addr` array's values are still being initialized.

35: Scatter comments throughout your code.

36: The parallel array that holds the broker's commission.

37: The `commPer` array's values are still being initialized.

21: All data is assigned in advance.

29: Squeezing too much data on one line makes your programs harder to read.

continues

Project 9 Listing. continued

```c
38:     clrscr();

39:     do

40:     {

41:       dispMenu();

42:       ans = getAns();

43:

44:       switch (ans)

45:       { case (1) : { diProps(code, price, addr, commPer);

46:                      break; }

47:         case (2) : { seProps(code, price, addr, commPer);

48:                      break; }

49:         case (3) : { exit(1);

50:                      break; }    // Unnecessary break but a good habit

51:       }    // If user entered bad value, while loop will repeat

52:     } while (ans != 3);    // Keep looping until exit() takes over

53:     return 0;

54: }

55: //*****************************************************

56: void dispMenu(void)

57: {    // Display a menu for the user

58:     puts("\n\n\t\t** Property Database Menu **\n");
```

Description

38: Erases the screen.

38: The code in main() is kept simple.

39: Start of the loop that displays a menu.

40: All loop bodies should contain braces.

41: Displays a menu for the user.

42: Gets the user's menu response from the getAns() function.

43: A blank line helps separate the switch statement.

44: switch will determine what code executes in response to the user's answer.

45: If the user entered a 1, calls the property-displaying function and passes the parallel arrays to the function to be printed.

46: break keeps the rest of the case code from executing.

47: If the user entered a 2, calls the property-searching function and passes the parallel arrays to the function to be printed.

48: break keeps the rest of the case code from executing.

49: If the user entered a 3, terminates the program.

50: This break is for completeness. If exit() executes, execution will never get here.

51: Close all switch statements with a right brace.

52: Keeps displaying the menu as long as the user doesn't enter a 3.

53: Returns to the IDE, even though the exit() in line 49 actually keeps this return from ever executing.

54: All functions end with a closing brace.

55: The asterisk comment helps separate functions from each other.

56: The definition line for the menu-displaying function.

56: Each function should perform a single task.

57: All functions begin with an opening brace.

58: Prints the menu text.

continues

Project 9 Listing. continued

```
59:    puts("Here are your choices:\n");

60:    puts("\t1. Look at the property listing");

61:    puts("\t2. Search for a property by its code");

62:    puts("\t3. Quit the program");

63:    puts("\nWhat is your choice? ");

64:    return;

65: }

66: //************************************************************

67: int getAns(void)

68: {   // Get the user's menu choice

69:    int ans;    // Local variable also named ans

70:    scanf(" %d", &ans);    // Answer to menu

71:    return (ans);

72: }

73: //************************************************************

74: void diProps(char * code[], float price[],

75:                char * addr[], float commPer[])

76: {   // Display a list of properties

77:    int ctr;    // for-loop control variable

78:    for (ctr = 0; ctr < NUM; ctr++)

79:        { printf("\nCode: %s\t Price: $%.2f\n",
```

Description

59:   Prints the menu text.

60:   Prints the menu text.

61:   Prints the menu text.

62:   Prints the menu text.

63:   Prints the menu text.

64:   Returns to `main()`.

65:   All functions end with a closing brace.

66:   The asterisk comment helps separate functions from each other.

67:   The definition line for the menu-answer function.

68:   All functions begin with an opening brace.

69:   A local variable is defined for the function's answer.

70:   Gets the user's answer.

71:   Returns the answer to `main()`'s line 42.

72:   All functions end with a closing brace.

73:   The asterisk comment helps separate functions from each other.

74:   The definition line for the property-displaying function. A loop in the body of this function prints all the property data.

75:   The rest of the function's argument list.

76:   All functions begin with an opening brace.

77:   A `for` loop always needs a control variable.

78:   Starts the counting through the property's parallel values.

79:   Prints the first line of property-data output with the property code and price.

continues

Project 9 Listing. continued

```
80:              code[ctr], price[ctr]);

81:       printf("Address: %s\n", addr[ctr] );

82:       printf("Commission percentage: %.2f%%\n\n",

83:              commPer[ctr] * 100.0);    // Show as a percent

84:       if (ctr == 3)    // Don't scroll off too fast

85:          { puts("Press any key to continue...");

86:            getch(); }

87:       }

88:    puts("Press any key to continue...");

89:    getch();

90:

91:    return;

92: }

93: //********************************************************

94: void seProps(char * code[], float price[],

95:              char * addr[], float commPer[])

96: {    // Ask the user for a property code and display match

97:    int ctr;          // for-loop control variable

98:    int found = 0;    // Initially not found

99:    char buf[6];       // Code plus null zero size

100:    // Get the search key
```

Description

80: Line 79's `printf()` concludes.

81: Prints the second line of property-data output with the property address.

82: Prints the third line of property-data output with the commission percentage.

83: The commission is stored as a decimal, so the percentage is multiplied by `100.0` to display the value as a decimal.

84: If three properties are on-screen, temporarily pauses the output to give the user a chance to read the screen's contents.

85: Tells the user how to proceed.

86: Waits for the user's keystroke.

87: All `for` loops end with a closing brace.

88: Once the list is finished displaying, gives the user another chance to read the screen's contents.

89: Waits for the user's keystroke.

90: Blank lines help separate parts of the program.

91: Returns to `main()`'s line 46.

92: All functions end with a closing brace.

93: The asterisk comment helps separate functions from each other.

94: The definition line for the property-searching function.

95: The argument list continues.

96: All functions begin with an opening brace.

97: The `for` loop control variable.

98: Until a match is found, the `found` trigger variable will remain false.

99: Reserves a place for the user's search code (the key).

100: Scatter comments throughout your code.

94: The user's property code will be asked for, and a search for that property will be made.

continues

Project 9 Listing. continued

```
101:    puts("I will now search for a property based on your code.");

102:    printf("What is the code of the property you want to see? ");

103:    fflush(stdin);    // Flush the buffer

104:    fgets(buf, 6, stdin);

105:    for (ctr = 0; ctr < NUM; ctr++)

106:      { if (!strcmp(code[ctr], buf))

107:        { printf("\nCode: %s\t Price: $%.2f\n",

108:                  code[ctr], price[ctr]);

109:          printf("Address: %s\n", addr[ctr] );

110:          printf("Commission percentage: %.2f%%\n\n",

111:                  commPer[ctr]*100.0);    // Show as a percent

112:          found = 1;

113:          break;

114:        }

115:    }

116:    if (!found)

117:      { printf("\n* I'm sorry, but I don't find code %s",

118:              buf);

119:      }

120:    return;

121: }
```

Description

101: Tells the user what to do.

102: Prompts the user for the search code.

103: Flushes the input buffer in case a carriage return from the menu answer is still on the input buffer.

104: Gets no more than six characters from the user for the search code.

105: Starts the loop that begins the property search.

106: Compares the user's search code to each code in the parallel arrays. strcmp() compares strings and returns 0 if they match.

106: strcmp() tests strings for equality.

107: If the search code is found, starts printing the property data.

108: Continues printing the found property's data.

109: Continues printing the found property's data.

110: Continues printing the found property's data.

111: Continues printing the found property's data.

112: Sets the found variable to true because a match was made.

113: Stops the search because the match was found.

114: All if tests end with a closing brace.

115: All for loops end with a closing brace.

116: In case no match was made, prepares to apologize to the user.

117: Prints the message telling the user no match was made.

118: Continues the message.

119: Ends the if with a closing brace.

120: Returns to main()'s line 48.

121: All programs end with a closing brace.

▼ **OUTPUT**

```
                ** Property Database Menu **

Here are your choices:

        1. Look at the property listing
        2. Search for a property by its code
        3. Quit the program

What is your choice?

1

Code: 231DV      Price: $89432.34
Address: 919 N. Elm
Commission percentage: 7.20%

Code: 821WQ       Price: $123029.34
Address: 2202 West Sycamore
Commission percentage: 7.00%

Code: 1990I      Price: $321293.95
Address: 7560 E. 26th Pl.
Commission percentage: 6.50%

Code: 294JU      Price: $214293.20
Address: 213 W. 104th Ave
Commission percentage: 9.10%

Press any key to continue...

Code: 901RE      Price: $68402.92
Address: 123 Willow Rd.
Commission percentage: 7.80%

Code: 829BN      Price: $421034.53
Address: 5629 S. 188th
Commission percentage: 5.64%

Code: 483LQ      Price: $232456.54
Address: 45 North Harvard
Commission percentage: 10.20%

Code: 778AS      Price: $432123.40
Address: 17093 Lansford
Commission percentage: 8.34%

Press any key to continue...
```

```
        ** Property Database Menu **

Here are your choices:

        1. Look at the property listing
        2. Search for a property by its code
        3. Quit the program

What is your choice?

2

I will now search for a property based on your code.
What is the code of the property you want to see? 483LQ

Code: 483LQ      Price: $232456.54
Address: 45 North Harvard
Commission percentage: 10.20%

            ** Property Database Menu **

Here are your choices:

        1. Look at the property listing
        2. Search for a property by its code
        3. Quit the program

What is your choice?
```

10

Consolidating Items

Unit 19: Structure with *struct*

Unit 20: Allocating Memory

Lesson 10 Project

19

Structure
with *struct*

dot operator

member

structure

structure pointer
operator

structure tag

► What You'll Learn About

► Grouping in a structure
► Initializing structure variables

This unit teaches you how to build your own data types! In addition to the regular data types such as `int`, `float`, `double`, you can now have data types called `George`, `Paul`, and `Ringo` if you want!

The most important reason for defining your own data types is to group other data types together. As a matter of fact, that's in a nutshell what this unit is all about. C gives you primary data types from which you can represent virtually any low-level value such as a single number, character, or string (through an array). After you finish this unit, you'll be able to define data types that are aggregate collections of C's fundamental data types.

Tip   Sometimes, defining your own data types eliminates the need to program using parallel arrays. Instead of a parallel array that represents several types of data, you can define an array of your own data types that represents data. However, your excursion through parallel arrays was not in vain. Advanced C programmers often create parallel arrays of their own data types to perform high-level database access.

► Grouping in a Structure

Concept   **What You Will Learn**

Use the `struct` statement to define your own data types. `struct` tells C to treat a collection of fundamental data types as a single data type from which you can define variables and arrays of variables.

Arrays (and also pointers to data lists) are powerful, but they have one drawback: All data elements must be of the same data type. You can't create a 10-element array in which half the elements are integers and half are floating-point values.

There might be times, however, when such a mixed data-typed array would come in handy. A local television station wants to track its weekday broadcast audience (an `int` or `long int`) and the cost of each average airtime hour per day (a `float`). You'd need five integer values and five floating-point values, and you would pair two at a time for each day of the week. Two parallel arrays are the only means for achieving such a database that you know of right now.

definition

A *structure* is a programmer-defined collection of other data types.

Such combined data almost always works better and makes for easier coding when you store it in structures instead of parallel arrays. One of the easiest ways to begin thinking about structure data is to picture the 3 x 5 cardfiles you've seen or used. Such cardfiles usually contain names of contact people, their phone numbers, possibly their ages, and all sorts of other related but differently formatted data.

> **Note** Structures are often called *records* in other programming languages and in database systems.

Another good example of the perfect data for C structures is a stack of rental applications for an apartment. Each application contains the same format and collection of information: the prospective tenant's name, address, income, Social Security number, and so on. Each application contains completely different facts and figures, but they all have the same format.

When you define a structure, you define the format (similar to a blank form) of the data you want the structure to hold. When you ask C to define a structure variable, C makes a place in memory that combines all the data types in each structure member. The members in the structure correspond to each blank on a form. Through assignment statements, user input, and file input, programs initialize structure variables with unique data in each of the structure variable's fields.

> **Note** Members are often called *fields* in other programming languages and in database systems.

definition
A *member* is an individual data value within a structure.

The *struct* Statement

When you define a structure, you tell C exactly what format you want that structure to take. For example, suppose that your company currently keeps its inventory on 3 x 5 cards that look like the one in Figure 19.1. It would be your job to convert that cardfile system to a C program.

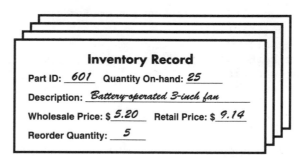

FIGURE 19.1.
Each cardfile contains the same structure.

Each card in the cardfile has the same format. In other words, each card has a place for a product description, a retail price, and so on. Each card shares a uniform format, or structure, with the other cards. Each card contains the same details. Therefore, each card could be considered a structure variable, and each data item on each card would be a member of that structure variable. Your job is to convert the card into a structure, convert the card's items into members, and convert each card's facts and figures into data for the structure variables.

The first thing you must do to convert the cardfile to a program using C structures is determine the data types for each of the members. Table 19.1 lists good data type suggestions for the card inventory. If a data type is `char *`, that can mean either a character array holding a string or a character pointer pointing to a string.

UNIT
19
Structure with struct

Warning You must decide in advance how much space to allow for each text member that will hold string data. You'll store each string member in an array, so you must decide in advance how long that array will be. Make the array long enough to hold the longest but most reasonable data value you expect. In other words, don't make the array too short, because you won't be able to hold needed descriptions, but at the same time, don't allow for a lot of unused space by making the array too large.

Table 19.1. The parts inventory members.

Member Name	Data Type	Length of String	Description
partID	char *	4	Unique part ID. No duplicates are allowed.
descrip	char *	15	Description of the item.
quant	int		Quantity in inventory currently.
retPrice	float		Retail price.
whoPrice	float		Wholesale price.
reorder	int		Reorder quantity. When the quantity gets to this level, the item should be reordered.

If you were defining the data in Table 19.1 in separate variables, you might do so like this:

```
char partID[5];    // Leave room for the null zero
char descrip[16];
int quant;
float retPrice;
float whoPrice;
int reorder;
```

Instead of using separate variables, it would be nice to be able to refer to these items as a whole. When you pick up one of the 3 x 5 inventory cards, you're manipulating all the data at once. If you were to define a structure variable from these items, you could manipulate the single structure variable and treat the collection as a single entity instead of as six separate variables.

The struct statement defines structures. As mentioned earlier, when you define a structure, you don't actually define variables at that time. (Technically, there's a way to define both the structure and variables at once, but it's rarely done.) Defining structure variables requires two steps:

1. Define the structure so that C knows what the collection of data types in the structure looks like.

2. Define one or more structure variables from that structure.

You must use the struct statement in both steps. Therefore, struct has two purposes: to define structure formats and to define structure variables.

Here is the format of the `struct` statement that you must use when defining the format of data:

```
struct [structureTag] {
  member definition;
  member definition;
      // One or more member definitions can follow
  member definition;
};   // Remember the required semicolon!
```

Putting the inventory items in a structure definition is easy. All you have to do is take the separate variable definitions shown earlier and surround them with the opening and closing lines of the `struct` statement. You don't have to supply a structure tag. The brackets around `structureTag` in the format indicate that the tag is optional. A tag name is required if you define the structure format in one place and a structure variable in another. Most C programmers supply a tag name so that they can define structure variables throughout the code and use the tag name as a reference. You'll see how to use the tag name in the examples that follow.

definition

A *structure tag* is a name you can assign to a structure's format.

Here is an example of a structure definition for the inventory described earlier:

```
struct invent {         // Defines a new data type named invent
  char partID[5];       // A part ID code. Leave room for the null zero.
  char descrip[16];     // A description of the item
  int quant;            // The number of items in the inventory
  float retPrice;       // Rctail price
  float whoPrice;       // Wholesale price
  int reorder;          // Level reached before reordering
};                      // The semicolon is required
```

Remember that this `struct` statement defines *only* the format of the structure, not the structure variable. After this `struct` statement executes, the program can define `int` variables, `float` variables, and also `invent` variables. Before this `struct`, C knew about the built-in data types, but it had no idea what an `invent` data type was.

> ***Tip*** Put comments to the right of members to describe the data each member holds.

Now that C recognizes the `invent` data type, you can use the structure tag `invent` to define variables. The following statement defines three inventory structure variables:

```
struct invent item1, item2, item3;
```

When you define an integer variable, you precede the variable name with `int` like this:

```
int i;
```

When you define a structure variable, you precede the variable name with `struct` *structureTag*, as done for the three inventory parts. Figure 19.2 shows what the variable `item1` looks like. The boxes next to the members represent how many bytes of memory each member consumes using the Turbo C++ compiler.

What does C put in the structure variable's members? The answer is the same as for any other kind of variable: C doesn't put anything in the structure automatically. The structure will contain garbage. If you want data in the structure variable members, you have to put data in the structure variable, as described in the next section.

UNIT

19

Structure with struct

item1

partID		
descrip		
quant		
retPrice		
whoPrice		
reorder		

FIGURE 19.2.
The format of the `item1`
structure variable.

Tip You're about done with C, so take a deserved break! There are only 32 commands in C, and with `struct`, you've now learned all the important ones!

STOP&TYPE Listing 19.1 doesn't contain a complete program, but it demonstrates how to define a structure for a radio station's listener database. Instead of defining individual, separately named structure variables, this program defines an array of structure variables.

Review   **What You Have Learned**

The `struct` statement defines a structure and also defines variables from structures.

▼ INPUT   LISTING 19.1. DEFINING AN ARRAY OF STRUCTURE VARIABLES.

```
1:   /* Filename: RADIOST.C */
2:   // Defines a structure for a radio station listener
3:   // database and defines an array of structure
4:   // variables for that database
5:
6:   // Before defining structure variables,
7:   // you must define the structure's format
8:   struct radioList {
9:     char listName[25];   // Listener name
10:    char dateFirst[9];   // Date first tuned in (i.e., 11/02/93)
11:    int age;
12:    char sex;
13:    int progSegment;     // Favorite daily program segment number
14:   };
15:
16:   main()
17:   {
18:     struct radioList listeners[100];   // Define 100 variables
19:     struct radioList *owner;           // A pointer to a structure
20:                                        // variable
21:   // Rest of program would follow
```

Note There is no output because this program is incomplete.

▼ **ANALYSIS**

You'll see the pattern in Listing 19.1 throughout your career as a C programmer. Most C programmers define their structures globally before the `main()` function. Remember, the structure definition doesn't define variables, so you won't be defining global variables just because the structure definition appears before `main()`.

> *Tip* If you use the same structure definitions often, put them in their own header files and include them at the top of whatever programs need to define structure variables. If you must make a change to the structure definition, you can do so in one place without changing all the source code files that use the structures.

Line 18 uses the structure definition to define 100 occurrences of the `listener` variables in an array. (Of course, you could define 100 separately named variables, but that wouldn't be useful, as you already know.) Keep in mind, however, that line 18 defines *a lot* of data! Not only does line 18 define 100 variables, but each variable is actually a collection of five other member variables, two of which are also arrays. A single element of the `listeners` array, such as `listeners[16]`, takes approximately 39 bytes of data!

> *Warning* You can't predict by adding individual data sizes exactly how much memory a structure variable will consume. C might add hidden padding between members to help with memory organization. There is always only one way to determine the size of any data in C—by using the `sizeof` operator.

Figure 19.3 shows what the `listeners` array looks like. Each element in the array contains an individual set of five members that look like the `radioList` structure's format.

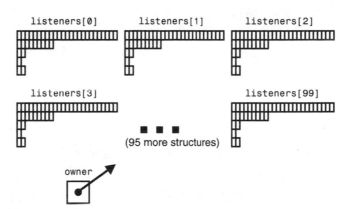

FIGURE 19.3.
The organization of the `listeners` array.

Line 19 of Listing 19.1 defines a pointer to a structure. Not only can you define pointers to the built-in data types, but you also can define pointers to the data types that you define. (You must first define the structure before defining a pointer to a non-built-in structure.) You won't see the full advantage of using pointers to structures in this unit, but in the next unit, you'll fully understand how pointers to your structures can help you manage memory effectively.

Warning   A pointer to a structure can point *only* to data with that particular format. In other words, if Listing 19.1 defined a second structure in addition to the `listener` structure, `owner` couldn't point to variables defined from that second structure; `owner` could point only to variables defined from the `listeners` structure.

▶ Initializing Structure Variables

Concept   **What You Will Learn**

The dot operator and structure pointer operator store data in the members of structure variables.

There are two places in a program that you can initialize structure variables. You can initialize structure variables when you define them and also in the body of the program through the usual mechanisms of assignment, user input, and file input.

Rarely will you initialize structures when you define them, but for completeness, you should know how to put data in structure variables at definition time. You'll see a pattern here, because you initialize structure variables the same way you initialize array data: using braces. The following `struct` defines a simple structure that contains a `float`, an `int`, and a `char` array:

```
struct s {
  float f;
  int i;
  char name[15];
};   // Define the structure
```

To define a structure variable without initializing the data, you already know that this will work:

```
struct s aVar;
```

To assign and initialize at the same time you define the variable, do this:

```
struct s aVar = {10.5, 14, "Paul Jones"};
```

The order of the data in the braces must match the order of the members. This kind of assignment is available only at the time you define the structure variable, just as assigning a list of values to arrays is possible only when you define arrays.

If you want to define and initialize an array of structures, list the data values consecutively:

```
struct s aVars[3] = { {10.5, 14, "Paul Jones"},
                      {73.4, 8, "Kim London"},
                      {19.5, 56, "William Meck"} };
```

Each group of inner braces initializes a new structure variable.

Warning You can't initialize structure variables directly using the assignment statement once you've defined the variables.

Inside the program's body, assigning data to structures takes just a little more effort. You must learn about two new operators before you put data in structure variables. They are the dot operator and the structure pointer operator. Table 19.2 describes each of these operators.

Table 19.2. The structure assignment operators.

Operator	Description
.	Stores data in a member of an individual structure variable.
->	Stores data in a member of a structure *pointed to* by a pointer.

The dot operator and the structure pointer operator store data one member at a time. Therefore, if the structure variable contains 15 members, you'll need 15 statements to assign data to the entire structure variable.

 Note Even though these operators are called *structure assignment operators*, you'll also use them to store data from user input and from disk file input in structure variables.

Here is the format of the dot operator's usage:

```
structureVariableName.memberName
```

Here is the format of the structure pointer operator's usage:

```
pointerToStructure->memberName
```

You'll never see a structure variable on the left of the -> operator, only a pointer to a structure. That's how you know which to use: If you want to store data in a specific structure variable's member, use the dot operator. If you want to store data in a member of a structure that's pointed to by a structure pointer, use the -> operator.

Newcomers to C programming often feel that the dot operator is easier to understand than the structure pointer operator. Part of the reason they feel this way is that they don't see the need for pointers to structures until they learn about dynamic memory allocation (which you'll learn about in the next unit). Until we get to the next unit, we'll leave the -> alone and concentrate on the dot operator.

Given the s structure definition repeated here:

```
struct s {
  float f;
  int i;
  char name[15];
};   // Define the structure
```

if you were to define three nonarray variables like this:

```
struct s aVar1, aVar2, aVar3;   // Define three nonarray variables
```

UNIT

19

Structure with *struct*

you could put data in the members of aVar1 like this:

```
aVar1.f = 12.34;    // Fills up the first member
aVar1.i = 23;       // Fills up the second member
strcpy(aVar1.name, "Sally Lake");    // Fills up the third member
```

Once you grab the correct structure variable by putting it on the left side of the dot operator, the right side of the dot operator tells C exactly which member from that particular operator is to be assigned. As usual, if you want to store data in character arrays, you'll have to use the strcpy() function, because you can't assign to arrays directly.

Here's some code that would fill the other two variables:

```
aVar2.f = 84.5;
aVar2.i = 3;
strcpy(aVar2.name, "Tim Deer");
aVar3.f = 56.3;
aVar3.i = 16;
aVar3.name[0] = 'A';
aVar3.name[1] = 'n';
aVar3.name[2] = 'n';
aVar3.name[3] = ' ';
aVar3.name[4] = 'H';
aVar3.name[5] = 'u';
aVar3.name[6] = 'f';
aVar3.name[7] = 'f';
aVar3.name[8] = '\0';
```

Do you understand the last few assignments? You don't *have* to assign strings to character arrays using strcpy(). If you like, you can store one character at a time. Just because the character array is part of a structure variable, that doesn't affect what you can do with the array. The existence of the structure variable simply affects how to get to the data, because you must preface the data with the name of the structure variable using the dot operator.

If an array of s variables were defined instead of separately named nonarray variables, the dot operator would work exactly as it does with nonarray variables. The only thing you must be sure of is to put the variable's subscript to the left of the dot, because the subscript goes with the structure variable and not with the member. For example, the following definition defines an array of three s variables:

```
struct s aVar[3];    // An array of three variables
```

The following code assigns each of these array elements the same data just assigned to the individual variables. However, the subscripts determine which structure variable is being assigned:

```
aVar[0].f = 12.34;    // Fills up the first member
aVar[0].i = 23;       // Fills up the second member
strcpy(aVar[0].name, "Sally Lake");    // Fills up the third member
aVar[1].f = 84.5;
aVar[1].i = 3;
strcpy(aVar[1].name, "Tim Deer");
aVar[2].f = 56.3;
aVar[2].i = 16;
aVar[2].name[0] = 'A';
aVar[2].name[1] = 'n';
aVar[2].name[2] = 'n';
```

```
aVar[2].name[3] = ' ';
aVar[2].name[4] = 'H';
aVar[2].name[5] = 'u';
aVar[2].name[6] = 'f';
aVar[2].name[7] = 'f';
aVar[2].name[8] = '\0';
```

Note Yikes! The last few assignments show subscripts on *both* sides of the dot operator. Nothing is really new here. The left side of the dot indicates which of the array structure variables is being assigned to, and the subscript on the right of the dot operator determines the member's individual element you're assigning to.

STOP&TYPE Listing 19.2 contains a fully working version of the radio listener database. The user can enter data and print it via the menu.

Review

What You Have Learned

The dot operator lets you assign data to individual members of structure variables.

▼ INPUT   LISTING 19.2. COMPLETING THE RADIO LISTENER DATABASE.

```
 1:  /* Filename: RADIOST2.C */
 2:  // Defines a structure for a radio station listener
 3:  // database and defines an array of structure
 4:  // variables for that database. The user can then
 5:  // enter and display data from the structures.
 6:
 7:  // Before defining structure variables,
 8:  // you must define the structure's format
 9:  struct radioList {
10:    char listName[25];    // Listener name
11:    char dateFirst[9];    // Date first tuned in (i.e., 11/02/93)
12:    int age;
13:    char sex;
14:    int progSegment;      // Favorite daily program segment number
15:  };
16:
17:  #include <stdio.h>
18:  #include <conio.h>
19:  #include <stdlib.h>
20:  // The number of array elements to be defined follows
21:  #define NUM 100
22:
23:  void dispMenu(void);
24:  int getAns(void);
25:  void addList(struct radioList listeners[NUM]);
26:  void dispList(struct radioList listeners[NUM]);
27:  void pressKey(void);
28:
29:  // What? A global variable?? This variable really is global to
```

UNIT

19

Structure with struct

continues

LISTING 19.2. CONTINUED

```
30:   // the program because there is only one listener array and
31:   // each function that accesses that array (plus any you might
32:   // later add) needs to know how many elements are currently in
33:   // the array.
34:   int numList;   // The number of listeners added so far
35:
36:   main()
37:   {
38:     struct radioList listeners[NUM];   // Defines an array
39:                                        // of structure variables
40:     int ans;
41:     clrscr();
42:     do
43:     { dispMenu();
44:       ans = getAns();
45:       switch (ans)
46:       { case (1) : addList(listeners);
47:                    break;
48:         case (2) : dispList(listeners);
49:                    break;
50:         case (3) : exit(1);
51:                    break;   // Just for completeness
52:         default : printf("\n** You must enter 1, 2, or 3\n");
53:                    break;
54:       }
55:     } while ((ans >= 1) && (ans <= 3));
56:     pressKey();   // The "Press any key..." prompt
57:     return 0;
58:
59:   }
60:   //***********************************************************
61:   void dispMenu(void)
62:   {
63:     printf("\n\n\n\t\t** Radio Listener Database **\n\n");
64:     printf("Here are your choices:\n");
65:     puts("\t1. Enter listener data");
66:     puts("\t2. Display listener data");
67:     puts("\t3. Quit the program");
68:     printf("What is your choice? ");
69:     return;
70:   }
71:   //***********************************************************
72:   int getAns(void)
73:   {
74:     int ans;   // Temporary housing for the scanf() variable
75:     fflush(stdin);
76:     scanf(" %d", &ans);
77:     return (ans);
78:   }
79:   //***********************************************************
80:   void addList(struct radioList listeners[NUM])
81:   {
82:     if (numList == NUM)
83:       { printf("\nThe listener list is full; you cannot add more\n");
84:         pressKey();
85:         return;   // Return from the function early
86:       }
```

```
 87:        fflush(stdin);
 88:        printf("\nWhat is the name of the listener? ");
 89:        gets(listeners[numList].listName);
 90:        printf("What date did %s first listen to us ",
 91:                listeners[numList].listName);
 92:        printf("(i.e., 11/10/92)? ");
 93:        gets(listeners[numList].dateFirst);
 94:        printf("How old is %s? ", listeners[numList].listName);
 95:        scanf(" %d", &listeners[numList].age);
 96:        printf("Is %s male (M) or female (F)? ",
 97:                listeners[numList].listName);
 98:        scanf(" %c", &listeners[numList].sex);
 99:        fflush(stdin);
100:        printf("What is %s's favorite segment (1, 2, or 3)? ",
101:                listeners[numList].listName);
102:        scanf(" %d", &listeners[numList].progSegment);
103:        numList++;   // Increment the counter for the next entry
104:        return;
105:    }
106:    //***********************************************************
107:    void displList(struct radioList listeners[NUM])
108:    {
109:        int ctr;
110:        if (numList == 0)
111:          { printf("\n\nThere are no listeners in the list!\n\n");
112:            return ; }    // Return early
113:        for (ctr = 0; ctr < numList; ctr++)
114:        { printf("\nListener #%d: \n", ctr + 1);
115:          printf("  Name: %s\n", listeners[ctr].listName);
116:          printf("  First listen date: %s",
117:                  listeners[ctr].dateFirst);
118:          printf("  Age: %d\tSex: %c\n", listeners[ctr].age,
119:                  listeners[ctr].sex);
120:          printf("  Program segment: %d\n",
121:                  listeners[ctr].progSegment);
122:          if (((ctr%3) == 0) && (ctr != 0))
123:          { pressKey(); }    // Scroll after 4 lines but not first time
124:        }
125:        return;
126:    }
127:    //***********************************************************
128:    void pressKey(void)
129:    {
130:        fflush(stdin);
131:        printf("\n\nPress any key to continue...");
132:        getch();
133:        return;
134:    }
```

UNIT

19

Structure with struct

▼ OUTPUT

```
                ** Radio Listener Database **

Here are your choices:
        1. Enter listener data
        2. Display listener data
        3. Quit the program
What is your choice? 1
```

```
What is the name of the listener? George Smith
What date did George Smith first listen to us (i.e., 11/10/92)? 09/12/91
How old is George Smith? 23
Is George Smith male (M) or female (F)? M
What is George Smith's favorite segment (1, 2, or 3)? 2


            ** Radio Listener Database **

Here are your choices:
        1. Enter listener data
        2. Display listener data
        3. Quit the program
What is your choice? 1

What is the name of the listener? Mary Lou
What date did Mary Lou first listen to us (i.e., 11/10/92)? 02/14/94
How old is Mary Lou? 43
Is Mary Lou male (M) or female (F)? F
What is Mary Lou's favorite segment (1, 2, or 3)? 1


            ** Radio Listener Database **

Here are your choices:
        1. Enter listener data
        2. Display listener data
        3. Quit the program
What is your choice? 1

What is the name of the listener? Joe Lisky
What date did Joe Lisky first listen to us (i.e., 11/10/92)? 07/06/93
How old is Joe Lisky? 32
Is Joe Lisky male (M) or female (F)? M
What is Joe Lisky's favorite segment (1, 2, or 3)? 1


            ** Radio Listener Database **

Here are your choices:
        1. Enter listener data
        2. Display listener data
        3. Quit the program
What is your choice? 1

What is the name of the listener? Laura Tinker
What date did Laura Tinker first listen to us (i.e., 11/10/92)? 01/02/94
How old is Laura Tinker? 41
Is Laura Tinker male (M) or female (F)? F
What is Laura Tinker's favorite segment (1, 2, or 3)? 3


            ** Radio Listener Database **

Here are your choices:
        1. Enter listener data
        2. Display listener data
        3. Quit the program
What is your choice? 2
```

```
Listener #1:
  Name: George Smith
  First listen date: 09/12/91   Age: 23   Sex: M
  Program segment: 2

Listener #2:
  Name: Mary Lou
  First listen date: 02/14/94   Age: 43   Sex: F
  Program segment: 1

Listener #3:
  Name: Joe Lisky
  First listen date: 07/06/93   Age: 32   Sex: M
  Program segment: 1

Listener #4:
  Name: Laura Tinker
  First listen date: 01/02/94   Age: 41   Sex: F
  Program segment: 3


Press any key to continue...


              ** Radio Listener Database **

Here are your choices:
        1. Enter listener data
        2. Display listener data
        3. Quit the program
What is your choice? 3
```

▼ ANALYSIS

Despite the fact that this program is longer than any you've seen so far, there is very little that is new. The primary structure activity lies in the functions named addList() (lines 79 through 105) and dispList() (lines 106 through 126).

In the addList() function, the user enters values that go directly to the array of structure variables. Both gets() and scanf() were chosen to get the user's data. As always, you must precede the scanf() data with an address of operator, even though you're passing to scanf() an individual member of a structure variable. Once the structure variable's members all have data, the program updates the one global variable named numList and returns to main().

The numList global variable keeps track of the number of listeners in the list at any one time. A global was used because if any additional routines are added to make this program even more functional, they will be working with the listener array and numList will have to be accessed from several different routines and either returned or passed by address or kept global, which is easiest here. If numList were passed by value to the functions that needed access to it, the functions might change numList, but no other function would know about that change.

The dispList() function simply uses a for loop to step through the array of structures. Despite the fact that structures contain aggregate data, you can see in dispList() that the code to print arrays of structure data varies little from the code to print data from any other kind of array.

The program often uses the dot operator to "get to" the member of the structure variable being worked with.

 Tip   When you learn about disk I/O in the next lesson, you'll be able to store user input so that the program can load from disk data that the user's already typed instead of forcing the user to reenter new values every time he or she runs the program.

▶ Homework

General Knowledge

1. What is a structure?
2. What's one advantage of a structure over a parallel array?
3. What are the individual names of a structure called?
4. Answer the next five questions based on this structure definition:

    ```
    struct s {
      int i;
      char * c;
      char c2[100];
      float x;
      long int l;
    };
    ```

    A. How many structures are being defined?

    B. How many members are being defined?

    C. How many structure variables are being defined? If any, what are their names?

    D. How many structure tags are being defined? If any, what are their names?

    E. Would you probably place this code locally or globally?

5. Which two operators perform structure assignment?
6. What's the advantage of defining a structure globally?
7. What always appears on the right side of . or ->?
8. What always appears on the left side of .?
9. What always appears on the left side of ->?
10. True or false: A structure tag defines the format of a structure but not a structure name.
11. True or false: You can initialize a structure format when you define it.
12. True or false: You can initialize a structure tag when you define it.
13. True or false: You can initialize a structure variable when you define it.

What's the Output?

14. Answer the next five questions based on this structure definition and initialization. Some have no valid answers, so be careful.

```c
struct aStruct {
  char c[10];
  char c2;
  int i;
  float x;
};
struct aStruct aVar = {"abc", 'X', 4, 34.3};
```

    A. What is the value of c?

    B. What is the value of aVar.c[2]?

    C. What is the value of aVar.x?

    D. What is the value of aVar[1].c?

    E. What is the value of aVar[1].c[4]?

Find the Bug

15. Study the following struct definition closely. What's missing?

```c
struct books {
  char title[25];
  char author[16];
  int quant;
  float retPrice;
  float whoPrice;
}
```

16. After you fixed the preceding struct, John J. Johnson decided to write a program using the structure. He defined a book variable like this:

```c
struct books myBook;
```

John then decided to store data in the variable one member at a time. However, he ran into a problem with this statement:

```c
strcpy(title.myBook, "A Thousand Tales");
```

See if you can help him.

Write Code That...

17. Add error checking to the RADIOST2.C program in Listing 19.2 so that the user has to enter 1, 2, or 3 in response to the program segment. As it now stands, the program doesn't contain error checking for the segment number.

18. Write a program that keeps track of Olympic skaters' names and scores. Use an array of eight structure variables to keep track of the eight competitors. Initialize the information when you define the variables. Print the average scores (assume that the scores can range from 0.0 to 10.0), the name of the skater with the

UNIT

19

Structure with *struct*

highest scores, the name of the skater with the lowest scores, and the name of the skater who makes the most from television movies about her life (just kidding!).

Extra Credit

19. Write a parts inventory system using the `inventory` structure described in this unit. You can use the radio listener program in Listing 19.2 as your guide. Before letting the user add an item to the inventory, check to see if that part ID already exists. If it does, display an error message and redisplay the menu. By checking for duplicate part IDs, you disallow duplicate keys in the array.

20

Allocating Memory

dynamic memory

free()

heap

malloc()

▶ What You'll Learn About

- ▶ The heap
- ▶ The heap functions
- ▶ Checking `malloc()` for errors
- ▶ Multiple allocations

This unit explores the memory management power of C. Storing data in variables is extremely important.bat, but variables aren't the only way to store data in memory. Through the techniques that you learn in this unit, you'll store data in unnamed memory locations. You won't have to keep track of memory addresses. You'll access the memory through pointers.

Some of the pointer discussion up to this point might have seemed, well, *pointless*. C pointers are far from pointless, however. Without pointers, you wouldn't be able to write the kinds of programs that commercial software developers write all the time. Named variables are simply too limiting to do everything you need to do when writing programs such as word processors. Variables are practical and necessary, as you've seen throughout this book, but they can't handle all data requirements by themselves.

The most important thing to realize about the material in this unit is that you will soon be able to request extra memory any time your program wants it. When your program is through with that memory, it can put the data right back where it found it and give the memory back to the system to dole out later or to give to other tasks now.

▶ The Heap

Concept   **What You Will Learn**

Learn what the heap is and why you need to learn how to control the heap's memory.

definition

The *heap* is your PC's unused memory.

The heap is your computer's leftover memory. In other words, the heap is any memory left after the following have consumed their share:

- ▶ The operating system
- ▶ Any terminate-and-stay-resident (*TSR*) programs that you or your AUTOEXEC.BAT file might have loaded
- ▶ Any windowing environment, such as Windows, that you might be running
- ▶ Device drivers such as the ones you must load before using a mouse or CD-ROM
- ▶ The C compiler you're running, such as Turbo C++
- ▶ The C program you're running
- ▶ The variables used by your C program

How much memory will be left, especially considering that we're keeping this discussion to the conventional 640K memory area (required by this book's compiler)? Not much memory will be left at all! If you use a network, you'll have even less.

Think for a moment about the implications of this discussion. First of all, you might not even think it matters to your C program if there is a little or a lot of memory left. After all, according to the preceding list, there's already room for your C program and its data. Why would a C program need more memory from this free area called the heap?

Up to this point, no program in this book has used heap memory. As a clue, if a program contains only variables and pointers to variables, it doesn't use the heap.

As mentioned in Lesson 9, this book sticks with conventional memory. The conventional memory limitation isn't just a requirement of the Turbo C++ compiler that you get here. DOS itself is closely tied to that 640K barrier. Even though you can run programs that use advanced memory schemes to access extended memory, there is still a lot of reliance on that first 640K. The more room you have under 640K, generally the better your programs run.

Eventually, perhaps sometime in the mid-1990s, Microsoft or somebody else will introduce an operating environment that will treat all PC memory equally, making access to extended memory less difficult than it is now. In the meantime, we've got to make the best of our memory.

MORE MEMORY WON'T SOLVE ANYTHING

As memory grows and as operating environments continue to use the PC's extended memory as a normal extension of the 640K conventional memory, your memory problems won't be solved. It seems that ample memory today won't be enough for tomorrow. (The same holds true for processor speeds as well.)

As memory grows, the programs we use get bigger, the more we use windowed operating environments, and the more likely it is that we'll connect to a network of some kind. As your memory increases, you'll begin to load more and more programs at once within your windowed environment, printing a word processor document while calculating a spreadsheet. The more memory we get, the more we use.

You shouldn't think of your PC as a stand-alone, one-task machine. Even if you never plan to network with other users, you're still going to be loading more and more programs and demanding that your computer keep track of more and more data at once. These days, even a background fax is common. It's easy to receive a fax while writing a C program or balancing your checkbook.

The bottom line is that you're going to be adding to that memory crunch with your own programs. When your program defines a variable, that variable will take memory away from another process that could have put the memory to good use. You've got to become more environmentally aware—of the environment within your PC's memory chips!

UNIT

20

Allocating Memory

This discussion leads to the following point: The heap might be small, but it's important. The heap, the available memory after everything running gets what it needs, is constantly being eroded by the operating system and other environments. Luckily, most programs that use memory from the heap put the memory back. That's what this unit is really all about: Use memory when you need it, and use as much as you need, but when you're done, put that memory right back on the free heap storage so that other tasks can have access to it.

When you begin to use memory as if it were an accordion, shrinking as you need more and growing as you put some back, you'll be optimizing your computer's memory use. Your programs will be able to give more to DOS when DOS needs it (DOS continually grabs and returns heap memory) and to other tasks that you might be running in Windows.

The Heap Is Critical for Software Developers

Programmers can't always predict how much memory their users will need. When you write a program to work with a specific amount of data, such as the previous year's temperature readings, you know at programming time how much memory is required, and you can define your arrays and variables accordingly. However, when you write a program such as a word processor, you have no idea when you write the program just how much memory the user will consume. The user doesn't even know until she or he writes a document.

You could reserve a tremendous amount of space ahead of time in a huge array, and the user would fill only the portion needed. However, most of the time—in fact, probably *all* of the time—the user will never fill all of your reserved memory. Therefore, when you define more than enough space, you waste too many memory resources that could be better utilized by the user's operating system, network, and windowing environment.

The goal of heap memory usage is to use only what the user needs. If the user begins typing a document into a word processing program that's based on the heap, the word processor can begin with very little memory reserved. As the user types more and more, the word processor can grab more memory from the heap. If the user deletes a bunch of pages, that memory can be sent back to the heap so that other programs can use it.

Understanding the Terms

When your program uses only named variables and arrays to hold data, it's not taking advantage of heap memory. The heap memory sits there, perhaps being used by other tasks, but not by your program.

Before learning how to work with the heap, you must understand some important terms associated with the heap. Table 20.1 lists the terms most often used.

Table 20.1. Terms associated with the heap.

Term	Definition
Allocate	To request memory from the heap. Once a program successfully allocates memory for data, the operating system makes sure that no other tasks can access that allocated memory. In other words, when you allocate heap storage, the available heap shrinks in size by that many bytes.
Available heap	The amount of memory on the heap at any one time.
Deallocate	To release heap memory from your program's use and return that memory to the available heap.
Dynamic memory allocation	The process of allocating and deallocating heap memory from within a program.
Free	Same as deallocate.
Free heap	Same as available heap.
Free store	Same as available heap.
Heap management	Making sure that you utilize the heap properly, checking for errors when you allocate and freeing heap memory that you no longer need.
Unallocated heap	Same as available heap.

When you read other books or articles about C programming, you'll run across these terms. The entire process of using the heap boils down to these two steps:

▶ Grab more heap memory when your program needs it.

▶ Put that heap memory back when your program is through with it.

The accordion-like growth and shrinkage of the heap produces dynamic memory allocation. Instead of defining all your variables in advance, you allocate memory dynamically on-the-fly (when you need it).

Often, a program you write needs lots of memory, but only for a small portion of the program. For example, a customer processing program might track customers as they purchase items throughout the day. The program runs all day. However, at any one time, the program needs very little memory, because as each customer finishes paying, the program stores that customer's data to the disk. The program doesn't need to be able to hold more than one customer's structure at any one time until the end of the day, when the store manager selects the menu option that will produce the evening reports. The day's customer data is then read into memory, statistics are computed, and reports are run. Only at the end of the day does the program need to allocate a lot of memory. There is simply no reason to keep that memory allocated throughout the day, especially if the PC is connected to a network, where memory is even more dear than on a stand-alone computer.

UNIT

20

Allocating Memory

definition
Dynamic means *changing,* as opposed to *static,* which means *constant.*

Note Local variables are *not* part of the heap, even though they disappear when their block ends, as described in Lesson 8. The memory for local variables comes from a section of memory known as the *stack*. You can't control the size of the stack in any way. A local variable's value disappears as soon as its block ends, but the memory reserved for that variable doesn't automatically become available to other tasks in the same way that the heap memory becomes available.

Review   **What You Have Learned**

You now know the importance of using the heap. When a program needs memory, it should get that memory from the heap. When the program is finished, it should free the memory back to the heap. The heap doesn't re-place the named variables that you've seen so far. Variables are needed to hold totals, counters, and often even data. The heap, however, is a better holding place when you must work with large or varying amounts of data, because it can grow and shrink as you use it.

Note There is no stop and type here due to this section's conceptual nature.

▶ **The Heap Functions**

Concept   **What You Will Learn**

The `malloc()` function allocates heap memory for your C programs, and `free()` deallocates memory by sending unwanted memory back to the heap's control.

From now on, when you think of the heap, forget about the concept of sequential memory. In other words, think of the heap as just, well, as just a pile of memory locations heaped on top of each other! This analogy is important if you are to use the heap effectively. When you allocate heap memory two times in a row, the second chunk of memory might or might not be close to the first. You can't predict just where from the heap your next allocation request will come. Likewise, when you deallocate memory, you don't know what C will do with that memory. Once the memory is deallocated, forget about it, because you have no idea where it went.

You must keep track of allocated heap space using pointers. You can't name heap memory, because allocated heap memory contains no variables to name. Allocated bytes from the heap might be located anywhere, and if you store data in that memory and then free that memory back to the heap, those values won't necessarily still be in the heap memory. Once it's freed, you must forget all about the memory. Again, the "pile of heap memory" analogy helps keep your management of the heap better focused. As Figure 20.1 shows, when you allocate from the heap, C might go anywhere to get the memory, and when you deallocate, you must act as if you don't know where that memory is going.

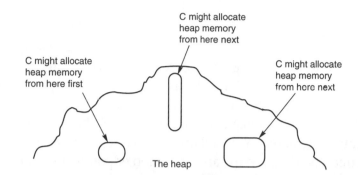

FIGURE 20.1.
Who knows where C will grab the next chunk? Who knows where C will put it back? Only C knows!

> **Warning** So far, this discussion might sound strange, but it's important, so heed its warnings. When you free memory, forget about it. If you'll need a value from that memory later, don't free it! Some C programmers deallocate the heap but expect to still use their pointers to read values they stored on the heap. Those programmers soon encounter lots of bugs. Always keep in mind that you share the heap with other tasks, especially the operating system. As soon as you free memory, that memory is available for another task to grab immediately. Therefore, whatever you put there usually is long gone if you try to read the value later.

Rarely will you allocate one byte at a time from the heap. Doing so would make the program tremendously inefficient and would take too much work on your part. Usually you'll allocate a chunk of memory at once, and your application will determine how many bytes that chunk should be. For example, if you were writing a word processing program, you wouldn't want to allocate a new byte each time the user typed a new character into the document. Instead, you might allocate 100 or 250 bytes at a time, then let the user fill that memory up. If the user needed more, you would allocate another chunk.

Although you don't know the address where C will get its next allocation, and although you can't rely on C's next allocated memory falling directly behind the memory you last allocated, *you can rely on C to give you contiguous memory within each allocation.* Whether you allocate 10 or 100 bytes of memory, C might go anywhere on the heap to get that memory, but those 10 or 100 bytes will all appear back-to-back sequentially in memory. You can rely on the memory being contiguous. As a matter of fact, you *have* to rely on the memory being contiguous, or the heap wouldn't offer much advantage to the programmer.

Figure 20.2 shows you what C does when you request eight bytes from the heap. C goes to the heap and finds where it wants to grab those eight bytes. When C gets the eight bytes, they're always together, with the address of the first byte appearing exactly seven bytes before the address of the last byte.

UNIT **20** Allocating Memory

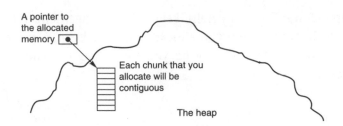

FIGURE 20.2.
The memory that you allocate will always be contiguous.

A pointer to the allocated memory

Each chunk that you allocate will be contiguous

The heap

If you understand this paragraph, you will have already gained a full understanding of the heap. When you allocate heap memory, you also provide a pointer variable. When the allocation is complete, C makes sure that the pointer variable points to the first byte of the memory you just allocated. The rest of the allocated memory will appear right behind that address. You end up with a contiguous set of new memory pointed to by a pointer. You then can use array notation or pointer notation on that memory. In other words, even though the allocated memory has no variable name, you can access that memory via the pointer as if it were an array that you defined. Unlike your program's defined arrays, however, this allocated array didn't begin taking up memory until you allocated it! Also, this array's memory will go back to the system as soon as you deallocate the array, even though your program won't be over yet.

The `malloc()` (which stands for *memory allocation*) function allocates memory. The `free()` function frees memory. Both of these functions require the STDLIB.H header file, so be sure to include this header when allocating heap memory.

`malloc()` always returns a pointer. Look again at Figure 20.2 and you'll see that the heap memory is shown pointed to by a pointer. Therefore, when you call `malloc()`, you must supply a pointer that `malloc()` can make point to the allocated memory.

 Warning   If you thought that `scanf()` was a strange function, wait until you see the format of `malloc()`!

`malloc()` will always allocate data based on the number of *bytes* you want allocated. You don't allocate characters, you don't allocate integers, and you don't allocate floating-point values, but you *do* allocate bytes. The end result is that you'll eventually store characters, integers, and floating-point values on the heap, but when you call `malloc()`, you must tell it how many bytes to allocate before it can properly allocate.

Here is the format of every `malloc()` that your C programs will call:

```
aPointerVar = (dataType *)malloc(numBytes * sizeof(dataType));
```

That's quite a mouthful. As you can see, you must assign the return value of `malloc()` to a pointer variable. The pointer variable must be the same data type as the kind of data you want to store on the heap. If you want to store 20 `double` values on the heap, you must assign `malloc()` to a `double` pointer. Both `dataType` values in the format of `malloc()` would also have to be that same `double` data type.

Let's look at a specific `malloc()` example. If you were to allocate 50 integers on the heap, you'd first need an integer pointer. The following definition defines an integer pointer:

```
int * hPtr;   // Define a pointer to integers
```

The following `malloc()` function call defines 50 integers on the heap and assigns the `hPtr` pointer to point to the first of those integers:

```
hPtr = (int *)malloc(50 * sizeof(int));
```

Don't worry; the `malloc()` function call is easier than it first looks! Study the value inside the `malloc()` parentheses. The argument you send `malloc()` has to be the number of bytes you want allocated. Therefore, this function tells `malloc()` to allocate `50 * sizeof(int)` bytes. How many bytes is `50 * sizeof(int)`? In Turbo C++, that's exactly 100 bytes, because 50 integers consume 100 bytes at two bytes each. Why not put 100 inside the parentheses? Data type sizes vary among compilers and computers. Your copy of Turbo C++ stores integers in two bytes, but the next version you buy might not, so you should always use `sizeof` instead of coding data type sizes directly.

Now that we've tackled `malloc()`'s argument, let's look at the parenthetical expression to the left of `malloc()`. Think for a moment what the expression `(int *)` must be. Previously, when you saw a data type inside parentheses, you saw a typecast. `(int *)` is also a typecast. Until now, however, you've never seen a pointer inside typecast parentheses, only nonpointer data types. `(int *)` simply takes the return value of `malloc()` and typecasts that return value to an integer pointer. After all, the statement assigns `malloc()`'s return value to an integer pointer variable, so you have to typecast that return value first.

`malloc()` returns a *void pointer*. In C, a void pointer is a pointer to an unspecified data type. C won't automatically convert a void pointer to another data type, so when you store a void pointer in a pointer variable, you must typecast that pointer to the variable's data type. Figure 20.3 shows the individual parts of this `malloc()` call. Using pseudocode, here is what the `malloc()` instructs C to do:

> *"Find enough contiguous bytes on the heap to hold 50 integers. Allocate that space so that it's no longer considered part of the free heap space. Assign the integer pointer named `hPtr` to the first of those allocated addresses. The typecast ensures that `malloc()`'s return value will work inside the `hPtr` integer."*

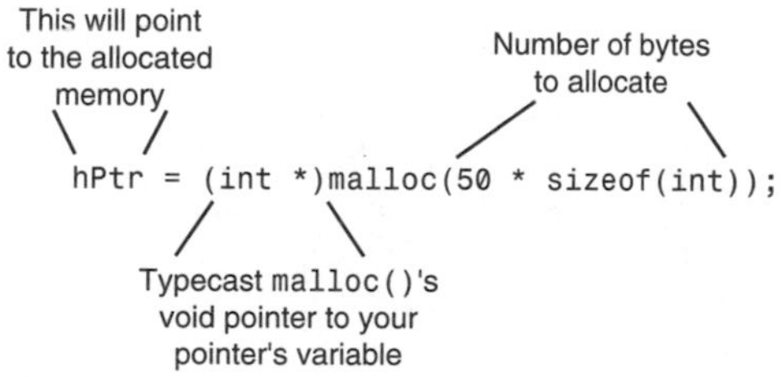

FIGURE 20.3.
Separating the parts of `malloc()` to ease the pain.

This will point to the allocated memory
Number of bytes to allocate

```
hPtr = (int *)malloc(50 * sizeof(int));
```

Typecast `malloc()`'s void pointer to your pointer's variable

Once you allocate memory, you can treat that memory *as if it were an array!* That's good news! Once you call `malloc()`, the allocated memory is just like an array. You can treat the memory as if it were an array, because an array is nothing more than a pointer to a list of contiguous data, and that's what you get from `malloc()`.

When you're done with the memory, be sure to put it back on the heap. Other tasks will then have access to the freed memory. Here is the format of `free()`:

```
free(aPointerVar);
```

To free the memory that was allocated earlier, you'd pass hPtr to free():

```
free(hPtr);   // Deallocate the allocated memory
```

After you free the memory, keep these three things in mind:

1. You can never use that memory again through the pointer that you originally allocated with.

2. hPtr is still visible, but its value is meaningless. Although the actual address in hPtr won't change, keep in mind that when C deallocates memory, you have to assume that you don't know where that memory will be put back. Right after your free() function call, your operating system or network or windowing environment might decide to allocate some heap memory. If so, another task might be using the address held in hPtr.

3. hPtr is still an active, visible variable, at least until its block ends. You can use hPtr for an integer pointer to hold addresses of other integers. You also can use hPtr for another allocation. free() frees the allocated memory but doesn't change the life of hPtr.

Note When you allocate memory with malloc(), C keeps track through an internal table of how many bytes you allocated. When you free the pointer pointing to those bytes, C remembers exactly how many bytes it allocated to that pointer and deallocates exactly that many bytes.

You can allocate your own structure data on the heap. If you had defined a structure variable named customer, you could define as many heap locations for as many customer structures as your program needs. The following malloc() defines 150 customer structures on the heap, assuming that custPtr is a defined pointer to your structure:

```
custPtr = (struct customer *)malloc(150 * sizeof(struct customer));
```

Once you allocate structures on the heap, you're left with a pointer to a structure, not a structure variable. Therefore, you must use the structure pointer operator (->), not the dot operator, to store and retrieve members within that structure. The following assignments would store four values in four of the customer members:

```
custPtr->purchase = 65.27;
strcpy(custPtr->name, "Sam Kane");
custPtr->balance +== custPtr->purchase;
custPtr->code = 'X';
```

STOP&TYPE Listing 20.1 contains a program that totals the checks written by the user in the previous month. Instead of defining a big array, this program allocates memory based on the number of checks the user actually wrote.

Review   **What You Have Learned**

malloc() dynamically allocates memory when your program needs it, and free() sends that memory back to the heap.

```
 1:  /* Filename: ALCHECK.C */
 2:  // Asks the user for the number of checks written
 3:  // last month, then allocates that many floating-point
 4:  // values. The user then enters each check into the
 5:  // allocated array. The program prints the total
 6:  // after all the checks have been entered.
 7:  #include <stdio.h>
 8:  #include <conio.h>
 9:  #include <stdlib.h>
10:  int howMany(void);
11:  void getChecks(int nChks, float * theChecks);
12:  float getTotal(int nChks, float * theChecks);
13:
14:  main()
15:  {
16:    int nChks;
17:    float total;
18:    float * theChecks;    // Will point to allocated memory
19:
20:    clrscr();
21:    printf("** Monthly Checkbook Program **\n\n");
22:    nChks = howMany();    // Ask the user how many checks
23:    // Allocate the memory, one float per check
24:    theChecks = (float *)malloc(nChks * sizeof(float));
25:    getChecks(nChks, theChecks);          // Get the values
26:    total = getTotal(nChks, theChecks);   // Add them up
27:    printf("\n\nYour total was $%.2f for the month.\n", total);
28:    free(theChecks);
29:    printf("Press any key to continue...");
30:    getch();
31:    return 0;
32:  }
33:  //************************************************************
34:  int howMany(void)
35:  {
36:    int ans;    // To hold the scanf() value
37:    printf("How many checks did you write last month? ");
38:    scanf(" %d", &ans);
39:    return (ans);
40:  }
41:  //************************************************************
42:  void getChecks(int nChks, float * theChecks)
43:  {
44:    int ctr;
45:    // No need or vehicle for passing allocated memory. The
46:    // memory doesn't go away between functions or blocks.
47:    printf("\nYou now must enter the checks, one at a time.\n\n");
48:    for (ctr = 0; ctr < nChks; ctr++)
49:    {
50:      printf("How much was check %d for? ", (ctr + 1));
51:      scanf(" %f", &theChecks[ctr]);    // Store value on the heap
52:    }
53:    return;
54:  }
55:  //************************************************************
56:  float getTotal(int nChks, float * theChecks)
```

UNIT

20

Allocating Memory

continues

LISTING 20.1. CONTINUED

```
57:  {
58:    // Add the check totals
59:    int ctr;
60:    float total = 0.0;
61:    for (ctr = 0; ctr < nChks; ctr++)
62:    {
63:      total += theChecks[ctr];
64:    }
65:    return total;
66:  }
```

▼ **OUTPUT**

```
** Monthly Checkbook Program **

How many checks did you write last month? 6

You now must enter the checks, one at a time.

How much was check 1 for? 17.82
How much was check 2 for? 109.28
How much was check 3 for? 536.49
How much was check 4 for? 9.80
How much was check 5 for? 3.73
How much was check 6 for? 84.08

Your total was $761.20 for the month.
Press any key to continue...
```

▼ **ANALYSIS**

As you can see, the only thing new about this program's code is the `malloc()` on line 24 and the `free()` on line 28. `main()` defines only three variables: `nChks`, `total`, and `theChecks`. `theChecks` is a pointer variable that is used to point to the allocated memory. Once you allocate the floating-point values in line 24, the program treats `theChecks` as if it were a defined array.

The `getChecks()` function uses a `for` loop in lines 48 through 52 to get its check values. As the user enters check values in line 51, those values go directly to the heap memory. There's no reason to pass the heap memory between functions because heap memory is neither local nor global. The heap memory is separate from the variables' memory. As long as you keep track of the pointer to the allocated memory, you can access the allocated heap from anywhere in the code.

 Warning If you ever lose track of the value stored in the allocation pointer, you'll never again gain access to that allocated memory, you'll never be able to use that allocated memory, and you'll never be able to free that allocated memory! Be sure that you pass the pointer to the heap between functions, because the pointer is the key to getting to the allocated memory.

Checking *malloc()* for Errors

Concept **What You Will Learn**

In rare circumstances, there might not be enough memory to allocate. `malloc()`'s return value tells you whether the allocation worked or failed.

There arc many reasons why a `malloc()` might fail. You might have too many device drivers and TSR programs loaded. You might be requesting far more than `malloc()` can deliver given your computer's memory limits. Whatever the reason, don't call `malloc()` without checking its return value for an error.

`malloc()` returns 0 if it fails. Even if `malloc()` could allocate 99% of your requested memory, the entire allocation process is a failure if you can't allocate every byte that you need to allocate.

After an allocation attempt like this:

```
hPtr = (float *)malloc(2500 * sizeof(float));
```

`hPtr` holds one of two values:

▶ The value of the allocated memory on the heap

▶ The value 0, which indicates that the allocation failed

To check `hPtr` for an error, you simply need to compare it against zero:

```
if (hPtr == 0)
  { printf("The allocation failed.\n");
    exit(1);
  }
// Rest of program can assume that the allocation worked
```

Given the fact that `hPtr` contains false (0) if the allocation failed, the following code is a little more efficient because the extra `==` doesn't have to be tested:

```
if (!hPtr)
  { printf("The allocation failed.\n");
    exit(1);
  }
// Rest of program can assume that the allocation worked
```

Warning If you fail to check for an allocation error and an error does occur, you will be storing data in memory that isn't allocated, using a zero-based pointer, and the results will be less than satisfactory (for example, your computer might freeze up at just the wrong moment).

STOP&TYPE Listing 20.2 contains a small allocation program that allocates far more memory than the Turbo C++ compiler can allocate. The error is found.

UNIT

20

Allocating Memory

Review

Check `malloc()`'s return vale against 0 to see if an error occurred.

▼ INPUT   LISTING 20.2. OVERALLOCATING AND DETECTING IT.

```
 1:  /* Filename: OVERALLO.C */
 2:  // Allocates too much memory and checks for the error
 3:  #include <stdio.h>
 4:  #include <conio.h>
 5:  #include <stdlib.h>
 6:  main()
 7:  {
 8:    long double * ldPtr;
 9:
10:    clrscr();
11:    ldPtr = (long double *)malloc(32767 * sizeof(long double));
12:    if (!ldPtr)
13:      { printf("Oops, there's no way that allocation will work!");
14:      }
15:    else
16:      { printf("This won't ever print.\n");
17:        free(ldPtr);   // This really isn't needed
18:      }
19:
20:    printf("\n\nPress any key to continue...");
21:    getch();
22:    return 0;
23:  }
```

▼ OUTPUT

```
Oops, there's no way that allocation will work!

Press any key to continue...
```

▼ ANALYSIS

32,767 `long double` values is a lot of data! There's no way that your Turbo C++ compiler will find that much room on the heap within conventional memory. The return value of `malloc()`, `ldPtr`, contains a 0 after line 11's `malloc()`. Therefore, the error message on line 13 prints as expected.

 Tip   You can use a C function named `farmalloc()` to access larger amounts of memory than `malloc()` allows.

► Multiple Allocations

You can allocate more than one group of heap memory, just as you can define several arrays. As long as you define more than one pointer, you can allocate more than one chunk of heap memory.

You could define three pointer variables like this:

```
char * cPtr;
int * iPtr;
float * fPtr;
```

and in the same program allocate three different chunks of memory with these `malloc()`s:

```
cPtr = (char *)malloc(150 * sizeof(char));
iPtr = (int *)malloc(45 * sizeof(int));
fPtr = (float *)malloc(188 * sizeof(float));
```

To be complete, you'd also want to check the return value of each `malloc()` just to be sure that all three allocations worked before you attempted to store data on the heap.

One of the most powerful data storage routines you can create is an array of pointers with each pointer pointing to allocated memory on the heap. An array of heap pointers is fairly common in advanced C programs. Such a program might need to keep track of several sets of data, with each set pointed to by a different pointer in the array. Figure 20.4 shows what such an array might look like in relation to the heap.

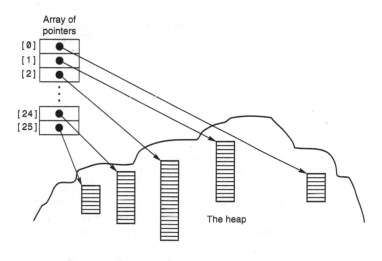

FIGURE 20.4.
An array of
pointers to
the heap.

When you allocate several times using an array of pointers, the rest of your program isn't any harder to code than if you had defined many arrays ahead of time. In addition, you gain memory-saving techniques through heap usage. The array of pointers gives you a means to step through several lists of data values via a `for` loop.

STOP&TYPE Listing 20.3 contains a program that tracks salespeople in five cities. Each city has three salespeople.

Review

An array of pointers lets you store several lists of allocated data on the heap.

▼ INPUT   LISTING 20.3. ALLOCATING AN ARRAY OF POINTER DATA.

```c
 1:  /* Filename: ARRHEAP.C */
 2:  // Allocates an array of heap pointers
 3:  #include <stdio.h>
 4:  #include <conio.h>
 5:  #include <stdlib.h>
 6:
 7:  void allMemory(float * cities[5]);
 8:  void getCity(float * cities[5]);
 9:  float calcCity(float * cities[5]);
10:  void freeAll(float * cities[5]);
11:  main()
12:  {
13:    float * cities[5];   // Five cities worth of data
14:    float avg = 0.0;
15:    clrscr();
16:    allMemory(cities);
17:    getCity(cities);
18:    avg = calcCity(cities);   // Total each city
19:    avg /= 15.0;   // Calculate average from total
20:    printf("\nThe average sales value is $%.2f\n", avg);
21:    freeAll(cities);   // Why not a simple free()?
22:
23:    printf("\n\nPress any key to continue...");
24:    getch();
25:    return 0;
26:  }
27:  //*********************************************************
28:  void allMemory(float * cities[5])
29:  {
30:    // Allocate each array's three values
31:    int ctr;
32:    for (ctr = 0; ctr < 5; ctr++)
33:      { cities[ctr] = (float *)malloc(3 * sizeof(float)); }
34:    return;
35:  }
36:  //*********************************************************
37:  void getCity(float * cities[5])
38:  {
39:    // This function gets the total number of
40:    // values for each city. Each city has three
41:    // salespeople covering its territories.
42:    int ctr1, ctr2;
43:    // Use a nested for-loop to get each city's values
44:    for (ctr1 = 0; ctr1 < 5; ctr1++)
45:      {  printf("City #%d:\n", (ctr1 + 1));
46:        for (ctr2 = 0; ctr2 < 3; ctr2++)
47:         { printf("What is value #%d? ", (ctr2 + 1));
48:            scanf(" %f", (cities[ctr1] + ctr2));
49:         }
50:      }
```

```
51:    return;
52:  }
53:  //********************************************************
54:  float calcCity(float * cities[5])
55:  {
56:    // Add up the total sales in each city
57:    int ctr1, ctr2;
58:    float totalCity = 0.0, total = 0.0;
59:    printf("\n");
60:    for (ctr1 = 0; ctr1 < 5; ctr1++)
61:   {
62:       for (ctr2 = 0; ctr2 < 3; ctr2++)
63:        { totalCity += *(cities[ctr1] + ctr2);
64:        }
65:       printf("City #%d total is $%.2f\n", (ctr1 + 1), totalCity);
66:       total += totalCity;   // Add to grand total
67:       totalCity = 0.0;       // Zero for next city
68:   }
69:    return total;
70:  }
71:  //********************************************************
72:  void freeAll(float * cities[5])
73:  {
74:    // Free each array's three values
75:    int ctr;
76:    for (ctr = 0; ctr < 5; ctr++)
77:      { free(cities[ctr]); }
78:    return;
79:  }
```

▼ OUTPUT

```
City #1:
 What is value #1? 434.56
 What is value #2? 554.21
 What is value #3? 231.78
City #2:
 What is value #1? 765.45
 What is value #2? 392.12
 What is value #3? 439.24
City #3:
 What is value #1? 1021.34
 What is value #2? 604.54
 What is value #3? 375.58
City #4:
 What is value #1? 778.09
 What is value #2? 605.77
 What is value #3? 542.23
City #5:
 What is value #1? 435.70
 What is value #2? 835.32
 What is value #3? 302.34

City #1 total is $1220.55
City #2 total is $1596.81
City #3 total is $2001.46
City #4 total is $1926.09
City #5 total is $1573.36
```

```
The average sales value is $554.55

Press any key to continue...
```

▼ **ANALYSIS**

The `allMemory()` function in lines 28 through 35 allocates all the city heap memory, with five cities and three values per city. Each of the five elements in the `cities` array points to a different set of three floating-point values. The rest of the program lets the user fill these heap values with 15 sales numbers.

The `getCity()` function in lines 37 through 52 contains a nested `for` loop. The outer loop steps through each of the five cities in line 44, and the inner loop in line 46 steps through each of the three sales figures in each city.

Line 48 requires a little more discussion than a typical `scanf()`. Unlike the `scanf()` function calls that you've seen so far, this `scanf()` doesn't have an & before its value. That's because (`cities[ctr1] + ctr2`) *is* an address, and that address is the location of the next city's sales total on the heap. (The `allMemory()` function filled up these addresses.)

As soon as the city values are in memory, `calcCity()` in lines 54 through 70 calculates each city's total sales (printed in line 65 at each iteration of the outer loop) and calculates a running grand total of all the city sales.

After `main()` prints the grand total, the `freeAll()` function steps through each of the city addresses, freeing them before the program ends.

 Note   If you don't free your allocated memory, the operating system will free that memory for you when you return to DOS. However, if you rely on DOS to do your job, you might as well not go to the trouble of using dynamic memory allocation, because your data will remain allocated and unavailable to the rest of the system.

▶ Homework

General Knowledge

1. What is the heap?
2. What is dynamic memory allocation?
3. What's the advantage of using the heap over using defined variables?
4. What function allocates memory?
5. What function deallocates memory?
6. What's the return value of `malloc()`?
7. How does `free()` know how many bytes to deallocate?
8. How do you access heap memory once you allocate it?
9. Why must you use the `->` operator when accessing structure members on the heap?

10. How does your use of the heap improve memory for other tasks that might need memory?

11. How can you ensure that `malloc()` works properly?

12. What happens to allocated memory values when you call `free()`?

13. What header file must you include before allocating memory?

14. True or false: You can name allocated memory.

15. True or false: An integer variable can point to heap memory.

16. True or false: If `malloc()` can't allocate all of the memory you request, it at least allocates as much as possible.

17. True or false: If you fail to deallocate memory, DOS will free the memory for you when your program terminates.

18. True or false: When you use `malloc()` to allocate a chunk of memory, all bytes in that allocated memory will be contiguous.

19. True or false: When you deallocate an array of pointers' heap memory, the array of pointers also goes away.

Note   There is no What's the Output? section for this unit.

Find the Bug

20. What's wrong with the following `malloc()` call?

    ```
    values = (int *)malloc(200 * sizeof(int *));
    ```

21. After allocating a structure like this:

    ```
    aStructPtr=(struct aStruct *)malloc(10*sizeof(struct aStruct);
    ```

    Linda tries to store a string value in the structure's member named `firstName` like this:

    ```
    strcpy(aStructPtr.firstName, "Linda");
    ```

    Help Linda find the problem with this code.

Write Code That...

22. Write a `malloc()` function call that allocates 300 characters on the heap that are pointed to by the `pChar` character pointer.

23. Write a `free()` function call that deallocates the `pChar` pointer you used to allocate in question 22.

24. Write a program to allocate an array of 10 country names. Allocate 15 letters for each country's name on the heap. Be sure to perform error-checking in case the allocation fails. With a `for` loop, store a different country on the heap in the 10 spaces that you allocate. Print the names in reverse order, from the last country name in the list to the first. Deallocate the list of names before your program terminates.

UNIT

20

Allocating Memory

Extra Credit

25. Write a program that stores three parallel arrays on the heap. The first array will hold your friends' names (in a heap array of no more than 20 characters each). The second array will hold your friends' ages. The third array will hold your friends' sex in a single character, M or F. Print a list of your friends and their data, and at the bottom of the list, print the average age. Deallocate all the data when you're done.

26. Rewrite the program in question 25 by using allocated structures instead of parallel arrays.

10

Consolidating Items

STOP&TYPE In this lesson, you learned about storing data using the advanced data techniques of structures and dynamic memory allocation. You saw the following:

▶ Structures are aggregate collections of data.

▶ You must define a structure, naming that structure with a structure tag, before you can define structure variables.

▶ A structure's members, its individual data parts, hold fundamental data types such as ints and chars.

Project 10 Listing. Allocating an array of structures on the heap.

```
1:   /* Filename: LESSON10.C */

2:   // A stockbroker's program that lets the broker enter a client's

3:   // stock portfolio into an array of pointers. Each of the

4:   // pointers in the array points to nothing when the program

5:   // begins, but the program allocates each pointer's structure

6:   // when needed for the next stock.

7:   #define NUM 150

8:   #include <stdio.h>

9:   #include <conio.h>

10:  #include <stdlib.h>

11:  struct stkStr {

12:     char stockID[4];

13:     float price;

14:     float divRate;

15:     int peRatio; };
```

▶ The dot operator and structure pointer operators access the members of a structure variable.

▶ The heap is your computer's free memory.

▶ When you allocate heap memory, your program then uses only as much memory as it needs at any one time.

▶ Allocate memory with malloc() and deallocate memory with free().

Description

1: A C comment that includes the program's filename.

2: A C++ comment that contains the program's description.

3: The program description continues.

4: The program description continues.

5: The program description continues.

6: The program description continues.

7: Defines a constant in case you want to limit the number of stocks to be analyzed.

8: The printf() and scanf() functions need information in the STDIO.H header file.

9: The screen-clearing function, clrscr(), needs information in the CONIO.H header file.

10: malloc() and free() require the STDLIB.H header file.

11: Defines the stock structure format.

12: Keeps track of a three-character string, leaving room for the null zero.

13: The stock price.

14: The dividend rate.

15: The price/earnings ratio.

7: For example, you might convert this to a disk file input program later.

continues

Project 10 Listing. continued

```
16:
17:  void getNumStks(void);
18:  void allocMemory(struct stkStr * stocks[]);
19:  void getData(struct stkStr * stocks[]);
20:  void calcStats(struct stkStr * stocks[]);
21:  void freeMemory(struct stkStr * stocks[]);
22:  int totalStks = 0;    // Total number of stocks entered
23:
24:  main()
25:  {
26:    struct stkStr * stocks[NUM];   // For use with larger arrays
27:    clrscr();
28:    puts("** Stock Analysis**\n\n");
29:    getNumStks();    // Ask broker how many stocks are in portfolio
30:    allocMemory(stocks);   // Allocate the stocks
31:    getData(stocks);       // Get the data from the broker
32:    calcStats(stocks);     // Print statistics
33:    freeMemory(stocks);    // Deallocate the stocks
34:    printf("\n\nPress any key to continue...");
35:    getch();
36:    return 0;
37:  }
```

PROJECT Consolidating Items

Description

16:	Blank lines help make your program more readable.
17:	You should prototype all functions.
18:	Prototype of another function.
19:	Prototype of another function.
20:	Prototype of another function.
21:	Prototype of another function.
22:	A global variable that controls the maximum number of stocks.
23:	Blank lines help make your program more readable.
24:	`main()` begins.
25:	All functions begin with an opening brace.
26:	`main()` defines a local array of pointers to the stock structures.
27:	Erases the user's output screen.
28:	Prints a title.
29:	Calls a function that asks the broker how many stocks are in the portfolio.
30:	Calls a function that allocates memory for each of the broker's stocks.
31:	Calls a function that loops until the broker's stock data is entered.
32:	Calls a function that computes statistics from the stock data.
33:	Always deallocate your program's allocated memory.
34:	Pauses long enough for the user to see the results.
35:	Waits for the user's keystroke.
36:	Always return from `main()` to the IDE.
37:	A final brace ends all `main()` functions.

Project 10 Listing. continued

```
38:   //*************************************************************
39:   void getNumStks(void)
40:   {
41:     printf("How many stocks to analyze? ");
42:     scanf(" %d", &totalStks);
43:     printf("\n");    // Blank line
44:     return;
45:   }
46:   //*************************************************************
47:   void allocMemory(struct stkStr * stocks[])
48:   {    // Allocate memory needed for the broker's stocks
49:     int ctr;
50:     for (ctr = 0; ctr < totalStks; ctr++)
51:     {
52:       stocks[ctr] = (struct stkStr *)malloc(sizeof(struct stkStr));
53:       if (!stocks[ctr])
54:         { printf("\n\nThe memory allocation failed.\n");
55:           exit(1);
56:         }
57:     }
58:     return;
59:   }
```

Description

38: A line of asterisks helps to separate functions.

39: The definition (first line) of `getNumStks()`. Receives no arguments because the function will update the single global variable.

40: All functions begin with an opening brace.

41: Asks the user how many stocks there are.

42: Gets the number of stocks.

43: Prints a blank line for subsequent output.

44: Returns to the `main()` function.

45: A final brace ends all functions.

46: A line of asterisks helps to separate functions.

47: Defines the function that allocates heap memory.

47: You must pass the array of pointers to `allocMemory()` because the array is local to `main()`. Notice that you don't have to specify a subscript when you receive an array.

48: Scatter comments throughout your code.

49: Defines a `for` loop control variable.

50: Steps through the stocks.

50: You must allocate each pointer's data in the array.

51: Always use braces in the body of `for` loops.

52: Allocates heap memory for each pointer in the array.

53: Always check for allocation errors! If there was an allocation error...

54: Prints an error message if the allocation failed.

55: Exits the program upon an allocation error.

56: Closes the body of the `if` loop.

57: Closes the body of the `for` loop.

58: Returns to `main()`.

59: All functions require a closing brace.

continues

Project 10 Listing. continued

```c
60:   //************************************************************

61:   void getData(struct stkStr * stocks[])

62:   {    // Get the stock data from the broker

63:      int ctr;

64:      for (ctr = 0; ctr < totalStks; ctr++)

65:      {

66:         fflush(stdin);

67:         printf("Stock #%d:\n", (ctr+1));

68:         printf(" What is the 3-letter ID of the stock? ");

69:         fgets(stocks[ctr]->stockID, 4, stdin);

70:         printf(" What is the price? ");

71:         scanf(" %f", &stocks[ctr]->price);

72:         printf(" What is the dividend rate? ");

73:         scanf(" %f", &stocks[ctr]->divRate);

74:         printf(" What is the integer P/E ratio? ");

75:         scanf(" %d", &stocks[ctr]->peRatio);

76:      }

77:      return;

78:   }

79:   //************************************************************

80:   void calcStats(struct stkStr * stocks[])

81:   {    // Calculate and print stock statistics
```

Description

60: A line of asterisks helps to separate functions.

61: Defines the function that will get the stock data. Passes `main()`'s local array of pointers.

62: Scatter comments throughout your code.

63: Defines a `for` loop control variable.

64: Steps through the stocks.

65: Always use braces in the body of `for` loops.

66: Deletes any unwanted characters from the input buffer.

66: The previous request for the number of stocks could have left an Enter keypress on the buffer.

67: Tells the user which stock he or she is entering.

68: Asks for the three-letter stock ID of the next stock.

69: Gets a three-character string from the user.

69: Use the structure pointer, `->`, with pointers to structures.

70: Asks for the price.

71: Gets the stock's price.

72: Asks for the stock's dividend rate.

73: Gets the dividend rate.

74: Asks for the price/earnings ratio.

75: Gets the P/E ratio.

76: The brace that closes the body of the `for` loop.

77: Returns to `main()`.

78: All functions end with a closing brace.

79: A line of asterisks helps to separate functions.

80: Defines a function that will calculate stock statistics based on `main()`'s local pointer array.

81: Scatter comments throughout your code.

continues

Project 10 Listing. continued

```c
82:     int ctr;

83:     int highPrice, lowPrice, highSub = 0, lowSub = 0;

84:     highPrice = stocks[0]->price;    // Set the initial values

85:     lowPrice = stocks[0]->price;

86:     float avgDiv = 0.0, avgPE = 0.0;

87:     for (ctr = 0; ctr < totalStks; ctr++)

88:     {

89:        if (stocks[ctr]->price > highPrice)

90:           { highSub = ctr; }

91:        if (stocks[ctr]->price < lowPrice)

92:              { lowSub = ctr; }

93:        avgDiv += stocks[ctr]->divRate;

94:        avgPE += stocks[ctr]->peRatio;

95:     }

96:     avgPE /= totalStks;

97:     avgDiv /= totalStks;

98:     printf("\nThe average P/E ratio is %.3f\n", avgPE);

99:     printf("The average dividend is %.3f\n", avgDiv);

100:    printf("The highest priced stock ID is %s\n",

101:           stocks[highSub]->stockID);

102:    printf("The lowest priced stock ID is %s\n",

103:           stocks[lowSub]->stockID);
```

Description

82:	Defines a `for` loop control variable.
83:	Defines variables that will keep track of the statistics.
84:	Initializes the high stock subscript with the first stock.
85:	Initializes the low stock subscript with the first stock.
86:	Defines two more variables that will hold statistics.
87:	Steps through the stocks.
88:	Begins the body of the `for` loop.
89:	If the current loop's stock is more than the highest stock price so far...
90:	Updates the high stock with the current stock.
91:	If the current loop's stock is less than the lowest stock price so far...
92:	Updates the low stock with the current stock.
93:	Adds to the dividend total for a subsequent average calculation.
94:	Adds to the price/earnings total for a subsequent average calculation.
95:	Closes the `for` loop.
96:	Divides the price/earnings total for a P/E average.
97:	Divides the dividend total for a dividend average.
98:	Prints the average P/E ratio.
99:	Prints the average dividend rate.
100:	Begins printing the highest stock price ID.
101:	The printing continues.
102:	Begins printing the lowest stock price ID.
103:	The printing continues.

continues

Project 10 Listing. continued

```
104:    return;
105:  }
106:  //*********************************************************
107:  void freeMemory(struct stkStr * stocks[])
108:  {    // Allocate memory needed for the broker's stocks
109:    int ctr;
110:    for (ctr = 0; ctr < totalStks; ctr++)
111:    {
112:      free(stocks[ctr]);
113:    }
114:    return;
115:  }
```

Description

104:	Returns to `main()`.
105:	Closes the function body.
106:	A line of asterisks helps to separate functions.
107:	Defines the function that will deallocate the heap memory.
108:	Scatter comments throughout your code.
109:	Defines a `for` loop control variable.
110:	Steps through the stocks.
111:	The opening brace of the `for` loop body.
112:	Deallocates each of the heap memory chunks pointed to by `main()`'s array of pointers.
113:	Closes the `for` loop.
114:	Returns to `main()`.
115:	Closes the function.

112: Free each pointer's heap memory.

▼ OUTPUT

```
** Stock Analysis**

How many stocks to analyze? 3

Stock #1:
 What is the 3-letter ID of the stock? BQS
 What is the price? 22.75
 What is the dividend rate? 2.31
 What is the integer P/E ratio? 4
Stock #2:
 What is the 3-letter ID of the stock? WWC
 What is the price? 32.50
 What is the dividend rate? 5.39
 What is the integer P/E ratio? 19
Stock #3:
 What is the 3-letter ID of the stock? XRU
 What is the price? 58.00
 What is the dividend rate? 6.21
```

```
What is the integer P/E ratio? 13

The average P/E ratio is 12.000
The average dividend is 4.637
The highest priced stock ID is XRU
The lowest priced stock ID is BQS

Press any key to continue...
```

Lesson ▶

Long-Term Storage

Unit 21: Sequential Files

Unit 22: Random Access Files

Lesson 11 Project

21

Sequential Files

access mode

disk file

fclose()

fopen()

fprint()

sequential access

▶ **What You'll Learn About**

- ▶ Disk files
- ▶ The first step: opening the file
- ▶ Closing the file with `fclose()`
- ▶ Writing data
- ▶ Adding to a sequential file
- ▶ Reading a sequential file

This unit teaches you how to store your program's data on the disk. There are several advantages to disk storage. The primary advantage is that you don't have to ask the user for all the data values every time he or she runs the program! The disk drive offers long-term data storage capabilities because the disk's contents, unlike your memory's, don't get erased every time you turn off the computer. The data stays in a file, safely tucked away until your program is ready to access it.

Your programs can't work with disk data directly. Just because you process disk files doesn't mean that you no longer need variables and heap memory. Before your program can work with data in a disk file, it must read that data from the file into variables or heap memory. When your program creates a disk file for the first time, it must have data in its variables (or in heap memory) before it can send the data to the file.

This unit is the first in a lesson on accessing the disk with C. There are two types of disk access:

- ▶ Sequential access
- ▶ Random access

Sequential access is useful for storing textual data to the disk drive. You also can store numeric data using sequential access, but most of today's true data-processing programs save numeric and formatted data using random access. Your applications' needs determine which method you use in your programs.

▶ **About Disk Files**

Concept   **What You Will Learn**

Programs must open disk files before they can access the data on the disk.

When you go to a filing cabinet to retrieve something, the first thing you do is open the cabinet drawer. After you open the drawer, you look at the file folder tabs, searching for the information you need. Once you find the proper file folder, you scan through the papers, retrieving the information that fits your needs. When you're done with the file, you put it away and close the drawer.

This filing cabinet analogy works perfectly for disk files. Here is the usual procedure for reading data from a file:

1. Open the disk file, locating the correct file by the filename.

2. Read the contents of the file.

3. When your program finds the data that meets your needs, it can calculate and print with that data.

4. After accessing the file, you must close it.

All disk files have names, and C uses the same file-naming conventions used by your operating system. DOS uses eight-character filenames with an optional three-character extension. Therefore, when you write Turbo C++ programs on a DOS-based machine, the files that you open, read from, and write to must conform to the DOS file-naming rules.

 Warning   You can't create two files on the same disk (in the same directory) with the same name. If two files had the same name, C wouldn't know which one you wanted when you tried to open one of them by name.

In this unit, you'll learn about sequential file access. Sequential files have the following properties:

▶ Programs can read sequential files in order from start to finish.

▶ Programs can append to sequential files.

▶ When creating sequential files, your program must write each file in order, from the first byte to the last.

Sequential files are good at handling lots of data, but they have several limitations. Here are the primary limitations:

▶ You can't insert data in the middle of a sequential file.

▶ You can't access a sequential file randomly. For example, you can't read the second byte, then the last byte, then the first byte, and so on.

▶ You can't change data in a sequential file. If you want to change something in a sequential file, you must copy the file to a new file after changing the needed data.

definition

To *append* means to add data to the end of a disk file.

Sequential file access is a lot like reading from and writing to cassette tapes. When you listen to such a tape, you listen from the beginning to the end. You can fast-forward to the middle of the tape, but you never know exactly what song you'll land on. In a computerized sequential file, there are ways to scan forward to the middle of a file, but you'll have no idea what data will be at that location, and you might even land in the middle of a two-byte integer. Scanning over sequential file data is a faulty task, and for all intents and purposes, it's meaningless in sequential file processing.

When you add songs to a cassette tape, you can only add (*append*) those songs to the end of the tape. You can't very well insert a song at the beginning! The same holds true for sequential files because you can't insert or change data in the middle of a sequential file. Even using the most advanced cassette decks available, changing a song would be impossible because changing music data using a tape format is too difficult. Even a digital tape machine couldn't change music on a tape unless the change were *exactly* the same length as the music being replaced.

As you read the cassette tape analogy, you might wonder just what advantage sequential files provide and why they're important to learn about. A sequential file is useful for textual data, such as a word processing file. Sequential files are useful if you will always read the entire file into arrays and process arrays (you can change array data without any of the sequential limitations listed here). Sequential files are useful for historical data that you don't access very often and that you never change.

> **Note**   Random access files, as you'll learn in the next unit, are perfect for nontextual data that you must access often in virtually any order. For example, a credit card company would want to use random access files for their customer records so that they could continually update specific customer account balances and search for specific customers without reading or writing the entire file. Random files are also great for storing structure data because each piece of data consumes an equal amount of the file, making searches easier.

When reading and writing disk files of any type, you do so with a special pointer called a *file pointer*. A file pointer is just like any other pointer that contains an address of data. Unlike a pointer variable, however, a file pointer contains on disk the location of the data that you want to access next. The file pointer is a central issue throughout all of the file I/O functions that you'll learn about in this lesson. The primary C difference between sequential files and random access files is in how you handle the file pointer.

Review   **What You Have Learned**

> You can read and write sequential files, but you must read and write them from the beginning, without skipping data. You can't change a sequential file, although you can append to one.

> **Note**   There is no stop and type here due to this section's conceptual nature.

▶ **The First Step: Opening the File**

Concept   **What You Will Learn**

> The `fopen()` function opens files.

`fopen()` is the first of several file I/O functions that you need in order to work with data files. All of the file I/O functions are prototyped in STDIO.H, so you don't need to include an additional header file when you want to perform file I/O.

As just mentioned, you perform file I/O using a file pointer. It's important to define the file pointer properly. Most C programmers define their file pointers globally. A global file pointer makes sense. After all, the file is global to every function in your program. Unlike variables in memory that can go away, the file stays intact until you delete it.

Here is the format of a file pointer definition:

```
FILE * filePtr;
```

FILE isn't a built-in data type. When you see an uppercase word in a C program, that word is almost always a defined constant. FILE is defined in the STDIO.H header file as a complicated file-related structure. When you define a file pointer, you're actually defining a pointer to a structure. The details of the structure aren't critical. All you need to know is that the structure lets the file pointer keep track of every byte's location within the file.

The following statement defines a file pointer named myFile:

```
FILE * myFile;   // Define a file pointer
```

Again, you should define your file pointers globally so that every function in your program can access the file. Define a file pointer for every file you want to open. If, for example, you were opening an existing file for reading and a new file for output, you might open these two file pointers:

```
FILE * fileRead;
FILE * fileWrite;
```

Tip   If you have several files to access, you can define an array of file pointers.

Once you define a file pointer, you can then open a file. When you open a file, C determines whether the file exists (if you're opening an existing file) and connects to the open file the file pointer that you specify. Once you open a file, you never refer to the filename again. After you open a file, you use the file pointer to access the file in the rest of the program.

Here is the format of the fopen() function:

```
filePtr = fopen(fileNameString, modeString);
```

Both arguments to fopen() must be strings. You can specify string literals, character arrays holding strings, or character pointers pointing to strings in memory. The modeString, often just called the *file mode,* can be any value in Table 21.1.

Table 21.1. Sequential file access mode values.

Access Mode	Description
"w"	Opens the file in write mode. If the file exists, the new file you're creating replaces the old one.
"r"	Opens the file in read mode. If the file doesn't exist, fopen() returns an error that you should always check for.
"a"	Opens the file in append mode, letting you add to the end of the file. If the file doesn't exist, a new file is created.

The following `fopen()`s open three files, one in each mode, assigning to file pointers already assumed to be defined:

```
file1 = fopen("sales.94", "w");   // Open a new file for output
file2 = fopen("d:\\mary\\account.dat", "r");   // Open for reading
file3 = fopen("c:\\names.txt", "a");   // Add to the file
```

Note   As with all DOS filenames, you can specify the `fopen()` filename in uppercase or lowercase letters.

Notice the double backslashes in the last two `fopen()` calls. As you already know, the backslash is the special C character used for escape sequences such as `\n`. When you must specify a drive or a pathname, use two backslashes, `\\`, so that C won't interpret the filename as if it contained an escape sequence.

Without the double backslash, the following `fopen()` would fail:

```
file3 = fopen("c:\names.txt", "a");   // Add to the file
```

because C would think that you wanted to open a filename that began with a newline character, and that is simply not possible.

The file pointer that receives the `fopen()` return value will contain either the pointer to the open file or 0. If the pointer contains 0, an error occurred when opening the file. Often, you'll see error-checking code following an `fopen()`:

```
aFile = fopen("c:\\names.txt", "r");
if (aFile == 0)
  { printf("A file open error occurred.\n");
    exit(1);
  }
```

It's not too unreadable to combine the check against the 0 with the `!` operator, like this:

```
aFile = fopen("c:\\names.txt", "r");
if (!aFile)   // More efficient
  { printf("A file open error occurred.\n");
    exit(1);
  }
```

Note   In Lesson 4, you learned that the `!` operator is difficult to use. However, `!` plays an important and easy-to-understand role in file I/O operations. In a way, the preceding `!` reads like this: *"If not `aFile`..."*, meaning that if the file pointer isn't there, an error occurred.

Other C programmers prefer to eliminate the separate error test altogether and combine the error checking with the actual `fopen()`:

```
if (!(aFile = fopen("c:\\names.txt", "r")));
  { printf("A file open error occurred.\n");
    exit(1);
  }
// If code gets here, the fopen() worked
```

Listing 21.1 contains the first part of a file opening program. The user wants to create a new data file to hold lines from the poems he writes (the perfect combination of man and machine?).

Review   **What You Have Learned**

Use `fopen()` to open files before you access them. Whether you're creating, reading, or appending a file, you must open that file first.

▼ **INPUT   LISTING 21.1. OPENING A FILE VIA A FILE POINTER.**

```
1:   /* Filename: OPEN1ST.C */
2:   // Opens a file for output. If the file exists, the
3:   // existing version of the file will be overwritten.
4:   #include <stdio.h>
5:   #include <conio.h>
6:   #include <stdlib.h>    // For exit()
7:
8:   // Define the file pointers globally
9:   FILE * poemFile;
10:
11:  main()
12:  {
13:    clrscr();
14:    poemFile = fopen("C:\\poems.txt", "w");
15:    if (!poemFile)
16:      { puts("An error occurred while opening the file!");
17:        exit(1);
18:      }
19:    // Code gets here if the file opened properly
20:    //
21:    // Body of program to write the file's contents would follow
```

Note   There is no output because the code is incomplete.

▼ **ANALYSIS**

Line 9 defines a file pointer named `poemFile`. From a file pointer's definition, you can't tell whether the file will be opened in read, write, or append mode. You'll request the proper mode in an `fopen()` call such as the one in line 14. The program will create the file named POEMS.TXT, which will reside on drive C:.

If an error occurred, the `if` catches it in line 15. Perhaps drive C: has a problem or there are too many files already in the root directory. Whatever the problem, the `if` ensures that the program doesn't try to write data to a file that wasn't really opened.

Note   You must perform much more error-checking with file I/O because so many problems can occur with a physical device such as a disk drive.

▶ Closing the File with *fclose()*

Concept   **What You Will Learn**

When your program is finished with a file, close the file with `fclose()` to safely tuck the file's data away.

The `fclose()` function works the opposite of `fopen()`. `fclose()` closes a disk file. Here is the format of the `fclose()` function:

```
fclose(filePtr);
```

`filePtr` must be pointing to a file you opened earlier. No matter which mode you opened the file in, `fclose()` closes the file. `fclose()` writes to the file any data still left on the file buffer, updates the file's directory with the file's vital statistics such as the file size, and releases the file pointer so that you can assign it to another `fopen()` if you want to.

> ▶ *Tip*   You can use the same file pointer for two different files in the same program, but you must close the first file before opening the second one. Likewise, you can open the same file in different modes within the same program as long as you close the file before opening it a second time. Perhaps you'd like to create a file, store user input in it, then reread the file and print the contents to the printer, which would require that the file be opened and closed twice.

The following `fclose()` function call closes the file pointed to by the `salesFile` pointer:

```
fclose(salesFile);    // Close the file
```

Always close your open files when you're done with them. The longer a file stays open, the greater chance there is that something might happen to its contents. A power surge or someone accidentally tripping over the computer's plug will virtually ensure that your program's open files will be at best incomplete and at worst inaccessible. When you close your files, the data is safely tucked away. Keep your files open for reading, writing, and appending only as long as you need to.

If you fail to close your files, DOS will close them for you. Nevertheless, don't rely on DOS to do your work. When you close a file, you take active steps in preserving that file's contents.

Listing 21.2 contains the same poem-writing code that you saw in Listing 21.1. At the end of `main()`, this program closes the file before returning to the IDE.

Review   **What You Have Learned**

Use `fclose()` to close your files.

▼ INPUT   LISTING 21.2. CLOSING THE POEM FILE WHEN DONE.

```
 1: /* Filename: OPEN2ND.C */
 2: // Opens a file for output. If the file exists, the
 3: // existing version of the file will be overwritten.
 4: // Closes the file when finished with it.
 5: #include <stdio.h>
 6: #include <conio.h>
 7: #include <stdlib.h>   // For exit()
 8:
 9: // Define the file pointers globally
10: FILE * poemFile;
11:
12: main()
13: {
14:   clrscr();
15:   poemFile = fopen("C:\\poems.txt", "w");
16:   if (!poemFile)
17:     { puts("An error occurred while opening the file!");
18:       exit(1);
19:     }
20:   // Code gets here if the file opened properly
21:   //
22:   // Body of program to write the file's contents would follow
23:
24:   // Close the file when done
25:   fclose(poemFile);
26:   return 0;
27: }
```

Note   There is no output because the code is incomplete.

▼ ANALYSIS

Line 25 closes the file opened in line 15. This program outline assumes that the entire program will need access to that file. In reality, you would want to open the file right before you wrote to it and close the file when you were finished.

Don't go overboard with safety, however. In the next section, you'll learn how to write data to an output file. You shouldn't open the file right before each write and close it right after each write. Your programs would then lose a tremendous amount of efficiency. Just be sure that you open a file before your first access and close that file when your program is done with it.

 # Writing Data

Concept   **What You Will Learn**

Use familiar I/O functions to send output to a sequential data file.

The nice thing about writing, reading, and appending to files is that you already know how! There is little that is new in this section. The familiar I/O functions such as `fprintf()` work for files as well as for the screen and sometimes the printer. Two common functions used for file output are

▶   `fprintf()`

▶   `fputs()`

You can use `fprintf()` to write formatted data to a file. You need `fprintf()` when you want to write numeric data in a certain format provided by the format codes. `fputs()` is useful for writing string data to a file.

`fprintf()` was used earlier in this book for printer output. Use the printer pointer named `stdprn` for `fprintf()`'s first argument to route the output to the printer. To route the output to a file, use a file pointer as `fprintf()`'s first argument.

The following function calls write three lines of data to a file pointed to by the `fPtr` file pointer:

```
fprintf(fPtr, "Sales in the %s region were $%.2f \n",
            regName, sales);
fprintf(fPtr, "There were %d salespeople in the region.\n",
            people);
fprintf(fPtr, "The profit percentage is %.1f", percent);
```

The format of `fputs()` is similar to `puts()`, except that you must use the file pointer as the function's second argument instead of the first. The following function writes the string `Dallas, Texas` to a file pointed to by `fileCities`:

```
fputs("Dallas, Texas", fileCities);    // Writes a string to a file
```

`fputs()` drops the string's null zero so that the extra byte doesn't appear in the final data file. The dropping of the null zero sometimes makes it difficult to read strings back into memory later. Therefore, you'll find it useful to add a newline character to the end of strings that you output with `fputs()` so that a subsequent `fgets()` will be able to read each line of data back into a character array or allocated heap space. (You'll see this demonstrated in the last section of this unit).

 **STOP&TYPE** Listing 21.3 contains a fully functioning program that opens the poem file, writes a short poem, and closes the file.

Review

Use `fprintf()` and `fputs()` to output to an open file.

▼ INPUT   **LISTING 21.3. WRITING A POEM TO THE DISK.**

```
1:  /* Filename: POEMOUT.C */
2:  // Opens a file for output. If the file exists, the
3:  // existing version of the file will be overwritten.
4:  // Writes a short poem to the open disk file.
5:  // Closes the file when finished with it.
```

```
6:   #include <stdio.h>
7:   #include <conio.h>
8:   #include <stdlib.h>    // For exit()
9:
10:  // Define the file pointers globally
11:  FILE * poemFile;
12:
13:  main()
14:  {
15:    clrscr();
16:    poemFile = fopen("C:\\poems.txt", "w");
17:    if (!poemFile)
18:      { puts("An error occurred while opening the file!");
19:         exit(1);
20:      }
21:    // Code gets here if the file opened properly
22:    // Write the poem one line at a time
23:    fputs("I love C and C loves me.\n", poemFile);   // Note the \n
24:    fputs("We're as happy as two can be.\n", poemFile);
25:    fputs("But when C gives me a bug that I hate...\n",poemFile);
26:    fputs("I turn off my PC and go on a real date!\n", poemFile);
27:
28:    // Close the file when done
29:    fclose(poemFile);
30:    return 0;
31:  }
```

Note There is no output in the usual sense. Nothing appears on your blank screen as a result of this program because the poem goes to the disk instead. If you were to use the Windows File Manager or the DOS TYPE command to view the contents of the POEMS.TXT file, you'd see that this program wrote the following poem to the file:

```
I love C and C loves me.
We're as happy as two can be.
But when C gives me a bug that I hate...
I turn off my PC and go on a real date!
```

▼ ANALYSIS

Lines 23 through 26 write the four lines of the poem using the `fputs()` function. As you can see, the newlines were added to the end of the poem's lines so that a subsequent program could read the poem more easily.

Note Even though string literals are the only kinds of data written in Listing 21.3, you don't *have* to write string literals. With `fputs()`, you can write any string stored in a character array or pointed to by a character pointer. Also, you can write any kind of data with `fprintf()`. Whatever you can print to the screen with `printf()` you can write to a file with `fprintf()`.

You might be wondering how to add the newline to the end of strings entered by the user. If you use the `fgets()` function to get string data, `fgets()` automatically adds the newline right before the null zero. This makes `fgets()` the perfect function for getting user text input that you will later write to a file.

▶ **Adding to a Sequential File**

Concept   **What You Will Learn**

If a sequential file already exists, you can add to the end of the file by opening it using the `"a"` access mode.

To add to a file, you use the same output functions you used to create the file in the first
place. The only difference between creating a file from scratch and appending to an
existing file lies in which `fopen()` access mode you use.

Figure 21.1 shows the difference between the `"w"` and the `"a"` access modes. When you
open a file with the `"w"` access mode, the file pointer points to the beginning of the file.
If the file has any contents, they are wiped out and the file is re-created from scratch.
When you open a file using the `"a"` mode, C initially sets the file pointer to point to the
end of the file (EOF), making the file ready for adding to.

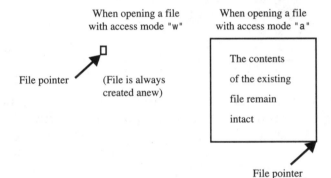

FIGURE 21.1.
The `"w"` and `"a"` access
modes direct the file
pointer differently.

 Tip   The append mode is safer than the write mode. If you're unsure
whether a file exists, opening it using the `"w"` access mode guarantees
that you'll overwrite whatever data is in the file. If you open the file
with the `"a"` access mode, C creates the file if necessary or saves the
original contents if the file already exists. The next section shows you
how to test whether a file exists before opening it.

STOP&**TYPE** Listing 21.4 adds a second stanza to the text file created in Listing 21.3.

Review   **What You Have Learned**

After you open a file in append mode, subsequent writes add data to the
end of the file.

▼ **INPUT   LISTING 21.4. ADDING A SECOND STANZA TO THE POEM.**

```
1:  /* Filename: POEMADD.C */
2:  // Opens a file for append and adds
```

```
3:   // additional text to the file
4:   #include <stdio.h>
5:   #include <conio.h>
6:   #include <stdlib.h>    // For exit()
7:
8:   // Define the file pointers globally
9:   FILE * poemFile;
10:
11:  main()
12:  {
13:    clrscr();
14:    poemFile = fopen("C:\\poems.txt", "a");
15:    if (!poemFile)
16:      { puts("An error occurred while opening the file!");
17:        exit(1);
18:      }
19:    // Code gets here if the file opened properly
20:    // Add to the poem
21:    fputs("\nWhen I program in C,\n", poemFile);
22:    fputs("I often think I'd like to be\n", poemFile);
23:    fputs("Somewhere in Italy...\n", poemFile);
24:    fputs("Instead of using the IDE!\n", poemFile);
25:
26:    // Close the file when done
27:    fclose(poemFile);
28:    return 0;
29:  }
```

Note   There is no output in the usual sense. Nothing appears on your blank screen as a result of this program because the poem goes to the disk instead. If you were to use the Windows File Manager or the DOS TYPE command to view the contents of the POEMS.TXT file, you'd see that this program wrote the following poem to the file:

```
I love C and C loves me.
We're as happy as two can be.
But when C gives me a bug that I hate...
I turn off my PC and go on a real date!

When I program in C,
I often think I'd like to be
Somewhere in Italy...
Instead of using the IDE!
```

▼ ANALYSIS

Line 14's fopen() is the only thing needed to turn a file-creation program into a file-appending program. The same kind of code appears here that appeared in Listing 21.3, which created the file named POEMS.TXT, but this program adds to the file.

The initial \n in line 21 adds a separating line between the file's original ending line and the additional lines that appear here. The \n makes the poem look more like a real poem with two stanzas.

▶ **Reading a Sequential File**

Concept   **What You Will Learn**

The `fgets()` function, as well as `fscanf()`, reads data from a sequential file into variables.

When you create a file, you must pay special attention to how you will eventually read from that file. For example, if you write to a sequential file using `fputs()`, you should read that data file using `fgets()`. `fscanf()` isn't great at reading text data for the same reason that `scanf()` isn't: `fscanf()` quits reading after the first word. Even if you attempt to read a line of text into an 80-character array using `fscanf()`, you'll get only the line's first word.

If you write only numeric data, such as an accounting file that doesn't contain text, you can use an `fprintf()` like this to write the data:

```
fprintf(filePtr, "%f%f%d\n", weekTotal, monthTotal, days);
```

A subsequent program can then use a mirror-image `fscanf()` to read the data back into the variables:

```
fscanf("%f%f%d\n", &weekTotal, &monthTotal, &days);
```

You'll find that even if you don't access a file randomly, if the file contains numeric data, you'll probably want to store that data in a random file, as described in the next unit. However, as long as you write only numeric data, using `fprintf()` and `fscanf()` as just shown works fine.

For reading textual data or complete lines from any file, the `fgets()` function is hard to beat. Here is the format of `fgets()`:

```
fgets(charArray, numBytes, filePtr);
```

`fgets()` reads a line of text until one of two things happens:

- ▶ A newline is reached. `fgets()` discards the newline, stops inputting, and doesn't make the newline part of the input character array that holds the rest of the line.
- ▶ `fgets()` reads *numBytes* worth of data without encountering a newline. Another one of your programs probably created the data file that you're reading, so you should be somewhat familiar with the longest possible line in the file.

Notice that `fgets()` doesn't stop reading at the first space. Most programmers use `fgets()` to read one line at a time from their files.

Tip   If you ever need to read a file one word at a time, use `fscanf()` and the `%s` conversion code inside the format string.

If you open a file for reading using the `"r"` access code, `fopen()` returns a 0 if the file wasn't found. When you attempt to read data from a file, one of two things will happen: either you'll get the data or you'll reach the end of the file where there is no more data. Therefore, you should check to see if you've reached the end of the file after each read. Test the fgets() function's return value for NULL (defined in STDIO.H) to see if an error occurred. If you get good data, everything is fine. However, if fgets() returns a NULL, you'll want to end the input. If you don't, the next attempt at fgets() will produce an error.

DOES THAT FILE EXIST?

The return value of fopen() lets you test to see if a file exists. Remember that if you attempt to open a file with the "r" access mode and the file doesn't exist, fopen() returns a 0, meaning that an error occurred.

To see if a file exists, open it using the "r" mode. If an fopen() error occurs, you know that the file doesn't exist. If an error doesn't occur, you know that the file exists. The following code shows how you would implement this file-checking process:

```
fPtr = fopen("afile.txt", "r");
if (fPtr == 0)
  { puts("The file does not exist."); }
else
  { puts("The file exists."); }
```

STOP&TYPE Listing 21.5 contains a program that reads the entire poem created earlier. fgets() reads up to 80 bytes of data. You know that no line in the poem comes close to being 80 bytes long, so the newlines at the end of each line will let fgets() know when the line ends.

Review

What You Have Learned

Use fgets() to read lines from a sequential text file. If the file contains only numbers that you wrote with fprintf(), you can use a mirror-image fscanf() to read the numbers into numeric variables.

▼ INPUT   LISTING 21.5. READING THE POEM WITH fgets().

```
 1:   /* Filename: POEMREAD.C */
 2:   // Reads a sequential text file from the
 3:   // beginning to the end, printing the contents
 4:   #include <stdio.h>
 5:   #include <conio.h>
 6:   #include <stdlib.h>   // For exit()
 7:
 8:   // Define the file pointers globally
 9:   FILE * poemFile;
10:
11:   main()
```

continues

LISTING 21.5. CONTINUED

```
12:  {
13:     char  inLine[80];    // Hold each line of file input
14:     clrscr();
15:     poemFile = fopen("C:\\poems.txt", "r");
16:     if (!poemFile)
17:       { puts("An error occurred while opening the file!");
18:         exit(1);
19:       }
20:     // Code gets here if the file opened properly
21:     // Read and print the poem
22:     while (fgets(inLine, 80, poemFile) != NULL)
23:       { printf(inLine); }
24:
25:     printf("\n\nPress any key when ready...");
26:     getch();
27:
28:     // Close the file when done
29:     fclose(poemFile);
30:     return 0;
31:  }
```

▼ **OUTPUT**

```
I love C and C loves me.
We're as happy as two can be.
But when C gives me a bug that I hate...
I turn off my PC and go on a real date!

When I program in C,
I often think I'd like to be
Somewhere in Italy...
Instead of using the IDE!

Press any key when ready...
```

▼ **ANALYSIS**

The file-reading process occurs in lines 22 and 23. The while loop keeps reading and printing until fgets() encounters an end-of-file condition.

Note   If fgets() encounters an error during the input, it returns a NULL condition. If you need to know if an error or end-of-file took place, you have to use either the ferror() or the feof() function, discussed in the next unit.

▶ **Homework**

General Knowledge

1. What is an advantage of using a file as a storage location?
2. How many types of files are there? What are they called?

3. How many ways can you access a sequential file?

4. What is a file pointer used for?

5. What function do you use to open a sequential file?

6. Why do you use a double backslash when opening files?

7. What function closes files?

8. What happens if you attempt to open a file for reading and the file doesn't exist?

9. What happens if you attempt to open a file for writing and the file already exists?

10. What happens if you attempt to open a file for appending and the file already exists?

11. What happens if you attempt to open a file for appending and the file doesn't exist?

12. Name one function that outputs data to files.

13. Name one function that reads data from files.

14. How can you tell if an `fopen()` function worked properly?

15. How can you tell if you've reached the end of the file when reading with `fgets()`?

16. What is a disadvantage of using `fscanf()` for getting textual input?

17. True or false: A file holds data for a shorter time than memory.

18. True or false: The file pointer indicates whether the file is open for reading or writing.

19. True or false: You can change data in a sequential file.

20. True or false: When you specify a filename, you must type the filename in uppercase letters.

Note There are no What's the Output? exercises for this unit.

Find the Bug

21. Lily's program is having problems. She can't get the following `fopen()` to work even though she has a drive C: and there is a sequential data file on that drive named VALUES.DAT. Tell Lily how to fix this `fopen()` so that it will work.

```
fPtr = fopen("C:\VALUES.DAT", "r");
```

22. Paul wants to open a file, but he's having problems with his `fopen()`. He simply wants to create a sequential output file. What's wrong with the following `fopen()`?

```
fPtrPaul = fopen("EMPS.93", "W");
```

23. After Paul listened to your advice and fixed his `fopen()`, he messed up his `fclose()`. (Paul needs to reread this unit!) Tell him what's wrong with the following `fclose()`:

```
fclose("EMPS.93");
```

24. Joe wrote a program that created a customer file that stores each customer's balance. When a customer pays a bill, Joe wants to update that customer balance. However, he keeps getting bugs and damaging his data file. Every time he opens the file to write the changed balance, he wipes out the file! Joe doesn't want to move to random access just yet. Explain to Joe the only method he can use to change data in a sequential file. Hint: A second file is needed.

Write Code That...

25. Rewrite POEMOUT.C, the program in Listing 21.3. Instead of writing string literals, ask the user for a four-line poem one line at a time, and write the user's poem to the disk file. After you write the poem, close the file and reopen it for read access so that you can print the poem for the user. Print Great poem! at the bottom of the prose.

26. Write a program that reads a file one line at a time and makes a backup of that file called BACKUP.FIL. You'll need to open two files—one for reading and one for writing.

27. The fgetc() function reads one character at a time from a file. (Some files are compressed and you must read their data one byte at a time.) When fgetc() gets to the end of the file, it returns the defined EOF constant. Write a program that asks the user for a filename and then reads the file one character at a time, printing the letters to the screen as the program reads them. To test the program, use the CONFIG.SYS file, located in drive C:'s root directory. (Be sure to back up the file first by copying it to a different name such as CONFIG.BAK using the DOS COPY command or the Windows File Manager.)

Extra Credit

28. You can write programs that contain both text and numeric data in sequential files, but doing so often requires a little coding finesse. For example, write a program that stores the names, mileage, and price of five automobiles in a sequential file. Write the name with a terminating newline, and on the next line write that car's mileage and price. The next car's name will begin on the third line. Continue writing in this manner, using a pair of fputs() and fprintf() functions, until all the data is in the file. Close the file and open it again for reading. Use fgets() and fprintf() function pairs to read the values back and print the data to the screen.

22

Random Access Files

fread()

fseek()

fwrite()

random access

▶ **What You'll Learn About**

- ▶ Opening random access files
- ▶ Seeking the correct position
- ▶ Doing the random I/O
- ▶ Other file-related functions

Although random access files require a little more work up front than sequential files, you can do a lot more with random access files. Once you master the random access functions, you'll probably think that storing and retrieving random data is easier than doing the same with sequential files.

The best thing about random access files (often simply called *random files*) is that you can change data in the files without rewriting all the rest of the data. It's easy to mix data types in a random file because structures are so easy to read and write.

Some C programmers use random files for all their file I/O. After all, you can read a random file sequentially, but you can't read a sequential file randomly.

▶ **An Introduction to Random Access**

 *Concept*   **What You Will Learn**

Plan how you'll access your file before you create it.

Figure 22.1 shows the primary difference between sequential files and random files. You must always access a sequential file from the beginning to the end whether you're reading or writing data in the file. Random access lets you skip around the file, reading or writing whatever data you wish without bothering the rest of the data.

Whereas you read or write sequential files from top to bottom…

you can access a random file in any order that you need.

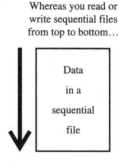

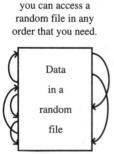

FIGURE 22.1.

Access sequential files sequentially and random files randomly.

With random files, you can even read and write to a file without ever closing the file. In other words, you can write customer information and, in the same program with the file still open, change the customer balances that you wrote earlier.

Note C doesn't store random and sequential files differently. To C, a file is just a stream of bytes going to or from the disk. The way your program accesses the file determines whether the file is random or sequential. If you plan to perform random access on a file, however, you must structure the file in such a way as to allow for the random access, as you'll see in this unit.

The format of a random access file must allow for random access. One of the ways to best structure a random file is to ensure that each piece of data consumes the same number of bytes. This might seem like a limitation, but it's not. After all, every time you define an array of structure variables, each of those variables will consume the same amount of space. As you saw in Lesson 10, structures are anything but limiting. Structures let you group all sorts of data types, and so do random files.

An inventory of parts, a phone book, a customer file, an employee database, and a store's accounts receivable records all share the same trait: Each of their records, or *structures* in C terminology, has the same format. This uniform format is what lets you skip around in a random file accurately. If there were no uniformity in a random inventory file, you couldn't easily skip to the 50th item and retrieve its data. Instead, you would have to read the file one character at a time, looking for some pattern of bytes, such as a part number, that indicated you found the item. Even then, reading the item's data would be difficult due to the different lengths of each item's data.

Once you structure a random file with all uniform data, you'll find that C provides many functions that you can use to skip forward, backward, and sideways (well, maybe not *sideways,* but randomly!), accessing the data however you need to for any given situation.

Review
What You Have Learned

Accessing random files requires that you make the file's values a uniform size. The best way to keep the data uniform is to store it in an array. If the data items contain different data types, store the random files as an array of structures.

Note There is no stop and type here due to this section's conceptual nature.

▶ Opening Random Access Files

Concept
What You Will Learn

Use a plus sign after the access mode to let C know that you're opening a file for random access.

The only difference in opening random access files and sequential files lies in the access mode you use. All of the access modes for random access files end with a plus sign (+). The + is a way of telling C that you want to do more with the file than ordinary sequential access.

definition

To *update* a file means to change or add to it.

Table 22.1 lists the random access modes available. There are some additional access modes as well, but the ones listed in Table 22.1 are the most common. The key difference from the sequential access modes is that the random access modes let you update a file, whereas the sequential access modes don't let you change the contents of the file without re-creating the file from scratch.

Table 22.1. The access modes for random access files.

Access Mode	Description
"r+"	Opens an existing file for reading and writing. The file pointer points to the beginning of the file when you first open the file.
"w+"	Opens a new file for writing and reading. If the file exists, the existing file will be erased and a new version created. Once you write data to the file, you can move the file pointer to a different location and read the data without reopening the file.
"a+"	Opens a new or existing file for appending, reading, and writing. The file pointer points to the end of the file if the file exists. The file is created if it doesn't exist.

 Note Perhaps you can now see why `fopen()`'s second argument, the access mode, is a string. In Unit 21, the access mode consisted of a single character, but the addition of the + requires that the argument be a string argument.

As you can see from the descriptions in Table 22.1, the access mode that you use depends on what you want to do with the file *first*. You can perform reading and writing with any of the random access modes. However, if you wanted to write data first, you'd use "w+". If you wanted to append to an existing file first, you'd use "a+". If you wanted to read from the file, searching for data before changing that data, you'd use "r+".

 Tip Use `fopen()` to check for random access file opening errors, just as you did in Unit 21 for sequential files.

Use `fclose()` to close random access files. The same `fclose()` function that you learned about in Unit 21 closes both sequential and random access files.

The following `fopen()` function call opens a file in a subdirectory for random file access. The file is assumed not to exist:

```
openErr = fopen("D:\\ACCT\\FIGURES.MAR", "w+");
```

The following `fopen()` function call might be used by another program to add to that file and, optionally, back up and read data:

```
openErr = fopen("D:\\ACCT\\FIGURES.MAR", "a+");
```

The following `fopen()` function call might be used to open the same file for reading and writing. This `fopen()` initially sets the file pointer to the beginning of the file:

```
openErr = fopen("D:\\ACCT\\FIGURES.MAR", "r+");
```

Review
What You Have Learned

The plus sign at the end of `fopen()`'s access mode specifies that you want to open the file using one of the random access modes.

Note There is no input, output, or analysis due to this section's conceptual nature.

▶ Seeking the Correct Position

Concept
What You Will Learn

Use the `fseek()` function to move the file pointer to the exact position you need to read or write next.

Once you open a random access file, you've got to be able to move the file pointer to the location you want to read or write next. All the standard `fgets()`, `fputs()`, and other I/O functions that you saw used for sequential files work for random access files as long as you first move the file pointer to the place where you want to do the I/O.

The `fseek()` function moves the file pointer back and forth through the file, preparing the file for I/O at the exact spot where you want to read or write. Here is the format of `fseek()`:

```
fseek(filePtr, longSeekVal, origin);
```

filePtr is the file pointer pointing to the file you want to work with. Of course, you must have opened the file using `fopen()` before `fseek()` can access the file. *longSeekVal* is the number of bytes that you want to move the file pointer from its current position. The value can be positive or negative, indicating the direction to move from the *origin*. *longSeekVal* should be a long integer or a long integer literal (such as `83940L`) because files are large. You might want to move the file pointer farther than 32767 bytes, because a number greater than 32767 won't fit in a regular integer data type. The *origin* must be one of the values from Table 22.2.

Table 22.2. The `fseek()` *origin* **values.**

origin	Description
SEEK_SET	The beginning of the file.
SEEK_CUR	The pointer's current position.
SEEK_END	The end of the file.

The three `origin` values tell `fseek()` exactly *from where* you want to move the pointer. In other words, you might have written 25 characters to the disk and want to back up the file pointer 10 bytes. To do that, you can either move –10 bytes from the current position (`SEEK_CUR`) or move 15 bytes from the beginning of the file (`SEEK_SET`).

 Warning   There is no `SEEK_BEG` origin value. Be sure to use `SEEK_SET` if you want to move the file pointer from the beginning of the file.

The `origin` values appear in uppercase because they're defined constant values from the STDIO.H header file. You'll use `fseek()` to move the file pointer to the location where you want to read or write, but the actual reading and writing *also* move the file pointer. If you were to read a character, the file pointer would move forward one byte due to the read.

Suppose that a newspaper company stored its last year's sales figures in a file. The 365 floating-point values represent each day of the year. After the file has been opened using the `"r+"` access mode using a file pointer named `daySalPtr`, the following `fseek()` moves the file pointer to the location of the last sales figure in the file so that the paper can then read the sales figure for New Year's Eve:

```
fseek(daySalPtr, -1L * sizeof(float), SEEK_END);
```

The second and third arguments of this `fseek()` tell C to move the file pointer to the end of the file (`SEEK_END`) and then back up one floating-point value (`-1L * sizeof(float)`). You'll almost always use an expression for `fseek()`'s second argument because you'll rarely want to move forward or backward in bytes. Usually you'll want to move in multiples of a data type or (more commonly) in multiples of a specific structure size.

After the New Year's Eve sales figure has been read, the file pointer points to the end of the file. The following `fseek()` moves the file pointer from that end-of-file position back 31 floating-point values to position the pointer at the sales value for December 1:

```
fseek(daySalPtr, -31L, SEEK_CUR);    // Move from current position
```

The following `fseek()` moves the file pointer back to the beginning of the file:

```
fseek(daySalPtr, 0L, SEEK_SET);
```

Of course, the programmer could have closed and reopened the file to move the file pointer to the beginning of the file, but using `fseek()` is more efficient.

Review

Use `fseek()` to move the file pointer around a file. The *origin* that you use determines the starting position of the seek.

Note There is no input, output, or analysis in this section. Before looking at a program that actually updates values in a file, you need to learn about the `fread()` and `fwrite()` functions.

▶ Doing the Random I/O

Concept

The `fread()` and `fwrite()` functions are the easiest functions for performing random I/O.

Although you can use all the file I/O functions that you learned in Unit 21 for random file access, the `fread()` and `fwrite()` functions generally are easier to use. Given the fact that you'll be storing structures in virtually all random access files, `fread()` and `fwrite()` read and write structures easily.

Note `fread()` and `fwrite()` read and write variables of *any* data type, not just structures. For example, if you seek to an integer that you want to read or write, substitute the integer's value or variable in place of the structure variable in this discussion.

The reason that `fwrite()` and `fseek()` are so popular is that they write data of any data type with the same syntax. Without `fwrite()`, if you were to write a character to a file, you'd use `fputc()`. If you were to write a string to a file, you'd use `fputs()`. If you were to write an integer to a file, you'd use `fprintf()`. One pair of functions, `fwrite()` and `fread()`, performs I/O on all data types.

Tip `fread()` and `fwrite()` even write complete arrays in one function call! If you needed to store an array of 150 structure variables, a single `fwrite()` would do the trick. If you wanted to read that array of structures back in from the disk in another program, a single `fread()` would take care of everything.

You should use `fwrite()` and `fread()` in pairs. Don't use `fread()` to read data that you wrote with `fprintf()`. An `fread()` that reads data written by `fwrite()` will always be the mirror image of that `fwrite()`, as you'll see in the next few examples.

Here is the format of fwrite():

```
fwrite(dataAddress, size, numBytes, filePtr);
```

dataAddress must be the starting address of whatever data you want to write. If you write a regular variable, put an & in front of it to pass the variable address to fwrite(). If you want to write an array using fwrite(), simply pass the array name (as you know, an array name is a pointer to the start of an array). If you want to write data from the heap, you only need to pass the name of the pointer that points to that heap data.

The *size* value is the size of the data you're writing. Obviously, most of the time you'll pass *size* using a sizeof() function call. If you were passing an array named figures, you'd use sizeof(figures) for fwrite()'s second argument.

numBytes tells fwrite() how many values you're passing. Usually *numBytes* is 1 because you're passing one array or one variable. However, if you're passing an array of 100 floating-point values, you can use sizeof(float) for the second argument and 100 for the *size* argument if you wish.

filePtr is a pointer pointing to the file that you've opened and positioned with fseek().

The format of fread() is identical to that of fwrite() (that's why they work so well in pairs). Here is the format of fread():

```
fread(dataAddress, size, numBytes, filePtr);
```

The following fwrite() writes an array named custs, of 150 customer structure variables, to the disk:

```
fwrite(custs, sizeof(custs), 1, cFilePtr);
```

The following would also work:

```
fwrite(custs, sizeof(custs[0]), 150, cFilePtr);
```

In the second fwrite(), the size of one of the structure variables was passed, and 150 of those were in the array to be written.

The following fread() would read those values into an array of structures named oldCusts:

```
fread(custs, sizeof(custs), 1, cFilePtr);
```

Of course, before this fread(), you would have to define the array of customer structure variables, and the structure must be the same format as the structures written with the fwrite().

> **Note**   The data file created with fwrite() isn't an ASCII text file such as the ones you created with sequential I/O. fwrite() compresses the data, giving you more disk space as a result.

STOP&TYPE   Listing 22.1 contains a program that initializes an array of 10 structure variables and writes that array to disk. The program then reads those same structures back into a second, uninitialized array, showing that the fread() easily reads the same data written by fwrite(). Finally, three records are selected to be read randomly in the file.

Review

Use `fwrite()` to write data to a random access file and `fread()` to read that same data. The `fseek()` function lets you jump directly to the place in the file you want to access next.

▼ **INPUT   LISTING 22.1.** `fseek()`, `fwrite()`, **AND** `fread()` **TAKE CARE OF VIRTUALLY ALL YOUR RANDOM ACCESS FILE NEEDS.**

```
1:   /* Filename: RANSTRS.C */
2:   // Writes an array of 10 structures to a disk
3:   // file and then rereads that file randomly
4:   #include <stdio.h>
5:   #include <conio.h>
6:   #include <stdlib.h>
7:
8:   struct cafeSt {
9:     char name[15];
10:    float avPrice;
11:    int seats;
12:  };
13:
14:  void prStruct(struct cafeSt prVar);
15:  void pKey(void);
16:
17:  FILE * fPtr;
18:
19:  main()
20:  {
21:    int ctr;
22:    // Keep the data alphabetical and sequential to
23:    // help verify that the data is read properly
24:    struct cafeSt cafes[10] = {{"Adam's Mark", 12.95, 135},
25:                               {"Berryhill", 20.15, 78},
26:                               {"Capricorn's", 18.40, 101},
27:                               {"Daybreak", 3.69, 63},
28:                               {"Even Steven", 13.90, 45},
29:                               {"Fike's Foods", 48.51, 73},
30:                               {"Great Gobs", 8.97, 28},
31:                               {"Ham Heaven", 5.49, 65},
32:                               {"Ike's Chili", 3.65, 40},
33:                               {"Jan's Drinks", 1.75, 25}};
34:    struct cafeSt cafesNew[10];   // A second, uninitialized array
35:    struct cafeSt aVar;   // A single structure variable
36:
37:    clrscr();
38:    puts("Getting ready to write the data...");
39:    // Didn't open the file until ready to write
40:    fPtr = fopen("c:\\cafe.dat", "w+");
41:    if (!fPtr)
42:      { puts("\n** Error opening file**\n");
43:        exit(1);
44:      }
45:    // A single function call writes all the data
46:    fwrite(cafes, sizeof(cafes), 1, fPtr);
47:    puts("Just wrote the data");
48:    fclose(fPtr);
```

continues

LISTING 22.1. CONTINUED

```
49:
50:     // Open the file again to show that the fwrite() worked
51:     fPtr = fopen("c:\\cafe.dat", "r+");
52:     if (!fPtr)
53:       { puts("\n** Error opening file**\n");
54:         exit(1);
55:       }
56:
57:     fread(cafesNew, sizeof(cafesNew), 1, fPtr);
58:
59:     for (ctr = 0; ctr < 10; ctr++)
60:       { prStruct(cafesNew[ctr]);
61:         if (ctr == 4)
62:           { pKey(); }
63:       }
64:     fseek(fPtr, (4L * sizeof(aVar)), SEEK_SET);    // Fifth cafe
65:     fread(&aVar, sizeof(aVar), 1, fPtr);
66:     printf("\nFifth structure:");
67:     prStruct(aVar);
68:
69:     fseek(fPtr, (-3L * sizeof(aVar)), SEEK_CUR);   // Third cafe
70:     fread(&aVar, sizeof(aVar), 1, fPtr);
71:     printf("\nThird structure:");
72:     prStruct(aVar);
73:
74:     fseek(fPtr, -1L * sizeof(aVar), SEEK_END);    // Last cafe
75:     fread(&aVar, sizeof(aVar), 1, fPtr);
76:     printf("\nLast structure:");
77:     prStruct(aVar);
78:
79:     fclose(fPtr);
80:     pKey();
81:     return 0;
82:   }
83: //********************************************************
84: void prStruct(struct cafeSt prVar)
85: {
86:   printf("\nName: %s\n", prVar.name);
87:   printf("Average menu price: %.2f\n", prVar.avPrice);
88:   printf("Seating: %d\n", prVar.seats);
89:   return;
90: }
91: //********************************************************
92: void pKey(void)
93: {   // Gives the user a chance to pause
94:   printf("\nPress any key to continue...");
95:   getch();
96:   return;
97: }
```

▼ OUTPUT

```
Getting ready to write the data...
Just wrote the data
```

```
Name: Adam's Mark
Average menu price: 12.95
Seating: 135

Name: Berryhill
Average menu price: 20.15
Seating: 78

Name: Capricorn's
Average menu price: 18.40
Seating: 101

Name: Daybreak
Average menu price: 3.69
Seating: 63

Name: Even Steven
Average menu price: 13.90
Seating: 45

Press any key to continue...

Name: Fike's Foods
Average menu price: 48.51
Seating: 73

Name: Great Gobs
Average menu price: 8.97
Seating: 28

Name: Ham Heaven
Average menu price: 5.49
Seating: 65

Name: Ike's Chili
Average menu price: 3.65
Seating: 40

Name: Jan's Drinks
Average menu price: 1.75
Seating: 25

Fifth structure:
Name: Even Steven
Average menu price: 13.90
Seating: 45

Third structure:
Name: Capricorn's
Average menu price: 18.40
Seating: 101

Last structure:
Name: Jan's Drinks
Average menu price: 1.75
Seating: 25

Press any key to continue...
```

▼ **ANALYSIS**

When you compile this program, you receive four compiler warnings. Turbo C++ always warns you when you pass a structure by value. A copy of the structure is passed when you pass the structure by value instead of by address. Turbo C++ lets you know that, if the structure is long (which this one really isn't), the program would be more efficient if you passed the structure by address. This structure is small, so the efficiency loss is insignificant. Also, the syntax required to pass a structure variable by address is too tedious to deal with now (you'd have to precede all the structure variables in prStruct() with asterisks).

Lines 24 through 33 define and initialize an array of structure variables that will be written to the disk. Line 34 defines an identical array of structures but doesn't initialize the array. Line 35 defines a single nonarray structure variable.

Once the file is opened, line 46 writes the entire array of structures to the disk file using a single fwrite().

The file is opened again in line 51, and the entire file is read into the second array named cafesNew in line 57. Just to show that the file was read completely, the for loop in lines 59 through 63 prints the newly read array.

The program ends by reading three different records—the fifth, third, and last—into a nonarray structure variable named aVar. The result is displayed after each print.

▶ Other File-Related Functions

Concept _____ **What You Will Learn**

Wrap up your knowledge of fundamental file functions by learning about a few functions you might need sometime.

Table 22.3 lists four more file-related functions. As you can see from this table, you can delete files from C programs, reposition the random access pointer, check for the end of the file, and check for errors.

Table 22.3. File-related functions.

Function Name	Description
feof()	Returns true if the file pointer points to the end of the file.
ferror()	Returns true if an error occurred on the most recent file I/O function call. Most useful for fgets(), which doesn't distinguish between end-of-file and error conditions.
remove()	Removes the filename pointed to by its string argument. If the file can't be removed because it doesn't exist or because the filename specification is invalid, remove() returns a –1.
rewind()	Repositions the file pointer to the beginning of the file.

Note You now know three different ways to set the file pointer to the beginning of a file:

1. `fseek(fPtr, 0L, SEEK_SET);`

2. `fclose(fPtr);`
   `fopen();`

3. `rewind(fPtr);`

`fgets()` returns a STDIO.H-defined `NULL` value if an error occurs or if an end-of-file condition is reached. In order to tell the difference, you can use `ferror()` to see what the `NULL` means:

```
while (fgets(name, 150, fPtr) != NULL)
{
   puts(name);   // Print the line just read
}

if (ferror(fPtr))
  { printf("\n** An error appeared**"); }
else
  { printf("\n** End of file**"); }
```

Listing 22.2 contains a function named deleteIt() that accepts a character array as its argument and deletes the file or prints an error message if the file can't be deleted.

Review

What You Have Learned

`remove()` erases the filename pointed to by its argument.

▼ INPUT   LISTING 22.2. A FUNCTION THAT ERASES A FILE.

```
void deleteIt(char fName[])
{
  int errorVal;
  errorVal = remove(fName);   // Attempt to erase the file
  if (errorVal == -1)
    { printf("** Warning.. I could not delete %s\n", fName); }
  return;
}
```

Note There is no output because the program is incomplete as shown.

▼ ANALYSIS

Unlike the other file I/O functions, `remove()` doesn't take a file pointer argument. Instead, you must tell `remove()` which file to erase by passing the file's filename to `remove()`.

▶ Homework

General Knowledge

1. What's the physical difference between random access files and sequential files?

2. How can you read a random access file sequentially?

3. Why should all values in a random access file be the same size?

4. What's the primary difference between an `fopen()` call for a random access file and a sequential file?

5. What does it mean to update a file?

6. If you try to open a file that doesn't exist by using the `"w+"` mode, what does C do?

7. If you try to open a file that does exist by using the `"w+"` mode, what does C do?

8. If you try to open a file that doesn't exist by using the `"a+"` mode, what does C do?

9. If you try to open a file that doesn't exist by using the `"r+"` mode, what does C do?

10. How do you check for `fopen()` errors when opening random access files?

11. How do you close random access files?

12. What does the `fseek()` function do?

13. What is the *origin* in relation to the `fseek()` function?

14. What is the name of the function that erases files?

15. How can you reliably determine whether an `fgets()` got to the end of a file?

16. How can you reliably determine whether an `fgets()` encountered an error during input?

17. True or false: Random file I/O requires that you plan your file's contents more than when you use sequential file access.

18. True or false: There are usually several ways to seek to the same location in a file.

19. True or false: The `fread()` that reads `fwrite()`-produced data files usually contains the same arguments as `fwrite()`.

20. True or false: If you write a file using `fprintf()`, you can read that file using `fread()`.

21. True or false: If you write a file using `fwrite()`, you can read that file using `fgets()`.

22. True or false: `fwrite()` and `fread()` write and read entire arrays with one function call.

23. True or false: There are three ways to position the file pointer at the beginning of a file.

There is no What's the Output? section.

Find the Bug

24. Raymond wants to position his random access file pointer at the beginning of his file. Help him fix the following `fseek()` function call:

```
fseek(fPtr, 0L, SEEK_BEG);
```

25. Mark wants his C program to erase a file called MYDATA.DAT that is open and pointed to by the `fPtr` file pointer. Help him erase the file by fixing this `remove()`:

```
remove(fPtr);
```

Write Code That...

26. Linda is writing an array of 2,000 integers to the disk. The array is called `timeVals`. Rewrite the following `fwrite()` so that the third argument is 1 instead of 2000:

```
fwrite(timeVals, sizeof(int), 2000, fPtr);
```

27. Write Linda's `fread()` function in question 26 so that it will read her values back into the array.

28. Write a program that writes a random access file, then reads that file twice. Use only a single `fopen()` and `fclose()`. Use `rewind()` to reposition the file pointer at the beginning for the second printing.

29. Write a program that writes the letters a through z to a random access file. When that's finished, without closing the file, change the h, p, and t in the file to asterisks. Read and print the file's contents toward the end of the program to show that the three changes took place.

Extra Credit

30. Write a program that lets the user enter five customers' names and balances in a disk file. The program should assign each customer a sequential number, beginning at 0. Once all five customer names, balances, and numbers are stored on disk, set up a loop that asks the user for a customer number (from 0 to 4) and a sales total. Update that customer's balance on the disk by adding the entered sales total to that customer's stored balance. When the user enters –99 for a customer number, stop the loop and print all five customer numbers, names, and current balances on-screen.

Long-Term Storage

STOP&TYPE In this lesson, you learned how to store data in sequential and random access files. You saw the following:

▶ How disk files relate to C programs.

▶ The types of disk file access: sequential and random.

▶ Opening and closing files.

Project 11 Listing. Changing values in a random access file.

```
 1:   /* Filename: LESSON11.C */

 2:   // This program assigns data to an array of floats, then writes

 3:   // that data to a random access file, then rewinds the file

 4:   // pointer to the beginning and reads each float once more,

 5:   // doubling the value that's stored in the file.

 6:

 7:   #define NUM 6

 8:   #include <stdio.h>

 9:   #include <conio.h>

10:

11:   void wrData(float totals[NUM]);

12:   void chData(void);

13:   void prData(void);

14:   FILE * fPtr;

15:

16:   main()
```

▶ Specifying the access mode.

▶ Creating, appending to, and reading from a sequential file.

▶ Creating and changing a random access file.

▶ Using `fseek()` to move the random access file pointer.

Description

1: A C comment that includes the program's filename.

2: A C++ comment that contains the program's description.

3: The description continues.

4: The description continues.

5: The description continues.

6: Put blank lines in your programs to separate sections of code.

7: Defines a constant that tracks the total number of values in the array and file.

8: The `printf()` and `scanf()` functions need information in the STDIO.H header file.

9: The screen-clearing function, `clrscr()`, needs information in the CONIO.H header file.

10: Put blank lines in your programs to separate sections of code.

11: You should prototype all functions.

12: Prototype of another function.

13: Prototype of another function.

14: A file-pointer definition that the program uses to keep track of the open file.

14:　Define file pointers globally because files are entities separate from your program to which all functions should have access.

15: Put blank lines in your programs to separate sections of code.

16: `main()` begins.

continues

Project 11 Listing. continued

```
17:   {

18:      float totals[NUM] = {2.32, 4.55, 7.43, 2.18, 9.01, 2.34};

19:      clrscr();

20:      wrData(totals);    // Create a random file and write the array

21:      puts("Here are the totals:");

22:      prData();          // Print the totals before doubling them

23:      puts("\nJust wrote the data to the file.");

24:      puts("Getting ready to change the data...");

25:      chData();          // Double each of the total values

26:      puts("Just changed the data in the file.");

27:      puts("\nHere are the totals doubled:");

28:      prData();          // Read and print the data

29:      fclose(fPtr);

30:

31:      printf("\n\nPress any key to continue...");

32:      getch();

33:      return 0;

34:   }

35:   //**************************************************

36:   void wrData(float totals[NUM])

37:   {
```

Description

17: All functions begin with an opening brace.

18: `main()` defines a local array of floating-point values that will be written to a random access file later.

19: Erases the user's output screen.

20: Calls the function that writes the floating-point values to the disk.

21: Prints a title on-screen.

22: Calls a function that prints the floating-point values on-screen in the order that they're written in the file.

23: Prints a title on-screen.

24: Prints a title on-screen.

25: Calls a function that changes data in the random file.

26: Prints a title on-screen.

27: Prints a title on-screen.

28: Calls a function that prints the floating-point values on-screen in the order they're written in the file after they're doubled.

29: Always close all open files as soon as the program is finished accessing them.

30: Put blank lines in your programs to separate sections of code.

31: Prompts the user to press a key when he or she is finished viewing the output.

32: Waits for the user's keypress.

33: Always return from `main()` to the IDE.

34: A final brace ends all `main()` functions.

35: A line of asterisks helps to separate functions.

36: The definition (first line) of `wrData()`. Receives `main()`'s floating-point array of values.

37: All functions begin with an opening brace.

22: `prData()` prints values read from the file, not values from the array.

continues

Project 11 Listing. continued

```c
38:    int ctr;    // for-loop control variable

39:    // Open the file for writing and send the array to it

40:    fPtr = fopen("C:\\sales.dat", "w+");

41:    for (ctr = 0; ctr < NUM; ctr++)

42:      { fwrite(&(totals[ctr]), sizeof(float), 1, fPtr); }

43:

44:    return;

45:  }

46:  //********************************************************

47:  void chData(void)

48:  {

49:    float aTotal;

50:    int ctr;    // for-loop control variable

51:    // Reposition the file pointer to the file's start again

52:    fseek(fPtr, 0, SEEK_END);    // End of file

53:    for (ctr = NUM - 1; ctr >= 0; ctr--)

54:      {

55:        fseek(fPtr, (ctr) * (sizeof(float)), SEEK_SET);

56:        fread(&aTotal, sizeof(float), 1, fPtr);

57:        aTotal *= 2.0;

58:        // The next fseek() seeks to the same position in
```

Description

38: Defines the `for` loop control variable.

39: Scatter comments throughout your programs.

40: Opens the file for output in random-access write/update mode.

40: Open random files using a + at the end of the access mode.

41: Steps through each element in the array.

42: Writes each array value one at a time.

42: A single `fwrite()` could have written the entire array at once, but each element will be read individually later. `fread()`s should match `fwrite()`s in format.

43: Put blank lines in your programs to separate sections of code.

44: Returns to `main()`.

45: A final brace ends all functions.

46: A line of asterisks helps to separate functions.

47: Defines the function that reads the file one value at a time, doubling each value and writing that value right back where it was.

48: All functions begin with an opening brace.

49: Defines a floating-point variable that will hold values as they are read individually from the file.

50: Defines the `for` loop variable.

51: Scatter comments throughout your programs.

52: Moves the file pointer to the *end* of the file (zero bytes from the file's end).

52: Just to demonstrate the randomness of random access files, the values will be read *backwards*, something impossible with sequential files.

53: Steps through the file.

54: `for` loop bodies should begin with a brace.

55: Seeks to the start of the last floating-point value in the file.

55: `fseek()` moves the file pointer to the correct location in the file.

56: Reads the value at the pointer's position.

57: Doubles the value just read.

58: Scatter comments throughout your programs.

continues

Project 11 Listing. continued

```
59:      // the file where this float value was read from

60:      fseek(fPtr, (ctr) * (sizeof(float)), SEEK_SET);

61:      // Write over the old total

62:      fwrite(&aTotal, sizeof(float), 1, fPtr);

63:    }

64:    return;

65:  }

66:  //*********************************************************

67:  void prData(void)

68:  {

69:    float aTotal;

70:    int ctr;    // for-loop control variable

71:    // Reposition the file pointer to the file's start again

72:    fseek(fPtr, 0, SEEK_END);    // End of file

73:    for (ctr = 0; ctr < NUM; ctr++)

74:     {

75:      fseek(fPtr, (ctr) * (sizeof(float)), SEEK_SET);

76:      fread(&aTotal, sizeof(float), 1, fPtr);

77:      printf("Total: %.2f\n", aTotal);

78:     }

79:    return;

80:  }
```

Description

59: Scatter comments throughout your programs.

60: Seeks back to the beginning of the floating-point that you just read.

61: Scatter comments throughout your programs.

62: Writes the doubled value over its original value in the file.

63: Closes the body of the for loop.

64: Returns to main().

65: The end of the function.

66: A line of asterisks helps to separate functions.

67: Defines the function that prints data from the file.

68: The function's opening brace.

69: Defines a floating-point variable that will hold each value from the file one at a time.

70: Defines the for loop control variable.

71: Scatter comments throughout your programs.

72: Positions the file pointer to the end of the file (SEEK_END).

73: Steps through the file one floating-point value at a time.

74: The opening brace of the for loop.

75: Seeks to the next value in the file.

76: Reads the value at the file's current position.

77: Prints the value just read from the file.

78: Closes the body of the for loop.

79: Returns to main().

80: The closing brace of the function.

62: Once fseek() positions the file pointer, you can write back over file data.

75: This function steps through the file's values in forward order, unlike chData(), which stepped through the file backwards. Remember that the file has never been closed and that all the moving of the file pointer is done while the file is still open.

▼ **OUTPUT**

```
Here are the totals:

Total: 2.32

Total: 4.55

Total: 7.43

Total: 2.18

Total: 9.01

Total: 2.34

Just wrote the data to the file.

Getting ready to change the data...

Just changed the data in the file.

Here are the totals doubled:

Total: 4.64

Total: 9.10

Total: 14.86

Total: 4.36

Total: 18.02

Total: 4.68

Press any key to continue...
```

12

Your C Future

Unit 23: Advanced Issues in C

Unit 24: What's This C++ All About?

Lesson 12 Project

23

Advanced Issues in C

algorithm

bubble sort

pass

sorting structure

string sort

▶ What You'll Learn About

- ▶ Sorting for order
- ▶ Sorting string data
- ▶ Sorting structures
- ▶ Finding the minimum and maximum

Congratulations! There's very little about the C language that you don't now know. This unit applies the power of C by showing you some ways to perform useful tasks that will come in handy as you write programs. The techniques you'll learn in this unit are the "staple" routines found in every programmer's tool belt.

definition

Sorting means to put data in order, either numerically or alphabetically.

One of the most important jobs a computer does is sort data. Often you'll want a list of addresses printed in zip-code order or a list of customers printed in last-name order, or perhaps you'll want to sort an array of structures in the order of one of the structure members.

definition

An *algorithm* is a programming method that performs a specific job.

This unit teaches you one popular sorting algorithm called the *bubble sort*. The bubble sort is one of the easiest sorting methods to understand. One drawback to the bubble sort is that it isn't extremely efficient. However, for your first sorting algorithm, the bubble sort works well enough while still being easy to understand. Complete books have been written on advanced sorting algorithms, each one trying to squeeze a microsecond of performance out of a new sorting routine, but the bubble sort is always a great algorithm for beginners.

This unit also shows you one of the most popular ways to search for the highest and lowest values in an array. You can use the algorithms shown here to find the salesperson with the highest sales or the regional office with the lowest profit margin. Along with sorting, searching for extreme values is one of the staple algorithms of computer programs.

▶ Sorting for Order

Concept   **What You Will Learn**

In a bubble sort, you swap pairs of values, with the higher or lower value floating to the top of the array just as bubbles float to the top of a drink.

There are two ways to sort values: in *ascending* or *descending* order. An ascending sort orders the values from the lowest to the highest. A descending sort orders the values from the highest to the lowest. The following numbers are sorted in ascending order:

10
13
21
25
37

```
45
57
62
63
64
98
```

Here are the same numbers sorted in descending order:

```
98
64
63
62
57
45
37
25
21
13
10
```

You can sort numbers or text. You almost always sort text in alphabetical order. Luckily, C's ASCII table (see Appendix B) appears in alphabetical order, so comparing C's character values for their order always produces correct results. For example, according to the ASCII table, the following if produces a true result:

```
if ('A' < 'C')
```

The ASCII value for 'A' is 65, and the ASCII value for 'C' is 67. 65 is less than 67, so the comparison is true. Alphabetically, 'A' is less than 'C', so the ASCII table maintains proper alphabetical ordering.

When sorting strings, you'll have to use the strcmp() function. The ASCII table's sequence is correct for sorting strings as well. The ASCII table provides sorted string values that produce the same order that a phone book would produce.

Note   According to the ASCII table, lowercase letters sort higher than uppercase letters. Therefore, MacNutty would be considered higher than MCDonald in a sorted list. MCDonald would appear first in a sorted list of names because it's lower in the ASCII sequence.

The bubble sort algorithm uses a nested for loop to achieve proper sorted order. The program performing the bubble sort must make several passes through the data, looking at pairs of values it encounters. For an ascending sort, if the first value in the list of numbers is more than the second, the bubble sort swaps the values and then moves to the next value in the list, comparing it against the first value, and so on.

Suppose you wanted to apply an ascending bubble sort to the following list of four values:

```
30
10
40
20
```

The first two values, 30 and 10, aren't in order. Therefore, the bubble sort would swap them, producing this list:

UNIT

23

Advanced Issues in C

definition

A *pass* is one scan through an array, usually accomplished by a for loop.

```
10
30
40
20
```

The bubble sort then looks at the third value in the list to see how it compares against the first. 40 is more than 10, so the bubble sort leaves it alone. Finally, 20 is more than 10, so 20 is left alone.

Obviously, the sorting isn't complete, but the list is in better shape than before. We've made just one pass through the list. The longer the list, the more passes that are needed to sort the values.

 Note   Did you notice that the smallest value, 10, floated to the top of the list? No matter how many values are in the list and no matter how out of order they are to begin with, the smallest value will always float to the top of the list during the first pass, the second pass will always float the second-smallest value to the second position, and so forth.

The next pass begins one down from the first. With each pass, the bubble sort can look at one less value because each pass floats the smallest value of the pass to the top. The second pass begins at 30. Because 30 is less than 40, nothing happens. The bubble sort moves to the next value, 20, and finds that 20 is less than 30. Therefore, the swap takes place, producing this list:

```
10
20
40
30
```

The third pass begins at the third value. 40 is more than 30, so the values are swapped, producing this list:

```
10
20
30
40
```

The values are now sorted. If the list had more values, more passes probably would be necessary. Also, if the list were in better order to begin with, fewer passes would have to be made (see the following tip).

 Tip   The maximum number of passes required will be one less than the number of values in the list (the total number of pairs in the array). A list of values might already be in order before a sort. Therefore, you can make your sorting routine much more efficient by checking to see if a swap took place during each pass. If a complete pass through the list produces no swapping, the list is sorted and no more passes have to be made. Also, each pass floats the smallest value to the top of the list, so each subsequent pass can check a smaller number of values, thus improving efficiency even more.

> **Note** A *worst-case sort* occurs when the list is in an order opposite of the desired order. The maximum number of swaps and passes is then required to sort the list.

The key to sorting an array is the swapping of the value pairs. A second array is never necessary to sort a list of values. The list can be sorted in place with the bubble sort algorithm just described. Think for a moment about how you would swap two values. Given the following variable definitions:

```
int i = 10;
int k = 20;
```

how would you swap their values? Would the following work?

```
i = k;
k = i;
```

This pair of assignment statements would *not* swap the values, even though at first glance it would appear to. In the first assignment, the value of k ends up in *both* i and k. The original value of i is lost, so the second assignment doesn't work as it first appears to. You need to define a *third* variable when swapping pairs of variables. Here is code that will swap i and k properly:

```
t = i;
i = k;
k = t;
```

t safely holds the value of i so that the second assignment can overwrite i's old value. The third assignment then stores i's old value in k, and the swap takes place correctly.

STOP&TYPE Listing 23.1 contains a program that assigns 20 values to an array, sorts the array in ascending order, and prints the values. A descending sort then occurs that reverses the array's order. The descending sort performs a worst-case sort because the values are in ascending order before the descending sort.

Review

What You Have Learned

The bubble sort makes several passes through an array, swapping pairs of values until the entire array is sorted.

▼ INPUT LISTING 23.1. SORT VALUES IN A LIST IN BOTH ASCENDING AND DESCENDING ORDER.

```
1:  /* Filename: NUMSORT.C */
2:  // Initializes and sorts an array of 20 values.
3:  // First, an ascending sort is done. Then the
4:  // program takes those sorted values and
5:  // performs a descending sort.
6:  #define NUM 20
7:  #include <stdio.h>
8:  #include <conio.h>
```

continues

LISTING 23.1. CONTINUED

```
 9:   // Program prototypes follow
10:   void prAra(int ara[NUM]);
11:   void ascSort(int ara[NUM]);
12:   void desSort(int ara[NUM]);
13:   main()
14:   {
15:     int ara[NUM] = {53, 23, 12, 56, 88,  7, 32, 41, 59, 91,
16:                     88, 62,  4, 74, 32, 33, 42, 26, 80,  3};
17:     clrscr();
18:     printf("Before the sort, here are the values: \n");
19:     prAra(ara);
20:
21:     // Perform an ascending sort
22:     ascSort(ara);
23:     printf("\n\nAfter the ascending sort:\n");
24:     prAra(ara);
25:
26:     // Perform a descending sort
27:     desSort(ara);
28:     printf("\n\nAfter the descending sort:\n");
29:     prAra(ara);
30:
31:     printf("\n\nPress any key to continue...");
32:     getch();
33:     return 0;
34:   }
35:   //**********************************************************
36:   void prAra(int ara[NUM])
37:   {
38:     int ctr;   // for-loop control variable
39:     for (ctr = 0; ctr < NUM; ctr++)
40:       { if ((ctr % 10) == 0)    // Print a newline after
41:           { printf("\n"); }     // every 10 values
42:         printf("%4d", ara[ctr]);   // Print values in four spaces
43:       }
44:     return;
45:   }
46:   //**********************************************************
47:   void ascSort(int ara[NUM])
48:   {
49:     int inner, outer;   // for-loop control variables
50:     int temp;           // Temporary value for swapping
51:     int didSwap;        // 1 if a swap took place in each pass
52:     for (outer = 0; outer < (NUM - 1); outer++)
53:       {
54:         didSwap = 0;    // Initialize after each pass
55:         // Next loop steps through each pair of values
56:         for (inner = outer; inner < NUM; inner++)
57:           {
58:             if (ara[outer] > ara[inner])    // First of two is higher
59:               { temp = ara[outer];    // Swap
60:                 ara[outer] = ara[inner];
61:                 ara[inner] = temp;
62:                 didSwap = 1;    // Indicate that a swap occurred
63:               }
64:           }
65:         if (!didSwap)    // If no swap happened,
66:           { break; }     // terminate the sort
```

```
67:      }
68:    return;
69:  }
70:  //*********************************************************
71:  void desSort(int ara[NUM])
72:  {
73:    // Only one change is needed for a descending sort
74:    int inner, outer;   // for-loop control variables
75:    int temp;           // Temporary value for swapping
76:    int didSwap;        // 1 if a swap took place in each pass
77:    for (outer = 0; outer < (NUM - 1); outer++)
78:      {
79:        didSwap = 0;   // Initialize after each pass
80:        // Next loop steps through each pair of values
81:        for (inner = outer; inner < NUM; inner++)
82:          {
83:            if (ara[outer] < ara[inner])    // First of two is higher
84:              { temp = ara[outer];   // Swap
85:                ara[outer] = ara[inner];
86:                ara[inner] = temp;
87:                didSwap = 1;   // Indicate that a swap occurred
88:              }
89:          }
90:        if (!didSwap)   // If no swap happened,
91:          { break; }    // terminate the sort
92:      }
93:    return;
94:  }
```

UNIT

23

Advanced Issues in C

▼ OUTPUT

```
Before the sort, here are the values:

 53  23  12  56  88   7  32  41  59  91
 88  62   4  74  32  33  42  26  80   3

After the ascending sort:

  3   4   7  12  23  26  32  32  33  41
 42  53  56  59  62  74  80  88  88  91

After the descending sort:

 91  88  88  80  74  62  59  56  53  42
 41  33  32  32  26  23  12   7   4   3

Press any key to continue...
```

▼ ANALYSIS

This program's power appears in the last two functions, ascSort() and desSort(). The nested for loops are tricky. The for in line 52 steps through the array, from the first to the next-to-last value. The outer loop doesn't need to check the last value because the inner loop will do that, and the sorting routine always checks the two values controlled by each loop.

The inner loop begins at the outer loop's current control variable. Line 56 shows the inner loop's initial value as outer. outer keeps increasing due to the outer for loop. There is no reason to start at the beginning of the array each time the inner loop begins. As mentioned earlier, the smallest value of each pass always floats to the top during each pass.

The didSwap variable in line 62 becomes 1 (indicating true) if a swap takes place during the outer loop's pass. If a swap ever fails to take place, the list is sorted and the outer loop can quit earlier than usual. If, however, the values were backwards, producing a worst-case sort, every iteration of the outer loop would be necessary. The didSwap variable would be useless in that special case.

Notice that the two sorting methods differ by a single character! Line 58 contains the comparison for the ascending sort, and line 83 contains the comparison for the descending sort. An ascending sort checks to see if the outer loop's value (the top value in the current pass) is more than the value being checked, and the descending sort checks to see if the outer loop's value is less.

> *Note*   If two or more values are the same, they will appear consecutively in the final sorted list.

▶ Sorting String Data

Concept   **What You Will Learn**

> The algorithm that you use to sort string data is identical to that for numerical sorting, except that you must use strcmp() for the comparison.

After you define an array of string data, sorting that array is simple. Just be sure to use the strcmp() function that you learned in Lesson 8 to make the comparison. strcmp() returns 0 if its two string arguments are equal, a negative value if the first string argument comes before the second string argument alphabetically, and a positive value if the first string argument comes later in the alphabet than the second.

> *Tip*   To remember strcmp()'s return values, imagine a minus sign between the arguments. For example, the comparison strcmp("A", "B"); produces a negative value because if you subtract the ASCII value of B (66) from the ASCII value of A (65), you get −1.

It doesn't matter if the strings are in variable memory or on the heap. strcmp() expects you to pass it the addresses of two strings.

> *Note*   Sorting an array of strings is extremely efficient. Unlike most programming languages that support string variables, C requires a little more work to set up an array of character pointers to strings. Unlike those other languages, however, when the sort makes a swap, you swap only pointers, not the actual strings themselves!

STOP&TYPE   Listing 23.2 contains a program that asks the user for the names of eight song titles. This program uses an 80-byte buffer to hold the user's response, but it allocates just enough heap memory to hold the string entered and updates the character pointer array to point to each string on the heap.

> **Note** This program's allocation of individual strings is a fairly common (and advanced) way to put strings on the heap efficiently.

Review — What You Have Learned

Use the bubble sort algorithm to sort strings. For the comparison, use strcmp().

▼ INPUT   LISTING 23.2. SORTING AN ARRAY OF STRINGS THAT RESIDE ON THE HEAP.

```
1:  /* Filename: STRSORT.C */
2:  // Asks the user for eight song titles and stores
3:  // each title on the heap as the user enters the
4:  // song. When all eight have been entered, sorts
5:  // the songs and prints them in alphabetical order.
6:
7:  #define NUM 8
8:
9:  #include <stdio.h>
10: #include <conio.h>
11: #include <string.h>
12: #include <stdlib.h>
13: void getSongs(char * songs[NUM]);
14: void sortSongs(char * songs[NUM]);
15: void prSongs(char * songs[NUM]);
16:
17: main()
18: {
19:   char * songs[NUM];   // To point to the songs
20:
21:   clrscr();
22:   puts("Song Sorter\n\n");
23:   getSongs(songs);
24:   sortSongs(songs);
25:   prSongs(songs);
26:
27:   printf("\n\nPress any key to continue...");
28:   getch();
29:   return 0;
30: }
31: //********************************************************
32: void getSongs(char * songs[NUM])
33: {
34:   int ctr;   // for-loop control variable
35:   char inBuffer[80];   // To hold an entered string
36:
37:   for (ctr = 0; ctr < NUM; ctr++)
38:     { printf("Please enter a song title: ");
39:       gets(inBuffer);
40:       // Allocate enough heap to hold that song
41:       // and leave enough room for the null zero
42:       songs[ctr] = (char *)malloc(strlen(inBuffer)+1);
43:       // Now that room is reserved, copy the string
44:       strcpy(songs[ctr], inBuffer);
45:     }
46:   return;
```

continues

LISTING 23.2. CONTINUED

```
47:  }
48:  //************************************************************
49:  void sortSongs(char * songs[NUM])
50:  {
51:     int inner, outer;    // for-loop control variables
52:     char * temp;          // Temporary value for swapping
53:     int didSwap;          // 1 if a swap took place in each pass
54:     for (outer = 0; outer < (NUM - 1); outer++)
55:       {
56:         didSwap = 0;    // Initialize after each pass
57:         // Next loop steps through each pair of values
58:         for (inner = outer; inner < NUM; inner++)
59:           {
60:             // Use strcmp() to see if first string is higher
61:             if (strcmp(songs[outer], songs[inner]) > 0)
62:               { temp = songs[outer];    // Swap pointers
63:                 songs[outer] = songs[inner];
64:                 songs[inner] = temp;
65:                 didSwap = 1;    // Indicate that a swap occurred
66:               }
67:           }
68:         if (!didSwap)    // If no swap happened,
69:           { break; }    // terminate the sort
70:       }
71:     return;
72:  }
73:  //************************************************************
74:  void prSongs(char * songs[NUM])
75:  {
76:     int ctr;    // for-loop counter
77:     puts("\n\nHere are the songs alphabetized:");
78:     for (ctr = 0; ctr < NUM; ctr++)
79:       { puts(songs[ctr]); }
80:     return;
81:  }
```

▼ **OUTPUT**

```
Song Sorter

Please enter a song title: Oh, say can you C?
Please enter a song title: The waves by the C
Please enter a song title: C'ing is believing
Please enter a song title: C, he, and she
Please enter a song title: Speak C like a professional!
Please enter a song title: Let's C
Please enter a song title: A C breeze just rolled in
Please enter a song title: Gentle C, forceful C


Here are the songs alphabetized:
A C breeze just rolled in
C'ing is believing
C, he, and she
Gentle C, forceful C
Let's C
Oh, say can you C?
```

```
Speak C like a professional!
The waves by the C

Press any key to continue...
```

▼ **ANALYSIS**

One of the most interesting parts of this program isn't the sort—which is nothing more than the bubble sort you saw earlier, with `strcmp()` used for the comparison in line 61—but the way the songs get to the heap.

In the `getSongs()` function, line 35 defines an 80-byte character array that holds one string at a time. The string is the user's input of a song title in line 39. Once the user enters a title into the `inBuffer` array, line 42 reserves enough room on the heap to hold that song plus one extra character for the null zero.

Line 44 copies the buffer's song to the heap at the location pointed to by the pointer. The loop continues until all eight songs (defined as `NUM` in line 7) are entered.

Note that, in lines 62 through 64, no song data is swapped. Only pointers to the individual songs are swapped. This efficiency becomes critical when you're sorting a huge number of string values and many swaps have to be made.

► Sorting Structures

Concept — **What You Will Learn**

> Select a value in your structure that you want to use for the comparison, such as a customer balance member. Compare that member to determine if a swap needs to take place.

Sorting an array of structures takes very little effort, despite the fact that you might be sorting a much larger amount of data. When you sort an array of numbers or strings, each element of that array is the same data type, so you compare and swap based on the same data. However, when you sort an array of structures, you compare against one of the structure members but swap the entire structure.

Warning If you swapped only the member of the sort comparison, you'd end up with structure variables whose members didn't go together!

STOP&TYPE Listing 23.3 contains a program that stores some sample inventory data in an array of five structures. The inventory is then sorted by price from high to low (a descending sort) and a listing is printed.

Note   If the inventory were stored in a disk file, which would be more common, the sorting algorithm wouldn't change at all. After you read the data from the disk into heap memory pointed to by the array of structure pointers, the rest of this program would stay the same and produce the sorted list—only the list would be much longer.

Review   **What You Have Learned**

Pick a member to sort by when sorting arrays of structure variables. Make the comparison on that member, but be sure to swap the entire structure variable.

▼ INPUT   LISTING 23.3. SORTING AN ARRAY OF FIVE SIMPLE INVENTORY STRUCTURE VARIABLES.

```
 1:  /* Filename: STRUSORT.C */
 2:  // Defines and initializes an array of five structure
 3:  // variables. The price member is then used as a
 4:  // comparison for the descending sort that follows.
 5:  #define NUM 5
 6:
 7:  struct inv {
 8:    char partID[6];
 9:    int quantity;
10:    float price;
11:  };
12:  void invSort(struct inv items[NUM]);
13:  void invPrint(struct inv items[NUM]);
14:  #include <stdio.h>
15:  #include <conio.h>
16:
17:  main()
18:  {
19:    struct inv items[NUM] = {{"HDWR9", 13, 4.53},
20:                             {"WDGT4", 2, 15.82},
21:                             {"POPL0", 4, 8.32},
22:                             {"RTYN6", 7, 5.40},
23:                             {"LOUN4", 61, 7.43}};
24:    clrscr();
25:    printf("Inventory Listing from High Price to Low Price\n\n");
26:    invSort(items);
27:    invPrint(items);
28:
29:    printf("\n\nPress any key to continue...");
30:    getch();
31:    return 0;
32:  }
33:  //*******************************************************
34:  void invSort(struct inv items[NUM])
35:  {
36:    int inner, outer;   // for-loop control variables
```

```
37:      struct inv temp;     // Temporary value for swapping
38:      int didSwap;            // 1 if a swap took place in each pass
39:      for (outer = 0; outer < (NUM - 1); outer++)
40:        {
41:          didSwap = 0;    // Initialize after each pass
42:          // Next loop steps through each pair of values
43:          for (inner = outer; inner < NUM; inner++)
44:            {
45:              if (items[outer].price < items[inner].price)
46:                { temp = items[outer];     // Swap
47:                  items[outer] = items[inner];
48:                  items[inner] = temp;
49:                  didSwap = 1;    // Indicate that a swap occurred
50:                }
51:            }
52:          if (!didSwap)  // If no swap happened,
53:            { break; }   // terminate the sort
54:        }
55:      return;
56:  }
57:  //**********************************************************
58:  void invPrint(struct inv items[NUM])
59:  {
60:    int ctr = 0;   // for-loop control variable
61:    for (ctr = 0; ctr < NUM; ctr++)
62:      { printf("Part ID: %s, Quantity: %2d, Price: $%6.2f\n",
63:        items[ctr].partID, items[ctr].quantity,
64:        items[ctr].price);
65:      }
66:    return;
67:  }
```

▼ OUTPUT

```
Inventory Listing from High Price to Low Price

Part ID: WDGT4, Quantity:  2, Price: $ 15.82
Part ID: POPL0, Quantity:  4, Price: $  8.32
Part ID: LOUN4, Quantity: 61, Price: $  7.43
Part ID: RTYN6, Quantity:  7, Price: $  5.40
Part ID: HDWR9, Quantity: 13, Price: $  4.53

Press any key to continue...
```

▼ ANALYSIS

The sorting function compares each part's price in line 45 but then swaps *all* the structure variable's members in lines 46 through 48. Only a single member, price, is used in the comparison, and then all data related to that price is swapped.

This program swaps the structure data itself, not pointers. If items were an array of pointers, you'd use the structure pointer operator (->) in place of the dot operator, but the program would still work as you see it here.

▶ Finding the Minimum and Maximum

Concept

Through a common algorithm, you can find the largest and smallest values in a list.

A couple of exercises in earlier units asked you to write programs that found the highest and lowest values in arrays of data. Several algorithms can find extreme data values. Now that you can sort arrays, another way to find the highest and lowest values in an array is to apply an ascending sort to the array. Once the array is sorted, the first element will be the smallest value and the last element will be the largest.

 Note The largest value in a series of numbers usually is referred to by programmers as the *maximum,* or simply *max,* and the smallest value is called the *minimum* or *min.*

If all you want to do is find the minimum or maximum values in an array, sorting the array first is severely inefficient. There's a quick way to find an array's highest and lowest values via one pass through the array.

The method most used to find extreme values is by starting the comparison at the other end of the extreme. In other words, when you want to find the largest value in an array, begin by storing the smallest possible value in a variable and compare each array element to that value, saving any value that's higher.

Therefore, to find the maximum value in an array of integers, begin by storing the value –32768 (the smallest possible integer) in a variable named max. Then compare each element of the integer array to max, replacing the value of max with any element that's higher. The first element will be higher than max because max is so small. Therefore, the first value will be used as the maximum value for the comparison, starting with the second element.

The opposite effect works for finding the minimum integer in the array. Store the *largest* possible integer, 32767, in a variable named min and step through the array, comparing each element against min.

Warning C treats all numeric literals as float, even if you don't specify a decimal point. Therefore, C will warn you when you store 32767 in an integer variable even though integers can hold 32767. C is letting you know that 32767 is being converted to an integer before C stores the value in the integer variable. This is another one of those compiler warnings that's safe to ignore in this case.

The initial minimum and maximum values you use don't have to be the extreme ranges of the data. Just be sure that the initial value for min is larger than any data that appears in the array and that the initial value for max is smaller than any of the array's values. The next program shows how to implement this min/max algorithm.

STOP&TYPE Listing 23.4 initializes a 20-element array with 20 values. The min function finds the lowest value and the max function finds the highest.

Review
What You Have Learned

To find the maximum, initially compare against a small value. To find the minimum, initially compare against a large value.

▼ INPUT   LISTING 23.4. FINDING THE HIGHEST AND LOWEST INTEGER IN AN ARRAY.

```
 1:  /* Filename: MINMAX.C */
 2:  // Finds the minimum and maximum values in an array
 3:  #define NUM 20
 4:
 5:  #include <stdio.h>
 6:  #include <conio.h>
 7:  void prAra(int ara[NUM]);
 8:  int min(int ara[NUM]);
 9:  int max(int ara[NUM]);
10:
11:  main()
12:  {
13:    int ara[NUM] = {53, 23, 12, 56, 88,  7, 32, 41, 59, 91,
14:                    88, 62,  4, 74, 32, 33, 42, 26, 80,  3};
15:    clrscr();
16:    printf("Here is the array:\n");
17:    prAra(ara);
18:    printf("\n\n\nThe lowest value is %d\n\n", min(ara));
19:    printf("The highest value is %d\n", max(ara));
20:
21:    printf("\n\nPress any key to continue...");
22:    getch();
23:    return 0;
24:  }
25:  //***********************************************************
26:  void prAra(int ara[NUM])
27:  {
28:    int ctr;   // for-loop control variable
29:    for (ctr = 0; ctr < NUM; ctr++)
30:      { if ((ctr % 10) == 0)   // Print a newline after
31:          { printf("\n"); }    // every 10 values
32:        printf("%4d", ara[ctr]);   // Print values in four spaces
33:      }
34:    return;
35:  }
36:  //***********************************************************
37:  int min(int ara[NUM])
38:  {
39:    int lowInt = 32767;
40:    int ctr;
```

continues

UNIT **23** Advanced Issues in C

LISTING 23.4. CONTINUED

```
41:    for (ctr = 0; ctr < NUM; ctr++)
42:      { if (ara[ctr] < lowInt)
43:          { lowInt = ara[ctr]; }
44:      }
45:    return lowInt;
46:  }
47:  //*********************************************************
48:  int max(int ara[NUM])
49:  {
50:    int highInt = -32768;
51:    int ctr;
52:    for (ctr = 0; ctr < NUM; ctr++)
53:      { if (ara[ctr] > highInt)
54:          { highInt = ara[ctr]; }
55:      }
56:    return highInt;
57:  }
```

▼ **OUTPUT**

```
Here is the array:

  53  23  12  56  88   7  32  41  59  91
  88  62   4  74  32  33  42  26  80   3


The lowest value is 3

The highest value is 91

Press any key to continue...
```

▼ **ANALYSIS**

There is no data value as large as 32767 or as small as –32768 in the ara array. Therefore, the min() and max() functions can safely use these values for the initial low and high values.

The min() function in lines 37 through 46 steps through every element in ara, comparing each value to lowInt. The first time through, the first element is lower than 32767, so lowInt becomes the first element in the array. For the rest of the for loop, each succeeding value in ara is compared against lowInt and stored there if needed.

The max() function in lines 48 through 57 does the same job, only for the highest value instead of the lowest.

▶ **Homework**

General Knowledge

1. What does it mean to sort data?

2. What are the two ways in which you can sort data?

3. What is an algorithm?

4. What's the most popular and easiest sorting algorithm?

5. Name a way you can improve the bubble sort's efficiency.

6. Where does the bubble sort get its name?

7. What function must you use to compare strings?

8. What determines how string data will compare?

9. What is a pass?

10. What is a worst-case sort?

11. What is the maximum number of passes required to sort an array?

12. Why is C's method of sorting strings more efficient than that of other languages that support string variables?

13. According to the ASCII table, which is lower: `St. John` or `Saint John`?

14. Why is a third variable needed when you swap variable values?

15. Name two ways to find the highest and lowest values in an array.

16. What is the highest value in an array called?

17. What is the lowest value in an array called?

18. True or false: You can't sort character data, only numeric data.

19. True or false: When you sort structures, only the member being compared should be swapped.

20. True or false: To find the maximum number, first store the largest possible value in a comparison variable.

21. True or false: To find the minimum number, first store the largest possible value in a comparison variable.

> **Note** There are no What's the Output? and Find the Bug parts for this unit.

Write Code That...

22. Shorten Listing 23.1. The ascending and descending sorts differ in only one statement each. Put those statements in a function called `Test()` that returns 1 or 0 based on whether the first argument is more or less than the second argument. Pass to the larger sorting routine an extra argument that specifies whether the sort is to be ascending or descending.

Extra Credit

23. Don Dickens is on a diet. He is tracking his daily calorie count for the last 10 days. Write a program that through initialization stores 10 days' worth of calorie counts (from 1,200 to 2,850 calories) in an array, and print those calorie counts from low to high. Print the day number of each count next to the sorted list.

24. Write a program that contains two parallel arrays. One is a classroom's student roster (stored in an array of character pointers), and the other is a floating-point array with each student's average to date. Write a program that prints a descending list of student scores from high to low. Print each student's name next to the score.

24

What's This C++ All About?

C++

cin

cout

delete

new

OOP

▶ What You'll Learn About

- ▶ Building on C
- ▶ Don't repeat struct
- ▶ Define variables anywhere
- ▶ Simple I/O
- ▶ Allocate and deallocate without headaches
- ▶ A third way to pass data

Once you learn C, what's next? C++! With this book's compiler, you get the best of both worlds. After you learn to program in C, you can move to C++. Despite industry disagreement over whether people need to learn C first, most C programmers learn C++ faster than people who start with C++.

This disagreement arises due to the *object-oriented programming* aspect of C++. This funny thing called *OOP* can't be nailed down with one simple definition. The concepts and nature of OOP aren't always intuitive at first. OOP approaches programming from a different angle than the one you've read about throughout this book. OOP basically makes your data more active, letting variables perform some of their own tasks, such as initialization.

One of the nice things about C++ is that you don't have to study the OOP aspects of it to use it effectively. C++ provides lots of small language improvements. You'll learn about some of these advantages here and see several benefits of C++. This unit will whet your appetite and plant a seed that sometime in the future will grow into a desire for you to move to C++. C++ is considered a better programming language than C, despite the fact that C++ is more difficult to learn.

 Warning   C is not dead! Despite all the C++ and OOP publicity, a huge number of data processing departments program using C, and C jobs still abound. Nevertheless, C++ is coming on strong, and this book wouldn't be complete if it didn't explain something about C++.

▶ Building on C

Concept   **What You Will Learn**

C++ has many non-OOP improvements.

Not all of C++'s new features are directly related to OOP. A lot of commands and functions simply give the programmer easier program-writing tools. Because the compiler that comes with this book compiles both C and C++ programs, you can begin using any of the C++ features whenever you like. Keep in mind, however, that your programs won't be compatible with other C programs if you add C++-only features.

Note The compiler that comes with this book is actually a C++-only compiler. C++ compilers can compile C programs, but C compilers can't compile C++ programs.

When you save your C++ programs, use the .CPP filename extension instead of C's .C extension. .CPP is the standard extension for C++ programs. Many C++ compilers require that C++ source code filenames end with .CPP.

Note The Review and Stop and Type parts appear at the end of this unit.

► Don't Repeat *struct*

Concept   **What You Will Learn**

In C++, `struct` defines a structure, but it's not needed for structure definitions.

In C, when you define a new data type using a structure definition like this:

```
struct myStruct {
  char name[20];
  int age;
  float salary;
};
```

you define variables from the structure like this:

```
struct myStruct person;   // Defines a variable named person
```

C requires the `struct` keyword because there is no built-in data type called `myStruct`. The `struct` keyword in C++ is used for only one thing—defining structures. The designers of C++ decided that the repetition of `struct` was a waste of programmers' time, so C++ lets you drop `struct` when defining structure variables. The following C++ variable definition is identical to the preceding one:

```
myStruct person;   // Defines a variable named person
```

One of the reasons that C++ was invented was to increase coding speed and eliminate errors that can appear in traditional C code. A top-notch C++ programmer usually can write a C++ program more quickly and with fewer bugs than he or she could write a C program.

▶ Define Variables Anywhere

Concept   **What You Will Learn**

You don't have to define all local variables at the top of a block.

C requires that you define all variables immediately after the opening brace of a block. C++ lets you define local variables anywhere in a function as long as you define them before you use them.

There are times when you need a variable for only a small section of a function. Defining all the variables at the top of the function means that some variables are defined far from their actual use. Being able to define a variable right before its first use often lets you keep better track of the variable's data type.

One of the best uses for defining variables close to their use is in `for` loops. As has been done throughout much of this book, programmers often define a single `for` loop control variable at the top of a function and then use that variable in a single `for` loop. In C++, you can define the control variable right inside the loop:

```
for (int var = 0; var < NUM; var++)
  { printf("%d \n", var); }
```

After you define `var`, the variable is visible until the block containing the `for` loop ends.

▶ Simple I/O

Concept   **What You Will Learn**

No complicated `scanf()` and `printf()` functions are needed in C++.

Now that you've mastered the `printf()` and `scanf()` conversion characters such as `%d`, throw them away! C++ doesn't need them because its I/O approach differs from C's. C++ contains two new operators, `<<` and `>>`, that work with special data values named `cout` and `cin` that do all your I/O.

 Tip   When you see `cout` and `cin` discussed, think of `cout` as representing your screen and `cin` as representing your keyboard. You'll then learn C++ I/O faster.

To print a message to the screen in C, you'd do this:

```
printf("I am %d years old\n", age);
```

To print the same message in C++, you'd do this:

```
cout << "I am " << age << " years old\n";
```

If you think of `cout` as being the screen, you can see the data being routed to the screen by the `<<` operator. No `%d` conversion character is needed because C++ knows how to print numeric data.

Note There are ways, through the use of *I/O manipulators,* to format numeric data by specifying how many decimal places you want and the output width of the data. However, for many I/O tasks, you don't need to use these manipulators. C++'s default I/O behavior often works exactly the way you want.

You can print any kind of built-in data type using `cout` without having to use a conversion character. Input is just as easy. You don't have to remember all the nuances of `scanf()`! If you define an integer variable and want the user to enter a value, prompt the user and get the value like this:

```
cout << "How many were sold? ";
cin >> numSold;
```

If `numSold` is defined as an integer, C++ stores the user's integer value. You can input any built-in data type using `cin >>`. Again, think of `cin` as being the keyboard, and you'll be able to picture the keyboard's data being routed, via `>>`, to the variable.

Warning When you use `cout` and `cin`, be sure to include the IOSTREAM.H header file. IOSTREAM.H is included more than any other header in C++ programs. IOSTREAM.H is to C++ programs what STDIO.H is to C programs.

`cout` AND `cin` CAN RECOGNIZE YOUR DATA TYPES TOO!

`cout` and `cin` don't just simplify your I/O syntax. Through a C++ process known as *operator overloading,* you can teach the `<<` and `>>` operators to output and input your own data types (those that you define with `struct`).

With one single line such as this one:

```
cout << customer;
```

C++ can output a structure of 25 members that contains all kinds of built-in data types, with a title, headings, and formatting! This magic is another example of how C++ can increase your programming efficiency. Any time you want to output the `customer` structure variable, just output it using this `cout <<` statement and C++ does the rest of the work.

By the way, this isn't really as magical as it sounds. You must first teach C++ how you want the output, titles, and formatting to appear. Once you do that, however, outputting the variable is simple throughout the rest of the program.

All of C's functions work in C++. If you want to use `printf()`, you can do so as long as you include the STDIO.H header file. All of the I/O, string, character, and numeric functions that work in C also work in C++.

▶ Allocate and Deallocate Without Headaches

Concept   **What You Will Learn**

C++ lets you allocate and deallocate heap memory without the hassle of
`malloc()` and `free()`.

C++ includes two new operators named `new` and `delete` that replace the `malloc()` and
`free()` functions. The `new` operator has some built-in OOP features that you'll need once
you begin programming using objects. The syntax of `malloc()` requires a lot of typing
and is prone to errors. `malloc()` is simply outdated in C++ programs and is a lot harder
to use than its younger cousin `new`.

If you want to allocate 250 characters on the heap using `malloc()`, you must define a
character pointer and assign the pointer the return value of `malloc()`:

```
char * cPtr;
cPtr = (char *)malloc(250 * sizeof(char));
```

Here's how you would do the same thing in C++:

```
char *cPtr;
cPtr = new char[250];    // Allocate 250 characters
```

The `new` syntax is much cleaner than the equivalent `malloc()` function call. Reading this
statement is easy: *"C, I want cPtr to point to 250 new characters from the heap."*

To delete the memory allocated with `new`, you would use `delete` like this:

```
delete cPtr;    // Release the 250 characters back to the heap
```

 Warning   Never mix the C++ allocation operators with the functions `malloc()`
and `free()`. If you allocate with `new`, deallocate with `delete`.

The `new` allocation can fail just as `malloc()` might fail if there weren't enough heap
memory. `new` returns the defined NULL value if the allocation fails so that you can check
for the problem and exit the program accordingly.

▶ A Third Way to Pass Data

Concept   **What You Will Learn**

There is a way to pass nonarrays by address without using C's special syntax.

In C, there are two ways to pass data: by value and by copy. C++ brings a third method to the programming table with *passing by reference*. Passing by reference lets you pass nonarrays by address without extra syntax.

Listing 24.1 contains a C program that passes the user's value, in pf, to a function by address. The function multiplies the variable by 3.14159. Due to the passing by address, pf is changed in both main() and in the called function.

▼ INPUT   LISTING 24.1. PASSING A FLOATING-POINT BY ADDRESS.

```
/* Filename: BYADDRES.C */
// Passes a variable by address
#include <stdio.h>
#include <conio.h>
void mult(float *pf);

main()
{
  float pf;
  clrscr();

  printf("What is the PI factor? ");
  scanf(" %f", &pf);

  // Pass pf by address to the mult() function
  mult( &pf );

  // Print pf to show that it's now changed in main()
  printf("\nAfter the multiplication, the PI factor is %.5f\n", pf);
  return 0;
}
//*********************************************************
void mult(float *pf)
{
  // When you pass nonarrays by address, you must precede
  // them with asterisks everywhere they appear. The extra
  // syntax is messy.

  *pf = *pf * 3.14159;
  return;
}
```

▼ OUTPUT

```
What is the PI factor? 5.0

After the multiplication, the PI factor is 15.70795
```

When you pass by reference in C++, you only need to precede the receiving argument with a single ampersand, &. When you pass data by reference, no special syntax is necessary. Look how much easier Listing 24.2's passing of pf is now that C++ is used.

▼ INPUT   LISTING 24.2. USING C++ TO PASS BY REFERENCE.

```
/* Filename: BYREF.CPP */
// Passes a variable by reference
#include <iostream.h>
#include <conio.h>
void mult(float & pf);    // Notice the ampersand

main()
{
  float pf;
  clrscr();

  cout << "What is the PI factor? ";
  cin >> pf;

  // Pass pf by address to the mult() function
  mult( pf );    // No extra syntax needed

  // Print pf to show that it's now changed in main()
  cout<<"\nAfter the multiplication, the PI factor is "<< pf <<"\n";
  return 0;
}
//********************************************************
void mult(float & pf)    // & indicates by reference
{
  // When you pass nonarrays by reference,
  // you need no special syntax

  pf = pf * 3.14159;
  return;
}
```

Note   The output for Listing 24.2 is identical to that for Listing 24.1.

Note   Before C++, *passing by address* was sometimes called *passing by reference*. As you can see, C++'s terminology causes a little confusion for some people.

STOP&TYPE Listing 24.3 contains a program that uses the C++ features discussed in the previous sections. As you can see, C++ is fully based on C, and knowing C helps you learn C++ even faster.

Review   **What You Have Learned**

C++ offers many shortcut features that save you programming time and make your coding easier.

```
 1:  /* Filename: CPPADV.CPP */
 2:  // Shows some advantages and shortcuts of C++
 3:  #include <iostream.h>
 4:  #include <conio.h>
 5:  #include <string.h>
 6:
 7:  struct People {
 8:    char * name;    // Will allocate each name
 9:    int weight;
10:  };
11:
12:  void getData(People dieter[4]);
13:  void calcData(float & weight);
14:  void prData(People dieter[4]);
15:  void dealData(People dieter[4]);
16:
17:  main()
18:  {
19:    clrscr();
20:
21:    cout << "** Calculating a diet's weight loss **\n\n\n";
22:    cout << "I'll ask for four people's names and";
23:    cout << " weights and\nthen calculate their expected";
24:    cout << " weight loss after two weeks.\n\n";
25:
26:    // Define the four structure variables in the middle
27:    // C++ programmers often use initial
         // uppercase letters for structures
28:    People dieter[4];
29:
30:    // Pass the variables to a function to
31:    // allocate each name and fill the variables
32:    getData(dieter);
33:
34:    // Pass the weights, by reference, to a calculate function
35:    for (int ctr=0; ctr<4; ctr++)    // Don't redefine control variable
36:      {  // Pass just the weight of each array variable
37:          // Due to a structure-passing conversion, save
38:          // the structure's weight in a stand-alone variable
39:          // before passing it. You can't pass the middle of
40:          // a structure by reference.
41:          float passWeight = dieter[ctr].weight;
42:          calcData(passWeight);
43:          calcData(passWeight);
44:          dieter[ctr].weight = passWeight;  }
45:    // Pass the variables to a print function
46:    prData(dieter);
47:
48:    // Pass the variables to deallocate names
49:    dealData(dieter);
50:
51:    return 0;
52:  }
53:  //*********************************************************
54:  void getData(People dieter[4])
55:  {
56:    char buffer[80];    // For temporary input
```

continues

LISTING 24.3. CONTINUED

```
57:      for (int ctr = 0; ctr < 4; ctr++)
58:        { cout << "What is dieter #" << (ctr + 1) << "'s name? ";
59:          cin >> buffer;
60:          // Make name pointer in each variable point to heap
61:          dieter[ctr].name = new char[strlen(buffer) + 1];
62:          strcpy(dieter[ctr].name, buffer);
63:          cout << "What is dieter #" << (ctr + 1) << "'s weight? ";
64:          cin >> dieter[ctr].weight;
65:        }
66:      return;
67:    }
68:    //**********************************************************
69:    void calcData(float & weight)
70:    {
71:      weight *= .85;
72:      return;
73:    }
74:    //**********************************************************
75:    void prData(People dieter[4])
76:    {
77:      cout << "\nHere are the predicted results after three weeks:";
78:      for (int ctr = 0; ctr < 4; ctr++)
79:      {
80:        cout << "\n" << dieter[ctr].name << " will weigh "
81:            << dieter[ctr].weight;
82:      }
83:      return;
84:    }
85:    //**********************************************************
86:    void dealData(People dieter[4])
87:    {
88:      for (int ctr = 0; ctr < 4; ctr++)
89:        { delete dieter[ctr].name; }
90:      return;
91:    }
```

▼ **OUTPUT**

```
** Calculating a diet's weight loss **

I'll ask for four people's names and weights and
then calculate their expected weight loss after two weeks.

What is dieter #1's name? Wendy
What is dieter #1's weight? 132
What is dieter #2's name? Kerry
What is dieter #2's weight? 141
What is dieter #3's name? William
What is dieter #3's weight? 218
What is dieter #4's name? Fred
What is dieter #4's weight? 187

Here are the predicted results after three weeks:
Wendy will weigh 95
Kerry will weigh 101
William will weigh 157
Fred will weigh 135
```

▼ **ANALYSIS**

Line 3 includes the IOSTREAM.H header file, which is needed for `cout` and `cin` operations.

The `struct` command is used only once (in line 7) because `struct` isn't needed when you define variables. The `People` structure format is really considered to be a data type newly added to C++ as soon as you define the structure. Virtually anywhere you use `int` or `float`, you can use `People` without having to preface the data type with `struct` as you'd have to in C.

`cout` and `cin` are used throughout the code. You won't find any `printf()` or `scanf()` function calls because they're unnecessary and cause extra work for C++ programmers.

A lot of work seems necessary to pass one of the structure members, `weight`, by reference. There are more-advanced ways to get around the extra code, but this example uses the most straightforward method. In line 41, a stand-alone `float` variable named `passWeight` is defined and assigned each structure's weight before passing that `float` variable by address to `calcData()`. The passed data gets changed because of the passing by reference. Once the function returns, the program assigns the changed variable to the structure's `weight` in line 44.

Notice that the `getData()` function contains the `new` operator. The `name` character pointer inside each structure variable will point to heap memory that is assigned the user's input value in line 62. Of course, the `new` means that there must be a `delete` somewhere in the program. You'll find the deallocation in the `dealData()` function in line 89. Notice that the entire structure variable isn't deleted because the structure variable was not allocated. Only the allocated `name` data is deallocated before the program terminates in `main()`.

 Tip If you like what little you've seen of C++, you'll want more details. The object-oriented aspect of the language requires careful study but raises your level of programming productivity. If you'd like to learn C++, you're now ready for the book *Moving from C to C++* (Sams Publishing, 1992). *Moving from C to C++* uses your current base of C knowledge as a framework for teaching the beginning and advanced object-oriented aspects of C++.

▶ # Homework

General Knowledge

1. What does OOP stand for?
2. Name an advantage of C++ over C.
3. Name three non-OOP improvements in C++ over C.
4. What extension should all C++ files have?
5. Where can you define local variables in C++?

6. Name the two new C++ operators that help with I/O.

7. What is your output device (usually the screen) known as in C++?

8. What is your input device (usually the keyboard) known as in C++?

9. Name the two new C++ operators that help with memory allocation and deallocation.

10. If you use `new` to allocate, how should you deallocate?

11. If you use `malloc()` to allocate, how should you deallocate?

12. What are the three ways to pass data in C++?

13. How do you pass data by reference in C++?

14. True or false: C++ was the predecessor of C.

15. True or false: You must use formatting conversion characters when outputting with `cout`.

16. True or false: There is a way to teach C++ how to input and output variables of your own data types.

What's the Output?

17. This is easy: What's the output of the following `cout`?

    ```
    cout << "PI: " << 3.14159 << ", Area: " << 76.42234 <<
        << ", Number: " << 42;
    ```

Find the Bug

18. Terrie coded the following structure variable definition in her program. Although this code doesn't have any bugs, Terrie didn't have to do so much work. Help her simplify this code.

    ```
    struct CompStruct businesses[25];   // Define an array of structures
    ```

19. Frank is outputting a message in a C++ program, but he gets a strange error message on the following statement:

    ```
    cout >> "End of report";
    ```

    Help Frank fix the problem.

Write Code That...

20. Convert the following `printf()` and `scanf()` functions into `cout` and `cin` statements:

    ```
    printf("Are you still in the %f tax bracket (Y/N)? ", brack);
    scanf(" %c", &ans);
    ```

21. Write a statement using `new` that allocates an array of 25 integers. Call `exit()` if the allocation failed.

22. Write a program that uses `cin` and `cout` to ask the user for three prices. Print the dollar total of those prices on-screen.

Extra Credit

23. Convert the following cout statements into a single cout statement:

```
cout << "Sales: ";
cout << 54.56;
cout << "Total sold: ";
cout << 27;
```

12

Your C Future

STOP&TYPE In this lesson, you looked into your programming future. By seeing how to sort both numeric and textual data, you learned some advanced algorithms that you'll find useful as you write more-advanced programs. After you saw some rather long programs in Unit 23, Unit 24 showed you how the C++ language improves upon C by providing shortcuts that eliminate some programming details. You saw the following:

▶ How to sort data both numerically and alphabetically.

▶ How to find the smallest and largest elements in an array.

▶ C++ improves upon C by providing shortcut commands and functions.

▶ C++ doesn't require struct when defining structure variables.

Project 12 Listing. Using some C++ shortcuts.

```
 1:  /* Filename: LESSON12.CPP */

 2:  // A C++ program that allocates an array of 100 integers

 3:  // on the heap, sorts the array in backwards order, and

 4:  // prints the results

 5:  #define NUM 100

 6:  #include <iostream.h>

 7:  #include <conio.h>

 8:  void allMemory(void);

 9:  void sortMemory(void);

10:  void prMemory(void);

11:  void deallMemory(void);

12:

13:  // Initialize iPtr globally only because all functions use it

14:  int * iPtr;

15:  main()
```

▶ You can define variables anywhere in a C++ program.

▶ C++ offers easier I/O using `cout` and `cin`.

▶ The C++ allocation operators, `new` and `delete`, make allocating data easier.

Description

1: A C comment that includes the program's filename.

2: A C++ comment that contains the program's description.

3: The program description continues.

4: The program description continues.

5: Defines the number of values to be allocated.

6: `cout` and `cin` need information in the IOSTREAM.H header file.

7: The screen-clearing function, `clrscr()`, needs information in the CONIO.H header file.

8: You should prototype all functions.

9: Prototype of another function.

10: Prototype of another function.

11: Prototype of another function.

12: Put blank lines in your programs to separate sections of code.

13: Scatter comments throughout your code.

14: The heap's memory pointer.

15: `main()` begins.

continues

Project 12 Listing. continued

```
16:  {

17:      clrscr();

18:      allMemory();        // Allocate memory and initialize it

19:      sortMemory();       // Sort the memory values backwards

20:      prMemory();         // Print the memory as sorted

21:      deallMemory();      // Deallocate the memory

22:      cout << "\n\nPress any key to continue...";

23:      getch();

24:      return 0;

25:  }

26:  //*********************************************************

27:  void allMemory(void)

28:  {

29:      iPtr = new int[NUM];

30:      // Step through each value, initializing them

31:      // with the even numbers from 0 to 198

32:      for (int ctr = 0; ctr < NUM; ctr++)

33:      {   iPtr[ctr] = ctr*2; }

34:      return;

35:  }

36:  //*********************************************************

37:  void sortMemory(void)
```

Description

16: All functions begin with an opening brace.

17: Erases the user's output screen.

18: Calls the function that allocates all of the heap memory with `new`.

19: Calls the function that sorts the numbers in descending order.

20: Calls the function that prints the values on the heap after the sort.

21: Calls the function that deallocates the memory.

22: Prompts the user to press a key when finished viewing the output.

23: Waits for the user's keypress.

24: Always return from `main()` to the IDE.

25: A final brace ends all `main()` functions.

26: A line of asterisks helps to separate functions.

27: The definition (first line) of the function that allocates the heap memory.

28: All functions begin with an opening brace.

29: Allocates 100 integers on the heap and makes `iPtr` point to the first one.

    29: Allocating with `new` is simpler than allocating with `malloc()`.

30: Scatter comments throughout your code.

31: Scatter comments throughout your code.

32: Steps through each element in the heap array.

33: Assigns to each value 2 times the value of the loop control variable.

34: Returns to `main()`.

35: A final brace ends all functions.

36: A line of asterisks helps to separate functions.

37: Defines the function that sorts the heap's memory values.

continues

Project 12 Listing. continued

```
38:  {

39:     int temp;         // Temporary value for swapping

40:     int didSwap;      // 1 if a swap took place in each pass

41:     for (int outer = 0; outer < (NUM - 1); outer++)

42:        {

43:        didSwap = 0;    // Initialize after each pass

44:        // Next loop steps through each pair of values

45:        for (int inner = outer; inner < NUM; inner++)

46:           {

47:           if (iPtr[outer] < iPtr[inner])    // First of two is higher

48:              { temp = iPtr[outer];    // Swap

49:                iPtr[outer] = iPtr[inner];

50:                iPtr[inner] = temp;

51:                didSwap = 1;    // Indicate that a swap occurred

52:              }

53:           }

54:        if (!didSwap)    // If no swap happened,

55:           { break; }    // terminate the sort

56:        }

57:     return;

58:  }

59:  //**************************************************
```

Description

38: All functions begin with an opening brace.

39: Defines a temporary variable that will help swap two integers during the sorting.

40: Defines the swapping test variable.

41: Steps through the values. Notice that the for loop control variable is defined inside the for loop.

42: for loop bodies should begin with a brace.

43: No values have been swapped yet.

44: Scatter comments throughout your code.

45: Starts the inner for loop so that pairs of values can be compared.

46: for loop bodies should begin with a brace.

47: If the pair of values is out of order, begins the code that swaps them.

48: Stores in a third variable one of the two values to be swapped.

49: Begins the swap.

50: Concludes the swap.

51: Sets the swapping test variable to true.

52: Closes the if body.

53: Closes the inner for loop body.

54: If a swap took place...

55: Exits the loop and returns to main(). This keeps the sort routine from looping needlessly.

56: Closes the outer for loop.

57: Returns to main().

58: All functions end with a closing brace.

59: A line of asterisks helps to separate functions.

41: The bubble sort is one of the easlest sorting algorithms.

48: A third variable is needed to swap two values.

continues

Project 12 Listing. continued

```
60:   void prMemory(void)

61:   {

62:     cout << "Here are the values sorted backwards:\n";

63:     for (int ctr = 0; ctr < NUM; ctr++)

64:       { cout << iPtr[ctr] << "\t"; }

65:     return;

66:   }

67:   //********************************************************

68:   void deallMemory(void)

69:   {

70:     delete iPtr;

71:     return;

72:   }
```

Description

60: Defines the function that prints data from the heap.

61: The function's opening brace.

62: Prints a title.

63: Steps through the heap memory.

64: Prints each value from the heap, separating the values with a tab character.

65: Returns to main().

66: All functions end with a closing brace.

67: A line of asterisks helps to separate functions.

68: Defines the function that deallocates data from the heap.

69: The function's opening brace.

70: Deletes the memory pointed to by iPtr.

70: Deallocate with free because of new.

71: Returns to main().

72: The function's closing brace.

▼ OUTPUT

```
Here are the values sorted backwards:
198     196     194     192     190     188     186     184     182     180
178     176     174     172     170     168     166     164     162     160
158     156     154     152     150     148     146     144     142     140
138     136     134     132     130     128     126     124     122     120
118     116     114     112     110     108     106     104     102     100
98      96      94      92      90      88      86      84      82      80
78      76      74      72      70      68      66      64      62      60
58      56      54      52      50      48      46      44      42      40
38      36      34      32      30      28      26      24      22      20
18      16      14      12      10      8       6       4       2       0
```

Appendix ▶

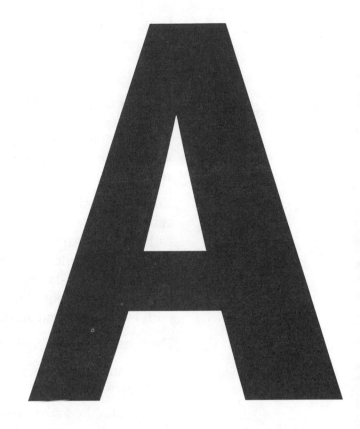

Installing
Your C
Compiler

Before you can run C programs, you must install the C compiler that comes with this book. Turn on your computer if it's not already on. Locate the disk that comes with this book, and you're ready to begin the installation.

▶ What Will Happen

The C compiler that you get with this book is actually more than just a C compiler. It will compile C++ code as well as C code. Someday, when you move from C to C++, you'll already have the C++ compiler.

Until then, you'll be working in C, writing powerful programs with the help of this book and the compiler. The name of the compiler is Turbo C++ Lite 1.0. The version that comes with this book isn't considered the full-featured version, primarily because no auxiliary documentation files are included. Lesson 1 explains a few more limitations of the compiler you get here, but be assured that nothing in the C language (or in C++, of which C is a subset) is left out. You get a full implementation of C. The enclosed compiler supports every command and function in the C language.

The installation procedure does the following:

▶ Creates all the necessary directories for the compiler under the primary directory name TCLITE.

▶ Copies the source code, answer, and compiler files from the disk to your hard disk.

▶ Expands the files. The files are compressed so that they all will fit on one disk. You can't run the programs in their compressed state.

After you install the compiler, you'll be ready to begin entering and running C programs on your computer.

 Note This book's Turbo C++ compiler requires that you use the IDE (integrated development editor) as described in Lesson 1 to enter, edit, and run your C programs. You won't be able to write stand-alone C programs (programs that can run outside of the IDE) as you can with other versions of Turbo C++.

▶ Begin at DOS

This book's C compiler installs from the DOS prompt. On many people's computers, the DOS prompt looks like this:

```
C:\>
```

If you run Windows or OS/2, you must do one of two things before installing the C compiler:

▶ Open a DOS window.

▶ Completely exit Windows or OS/2 and return to DOS.

Tip Due to memory shortages that can appear after a long Windows or OS/2 session, you're probably better off exiting these windowing environments completely before installing C. After you install the compiler, you can return to Windows or OS/2 and compile your C programs from a DOS window if you like.

Before installing, you must insert the disk in a disk drive, such as drive A:, and make that disk drive the default disk drive. In other words, if your C: drive shows at the DOS prompt, but you put the disk in drive A:, type A: at the DOS prompt to change the default drive to A:. Your DOS prompt would now look like this:

```
A:\>
```

The C compiler installs to a directory named TCLITE. Therefore, if you were to install the C compiler to drive C:, then displayed drive C:'s directory, you would see a directory named TCLITE in the listing. Under TCLITE, the installation program installs several more subdirectories as well.

▶ The Installation

Installing the C compiler is easy. The compiler does all the work! Once you've inserted the disk in the drive and made that drive the default drive, you only need to issue the install command.

Choose the hard disk where you want to install the program. Make sure that the disk has more than 2.5 megabytes free (that's about two-and-a-half million characters). The compiler itself takes about 2.5 megabytes, but you'll probably want additional space to hold the programs you write.

Assuming that you want to install the C compiler on your C: drive, type the following to start the installation:

```
INSTALL C:
```

Warning You must type a colon (:) at the end of the target installation hard disk.

The installation program will display a copyright message and begin the installation.

After you see the SUCCESSFULLY INSTALLED message, the installation program returns to the DOS prompt. Change to your C: hard disk drive once more by typing C: at the diskette drive's DOS prompt.

There are two ways to start the compiler. One requires that you change to the compiler's directory every time you run the program. Changing to the compiler's directory gets tedious, so the next section explains how to add the compiler's directory to your execution path.

▶ **Modifying Your Path**

Not everybody reading this book will be comfortable adding the C compiler's directory to their execution pathname. If you've never modified the DOS AUTOEXEC.BAT file, you might want to get some help the first time. Nevertheless, the things you'll be doing in the first two lessons of this book are far more advanced than modifying AUTOEXEC.BAT, so perhaps you should take the plunge and modify the file yourself.

After adding the compiler's execution directory to your AUTOEXEC.BAT pathname, you'll be able to start the compiler from any DOS prompt without having to first change to the C compiler's directory. The following steps explain how to add the path.

 Warning   These steps assume that you have DOS version 5.0 or later, as most people do these days. If you work with DOS 4.1 or earlier, you must be able to use the EDLIN line editor to change AUTOEXEC.BAT. EDLIN is not a trivial program. Get help from an experienced DOS advisor, or better yet, *run* to your nearest dealer and upgrade to a later version of DOS. Lots of goodies come with all DOS versions starting with 5.0. You'll be glad that you upgraded.

1. At the C:>\ prompt, type EDIT AUTOEXEC.BAT. As with all DOS commands, you can type the command in uppercase or lowercase. You'll see something like Figure A.1, although the contents of your file will differ from that of the figure's.

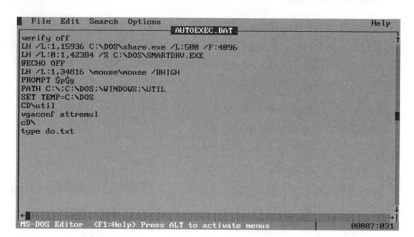

FIGURE A.1.
Getting ready to modify
AUTOEXEC.BAT.

2. Find the line that begins with PATH. Move the cursor, using the arrow keys or the mouse cursor, to the end of that line. At the very end of the line, without any spaces, type ;C:\TCLITE\BIN without pressing Enter. For example, if your PATH statement originally looked like this:

    PATH C:\;C:\DOS;C:\WINDOWS;C:\UTIL

    the PATH would now look like this:

    PATH C:\;C:\DOS;C:\WINDOWS;C:\UTIL;C:\TCLITE\BIN

3. Exit the editor by pressing Alt-F and then X and answering Yes when asked if you want to save the file.

4. You now must reboot your computer in order for the changes to take effect. If you completely exited to DOS from Windows or OS/2, you can reboot by pressing Ctrl-Alt-Delete. If you installed the compiler from a DOS window, you must exit your operating environment before rebooting.

Good luck, and enjoy your life as a C programmer!

ASCII Table

Appendix **B**

Dec X_{10}	Hex X_{16}	Binary X_2	ASCII Character
000	00	0000 0000	null
001	01	0000 0001	☺
002	02	0000 0010	☻
003	03	0000 0011	♥
004	04	0000 0100	◆
005	05	0000 0101	♣
006	06	0000 0110	♠
007	07	0000 0111	●
008	08	0000 1000	■
009	09	0000 1001	○
010	0A	0000 1010	■
011	0B	0000 1011	♂
012	0C	0000 1100	♀
013	0D	0000 1101	♪
014	0E	0000 1110	♪♪
015	0F	0000 1111	☼
016	10	0001 0000	►
017	11	0001 0001	◄
018	12	0001 0010	↕
019	13	0001 0011	‼
020	14	0001 0100	¶
021	15	0001 0101	§
022	16	0001 0110	‒
023	17	0001 0111	↨
024	18	0001 1000	↑
025	19	0001 1001	↓
026	1A	0001 1010	→
027	1B	0001 1011	←
028	1C	0001 1100	FS
029	1D	0001 1101	GS
030	1E	0001 1110	RS
031	1F	0001 1111	US
032	20	0010 0000	SP
033	21	0010 0001	!
034	22	0010 0010	"
035	23	0010 0011	#
036	24	0010 0100	$
037	25	0010 0101	%
038	26	0010 0110	&
039	27	0010 0111	'
040	28	0010 1000	(
041	29	0010 1001	)
042	2A	0010 1010	*

Dec X_{10}	Hex X_{16}	Binary X_2	ASCII Character
043	2B	0010 1011	+
044	2C	0010 1100	'
045	2D	0010 1101	-
046	2E	0010 1110	.
047	2F	0010 1111	/
048	30	0011 0000	0
049	31	0011 0001	1
050	32	0011 0010	2
051	33	0011 0011	3
052	34	0011 0100	4
053	35	0011 0101	5
054	36	0011 0110	6
055	37	0011 0111	7
056	38	0011 1000	8
057	39	0011 1001	9
058	3A	0011 1010	:
059	3B	0011 1011	;
060	3C	0011 1100	<
061	3D	0011 1101	=
062	3E	0011 1110	>
063	3F	0011 1111	?
064	40	0100 0000	@
065	41	0100 0001	A
066	42	0100 0010	B
067	43	0100 0011	C
068	44	0100 0100	D
069	45	0100 0101	E
070	46	0100 0110	F
071	47	0100 0111	G
072	48	0100 1000	H
073	49	0100 1001	I
074	4A	0100 1010	J
075	4B	0100 1011	K
076	4C	0100 1100	L
077	4D	0100 1101	M
078	4E	0100 1110	N

Dec X_{10}	Hex X_{16}	Binary X_2	ASCII Character
079	4F	0100 1111	O
080	50	0101 0000	P
081	51	0101 0001	Q
082	52	0101 0010	R
083	53	0101 0011	S
084	54	0101 0100	T
085	55	0101 0101	U
086	56	0101 0110	V
087	57	0101 0111	W
088	58	0101 1000	X
089	59	0101 1001	Y
090	5A	0101 1010	Z
091	5B	0101 1011	[
092	5C	0101 1100	\
093	5D	0101 1101	]
094	5E	0101 1110	^
095	5F	0101 1111	–
096	60	0110 0000	`
097	61	0110 0001	a
098	62	0110 0010	b
099	63	0110 0011	c
100	64	0110 0100	d
101	65	0110 0101	e
102	66	0110 0110	f
103	67	0110 0111	g
104	68	0110 1000	h
105	69	0110 1001	i
106	6A	0110 1010	j
107	6B	0110 1011	k
108	6C	0110 1100	l
109	6D	0110 1101	m
110	6E	0110 1110	n
111	6F	0110 1111	o
112	70	0111 0000	p
113	71	0111 0001	q
114	72	0111 0010	r
115	73	0111 0011	s
116	74	0111 0100	t
117	75	0111 0101	u
118	76	0111 0110	v
119	77	0111 0111	w
120	78	0111 1000	x

Dec X_{10}	Hex X_{16}	Binary X_2	ASCII Character
121	79	0111 1001	y
122	7A	0111 1010	z
123	7B	0111 1011	{
124	7C	0111 1100	¦
125	7D	0111 1101	}
126	7E	0111 1110	~
127	7F	0111 1111	DEL
128	80	1000 0000	Ç
129	81	1000 0001	ü
130	82	1000 0010	é
131	83	1000 0011	â
132	84	1000 0100	ä
133	85	1000 0101	à
134	86	1000 0110	å
135	87	1000 0111	ç
136	88	1000 1000	ê
137	89	1000 1001	ë
138	8A	1000 1010	è
139	8B	1000 1011	ï
140	8C	1000 1100	î
141	8D	1000 1101	ì
142	8E	1000 1110	Ä
143	8F	1000 1111	Å
144	90	1001 0000	É
145	91	1001 0001	æ
146	92	1001 0010	Æ
147	93	1001 0011	ô
148	94	1001 0100	ö
149	95	1001 0101	ò
150	96	1001 0110	û
151	97	1001 0111	ù
152	98	1001 1000	ÿ
153	99	1001 1001	Ö
154	9A	1001 1010	Ü
155	9B	1001 1011	¢
156	9C	1001 1100	£
157	9D	1001 1101	¥
158	9E	1001 1110	P_t
159	9F	1001 1111	ƒ
160	A0	1010 0000	á
161	A1	1010 0001	í
162	A2	1010 0010	ó

Dec X_{10}	Hex X_{16}	Binary X_2	ASCII Character
163	A3	1010 0011	ú
164	A4	1010 0100	ñ
165	A5	1010 0101	Ñ
166	A6	1010 0110	a
167	A7	1010 0111	o
168	A8	1010 1000	¿
169	A9	1010 1001	⌐
170	AA	1010 1010	¬
171	AB	1010 1011	½
172	AC	1010 1100	¼
173	AD	1010 1101	¡
174	AE	1010 1110	«
175	AF	1010 1111	»
176	B0	1011 0000	░
177	B1	1011 0001	▒
178	B2	1011 0010	▓
179	B3	1011 0011	│
180	B4	1011 0100	┤
181	B5	1011 0101	╡
182	B6	1011 0110	╢
183	B7	1011 0111	╖
184	B8	1011 1000	╕
185	B9	1011 1001	╣
186	BA	1011 1010	║
187	BB	1011 1011	╗
188	BC	1011 1100	╝
189	BD	1011 1101	╜
190	BE	1011 1110	╛
191	BF	1011 1111	┐
192	C0	1100 0000	└
193	C1	1100 0001	┴
194	C2	1100 0010	┬
195	C3	1100 0011	├
196	C4	1100 0100	─
197	C5	1100 0101	+
198	C6	1100 0110	╞
199	C7	1100 0111	╟
200	C8	1100 1000	╚
201	C9	1100 1001	╔
202	CA	1100 1010	╩

Dec X_{10}	Hex X_{16}	Binary X_2	ASCII Character
203	CB	1100 1011	╦
204	CC	1100 1100	╠
205	CD	1100 1101	=
206	CE	1100 1110	╬
207	CF	1100 1111	╧
208	D0	1101 0000	╨
209	D1	1101 0001	╤
210	D2	1101 0010	╥
211	D3	1101 0011	╙
212	D4	1101 0100	╘
213	D5	1101 0101	╒
214	D6	1101 0110	╓
215	D7	1101 0111	╫
216	D8	1101 1000	╪
217	D9	1101 1001	┘
218	DA	1101 1010	┌
219	DB	1101 1011	█
220	DC	1101 1100	▄
221	DD	1101 1101	▌
222	DE	1101 1110	▐
223	DF	1101 1111	▀
224	E0	1110 0000	α
225	E1	1110 0001	β
226	E2	1110 0010	Γ
227	E3	1110 0011	π
228	E4	1110 0100	Σ
229	E5	1110 0101	σ
230	E6	1110 0110	μ
231	E7	1110 0111	τ
232	E8	1110 1000	Φ
233	E9	1110 1001	θ

APPENDIX

B

ASCII Table

Dec X_{10}	Hex X_{16}	Binary X_2	ASCII Character
234	EA	1110 1010	Ω
235	EB	1110 1011	δ
236	EC	1110 1100	∞
237	ED	1110 1101	ø
238	EE	1110 1110	∈
239	EF	1110 1111	∩
240	F0	1111 0000	≡
241	F1	1111 0001	±
242	F2	1111 0010	≥
243	F3	1111 0011	≤
244	F4	1111 0100	⌠
245	F5	1111 0101	⌡
246	F6	1111 0110	÷
247	F7	1111 0111	≈
248	F8	1111 1000	°
249	F9	1111 1001	•
250	FA	1111 1010	·
251	FB	1111 1011	√
252	FC	1111 1100	η
253	FD	1111 1101	2
254	FE	1111 1110	■
255	FF	1111 1111	

Note   The last 128 ASCII codes listed in this table, numbers 128 through 255, are specific to IBM PCs and IBM compatibles.

Appendix ▶

C Operator Precedence Table

Precedence Level	Symbol	Description	Associativity
1	::	C++ scope access/ resolution	Left to right
2	()	Function call	Left to right
	[]	Array subscript	
	→	C++ indirect component selector	
	.	C++ direct component selector	
3 Unary	!	Logical negation	Right to left
	~	Bitwise (1's) complement	
	+	Unary plus	
	-	Unary minus	
	&	Address of	
	*	Indirection	
	sizeof	Returns size of operand in bytes	
	new	Dynamically allocates C++ storage	
	delete	Dynamically deallocates C++ storage	
	type	Typecast	
4 Member Access	.*	C++ dereference	Left to right
	→*	C++ dereference	
	()	Expression parentheses	
5 Multiplicative	*	Multiply	Left to right
	/	Divide	
	%	Remainder (modulus)	
6 Additive	+	Binary plus	Left to right
	-	Binary minus	
7 Shift	<<	Leftshift	Left to right
	>>	Rightshift	
8 Relational	<	Less than	Left to right
	<=	Less than or equal to	
	>	Greater than	
	>=	Greater than or equal to	

Precedence Level	Symbol	Description	Associativity
9 Equality	==	Equal to	Left to right
	!=	Not equal to	
10	&	Bitwise AND	Left to right
11	^	Bitwise XOR	Left to right
12	|	Bitwise OR	Left to right
13	&&	Logical AND	Left to right
14	||	Logical OR	Left to right
15 Ternary	?:	Conditional	Right to left
16 Assignment	=	Simple assignment	Right to left
	*=	Compound assign product	
	/=	Compound assign quotient	
	%=	Compound assign remainder	
	+=	Compound assign sum	
	-=	Compound assign difference	
	&=	Compound assign bitwise AND	
	^=	Compound assign bitwise XOR	
	|=	Compound assign bitwise OR	
	<<=	Compound assign left shift	
	>>=	Compound assign right shift	
17 Comma	,	Sequence point	Left to right

APPENDIX C — C Operator Precedence Table

Note Because of the confusion in most precedence tables, the postfix ++ and -- and the prefix ++ and -- don't appear here. The postfix operators usually appear in level 2, and the prefix operators appear in level 3. In practice, perform prefix before all other operators except for the scope resolution operator, and perform postfix right before the statement continues to the next executable statement in the program. C purists will cringe at this description, but it works 99.9 percent of the time, while the "technically correct" placements of these operators simply confuse programmers 99.9 percent of the time.

Index ▶

Symbols

! (not) logical operator, 164

!= (not equal to) relational operator, 153

#, preprocessor directives, 78

% (modulus operator), 172

%= compound operator, 146

%c format conversion character, printing single characters, 67-69

%d format conversion character, printing integer values, 70

%f format conversion character, printing floating-point values, 73-74

& (address of) operator
  passing nonarray variables by address, 345
  returning variable addresses, 388

& (ampersand)
  nonarray variables in scanf() function, 122
  passing data by reference, 547

& bitwise AND operator, 202

& truth table, 204

&& (AND) logical operator, 164

&= compound bitwise AND assignment operator, 203

" " quotation marks
  empty strings, 112
  string literals, 61

(, Left parenthesis in C programs, 41

'' apostrophes, character literals, 61

' single quote in C programs, 41

* dereference operator
    passing nonarray vari-
    ables by address, 345
    with pointers, 387
-> structure pointer opera-
    tor, assigning data to
    structures, 431
. dot operator, assigning
    data to structures,
    431-432
    not equal to sign, print-
    ing, 65
) right parenthesis in C
    programs, 41
* multiplication math
    operator, 53
*= compound operator, 146
+ addition math operator,
    53
+ unary operator, 137-138
+= compound operator,
    146
- subtraction math opera-
    tor, 53
- unary operator, 137-138
-= compound operator, 146
/ division math operator,
    53, 138-141
/, forward slash, comments
    in C programs, 41
/* (comments in programs),
    44, 79
// (two forward slashes),
    C++ comments, 45
/= compound operator, 146
: (colon) statement label
    separator, 268
; executable statement
    ending, 41
< (less than) relational
    operator, 153
< left angled bracket in C
    programs, 41
<< bitwise left shift opera-
    tor, 203
<<, bitwise leftshift opera-
    tor, 221

<< operator (C++), 545
<<= compound bitwise left
    shift operator, 203
<= (less than or equal to)
    relational operator, 153
= assignment operator, 99,
    144-148
== equal to relational
    operator, 153
> greater than relational
    operator, 153
> right angled bracket in C
    programs, 41
>= greater than or equal to
    relational operator, 153
>> bitwise right shift
    operator, 203
>> operator (C++), 545
>>= compound bitwise
    right shift operator, 203
?: conditional operator,
    190-193
[left bracket in C pro-
    grams, 41
\ backslash in C programs,
    41
\\ escape sequence charac-
    ter, 64
\a escape sequence charac-
    ter, 64
\b escape sequence charac-
    ter, 65
\n control character, 62
], right bracket in C pro-
    grams, 41
^ bitwise exclusive OR
    operator, 202
^ truth table, 205
{, left brace in C programs,
    41, 52
| bitwise OR operator, 202
| truth table, 205
|, vertical bar in C pro-
    grams, 41
|= compound bitwise OR
    assignment operator, 203
|| or logical operator, 164

}, right brace in C pro-
    grams, 41, 52
~ bitwise 1's complement
    operator, 203
~, tilde in C programs, 41
~ truth table, 206
~= compound bitwise
    exclusive OR assignment
    operator, 203
0 prefix, octal literals, 92
0x prefix, hexadecimal
    integer literal, 92
640K memory area, 443

A

\a escape sequence charac-
    ter, 64
a+ access mode, opening
    random access files, 498
About box (control menu),
    21
access mode
    opening random access
        files, 498-499
    sequential files, 481
adding to variables with
    increment (++) operators,
    194-198
addList() function, 437
address of (&) operator
    passing nonarray vari-
        ables by address, 345
    returning variable
        addresses, 388
addresses
    in memory, 385
    passing arrays by,
        343-347
advanced loop control, 296
advanced operators,
    218-220
aggregate initialization of
    character arrays, 119
ALCHECK.C program, heap
    arrays (listing 20.1),
    451-452

algorithms, bubble sort, 525

aligning columns of data escape sequence characters, 65

allMemory() function, 458

allocating
    heap memory, 445, 448, 455-458, 463
    structures on heap, 450

Alt-X keys, Quit command, 17

ampersand (&)
    nonarray variables in scanf() function, 122
    passing data by reference, 547

AND (&&) operator, 164, 221

angled brackets in C programs, 41

ANSI C standard, 11

API (application program interface), 19

apostrophes (')
    character literals, 61
    in C programs, 41

appending files, 481, 486-489

arguments
    data values in functions, 338
    passing by value, 339-341

ARRAYBEG.C program, defining/printing character arrays (listing 6.1), 115-116

arrays, 366-373, 407
    character, 113-120, 129, 366-367
    finding minimum/ maximum values, 536
    integer, 368
    memory space, 369
    multidimensional, 376

numeric, 366-368
parallel, 375
passing by address, 343-347
pointers, 399-403, 455
referencing with pointers, 391-395
searching, 373-379
single-dimensional, 376
structure, allocating on the heap (LESSON10.C), 462-472
subscript elements, 118

ARRHEAP.C program, allocating array of pointers (listing 20.3), 456-457

ARRTEMP.C program, array example (listing 17.1), 370-371

ascending sort order of values, 524

ASCII tables
    character, 65
    characters and integer values, 71

ASCII values for control characters, 315

ASCII zero, see null zero

ascSort() function, 529

assembly language, 10

assignment operator (=), 144-148
    data in variables, 99
    multiple statements, 144
    values in arrays, 370

ASSIGNS.C program, variables, storing/printing (listing 5.2), 101-102

associativity of expressions, 144-145

asterisk with forward slash (/*), program comments, 44

automatic data-type promotion, 183-184, 218

available heap, 445

B

\b escape sequence character, 65

backslash (\) in C programs, 41

binary numeric representation and bitwise operators, 209

binary operators, 137

binary zero, see null zero

BIT1.C program, bitwise operators example (listing 10.1), 206-207

BITEQUIV.C program, bitwise operators example (listing 10.3), 211-212

bitmask of programs, 219

BITSHIFT.C program, bitwise shift operators (listing 10.2), 208-209

bitwise operators, 202-203, 219
    compound AND, 221
    operations on user input, 209-212
    sample programs, 206-207, 211-212

bitwise shift operators, 207-209, 221

blank lines in output, 69

blank spaces in programs, 42

blocks of code
    in braces ({}), 52
    local/global variables, 334

Borland International Turbo C++ compiler, 12

braces
    case statements in switch statements, 284
    in C programs, 41
        function markers, 52

brackets in C programs, 41

branching to statement labels, 269

break statement, 232-236, 255
  end of case statement code, 287
  exiting for loops early, 262-264
  quitting for loops early (FORBREAK.C-listing 13.1), 263
  sample program (BREXIT.C-listing 11.3), 234-235
  with switch statement, 284-289
BREXIT.C program, break/exit() demo (listing 11.3), 234-235
bubble sort, 525
buffer, clearing of input, 310
buffered functions, 306
BYADDRES.C program, passing floating-points by address (listing 24.1), 547
BYREF.CPP program, passing by reference (listing 24.2), 548

C

.C file extension, 24
C programming language, 10-11
C++ programming language, 542
C++ shortcuts (LESSON12.CPP), 556-563
C:\> (DOS prompt), 16
calculating long math expressions, EXPRESS.C (listing 7.3), 143
calling functions, 54-56, 332
CARRINIT.C program, defining character arrays (listing 6.2), 119-120

cascading case code blocks, NOBREAKS.C (listing 14.3), 287-288
case statements
  break statements at end of code, 287
  enclosed in braces in switch statements, 284
CD command (DOS), 17
ceil() function, 322
char variable, 109
character arrays, 113-117, 129, 366-367
  data storage, 117-120
  defining, 113
    ARRAYBEG.C (listing 6.1), 115-116
    CARRINIT.C (listing 6.2), 119-120
  initializing one element at a time, 119
  printing, ARRAYBEG.C (listing 6.1), 115-116
  string storage, 118
  subscript numbers for elements, 115
character conversion functions, 316
character data, printing with %c, CHARCONV.C (listing 4.3), 69
character functions, PRODCODE.C (listing 15.2), 317
character I/O functions, 305-310
character literals, 61, 108
character strings, 108-112
character variables, 128
character zero, 110
character-testing functions, 315-316
characters
  integer values in ASCII table, 71
  pointers to, 395-399
  printing singly, 67-69

printing with INTPRINT.C (listing 4.4), 72
CHARCONV.C program, printing character data (listing 4.3), 69
CHARFUNS.C program, character pointers and arrays (listing 18.3), 398
check boxes in dialog boxes, 22
cin operator, 544-545
CITYNAME.C program, arrays of pointers (listing 18.4), 401-402
Clear desktop option (control menu), 21
clearing input buffer, 310
closing files, 484-485, 498
clrscr() function, 44, 219
code
  executable, 8
  source, 8
  syntax errors, 8
  see also programs
code blocks
  in braces ({}), 52
  local/global variables, 334
colon (:) statement label separator, 268
color monitors, color text output, 312-315
colorCode literal integer constants, 312
columns of data, aligning with escape sequence characters, 65
combining data types, 182-188
comma operator, 193
command buttons in dialog boxes, 22
commands
  Compile menu, 21
  Control menu, 21
  Debug menu, 21

DOS
    CD, 17
    TC, 32
    Edit menu, 21
    File menu, 20
        New, 23
        Open, 5
        Quit, 17
        Save, 24
    Help menu, 21, 28-29
    Options menu, Save, 23
    Project menu, 21
    Run menu, 21, 25
    Window menu, 21-23
    see also statements
comments in programs
    adding as program is
        written, 46-47
    C++ version, two for-
        ward slashes (//), 45
    denoting with forward
        slash and asterisk (/*),
        44, 79
    embedded, 45
    function-separating, 45
COMMENTS.C program,
    two styles of comments
    (listing 3.2), 47
compilation windows, 34
Compile menu, 25
Compile menu commands,
    21
compilers
    DOS programming
        support, 19
    functions, 11
compiling programs, 8, 342
compound bitwise AND
    operator, 221
compound bitwise opera-
    tors, 213-214
compound operators,
    146-148
compound relational
    operators, see logical
    operators

computer languages,
    syntax rules, 4
computing division results,
    MOREDIV.C (listing 7.2),
    140
computing interest with for
    loops (LESSON6.C pro-
    gram), 254
CONDIT.C program,
    conditional operator
    (listing 9.3), 192-193
conditional (?:) operator,
    190-193, 218
conditional statements,
    two-line, 221
CONIO.H header file, 50,
    304
conserving heap memory,
    443
constant pointers, 391
constant values, 61
constants, named, in
    programs, 50
contents of arrays, 118
contiguous memory
    allocation, 447
continue statements
    CONTINUE.C program
    (listing 13.2), 266
    reiterating loops,
        264-267
control character ASCII
    values, 315
control characters for
    output, 62
control menu commands,
    21
control variables
    countExpression of for
        loops, 245-246
    for loops (SEQUENCS.C-
        listing 12.2), 245-246
controls in dialog boxes, 22
conventional memory, 385
conversion characters
    printf() function, 93
    %s, printing strings, 117

cos() function, 324
counter variables in while
    loops, 228
countExpression, control
    variables of for loops,
    245-246
cout operator, 544-545
.CPP file extension, 25, 543
CPPADV.CPP program,
    advantages/shortcuts of
    C++ (listing 24.3),
    549-550
cprintf() function, 313
CPU (central processing
    unit), 4
cputs() function, 313
CSTUDY.C program,
    components of programs
    (listing 3.3), 55
Ctrl-F9 keys, Run com-
    mand, 25
CTYPE.H header file,
    character conversion
    functions, 316

D

data
    assigning to structures
        dot operator (.),
        431-432
        structure pointer
            operator (->), 431
    literal, printing with
        printf() function, 61
    passing between func-
        tions, LESSON8.C
        program, 356-360
    reading from disk files,
        478-480
    sorting for order,
        524-530
    storing in variables,
        99-102
data types
    combining, 182-188

defining personal with struct statements, 424-430
integer, 88
literal qualifiers, 93-94
memory requirements, 89
myStruct, 543
numeric, 86-95
outputting/inputting with operator overloading, 545
scientific notation, 87
unsigned, 89
variables, 97-98
data variables, 128
dealData() function, 551
deallocating heap memory, 445, 463, 546
Debug menu commands, 21
decimal ASCII numbers in ASCII character table, 65
declarations of variables, 53
decrement (-) operator, subtracting from variables, 194-198, 219
#define preprocessor directives, 43, 48-51
defining
file pointers, 481
global variables, 335
local variables, 334
pointer variables, 387
structure variables, 543
variables, 98-99
variables in C++, 544
defining character arrays
ARRAYBEG.C (listing 6.1), 115-116
CARRINIT.C (listing 6.2), 119-120
DEFPNTS.C program, pointers to variables (listing 18.1), 390

delete operator, 546
deleteIt() function, 507
dereference operator (*)
passing nonarray variables by address, 345
pointers, 387
descending sort order of values, 525
designing programs, 7-8
desSort() function, 529
dialog boxes, 22-24
directives, preprocessor, 48-51, 78
directories
INCLUDE, 49
PROGRAMS, 25
disk files, 478-480
dispList() function, 437
division, 172
computing results, MOREDIV.C (listing 7.2), 140
integers, INTDIV.C program (listing 7.1), 138
standard fractional, 139
division operator (/), 138-141
do-while loops, 230-232, 255
DOS
C:\> (prompt), 16
commands
CD, 17
TC, 32
compiler programming support, 19
errorlevel variable, 232
starting Turbo C++, 16
dot operator (.), 431-432, 463
double data type, 87
DOUSRAGE.C program, do-while loop (listing 11.2), 231-232
dynamic memory allocation, 445

E

%e, %E conversion characters, scientific notation, 91
Edit menu commands, 21
editing windows, 23, 32
editor for Turbo C++ compiler, 24
elements of arrays, 119, 366
else statements, 162-163
embedded comments in programs, 45
embedded if-else statements, 279
empty strings, 109, 112
equal to (==) relational operator, 153
erasing output screen, 297
error-checking memory allocation, with malloc() return values, 453-454
error-checking opening of files, 482
errorlevel variable (DOS), 232
errors
displaying in message window, 26
stack overflow, 334
escape sequences
characters, 62-67
hexadecimal, 109
ESCSEQS.C program, print output with escape characters (listing 4.2), 66
EVNTOODD.C program, compound bitwise operator (listing 10.4), 213-214
executable code, 8
executable statements, ending with (;), 41
exit() function, 232-236
exiting Turbo C++, 17
exp() function, 324

expanded memory, 384-386

exponents in scientific notation, 87

EXPRESS.C program, long expressions (listing 7.3), 143

expressions, associativity, 144-145

extended memory, 384-386, 443

F

F1 key, context-sensitive help, 28

F5 key, enlarging window, 23

fabs() function, 322

fclose() function, 484, 498

feof() function, 506

ferror() function, 506

fflush() function, 310

fgets() function, 311, 490

fields, *see* members of structures

file erasing function (listing 22.2), 507

file extensions, 543

file I/O functions, 480

File menu commands, 20
  New, 23
  Open, 5
  Quit, 17
  Save, 24

file pointers
  defining, 481
  moving with fseek() function, 499-501
  reading/writing disk files, 480

File Save dialog box, 24

file-naming conventions for programs, 479

file-related functions, 506-507

files
  appending, 486
  checking for existence, 491
  closing, 484-485
  disk, 478-480
  header, 49-50
  on program disk, 25
  opening, 480-482
  random access, 496-499, 512-518
  random I/O, 501-506
  reading, 486
  saving, 17
  sequential, 479, 488-489
  writing to, 486-487
  see also random access files; listings; sequential files

fillTemps() function, 372

findRetire() function, 52-54

float variables (C++), 551

floating-point data type, 87

floating-point values
  displaying with FLTPRINT.C (listing 4.5), 74
  fractional portions, storing with typecast operator, 187
  printing, %f format conversion character, 73-74

floating-point variables
  passing by address, BYADDRES.C (listing 24.1), 547
  pointers to, 387

floor() function, 322

FLOTARPT.C program, referencing arrays with pointers (listing 18.2), 394

flushing input buffer, 310

fmod() function, 323

fopen() function, 480-483, 498

for loops, 240-244, 255
  computing interest (LESSON6.C program), 254
  control variables (SEQUENCS.C-listing 12.2), 245-246
  countExpression of control variables, 245-246
  defining variables in C++, 544
  example program (FORAVG.C-listing 12.1), 243
  exiting early with break statements, 262-264
  nested, 247-249

FORBREAK.C program, quitting loops early (listing 13.1), 263

format conversion character (%c), single characters, 67-69

format conversion character (%d), integer values, 70

format conversion character (%f), floating-point values, 73-74

format of program structure, 48-56

format of random access files, 497

format strings, 65

formatted I/O functions, 305

forward slash and asterisk (/*), C comments, 44

forward slashes (//), C++ comments, 45

fprintf() function, 305, 486

fputs() function, 311, 486

fractional division, 139, 172

fractional portion of floating-point values, typecast operator, 187
fractional values for integers, 91
fread() function, 501-506
free() function, 446-449, 463
freeAll() function, 458
freeform style of C program writing, 42
freeing heap memory, 445, 450
fscanf() function, 490
fseek() function
   moving file pointer, 499-501
   origin values, 500
function-separating comments in programs, 45
functions
   addList(), 437
   allMemory(), 458
   ascSort(), 529
   braces as markers in programs, 52
   buffered, 306
   calling, 54-56, 332
   ceil(), 322
   character I/O, 305-310
   character-testing/conversion, 315-318
   clrscr(), 44, 219
   compiler-specific, 11
   cos(), 324
   cprintf(), 313
   cputs(), 313
   data values as arguments, 338
   dealData(), 551
   deleteIt(), 507
   desSort(), 529
   dispList(), 437
   exit(), 232-236
   exp(), 324
   fabs(), 322

fclose(), 484, 498
feof(), 506
ferror(), 506
fflush(), 310
fgets(), 311, 490
file erasing (listing 22.2), 507
file-related, 506-507
fillTemps(), 372
findRetire(), 52-54
floor(), 322
fmod(), 323
fopen(), 480-483, 498
fprintf(), 305, 486
fputs(), 311, 486
fread(), 501-506
free(), 446-449, 463
freeAll(), 458
fscanf(), 490
fseek(), 499-501
fwrite(), 501-506
getch(), 306-308
getchar(), 306
getche(), 306, 310
getCity(), 458
getData(), 551
getIt(), 339
getKey(), 379
gets(), 311
heap, 446-452
I/O (Input/Output), 54, 313-314
input, 304-315
integer, 322-323
isalpha(), 315
iscntrl(), 315
isdigit(), 315
islower(), 315
isspace(), 315
isupper(), 315
library, 11, 50-51, 304
log(), 324
log10(), 324
logarithmic, 324-326
main(), 51-52, 78
malloc(), 446-448, 453-454, 463

mathematical, 322-324
numeric, 322-326
output, 304-315
passing data between, 356-360
pow(), 323
prData(), 379
printf(), 54, 60, 79, 129
   outputting data, 60-63
   printing string literals, 61
prototypes, 341-343, 513
putc(), 306
putch(), 306-308
putchar(), 306-308
puts(), 311
recursive, 334
remove(), 506
returning values to with return statements, 347
rewind(), 506
scanf(), 54, 120-123, 129
self-prototyping, 341
separating in code, 331
separating in programs, 332
sharing local variables, 338-347
sin(), 324
sqrt(), 323
strcat(), 318
strcmp(), 318-319
   sorting strings, 525
   string data comparison, 530
strcpy(), 117-120
string I/O, 310-312, 318-322
strlen(), 318
tan(), 324
textbackground(), 312
textcolor(), 312
tolower(), 316
toupper(), 316
trigonometric, 324-326

unbuffered character I/O, 308
user-supplied, 51
fwrite() function, 501-506

G

%g, %G conversion characters, values in scientific notation, 92
getch() function, 306-308
getchar() function, 306
getche() function, 306, 310
getCity() function, 458
getData() function, 551
getIt() function, 339
getKey() function, 379
gets() function, 311
Glancing through a C program (listing 1.1), 6
global structure definitions, 429
global variables, 334-337
goto statement, 267-271
GOTO.C program, goto statement (listing 13.3), 270
greater than (>) relational operator, 153
greater than or equal to (>=) relational operator, 153
grouping data types in structures, 424

H

hard disks, saving programs, 18
hardware-dependent languages, 12
header files
    common code for programs, 50
    CONIO.H, 50, 304
    CTYPE.H, 316
    #include directive, 49

library function prototypes, 342
    MATH.H, 322
    STDIO.H, 50, 122, 304
    STDLIB.H, 233, 448
    STRING.H, 119, 318
heap, 463
    allocations
        memory, 448, 455-458
        new operator, 546
        structure arrays, 462-472
        structures, 450
    deallocating with delete operator, 546
    free memory, 442-446, 450
    functions, 446-452
    terminology, 444-446
Help menu commands, 21, 28-29
hexadecimal ASCII numbers, ASCII character table, 65
hexadecimal escape sequences, 109
hexadecimal integer literal (0x prefix), 92
hexadecimal values, printing, 93
high-level languages, 10
high-low-level languages, 10
HOTELIF.C program, if statement (listing 8.2), 160
HOTELELSE.C program, if/else statements (listing 8.3), 163

I

I/O (Input/Output), 54
    cin/cout operators, 544
    functions, 11, 54, 310-314

I/O manipulators, 545
IDE (Integrated Development Environment), 16
    practice program, 23-28
    screen, 17
    Using the Turbo C++ IDE (listing 2.1), 24
if command, 157
if conditional testing with LESSON4.C program, 172
if statements, 254
    hotel rate example, HOTELIF.C (listing 8.2), 160
    relational operators, 157-161
    with else statement, (HOTELELSE.C-listing 8.3), 163
if-else statements, 276-280
IFELSETV.C program, embedded if-else (listing 14.1), 279
INCDEC.C program, increment/decrement operators (listing 9.4), 197
INCLUDE directory, 49
#include preprocessor directives, 48-51
increment (++) operators, 194-198, 219
infinite loops, 227
INITIAL.C file, 25
initializing character arrays one element at a time, 119
initializing structure variables, 430-438
input buffer, clearing, 310
input from keyboard, scanf() function, 120-123
input functions, 304-315
input validation from users, 173
inputting data types with operator overloading (C++), 545

inside loop of nested loop, 247

instructions for programs, 4-5

INTDIV.C program, integer division (listing 7.1), 138

integer arrays, 368

integer data types, 86-88

integer division, 138, 172

integer functions, 322-323

integer values, 70-73

integer variables, 53

integers
fractional values, 91
long, 89
pointers to, 400
printing with INTPRINT.C (listing 4.4), 72
unsigned, 88

interest, computing
INTFIVE.C program, (listing 7.4), 147-148
with for loops, (LESSON6.C program), 254

INTPRINT.C program, printing program data (listing 4.4), 72

INTRO.C program (listing 1.1), 6

INVSRCH.C program, searching parallel arrays (listing 17.2), 377-378

isalpha() function, 315

iscntrl() function, 315

isdigit() function, 315

islower() function, 315

isspace() function, 315

isupper() function, 315

iterative approaches to programming, 9

K-L

keyboard input, scanf() function, 120-123

L qualifiers for integer literals, 90

labels of statements, 268

languages, hardware-dependent, 12

left brace in C programs, 41

left bracket in C programs, 41

left parenthesis in C programs, 41

left-to-right associativity in expressions, 145

length of strings, 111-112

less than (<) relational operator, 153

less than or equal to (<=) relational operator, 153

LESSON4.C program, operators and if testing, 172

LESSON5.C program, advanced operators, 218-220

LESSON6.C program, for loop computing interest, 254

LESSON7.C program, switch statement controlling menus, 296-298

LESSON8.C program, passing data between functions, 356-360

LESSON9.C program, property database, 406-416

LESSON10.C program, allocating structure arrays, 462-472

LESSON11.C program, values in random access file, 512-518

LESSON12.CPP program, C++ shortcuts, 556-563

library functions, 11, 50-51, 304
clrscr(), 219
prototypes in header

files, 342
strcpy(), 118

listings
1.1 Glancing through a C program, 6
2.1 Using the Turbo C++ IDE, 24
2.2 practice program for skill-building, 27
3.1 simple C program, 40-41
3.2 using two styles of comments, 47
3.3 common components of C program, 55
4.1 printing several messages with printf() (PRINTRO.C program), 62-63
4.2 print output using escape characters (ESCSEQS.C program), 66
4.3 printing character data (CHARCONV.C program), 69
4.4 printing strings, characters, and integers (INTPRINT.C program), 72
4.5 %f displaying floating-point values (FLTPRINT.C program), 74
5.1 Using qualifiers and conversion characters (CONVQUAL.C program), 94
5.2 variables for storing and printing (ASSIGNS.C program), 101-102
6.1 defining/printing character arrays (ARRAYBEG.C program), 115-116

6.2 assigning character arrays (CARRINIT.C program), 119-120

6.3 using scanf() for input of three values (SCANFBEG.C program), 122-123

7.1 integer division (INTDIV.C program), 138

7.2 computing divisional results (MOREDIV.C program), 140

7.3 calculating long expressions (EXPRESS.C program), 143

7.4 computing interest for five periods (INTFIVE.C program), 147-148

8.1 printing relational operator results (RELAT1ST.C program), 155-156

8.2 computing hotel rates (HOTELIF.C program), 160

8.3 if/else statements (HOTELSE.C), 163

8.4 data combinations (LOGICALS.C), 167

9.1 typecast operators example (TYPECAST.C program), 186

9.2 sizeof returning memory values (SIZEOF.C program), 189

9.3 conditional operator example (CONDIT.C program), 192-193

9.4 increment/decrement operators (INCDEC.C program), 197

10.1 printing results of bitwise operators (BIT1.C program), 206-207

10.2 bitwise shift operators (BITSHIFT.C program), 208-209

10.3 bitwise operators example (BITEQUIV.C program), 211-212

10.4 compound bitwise operator (EVNTOODD.C program), 213-214

11.1 while loop verifying user input (USERAGE.C program), 229

11.2 do-while loop (DOUSRAGE.C program), 231-232

11.3 break/exit() demo (BREXIT.C program), 234-235

12.1 for loop (FORAVG.C program), 243

12.2 for loop control variables (SEQUENCS.C program), 245-246

12.3 nested loops (NESTFOR.C program), 248-249

13.1 break statement quitting for loop early (FORBREAK.C program), 263

13.2 continue statement example (CONTINUE.C program), 266

13.3 goto statement (GOTO.C program), 270

14.1 embedded if-else statement (IFELSETV.C program), 279

14.2 switch statement (SWITCHV.C program), 283

14.3 cascading through case code blocks (NOBREAKS.C program), 287-288

14.4 switch statement for menus (MATHMENU.C), 290-291

15.1 I/O functions (LOTSIO.C program), 313-314

15.2 character functions (PRODCODE.C), 317

15.3 string functions (NAMESTR.C program), 320-321

15.4 math functions (MATHALL.C program), 325

16.1 outline of separate functions program, 332-333

16.2 local/global variables (LOCGLO.C program), 336

16.3 passing by value (VALUPASS.C program), 339-340

16.4 passing arrays by address (PASSADDR.C program), 343-344

16.5 passing by address and value (OVERRIDE.C program), 345-346

16.6 passing/returning values (PASSRET.C), 349-350

17.1 array example (ARRTEMP.C program), 370-371

17.2 searching parallel arrays (INVSRCH.C program), 377-378

18.1 pointers to variables (DEFPNTS.C program), 390
18.2 referencing arrays with pointers (FLOTARPT.C program), 394
18.3 character pointers and arrays (CHARFUNS.C program), 398
18.4 arrays of pointers (CITYNAME.C program), 401-402
19.1 structure variable arrays (RADIOST.C program), 428
19.2 radio listener database with dot operator (RADIOST2.C program), 433-435
20.1 allocating heap arrays (ALCHECK.C program), 451-452
20.2 overallocating memory and detection (OVERALLO.C program), 454
20.3 allocating array of pointers (ARRHEAP.C program), 456-457
21.1 opening files via file pointers (OPEN1ST.C program), 483
21.2 closing file example (OPEN2ND.C), 485
21.3 opening/writing to/ closing files (POEMOUT.C program), 486-487
21.4 append mode (POEMADD.C program), 488-489
21.5 fgets() function (POEMREAD.C program), 491-492

22.1 random access file (RANSTRS.C), 503-504
22.2 file erasing function, 507
23.1 ascending/descending sort order (NUMSORT.C program), 527-529
23.2 sorting heap string arrays (STRSORT.C program), 531-532
23.3 sorting structure arrays (STRUSORT.C program), 534-535
23.4 minimum/maximum array values (MINMAX.C program), 537-538
24.1 passing floating-points by address (BYADDRES.C program), 547
24.2 passing by reference (C++), 548
24.3 advantages/shortcuts of C++ (CPPADV.CPP program), 549-550
lists finding maximum/ minimum values, 536-538
literal data, printing with printf() function, 61
literal data type qualifiers, 93-94
literal qualifiers, numeric data types, 90-95
literals, character/string, 108-109
local variables, 334-347, 544
LOCGLO.C program, local/ global variables (listing 16.2), 336
log() function, 324
log10() function, 324
logarithmic functions, 324-326

logic errors in programs, 8
logical operators, 164-168, 173
LOGICALS.C program, logical operators (listing 8.4), 167
long data type, 87
long double data type, 87
long integer data type, 87
long integers, 89
loops, 254
    do-while, 230-232
    for, 240-244, 262-264
    infinite, 227
    nested, 247-249
    nesting, 255
    reiterating, 264-267
    while, 226-230
LOTSIO.C program, I/O functions (listing 15.1), 313-314
low-level languages, 10
lowercase letters in C programs, 42
lvalues in unary operators, 137
lvalues as variables, 100

M

main() function, 51-52, 78
maintenance of programs, 9
malloc() function, 446-448, 453-454, 463
manipulators, I/O, 545
math operators, 53, 172
    associativity of expressions, 145
    calculating long expressions, 143
    nested parentheses, 142
    precedence, 141-144
    precedence of operation order, 53
    primary operations, 136-141

MATH.H header file, math functions, 322

MATHALL.C program, math functions (listing 15.4), 325

mathematical functions, 322-324

MATHMENU.C program, menu switch statement (listing 14.4), 290-291

maximum values in lists, 536-538

members of structures, 425

memory
  addresses, 385
  allocating, 463
  array requirements, 369
  contiguous allocation, 447
  data type requirements, 89
  deallocating, 463
  error-checking allocation, 453-454
  expanded, 384-386
  extended, 384-386, 443
  heap, 442-446
    allocating, 448-450, 455-458, 546
    deallocating, 546
  overallocation detection, 454
  passing arrays by address, 343
  stack, 446
  storage determination, 188-190

memory buffer
  character I/O functions, 306
  clearing, 310

menu bar, 19-20

menus, 19-21
  controlling with switch statement (LESSON7.C program), 296-298

selection code with switch MATHMENU.C (listing 14.4), 290-291
  writing selection code with switch statements, 289-292

message bar, 19

message window, 26, 117

minimum values in lists, 536-538

MINMAX.C program, min/max array values (listing 23.4), 537-538

mixing data types, 182-188

% modulus (remainder) operator, 139, 172

monitors, color text output, 312-315

MOREDIV.C program, computing divisional results (listing 7.2), 140

moving file pointer, fseek() function, 499-501

multidimensional arrays, 376

multiple assignment statements, 144

multiple-choice program logic with switch statements, 277

myStruct data type, 543

N

\n control character, 62

named constants in programs, 50

NAMESTR.C program, string functions (listing 15.3), 320-321

naming variables, 96-97

nested if-else statements, 276-280

nested loops, 247-249

nested parentheses and math operators, 142

NESTFOR.C program, nested loops (listing 12.3), 248-249

New command (File menu), 23

new operator, allocating heap memory, 546

newline escape sequence, 62

newline keypress for getchar() function, 306

NOBREAKS.C program, cascading code blocks (listing 14.3), 287-288

NONAME00.CPP default filename, 24

nonarray variables
  in scanf() function, 122
  passing by address, 345

nonarrays, passing by address (C++), 547

not (!) logical operator, 164

not equal to (!=) relational operator, 153

not equal to sign ( ), printing, 65

null zero, 109-111

numeric arrays, 366-368

numeric data types, 86-95

numeric functions, 322-326

numeric literals, 61

numeric variables, 128

NUMSORT.C program, ascending/descending sorts (listing 23.1), 527-529

O

%o conversion character, printing octal values, 93

octal literals (0 prefix), 92

OOP (object-oriented programming), 542

Open command (File menu), 5

OPEN1ST.C program,
    opening files via file
    pointers (listing 21.1), 483
OPEN2ND.C program,
    closing files (listing 21.2),
    485
opening
    files, 480-482
    random access files,
        498-499
    program windows, 32
operator overloading, 545
operators, 10, 172
    <<, >>, 545
    address of (&)
        passing nonarray
            variables by address,
            345
        returning variable
            addresses, 388
    advanced, LESSON5.C
        program, 218-220
    assignment (=), 144-148
        storing data in vari-
            ables, 99
        storing values in
            arrays, 370
    binary, 137
    bitwise, 202-203,
        209-212
    bitwise leftshift (<<), 221
    bitwise shift, 207-209
    cin, 544-545
    comma, 193
    compound, 146-148
    compound bitwise,
        213-214, 221
    conditional (?:), 190-193
    cout, 544-545
    decrement (-), 194-198
    delete, deallocating heap
        memory, 546
    dereference (*), 345, 387
    division (/), 138-141
    dot (.), 431-432, 463
    increment (++), 194-198

LESSON4.C program,
    172
logical, 164-168
math, 53, 136-144
% modulus (remainder),
    139
new, allocating heap
    memory, 546
overriding with paren-
    theses, 141
precedence, 141
relational, 153-157
short-circuiting, 166
sizeof
    determining array
        space, 369
    memory storage
        determination,
        188-190
structure pointer (->),
    431, 463
typecast, 184-188
unary (+, -), 137-138
Options menu commands,
    21-23
or (||) logical operator, 164
origin values, fseek()
    function, 500
outline of separate func-
    tions program (listing
    16.1), 332-333
output
    blank lines, 69
    printing with escape
        characters, 66
output functions, 304-315
output of program, 5
output screen, 35, 297
outputting data types with
    operator overloading, 545
outputting data with
    printf() function, 60-63
outside loop of nested
    loop, 247
OVERALLO.C program,
    overallocating memory
    (listing 20.2), 454

overloaded operators, 387
OVERRIDE.C program,
    passing by address/value
    (listing 16.5), 345-346

P

parallel arrays, 375
parentheses
    in C programs, 41
    nested, and math
        operators, 142
    overriding operators,
        141
PASSADDR.C program
    (listing 16.4), 343-344
passing arrays by address,
    343-347
passing by value, 339-341
passing data by reference,
    BYREF.CPP program
    (listing 24.2), 548
passing data by reference
    (C++), 547-551
passing floating-points by
    address, BYADDRES.C
    (listing 24.1), 547
passing nonarray variables
    by address, 345
PASSRET.C program,
    passing/returning values
    (listing 16.6), 349-350
POEMADD.C program,
    append mode (listing
    21.4), 488-489
POEMOUT.C program,
    opening/writing to/
    closing files (listing 21.3),
    486-487
POEMREAD.C program,
    fgets() function (listing
    21.5), 491-492
pointers
    arrays, 399-403, 407, 455
    characters, 395-399
    defining, 387

dereference operator (*), 387

floating-point variables, 387

integers, 400

pointer variables, 384-391

referencing arrays, 391-395

structures, 430

tracking allocated heap space, 446

variables, 407

void, 449

postfix increment/decrement operators, 194

pow() function, 323

practice program (listing 2.1), 27

prData() function, 379

precedence

logical operators, 165

math operators, 53, 141-144

prefix increment/decrement operators, 194

preprocessor directives, 48-51, 78

primary math operators, 53, 136-141

printer output functions, 305

printf() conversion characters, 93

printf() function, 54, 60-63, 79, 129

printing

character arrays, ARRAYBEG.C program (listing 6.1), 115-116

character data with %c, CHARCONV.C program (listing 4.3), 69

data with printf() function, 60-63

floating-point values, 73-74

hexadecimal values, 93

integer values, 70-73

messages with printf() function, PRINTRO.C program (listing 4.1), 62-63

output with escape characters, ESCSEQS.C program (listing 4.2), 66

single characters, 67-69

strings/characters/integers, INTPRINT.C program (listing 4.4), 72

string literals, 61

strings, 117

values in scientific notation, 91-92

variables, 101

PRINTRO.C program, printing messages (listing 4.1), 62-63

PRODCODE.C program, character functions (listing 15.2), 317

program windows, 32

programming

heap memory considerations, 444

high-level, 10

high-low-level, 10

iterative approaches, 9

low-level, 10

Turbo Pascal, 12

programs

ALCHECK.C, allocating heap arrays (listing 20.1), 451-452

ARRAYBEG.C, defining/printing character arrays (listing 6.1), 115-116

ARRHEAP.C, allocating array of pointers (listing 20.3), 456-457

ARRTEMP.C, array example (listing 17.1), 370-371

ASSIGNS.C, variables for storing/printing (listing 5.2), 101-102

basic format of structure, 48-56

BIT1.C, bitwise operators example (listing 10.1), 206-207

BITEQUIV.C, bitwise operators example (listing 10.3), 211-212

bitmask of, 219

BITSHIFT.C, bitwise shift operators (listing 10.2), 208-209

braces as function markers, 52

BREXIT.C, break/exit() demo (listing 11.3), 234-235

BYADDRES.C, passing floating-points by address (listing 24.1), 547

BYREF.CPP, passing by reference (listing 24.2), 548

CARRINIT.C, defining character arrays (listing 6.2), 119-120

CHARCONV.C, printing character data (listing 4.3), 69

CHARFUNS.C, character pointers and arrays (listing 18.3), 398

CITYNAME.C, arrays of pointers (listing 18.4), 401-402

comments, 43-47, 79

COMMENTS.C, two styles of comments (listing 3.2), 47

common code in header files, 50

compiling, 8

CONDIT.C, conditional operator example (listing 9.3), 192-193

CONTINUE.C, continue statement example (listing 13.2), 266

CPPADV.CPP, advantages/shortcuts of C++ (listing 24.3), 549-550

CSTUDY.C, components of programs (listing 3.3), 55

DEFPNTS.C, pointers to variables (listing 18.1), 390

designing, 6-9

DOUSRAGE.C, do-while loop example (listing 11.2), 231-232

embedded comments, 45

ESCSEQS.C, print output with escape characters (listing 4.2), 66

EVNTOODD.C, compound bitwise operator (listing 10.4), 213-214

EXPRESS.C, calculating long expressions (listing 7.3), 143

file-naming conventions, 479

FLOTARPT.C, referencing arrays (listing 18.2), 394

FLTPRINT.C, floating-point values (listing 4.5), 74

FORAVG.C, for loop example (listing 12.1), 243

FORBREAK.C, break

quitting loop early (listing 13.1), 263

freeform style of writing, 42

function-separating comments, 45

GOTO.C, goto example (listing 13.3), 270

HOTELIF.C, if statement example (listing 8.2), 160

HOTELELSE.C, if/else statements (listing 8.3), 163

IDE practice session, 23-28

IFELSETV.C, embedded if-else (listing 14.1), 279

INCDEC.C, increment/decrement operators (listing 9.4), 197

instructions, 4

INTDIV.C, integer division (listing 7.1), 138

INTFIVE.C, computing interest (listing 7.4), 147-148

INTPRINT.C, printing strings/characters/integers (listing 4.4), 72

INVSRCH.C, searching parallel arrays (listing 17.2), 377-378

LESSON4.C, operators and if testing, 172

LESSON5.C, advanced operators demonstration, 218-220

LESSON6.C, for loop computing interest, 254

LESSON7.C, switch statement controlling menus, 296-298

LESSON8.C, passing data

between functions, 356-360

LESSON9.C, property database, 406-416

LESSON10.C, allocating structure array on the heap, 462-472

LESSON11.C, changing values in random access file, 512-518

LESSON12.CPP, C++ shortcuts, 556-563

LOCGLO.C, local/global variables (listing 16.2), 336

logic errors, 8

LOGICALS.C, logical operators example (listing 8.4), 167

LOTSIO.C, I/O functions (listing 15.1), 313-314

lowercase/uppercase letter usage, 42

main() function, 51-52

maintenance, 9

MATHALL.C, math functions (listing 15.4), 325

MATHMENU.C, switch statement for menus (listing 14.4), 290-291

MINMAX.C, min/max array values (listing 23.4), 537-538

MOREDIV.C, computing divisional results (listing 7.2), 140

named constants, 50

NAMESTR.C, string functions (listing 15.3), 320-321

NESTFOR.C, nested loops (listing 12.3), 248-249

NOBREAKS.C, cascading case code blocks

(listing 14.3), 287-288
NUMSORT.C, ascending/descending sorts (listing 23.1), 527-529
OPEN1ST.C, opening files via file pointers (listing 21.1), 483
OPEN2ND.C, closing file example (listing 21.2), 485
output, 5
OVERALLO.C, overallocating memory (listing 20.2), 454
OVERRIDE.C, passing by address/value (listing 16.5), 345-346
PASSADDR.C, passing by address (listing 16.4), 343-344
PASSRET.C, passing/returning values (listing 16.6), 349-350
POEMADD.C, append mode (listing 21.4), 488-489
POEMOUT.C, opening/writing to/closing files (listing 21.3), 486-487
POEMREAD.C, fgets() function (listing 21.5), 491-492
practice (listing 2.1), 27
PRINTRO.C, printing messages with printf() (listing 4.1), 62-63
PRODCODE.C, character functions (listing 15.2), 317
PROJECT1.C, 33-35
PROJECT2.C, 78-80
PROJECT3.C (data I/O), 128-130
prototyping functions before compiling, 342
pseudocode explaining logic, 277

RADIOST.C, structure variable arrays (listing 19.1), 428
RADIOST2.C, dot operator example (listing 19.2), 433-435
RANSTRS.C, random access file (listing 22.1), 503-504
RELAT1ST.C, relational operator results (listing 8.1), 155-156
saving, 17
SCANFBEG.C, scanf() input of values (listing 6.3), 122-123
SEQUENCS.C, for loop control variables (listing 12.2), 245-246
simple C example (listing 3.1), 40-41
SIZEOF.C, sizeof operator (listing 9.2), 189
statements, 5
STRSORT.C, sorting heap string arrays (listing 23.2), 531-533
STRUSORT.C, sorting structure arrays (listing 23.3), 534-535
SWITCHV.C, switch statement (listing 14.2), 283
text inside quotation marks, 42
TYPECAST.C, typecast operators (listing 9.1), 186
USERAGE.C, while loop example (listing 11.1), 229
users, 6
VALUPASS.C, passing by value (listing 16.3), 339-340
warning messages, 116
white space, 42

writing and separating code, 330-334
PROGRAMS directory, 25
Project menu commands, 21
PROJECT1.C program, 33-35
PROJECT2.C program, 78-80
PROJECT3.C program, data I/O, 128-130
property database (LESSON9.C program), 406-416
prototypes of functions, 341-343
prototyping functions, 513
pseudocode explaining program logic, 277
pull-down menus, 20
putc() function, 306
putch() function, 306-308
putchar() function, 306-308
puts() function, 311

Q

qualifiers
    literal data types, 93-94
    numeric literal data types, 90
Quit command (File menu), 17
quitting Turbo C++, 17
quotation marks
    in programs, 41-42
    string literals, 61

R

r (read mode) access mode, sequential files, 481-494
r+ access mode, opening random access files, 498

RADIOST.C program, structure variable arrays (listing 19.1), 428
RADIOST2.C program, dot operator example (listing 19.2), 433-435
RAM (Random Access Memory), 384
random access files, 496-499
changing values (LESSON11.C), 512-518
closing with fclose() function, 498
RANSTRS.C program (listing 22.1), 503-504
random I/O in files, 501-506
reading files, 478-480, 486, 490-492, 502
recursive functions, 334
references, passing data by (C++), 547-551
referencing arrays with pointers, 391-395
reiterating loops with continue statements, 264-267
relational operators, 153-157, 173
if statements, 157-161
printing results of tests, RELAT1ST.C (listing 8.1), 155-156
relational tests, 158
% remainder (modulus) operator, 139
remove() function, 506
Repaint desktop option (control menu), 21
repeating loops, 247
return statements, 55, 347-351
returning variable addresses, address of operator (&), 388

rewind() function, 506
right angled bracket in C programs, 41
right brace (}) in C programs, 41
right bracket (]) in C programs, 41
right parenthesis in C programs, 41
right-to-left associativity of expressions, 144
Ritchie, Dennis, C language co-creator, 10
Run command (Run menu), 25
Run menu commands, 21, 25
running programs, 5, 8
rvalues in unary operators, 137
rvalues as variables, 100

S
%s conversion character, printing strings, 117
sample programs, Turbo C++ compiler, 19
Save command (File menu), 24
Save command (Options menu), 23
saving programs, 17
scanf() function, 54, 120-123, 129
SCANFBEG.C program, scanf() input of values (listing 6.3), 122-123
scientific notation
data types, 87
printing values
%e, %E conversion characters, 91
wide ranges with %g, %G conversion characters, 92

screens
IDE, 17
output, 35, 297
Turbo C++, 19
user, 26
Search menu, 21
searching arrays, 373-379
SEEK_ origin values, fseek() function, 500
self-prototyping functions, 341
semicolons in statements, 240
separate functions in programs, 332
separate functions program outline (listing 16.1), 332-333
separating code when writing programs, 330-334
sequence point, see comma operator
SEQUENCS.C program, for loop control variables (listing 12.2), 245-246
sequential files, 479
access mode values, 481
appending (adding), 488-489
reading, 490-492
sequential searching of arrays, 373
short integer data type, 86
short-circuiting of operators, 166
signed integer data type, 86
signed long integer data type, 87
signed short integer data type, 87
simple C program (listing 3.1), 40-41
SIMPLE.C file (listing 3.1), 40-41

SIMPLE.C program (listing 3.1), 40-41
sin() function, 324
single quote (') in C programs, 41
single-dimensional arrays, 376
sizeof operator, 218
  determining array space, 369
  memory storage determination, 188-190
SIZEOF.C program, sizeof operator (listing 9.2), 189
small memory model, 18
sorting
  heap string arrays, STRSORT.C program (listing 23.2), 531-533
  order of values, 524-530
  string data, 530-533
  strings, 525
  structure arrays, STRUSORT.C program (listing 23.3), 534-535
source code, 8
spaghetti code, 271
special characters, typing in C programs, 41
sqrt() function, 323
stack memory, 446
stack overflow, 334
starting Turbo C++ compiler, 16-18, 32
statements
  break, 232-236, 255
    at end of case statement code, 287
    exiting for loops early, 262-264
    with switch statement, 284-289
  case
    break statements at end of code, 287
    enclosed in braces in

switch statements, 284
comments in programs, 43-45
continue, 264-267
#define, 43
else, 162-163
executable, 41
for, 240
goto, 267-271
if, 157-161, 254
if-else, 276-280
labels, 268
return, 55, 347-351
struct, 424-430
switch, 276, 281-284
  menu control (LESSON7.C program), 296-298
  menu selection code, 289-292
  SWITCHV.C program (listing 14.2), 283
  with break statement, 284-289
  two-line conditional, 221
  while, 226
stdin (standard input device), keyboard input, 311
STDIO.H header file, 50
  I/O functions, 304
  scanf() function inclusion, 122
STDLIB.H header file
  exit() function, 233
  heap functions, 448
stopping Turbo C++ compiler, 16-18
storing data values in variables, 95-102
strcat() function, 318
strcmp() function, 318-319
  sorting strings, 525
  string sort data compari-

son, 530
strcpy() function, 117-120
string functions, 318-322
string I/O functions, 310-312
string length, 111-112
string literals, 61, 109
  assigning to variables, 395
  printing, 61
string terminator, see null zero
string-delimiting zero, see null zero
STRING.H header file
  strcpy() function inclusion, 119
  string functions, 318
strings
  characters, 108-112
  printing with %s conversion character, 117
  printing with INTPRINT.C (listing 4.4), 72
  sorting, 525, 530-533
  storing in character arrays, 118
  zero-length, 109
strlen() function, 318
STRSORT.C program, sorting heap string arrays (listing 23.2), 531-533
struct statement, 424-430
structure arrays, allocating on heap (LESSON10.C), 462-472
structure of programs, 48-56
structure pointer operator (->), 431, 463
structure tags, 427
structure variables
  defining, 543
  initializing, 430-438
structured programming, 330

structures, 462
    assigning data
        dot operator (.),
            431-432
        structure pointer
            operator (->), 431
    global definitions, 429
    members, 425
    pointers to, 430
    sorting, 533-535
STRUSORT.C program,
    sorting structure arrays
    (listing 23.3), 534-535
submenus, *see* pull-down
    menus
subscript numbers for array
    elements, 115, 118, 366
subtracting from variables
    with decrement (-) opera-
    tors, 194-198
switch statement, 276,
    281-284
    menu selection code,
        289-292
    SWITCHV.C program
        (listing 14.2), 283
    with break statement,
        284-289
switch statements, menu
    control (LESSON7.C
    program), 296-298
SWITCHV.C program,
    switch statement (listing
    14.2), 283
syntax errors in code, 8
syntax rules in computer
    languages, 4

T

\t escape sequence charac-
    ter, aligning data col-
    umns, 65
tags for structures, 427
tan() function, 324
TC command (DOS), 32

terms associated with heap,
    444-446
text, color monitor output,
    312-315
text boxes in dialog boxes,
    22
text inside quotation marks
    in programs, 42
textbackground() function,
    312
textcolor() function, 312
Thompson, Kenneth, C
    language co-creator, 10
tilde (~) in C programs, 41
tolower() function, 316
total variables, while loops,
    228
toupper() function, 316
trigonometric functions,
    324-326
truth tables, 203-207
Turbo C++ programming
    language (Borland Inter-
    national), 4, 12
    compiler
        components, 18
        editor, 24
        sample programs, 19
        starting/quitting,
            16-17, 32
    screen, 19
Turbo Pascal language, 12
two-line conditional
    statement, 221
typecast operator, 184-188,
    218
TYPECAST.C program,
    typecast operators (listing
    9.1), 186
typecasting
    heap memory values,
        449
    values, 221

U

U qualifiers for integer
    literals, 90
unary operators (+, -),
    137-138
unbuffered character I/O
    functions, 308
uniform data in random
    access files, 497
UNIX operating system, C
    programming language,
    10
unsigned
    data types, 89
    integer data type, 86
    integers, 88
    long integer data type,
        87
    short integer data type,
        86
uppercase letters
    C programs, 42
    #define statements, 43
user input
    performing operations
        with bitwise operators,
        209-212
    validation, 173
user screens, 26
user-supplied functions, 51
USERAGE.C program,
    while loop example
    (listing 11.1), 229
Using the Turbo C++ IDE
    (listing 2.1), 24

V

validation of input from
    users, 173
values
    changing in random
        access file
        (LESSON11.C), 512-518
    comparing with rela-
        tional operators, 155

constant, 61
finding maximum/
minimum in lists,
536-538
integer, printing, 70-73
returning with return
statements, 347-351
searching arrays for
specific, 374
sorting for order,
524-530
typecasting, 221
VALUPASS.C program,
passing by value (listing
16.3), 339-340
variables, 53-54, 128
adding with increment
(++) operator, 194-198
assigning string literals,
395
char, 109
character, 113
counter, 228
data types, 97-98
declarations, 53
defining, 98-99
defining in C++, 544
errorlevel (DOS), 232
float (C++), 551
floating-point, 547
global, 334-337
integer, 53
local, 334-337
lvalues, 100
naming, 96-97
nonarray, 345
pointer, 407
pointers, 384-391, 407
printing, 101
returning addresses, 388
rvalues, 100
storing data values,
95-102
structure
defining, 425, 543
initializing, 430-438

subtracting from with
decrement (-) operator,
194-198
total, 228
value storage and
printing, ASSIGNS.C
(listing 5.2), 101-102
vertical bar in C programs,
41
void pointer, 449

W

w (write mode) access
mode, sequential files,
481
w+ access mode, opening
random access files, 498
warning messages, 116
while loops, 226-230, 254
counter variables, 228
example program
(USERAGE.C-listing
11.1), 229
total variables, 228
white space in programs,
42
Window menu commands,
21-23
windows
compilation, 34
editing, 23, 32
message, 26, 117
program, 32
Windows Program Man-
ager, starting Turbo C++,
16
worst-case sorts, 527
writing
data to files with fwrite()
function, 502
disk files with file
pointers, 480
menu selection code
with switch statements,
289-292

programs, separating
code, 330-334
to files, 486-487

X-Y-Z

%x conversion character,
printing hexadecimal
values, 93
zero as character, 110
zero-length strings, 109
Zoom command (Window
menu), 23

General Terms That Apply to Compiled Programs and Redistributables

The license granted in this statement for you to create your own compiled programs and distribute your programs and the Redistributables is subject to all of the following conditions:

▶ All copies of the programs you create must bear a valid copyright notice, either your own or the Borland copyright notice that appears on the original diskette label in this package.

▶ You may not remove or alter any Borland copyright, trademark, or other proprietary rights notice contained in any portion of Borland libraries, source code, Redistributables, or other files that bear such a notice. You may not remove or alter any identifying screen that is produced by a Borland Redistributable.

▶ Borland provides no warranty at all to any person, other than the Limited Warranty provided to the original purchaser of this package.

▶ You will remain solely responsible to anyone receiving your programs for support, service, upgrades, or technical or other assistance, and such recipients will have no right to contact Borland for such services or assistance.

▶ You will indemnify and hold Borland, its related companies, and its suppliers harmless from and against any claims or liabilities arising out of the use, reproduction, or distribution of your programs.

▶ Your programs must be written using a licensed, registered copy of this Borland product.

▶ Your programs may not be merely a set or subset of any of the libraries, code, Redistributables, or other files included in this package.

▶ You may not use Borland's or any of its suppliers' names, logos, or trademarks to market your programs, except to state that your program was written using this Borland product.

▶ All Borland libraries, source code, Redistributables, and other files remain Borland's exclusive property.

▶ Regardless of any modifications that you make, you may not distribute any files (particularly Borland source code files) except those that Borland has expressly designated as Redistributables. Nothing in this license statement permits you to derive the source code of files that Borland has provided to you in executable form only, or to reproduce, modify, use, or distribute the source code of such files. You are not, of course, restricted from distributing source code that is entirely your own. Code that you generate with a Borland code generator, such as AppExpert, is considered by Borland to be your code.

▶ All other requirements of the copyright law, international treaty, and Borland's No-Nonsense™ License Statement and Limited Warranty continue to apply except as provided otherwise above.

If you wish to distribute copies of your compiled programs or Redistributables on other terms, please call our OEM licensing department.

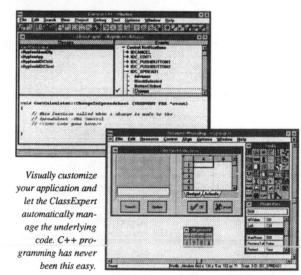

Borland Turbo C++ 3.0 for DOS

Turbo C++ is a full-featured compiler that makes programming in C and C++ easy. With context-sensitive help, color syntax highlighting, and the Programmer's Platform IDE, you can create great applications quickly. A complete tutorial helps you quickly navigate the development environment and gain insight into C and C++ languages. Novices and professionals alike will appreciate the intuitive help system that answers your questions instantly. There's even sample code that you can paste into your own applications.

Borland Turbo C++ 3.0 for DOS features:

- Easy-to-use Programmer's Platform IDE with color syntax highlighting
- Macro-based editor that supports full undo and redo, and editing of large files
- Integrated debugger with data and Object Inspectors,™ and conditional breakpoints
- 100% ANSI C-compatible runtime libraries
- Turbo Librarian™ for creating and managing .LIB files
- On-line, context-sensitive help system
- Hands-on tutorials on C and C++ programming

Name _____

Address _____

City _____

State/Province _____ Zip/Postal code _____

Phone (_____) _____ Fax (_____) _____

To redeem this coupon, mail the original coupon (no photocopies, please) along with payment and shipping information to: Borland, P.O. Box 660005, Scotts Valley, CA 95066-3249.

Select one:

❏ Borland® C++ 4.0 for DOS, Windows, and Windows NT (regularly $499)	❏ CD-ROM ❏ 3.5" HD disks	**$199.95**
❏ Borland Turbo C++ 3.0 for DOS (regularly $99.95)	❏ 3.5" and 5.25" disks	**$69.95**

Method of payment: ❏ Check enclosed†	Subtotal $ _____
❏ VISA ❏ MasterCard ❏ American Express	State sales tax* $ _____
___ ___ ___ - ___ ___ ___ - ___ ___ ___ - ___ ___ ___ card number	Freight ($10.00 per item) $ _____
Expiration date: __ __ / __ __ Z1136	Total order $ _____